Alice Stopford Green

Town Life in the Fifteenth Century

Volume 1

Alice Stopford Green

Town Life in the Fifteenth Century
Volume 1

ISBN/EAN: 9783337094577

Printed in Europe, USA, Canada, Australia, Japan

Cover: Foto ©ninafisch / pixelio.de

More available books at **www.hansebooks.com**

TOWN LIFE

IN

THE FIFTEENTH CENTURY

BY

MRS. J. R. GREEN

IN TWO VOLUMES

VOL. I

London
MACMILLAN AND CO.
AND NEW YORK
1894

The Right of Translation and Reproduction is Reserved

IN MEMORY OF
JOHN RICHARD GREEN
MARCH, 1894

PREFACE

IN the twenty years which have passed since Mr. Green drew his brilliant sketch of the early life of English towns, and of their influence on the history of English liberty, the study of the subject in this country has advanced but little; and it is not, I think, too much to say that the pages of his History still present the most vivid and suggestive picture which we possess of the mediæval boroughs—a picture inspired by ardent sympathy and emotion. In this rapid and original survey the true proportions of civic history in our national life are boldly drawn; and the burghers and shopkeepers of the towns, long neglected and despised, take their place in the distinguished ranks of those by whom our freedom has been won by their sturdy battle against oppression, leading the way in the growth and elevation of the English people, and carrying across the ages of tyranny the full tradition of liberty. But the history of this great civic revolution, which in Mr. Green's day cannot be said to have existed at all, has since then remained strangely neglected among us. While in foreign countries the study of the origin and growth of municipal institutions has been recognized as of overwhelming importance, and has already employed the erudition and tried the ingenuity of a long succession of scholars, English historians have stood aloof. No English name figures in the contests of the schools; nor is any English authority called to witness when a learned theory is advanced to solve the riddle; and if from time to time foreign scholars attempt to draw English towns within the range of their generalizations, the lack of sufficient or trustworthy materials at their disposal makes the result vain and unfruitful. No country indeed has been so backward as our own in municipal history, whether we take it from the popular or from the scientific side. The traveller who has asked at the bookshop of a provincial town for a local history or even for a local guide is as well able to realize the distance which parts us from France, Italy, or Germany, as is the student who inquires for a detailed account of how civic life or any one of its characteristic institutions grew up among us. A certain number of town histories do indeed exist, but they by no means always deal necessarily or even mainly with the life of the borough itself. To a considerable number of local antiquaries the buried relics of the Roman dominion have proved a permanent and pre-occupying interest. For the student of mediæval times the monastery and cathedral tower high above the squalid market-place and thatched town-hall which lie dwarfed and obscured under their vast shadow; and in modern as in older history the butchers and brewers who represent the secular corporations of York and Winchester are practically bid to stand aside before the presence of the spiritual corporations to whom the fame of S. Mary's or S. Swithun's is committed. Where ecclesiastical monuments of historic greatness are wanting, a fervent apologist may still find an excuse for the meanness and dulness of the municipal story, in the fact that at some time or other the town has lent its streets to serve as the stage for a critical scene in the national drama, and thus—through the lifting of a royal standard, or the tragedy of a conspicuous adventurer —derives a borrowed title to our interest. That the story of convent and chapter and solemn pageant should be told with full detail I do not question. I only urge that when the tale is finished we still wait for some notice of the city itself and the humble details of its common life. There are, it is true, signs of increasing interest in such matters, and some admirable studies in our municipal records have lately been made in England; nevertheless the work is still at its beginning, and how much need there is for further study I have had occasion to know in the course of an attempt to trace the developement of some forty or fifty provincial boroughs, so as to gain some idea of the condition of our mediæval towns, and the general drift of their history. The preparatory work which the foreign student finds already finished and organized for his use, the English worker has in almost every case to do for himself. Even the briefest sketch of a town history too often implies the long labour of seeking out a mass of scattered and isolated details, which must first be drawn together into some connected sequence before it is possible to study the general bearing and significance of the story in relation to the growth of neighbouring boroughs. Those who have attempted to find their way through the uncertainty and confusion of the materials as they at present exist, will probably be the most lenient judges of inevitable errors of detail such as must creep into the performance of so delicate and difficult a task.

It is evident, indeed, from the nature of the subject, that any writer who desires to give a survey of provincial town life as we can now picture it—from printed materials scattered in county histories, archæological journals, reports of commissions, imperfect abstracts of town documents, parliamentary records, charters, and stray pamphlets—must inevitably remain exposed to much correction in matters of detail from experts with local knowledge. At the same time it seems to me that without some effort to obtain a comprehensive view of the general subject, the student may leave himself open to the still graver errors that spring from the want of some ascertained measure of proportion, and from the incapacity to distinguish in each town that which is normal from that which is strange or characteristic. The question of origins I have deliberately set on one side, from the conviction that the beginnings of a society may be more fruitfully studied after we know something of its actual life. Avoiding therefore many dark questions, I have dealt in the first volume rather with the simpler and less contentious aspects of the growth of the borough to wealth and independence. In the second volume, however, the subjects which arise have long been familiar as matters of acute discussion; and it has sometimes happened, that in going over again the sources from which all our knowledge is derived, I have found myself gradually compelled to entertain views contrary to those which are commonly accepted. Thus, for example, in tracing the growth of self-government within the borough itself, I seem to discover in the phrases of the town records a new explanation for the position of the "communitas" side by side with the "cives"—a problem which, so far as I know, has never been really stated, and the difficulties of which are in no way met by the universally received interpretation. Moreover the theory of an early triumph and rapid decay of democratic government appears to me impossible to maintain, and I have suggested that in the growth of the common council we may find some evidence of a popular movement towards more effectual self-government which seems to have stirred the industrial classes of the fifteenth century. There are other burning questions in which impetuous economists have outrun the historians, and have not found it premature to set in order by the help of accepted theories the obscure chaos of social history in the Middle Ages. In spite of their zealous efforts, however, the whole problem (including even the ascertaining of the facts on which it depends) of the developement of English commerce and manufactures and of its effects on social life, still awaits the student; and it is in the confusion and ignorance which at present prevail, that I may find my best excuse for the fact that with regard to many questions—such, for instance, as the relation of internal traffic to free trade and protection, the general organization of labour, the position of the guild towards the hired worker, the attitude of the municipality to the industrial system, and of the capitalist to the town councillor—I have ventured to differ from conclusions which are commonly put forward.

I would add but one word of personal explanation before I close. The only training or guidance which I have ever had in historical work was in a very brief period during which I was able to watch the method and understand the temper in which Mr. Green's work was done. I never had the opportunity of visiting any English towns with him, or of following his studies in that direction. The most fruitful lesson which remains in my memory is that of a day spent in Ancona between two stages of an invalid journey, when I was able to see the intense enthusiasm with which, as was his habit, he made his way first to the Town-hall, and from the fragments of Greek and mediæval carving built into its walls, from harbour and pier, from names of streets, and the cathedral crypt, he extracted century by century some record of the old municipal life. It was doubtless some such remembrance as this that unconsciously led me in the course of reading, to turn to the story of the English boroughs. At the same time I have no doubt that I should always have been restrained from any idea of writing by my consciousness of the entire lack of adequate preparation for such a task, if I had not felt bound by an imperative obligation to make the attempt. When Mr. Green's work was over he asked of me a promise that I would try to study some of those problems in mediæval history where there seemed to him so much that still needed to be done, and so much to be yet discovered. In this book I have made my first beginning toward the fulfilling of that promise. Such a work can only be closed with feelings of compunction and dismay.

ALICE STOPFORD GREEN.

14, KENSINGTON SQUARE,
March, 1894.

CONTENTS

CHAPTER I.
THE ENGLISH TOWNS 1

CHAPTER II.
THE INDUSTRIAL REVOLUTION OF THE FIFTEENTH CENTURY . . . 35

CHAPTER III.
THE COMMERCIAL REVOLUTION OF THE FIFTEENTH CENTURY . . . 75

CHAPTER IV.
THE COMMON LIFE OF THE TOWN 124

CHAPTER V.
THE TOWNSPEOPLE 169

CHAPTER VI.
THE PROBLEM OF GOVERNMENT 197

CONTENTS

CHAPTER VII.
BATTLE FOR FREEDOM (TOWNS ON ROYAL DEMESNE) 226

CHAPTER VIII.
BATTLE FOR FREEDOM (TOWNS ON FEUDAL ESTATES) 250

CHAPTER IX.
BATTLE FOR FREEDOM (TOWNS ON CHURCH ESTATES) 277

CHAPTER X.
BATTLE FOR SUPREMACY 309

CHAPTER XI.
THE TOWNS AND THE CHURCH 333

CHAPTER XII.
CONFEDERATION 384

TOWN LIFE

IN

THE FIFTEENTH CENTURY

CHAPTER I

THE ENGLISH TOWNS

THERE is nothing in England to-day with which we can compare the life of a fully enfranchised borough of the fifteenth century. Even the revival of our local institutions and our municipal ambition has scarcely stirred any memory of the great tradition of the past, of the large liberties, the high dignities and privileges which our towns claimed in days when the borough was in fact a free self-governing community, a state within the state, boasting of rights derived from immemorial custom and of later privileges assured by law.

The town of those earlier days in fact governed itself after the fashion of a little principality. Within the bounds which the mayor and citizens defined with perpetual insistence in their formal perambulation year after year it carried on its isolated self-dependent life. The inhabitants defended their own territory, built and maintained their walls and towers, armed their own soldiers, trained them for service, and held reviews of their forces at appointed times. They elected their own rulers and officials in whatever way they themselves chose to adopt, and distributed among officers and councillors just such powers of legislation and administration as seemed good in their eyes. They drew up formal constitutions for the government of the community, and as time brought new problems and responsibilities, made and re-made and revised again their ordinances with restless and fertile ingenuity, till they had made of their constitution a various medley of fundamental doctrines and general precepts and particular rules, somewhat after the fashion of an American state of modern times. No alien officer of any kind, save only the judges of the High Court, might cross the limits of their liberties; the sheriff of the shire, the bailiff of the hundred, the king's tax-gatherer or sergeant-at-arms, were alike shut out. The townsfolk themselves assessed their taxes, levied them in their own way, and paid them through their own officers. They claimed broad rights of justice, whether by ancient custom or royal grant; criminals were brought before the mayor's court, and the town prison with its irons and its cage, the gallows at the gate or on the town common, testified to an authority which ended only with death.[1] In all concerns of trade they exercised

[1] The right of pit and gallows was never formally revoked. The last case was under Charles I. (Rogers's Agriculture and

the widest powers, and bargained and negotiated and made laws as nations do on a grander scale to-day. They could covenant and confederate, buy and sell, deal and traffic after their own will; they could draw up formal treaties with other boroughs, and could admit them to or shut them out from all the privileges of their commerce; they might pass laws of protection or try experiments in free trade. Often their authority stretched out over a wide district, and surrounding villages gathered to their markets and obeyed their laws;[1] it might even happen in the case of a staple town that their officers controlled the main foreign trade of whole provinces. In matters that nearly concerned them they were given the right to legislate for themselves, and where they were not allowed to make the law, they at least secured the exclusive right of administering it; the King and the Parliament might issue orders as to weights and measures, or the rules to be observed by foreign merchants, but they were powerless to enforce their decrees save through the machinery and with the

Prices, i. 132). The gallows at Southampton stood on the common; in Colchester at the end of East Street.

[1] The Inquisition de quo Warranto, Ed. I., proves that S. Martin's and other villages were under the jurisdiction of Canterbury; inquests at these places were held by the city coroner. York had a territory of 2,700 acres. (Agric. and Prices, iv. 579.) The burgesses of Dorchester claimed the right to weigh all goods within twelve miles of the town. A special statute was passed in 1430 "that they shall not be disturbed of their right," in consequence of the Act of 1429 ordering weights and measures in every town. (9th Henry VI. cap. vi.) Other instances, such as Norwich, Nottingham, &c., are too numerous to give.

consent of the town. Arduous duties were handed over to them by the state—the supervision of the waters of a river basin, the keeping of the peace on the seas. They sent out their trading barges in fleets under admirals of their own choosing, and leaned but lightly on state aid for protection or revenge, answering pillage with pillage, and making their own treaties with the mariners of other countries as to capture and ransom and redemption of goods, and the treatment of common sailors or of " gentlemen " prisoners.[1] The necessity of their assent and co-operation in greater commercial matters was so clearly recognized, that when Henry the Seventh in 1495 made a league of peace and free trade with Burgundy the treaty was sent to all the chief towns in England, that the mayor might affix to it the city seal, " for equality and stableness of the matter ; " and the same form was observed at the marriage of the Lady Mary.[2] Two hundred and twenty-six burghers sat in Parliament [3] beside the

[1] The mariners of the Cinque Ports drew up treaties with "French shipmen," as to ransom for mariners, sailors, or fishing boats that might be captured on either side; the people of the coast were to be set free without charge, while "gentlemen" and merchants were to pay whatever the captors chose to ask. The shipowners and merchants of each port signed the compact; and all the towns of the coast from Southampton to Thanet joined the league. The document which was drawn up was handed over to the keeping of the Lord Warden in Dover, and in case of dispute messengers from the Ports rode there to see its provisions, or to make a copy for their own guidance. Hist. MSS. Com. v. 537–8 ; iv. i. 434.

[2] Hist. MSS. Com. ix. 146 ; xi. 3, pp. 12–13, 171, 113. For 1340 see Ashley's Arteveldes, 126–7.

[3] Stubos Const. Hist. iii. 484—488. Hallam Const. Hist. iii.

seventy-four knights of the shire; and each borough freely decided for itself what the qualifications of its members should be, and by what manner of election they should be chosen, at a time when for country folk all such matters were irrevocably settled by the king's law. While the great lords with their armed bands of liveried retainers absolutely ruled the elections in the shires, in spite of all statutes of Parliament, the towns asserted their freedom to elect without fear or favour, and sent to the House of Commons the members who probably at that time most nearly represented the "people," that is so far as the people had yet been drawn into a conscious share in the national life.

Four hundred years later the very remembrance of this free and vigorous life was utterly blotted out. When Commissioners were sent in 1835 to enquire into the position of the English boroughs, there was not one community where the ancient traditions still lived. There were Mayors, and Town Councils, and Burgesses; but the burgesses were for the most part deprived of any share whatever in the election of their municipal officers, while these officers themselves had lost all the nobler characteristics of their former authority. Too often the very limits of the old "liberties" of the town were forgotten; or if the ancient landmarks were remembered at all it was only because they defined

36. Gneist, who gives different figures, considers that one of the greatest dangers of the fourteenth and fifteenth centuries was the irrational and meaningless increase of town representation. (Constitution Communale, tr. by Hippert, i. 333, 338; ii. 9.)

bounds within which the inhabitants had the right of voting for a member of Parliament; and in cases where the old boundaries now subsisted for no other reason, it was wholly forgotten that they might ever have had some other origin. In other boroughs where the right of voting was determined in another way, the townspeople had simply lost all remembrance of the ancient limits of their territory; or else, guided by some dim recollection of a former greatness with broader jurisdiction and wide-reaching subject estates, the corporation still yearly "walked the bounds" of lands over which they now claimed no authority. As the memory of municipal life died away there were boroughs where at last no one suspected that the corporate body had ever existed for any larger purpose than to choose members of Parliament. Knowing no other public honour or privilege and called to no other public service, the freemen saw in a single degraded political function the sole object of their corporate constitution; the representation of the people was turned by them into "a property and a commerce," and this one privilege, fed on corruption and private greed, survived the decay of all the great duties of the ancient civic life.[1]

There were it is true exceptions to this common apathy, and towns like Lynn might still maintain some true municipal life, while others like Bristol might yet show a good fighting temper which counted for much in the political struggles of the early nine-

[1] Rep. of Com. on Mun. Corp., 1835, 20, 21; 29-34; Papers relating to Parl. Representation, 93, 94. Vol. ix. No. 92. ii.; 31 x.

teenth century. But the ordinary provincial burghers had lost, or forgotten, or been robbed of the heritage bequeathed by their predecessors of the fifteenth century. With the loss of their municipal independence went the loss of their political authority; and the four hundred or so of members whom they sent to Parliament took a very different position there from that once held by their ancestors. In the Middle Ages the knights of the shire were the mere nominees of the wealthy or noble class, returned to Parliament by the power of the lord's retainers, while the burgesses of the towns preserved a braver and freer tradition.[1] At the time of the Reform Bill, on the other hand, a vast majority of the town members sat among the Commons as dependents and servants of the landed aristocracy, whose mission it was to make the will of their patrons prevail, and who in their corrupt or timid subjection simply handed back to the wealthier class the supreme political power which artisans and shopkeepers and " mean people " of the mediæval boroughs had threatened to share with them.

The true story of this singular growth of independence in the English boroughs and of its no less singular decay would form one of the most striking

[1] See Paston Letters, i. 160-1, 337, 339-40; ii. 78, 28, 31, 35-36; iii. 52-3. Richard the Redeless, passus iv. The great people occasionally exercised influence in towns; Hist. MSS. Com- v. 497; ix. 138. For various modes of voting in towns see Lynn, Hist. MSS. Com. xi. 3, 146-151; Chichester, Gross. Gild Merchant, ii. 48; Reading, Coates, 459; Sandwich, Boys, 402; Exeter, Freeman, 152; Worcester, Eng. Guilds, 373, 393; Bristol, Hunt, 86; Cinque Ports, Boy's Sandwich, 774, 796.

chapters in all our national history. But the materials for such a story, obscure, fragmentary, and scattered as they are, still lie hidden away in municipal archives, state rolls, and judicial records, as though the matter were one with which Englishmen had nothing to do. It is true indeed that the many ingenious expedients which the burghers devised to meet the peculiar difficulties of a past age would ill serve as models for our use to-day, nor can their success or failure be urged on either side of our modern controversies. They tell us nothing of the advantages or drawbacks of protection in our own time, or of the uses of state regulation of labour, or of the advisability of trade guilds. We cannot revive their courts or their privileges, any more than we can set up their gallows or call out modern citizens to dig a moat that shall be their defence from a hostile world. We cannot borrow their experience and live idly on the wisdom of the dead. But there is no more striking study of the perpetual adjustment and contrivance by which living communities adapt themselves to the changing order of the world than the study of our provincial boroughs in the Middle Ages; and Englishmen who now stand in the forefront of the world for their conception of freedom and their political capacity, and whose contribution to the art of government has been possibly the most significant fact of these last centuries, may well look back from that great place to the burghers who won for them their birthright, and watch with a quickened interest the little stage of the mediæval boroughs where their forefathers once played their part, trying a dozen schemes of representation, constructing plans of government, inventing constitutions, with a living energy which has not yet spent its force after traversing a score of generations.

There is no better starting point for the study of town life in England than the fifteenth century itself, when, with ages of restless growth lying behind them, and with their societies as yet untouched by the influences of the Renascence or the Reformation or the new commercial system, the boroughs had reached their prosperous maturity. It would be vain to attempt any reconstruction of their earlier history without having first stood, as it were, in the very midst of that turbulent society, and by watching the infinite variety of constitutional developement learned to search out and estimate the manifold forces which had been at work to bring about so complex a result; and no study of their later history is possible without an understanding of the prodigious vitality of the mediæval municipalities. There were the workshops in which the political creed of England was fashioned, where the notion of a free commonwealth with the three estates of king, lords, and commons holding by common consent their several authority, was proved and tested till it became the mere commonplace, the vulgar property of every Englishman. There the men who were ultimately to make the Reformation were schooled in all the vexed questions between church and state, and in the practical meaning of interference in civic matters by an alien power, so that the final crisis of religious excitement was but the dramatic declamation on a grand scale of lessons diligently repeated class by class for many a generation beforehand. There, too, long before the great national struggles of later centuries between England and the continental powers exalted patriotism to its highest ardour, men were already inspired by the vision of the English nation holding its post against the world, and by a passionate allegiance to its great destiny; and in every market and harbour the love of country was quickened by the new commerce with its gigantic ambition to win for England the dominion of the seas, its federations of merchants held together by the desperate struggle for supremacy, and its hordes of pirates who swept the ocean with the wild joy of their Norse ancestors. There is no break in our history when the old world merged into the new, for the spirit of the fifteenth century was the spirit of the sixteenth century as completely as it is the spirit of to-day.

The towns as we find them in the fifteenth century were the outcome of centuries of preparation. It was by a very slow and gradual process that England was transformed from a purely agricultural country, with its scattered villages of dependent tillers of the soil, into the England we know to-day —a land of industrial town communities, where agricultural interests are almost forgotten in the summing up of the national wealth. Our modern towns, indeed, can almost all trace back their history into the obscurity of a very distant past; but their record as we find it in Domesday, or under the Norman kings, is simply that of little country hamlets, where a few agricultural labourers gathered in their poor hovels, tilling by turns their lord's land and their own small holdings; or of somewhat bigger villages which lay at the branching of a great road, at a river ford, or at a convenient meeting-place for fair or market, and thus grew into some little consequence as the centres of a small local trade; while along the coast a few seaports were just beginning to draw merchants with their wares to a land that had long been almost forgotten by the traders of the Continent. It was not till the twelfth century[1] that our boroughs began to have an independent municipal history—from the time, that is, when the growth of the wool trade under Henry the First gave them a new commercial life; and the organization of local government under Henry the Second opened for them the way into a new world of political experiment and speculation.[2] From this time all went well with the municipalities for three hundred years. In the course of the thirteenth century the great majority of towns obtained rights of self-government, until finally these grants came to an end simply because there were no unenfranchised towns left.[3] Not indeed that the flow of royal charters ceased, for burghers who had got the first instalments of independence

[1] The first mention of burgesses in the Empire is in 1066 at Huy, in the bishopric of Liege. Pirenne, Dinant, 18.

[2] Dr. Gross gives a list of 150 towns which had gained the right of having a merchant gild—most of them in the twelfth and thirteenth centuries.

[3] Edward the First in the thirty years of his rule created fifty-four new boroughs. In the first eighty years of the fifteenth century the kings only issued nine charters of this kind.

were constant in pressing for all such further privileges as could magnify their authority or protect their dignity; and successive generations of patriotic citizens gathered into their town chests under the safe keeping of half a dozen locks piles of precious parchments, each of which conferred some new boon or widened the borders of liberty. Determined as it was by local circumstances the struggle for independence was carried on after an irregular fashion, first in one town, then in another ; here the burghers pressed forward riotously, and there loitered indifferently or stopped discouraged on their way. Some towns were allowed to elect their mayor before 1200,[1] others did not win the right till three or four centuries later; Bristol was made a shire in 1375, more than a hundred years before Gloucester; and in the fifteenth century there were still boroughs which had to gain their first charters, or else to exchange narrow and insufficient rights for full emancipation. But the forward movement never ceased ; every victory counted for liberty, and every success justified faith and inspired new zeal. The burghers went on filling their purses on the one hand, and drawing up constitutions for their towns on the other, till in the fifteenth century they were in fact the guardians of English wealth and the arbiters of English politics.

At first indeed municipal life, even at its best, was on a very humble scale. The biggest boroughs

[1] London was not apparently before other cities in the winning of liberties. (Round, Geoffrey de Mandeville, 372.) There were reasons enough for especial caution of Henry the Second in the matter of London.

could probably in 1300 only make a show of four or five thousand inhabitants, and of enfranchised burgesses a yet smaller number;[1] while the mud or wood-framed huts with gabled roofs of thatch and reeds that lined their narrow lanes sheltered a people who, accepting a common poverty, traded in little more than the mere necessaries of life.[2] It was not till the middle of the fourteenth century that the towns as they entered on a larger industrial activity began to free themselves from the indescribable squalor and misery of the early Middle Ages; but from this time forward we begin to detect signs of stirring prosperity, at first under the guise of a frugal well-being, and later carrying its luxury with happy ostentation. In the course of the next hundred years we see trading ports such as Lynn, Sandwich, Southampton, or Bristol, and centres of inland traffic such as Nottingham, Leicester, or Reading, and manufacturing towns like Norwich, Worcester, York, heaping up wealth, doubling and trebling their yearly expenditure, raising the salaries of their officers, building new quarters, adorning their public offices and churches, lavishing money on the buying of new privileges for their citizens, or on the extension of their trade. And while the bigger boroughs were thus enjoying their harvest of blessing and fat things, the small seaports and market towns also gathered

[1] Gross, Gild Merchant, i. 73, note; Archæologia, vii. p. 337-347; Stubbs, ii. 486.
[2] Burgage rents in the earliest times were accounted for by the officers not in a lump sum but "as the pennies come in." Rep. on Markets, 13.

in their share of the general good fortune by which all England was enriched.

Take, for example, the town of Colchester, where from the time of the Conquest a population of about 2,200 had found means to live, but in those two hundred and fifty years had never added to their numbers. Of their manner of life we can tell something from the records of a toll levied on their goods about 1300. One of the wealthiest tradesmen in the town was a butcher, whose valuation came to £7 15s. 2d.; while the stock-in-hand of his brethren in the trade consisted mostly of brawn, lard, and a few salting tubs, though one had two carcases of oxen at two shillings each, and another had meat worth thirty shillings in his shop. If we add to the butchers thirteen well-to-do tanners, and fourteen mercers who sold gloves, belts, leather, silk purses, and needle-cases, besides cloth and flannel, and one even girdles (which, with their silver ornaments, were costly articles), we have exhausted the list of the Colchester plutocrats. In the course of the fourteenth century, however, the makers of cloth came to settle beside the tanners and butchers. Card-makers, combers, clothiers, weavers, fullers, and dyers gathered to the town, and spread their trade out into the neighbouring villages. Wool-mongers pushed their business, till in 1373 the bailiffs made the under-croft beneath the old Moot Hall into a Wool Hall for the convenience of dealers, and added a fine porch with a vault overhanging the entrance to the Moot Hall, and some shops with solars over them. Before the century had closed the population had more than doubled. The poor houses that once lined the streets were swept away, and wealthy men built shops in the new style with chambers over them fronting the street, and let them to shopkeeping tenants.[1]

In the little trading town of Bridport we have the same story. In 1319 Bridport, with its one hundred and eighty burgesses, could not at a "view of arms," or muster of fighting men, produce a single burgher who bore bow and arrows, and sent out its motley regiment equipped with the universal knife or dagger, or, as it might chance, with staves, hatchets, pole-axes, forks, or spears, while an aristocrat or two actually bore a sword. Only sixty-seven burgesses out of the one hundred and eighty paid taxes, and the general poverty seems to have been extreme. The richest man had one cow, two hogs, two brass platters, a few hides, and a little furniture—the whole worth £4 8s.; and one of the most respectable innkeepers of the place owned two hogs, two beds, two tablecloths, two hand napkins, a horse, a brass pot, a platter, a few wooden vessels, and some malt.[2] In 1323 things were a trifle better, for eighty persons were then taxed, the property of some of them being valued only at six shillings, and this under a system in which the whole of each man's possessions was exactly reckoned up—his cards, yarn, shoes, the girths he was making or trying to sell, even his store of oatmeal. A century later, however, we find a new Bridport. Traders from Bristol had settled in its streets, and men of Holland and foreign merchants

---

[1] Cutt's Colchester, 111-117, 126-7.
[2] Two other inn-keepers had much the same stock-in-trade.

and craftsmen; and the townsfolk had grown prosperous and began to bind themselves together in fraternities—the brotherhood of S. Nicholas, the brotherhood of S. Mary and S. James, the brotherhood of the Two Torches, a brotherhood of the Light of the Holy Cross in S. Andrew's, and another in S. Mary's, and the brotherhood of the Torches in the Church of the Blessed Mary—apparently the offspring of the first half of the fifteenth century. The Toll Hall was repaired, the houses in the town set in order, and a new causeway made. The Guild Hall got its clock; the church was rebuilt and fitted up with organs, and sittings in it were let out to the wealthy burghers. When, finally, a "view of arms" was again held in the town in 1458, there was not a single name left of those who had appeared in the list of 1319. But these new traders came bravely set out with bows and arrows, as well as with daggers, bills, pole-axes, or spears, or marching proudly with their mails, jacks, salets, and "white harness with a basenet." The Bridport standard had changed, and one man who came carrying quite an armoury—a gun, besides a bow, twelve arrows, a sword, and a buckler—was ordered to have twelve more arrows at the next muster.[1]

[1] Hist. MSS. Com. vi. part i. 491-2, 478, 489. In Reading at the muster roll of 1311 there appeared eight men armed with sword, bow, arrows, and knife; thirty-three with bows, arrows, and knives; and over two hundred and thirty-five (besides some names lost at the foot of the roll) with hatchets and knives. In 1371 the town was able to raise a body of archers for service abroad; and under Edward the Sixth it sent fifty soldiers armed with bills, swords, daggers, bows, and arrows, and paid each

Even towns which like Rye had known all the calamities of war were only waiting for a moment of peace to win their share of the common prosperity. Burned by the French in 1377, burned and laid desolate again in 1448, Rye long remained on the level of poverty common in the Middle Ages. In 1414 it sheltered a mere handful of struggling people—twenty-one poor householders in Nesse Ward, twenty-eight in Water Melle Ward, and a somewhat larger number in Market Ward equally poor; within its walls, in fact, there was but one man—the lord of the manor—who was assessed at so great a sum as 6s. 8d., though there was the beginning of a fashionable suburb in the Ward without the Gate, where the Mayor lived with some dozen other well-to-do householders, two of whom besides the Mayor were assessed at the aristocratic figure of 6s. 8d. By the end of the century, however, Rye fishermen were known on distant seas and Rye traders in the fairs at home and abroad. London merchants had bought property in the thriving town, and new quarters had sprung up with names borrowed from the capital—Paternoster Ward and Bucklersbury Ward. In 1493 five of the burghers were assessed as owning £400 each, and the total value of the property possessed by the inhabitants was £6,303.[1]

Evidence of accumulating wealth indeed gathers on every side. The labour and enterprise which in earlier centuries had covered England with castles

---

soldier forty pence " for the King's affairs into Boulogne." Hist. MSS. Com. xi. 7, 171, 182.   [1] Ibid. v. 497.

and cathedrals and monasteries was now absorbed in the work of covering it with new towns. A journey through any part of the country to-day is enough to show us how ruthlessly the men of the fifteenth century swept away the parish churches which their fathers had built in the fourteenth century, to replace them with the big bare fabrics where size and ostentation too often did service for beauty, and in the building of which prosperous burghers gave more conspicuous proof of wealth and lavish generosity than of taste and feeling. In Canterbury and Worcester and Nottingham and Bristol and a host of other towns we may still admire the new houses that were being raised for the traders, with their picturesque outlines and fine carved work. Waste places in the boroughs were covered with buildings and formed into new wards. On every side corporations instinct with municipal pride built Common Halls, set up stately crosses in the market-place such as we still see at Winchester or Marlborough, paved the streets,[1] or provided new

[1] Act of Parliament for paving Gloucester, 1455; Fosbrooke's Gloucestershire, i. 157. For Exeter in 1466; Freeman's Exeter, 91. For Canterbury in 1474, because the "evil report" carried away by pilgrims "would be stopped if the roads were properly pitched with boulders and Folkestone stone"; Hist. MSS. Com. ix. 168, 144, 174. For Southampton in 1477, after a century of vain attempts to pave the streets; Davies, 119, 120; in 1384 a tax was levied for pavage; in 1441 accounts were rendered of paving stones provided; payments were made in 1457 to a London paviour. By the Act each citizen was ordered to pave before his own door as far as the middle of the street since "the town was full feebly paved and full perilous and jeopardous to ride or go therein, and in especial in the High Street," so that

water-supply for the growing population.[1] If we count up the new gates, and quays, and bridges, and wharves, and harbours, and sluices, and aqueducts, and markets of which the town records furnish accounts, we are filled with amazement at an activity which was really stupendous. Public duty and private enterprise went hand in hand. Sometimes the whole commonalty was called out to help at the church-building, or the digging of a new harbour; sometimes the charity once given to religious uses was turned into the channel of civic patriotism, and good citizens left money to found hospitals and almshouses and schools, to pave the streets, to pay the tolls of their town, to fee lawyers to defend its privileges, or buy a charter to protect its rights from invasion. Thus it was two traders of Canterbury who built in 1400 the first private bridge over the river; and in 1485 a mercer from London, William

"strangers thither resorting have been oftentimes greatly hurt and in peril of their lives." For Bristol in 1491 when the whole town seems to have been new paved. Ricart, 47-48.

[1] To take a single instance, in 1421 the water-supply of Southampton was undertaken by the council, and new leaden pipes provided by the grant of a burgess who had thus bequeathed his money "for the good of his soul." An aqueduct was made at considerable expense in 1428; 261 days' work at it was paid at from 4*d*. to 6*d*. a day; over £12 more was spent on an iron grating for it, and 27*s*. 2*d*. given to the plumber who fixed it; great stones from Wathe called "scaplyd stonys" were carried, with loads of chalk, quicklime, pitch, rosin, solder, wax, and wood. In 1490 a new well was made with a "watering-place for horse and a washing-place for women." Davies, 115, 117; Hist. MSS. Com. xi. 3, 138-40. In many towns wells were repaired, enclosed with a wall and covered with a roof and put under the care of wardens.

Pratt, constructed at his own expense the first main drain under the Old Street to carry off the rain-water into the river.[1] In Birmingham the whole community formed itself into a " guild and lasting brotherhood " for the doing of works of charity, and chiefly it would seem for the repairing of two great stone bridges and divers foul and dangerous ways on the high road to Wales—a work which the Corporation was too poor to undertake.[2]

Nor was this growth in wealth the only, or indeed the most striking part of the town's history during these three centuries from the time of Henry the Second to the time of Henry the Seventh. Trade is pretty much the same wherever it exists at all, and from its narrow dominion much of human energy will always make a way to escape. When Englishmen had spent a measure of their force in creating a nation of shopkeepers, there was still enough of buoyant and exuberant strength left to elaborate an art of government which has affected the history of the world; and the truly characteristic part of the mediæval story is that which enables us to measure the political genius with which the forerunners of our modern democracy shaped schemes of administration for the societies they had created of free workers. There was much to be done in the new ordering of life.[3] Already in the twelfth

---

[1] Hist. MSS. Com. ix. 137, 145.   See Paston, i. 434; Hist. MSS. Com. xi. 7, 169; x. 4, 529-30.

[2] English Guilds, 241, 249.

[3] For the contrast in this respect between the shire and the borough see Round's Geoffrey de Mandeville, 356-7.

century a new force had declared itself when in France the middle and lower classes for the first time found a voice in literature. From that time onwards poets of the people and teachers of socialism, writing in the vulgar tongue for common folk, proposed startling questions and boldly pressed home their conclusions. Nothing was safe from their criticism; as they discussed the original rights of men, the "social contract" between the people and their lords, the tyranny of nobles, or the rights of peasants,[1] these new thinkers among the people gave warning of growing energies too big and passionate to live at ease in the narrow bondage of mediæval custom and tradition. The inevitable changes however came slowly, and those who lived in the midst of the movement were themselves unconscious of the real transformation that was going on. Even at the end of the fourteenth century the writer of Piers Ploughman, when he paints for us the picture of the feudal world as it then was, has no dream that its bondage can ever be broken, that there is any escape out of the prison-house of mediæval society. For the first time we there see England, not as it appeared to historians and satirists of the court or the monastery, but as it looked to one standing in the very midst of that vast "field full of folk from end to other"—to the poet who walked among the people with his heart full of charity and pity, who by day mixed with the crowd at the fair, or watched the bargainings in the market-place, or travelled along country by-ways and entered the

[1] Luchaire, Communes Françaises, 22-25. See Piers Ploughman, passus i. 139-146; ii. 90-99; ix. 19-76; x. 223-227.

hovels of the poor, and at night sat in the ale-house among beggars and mendicant friars. But while he shows us all the trouble and confusion of that tumultuous crowd, the social order remains to him simple and unchangeable—fixed, in his belief, as firmly as the decrees of God and nature could establish it. He could only repeat the old time-honoured counsels of work and obedience as the final remedy for all social ills : " Counsel not the commons the King to displease." But it was more than possible that work and obedience might still leave, as it had left before, life empty of all but misery. Then the last solace lay in resignation.

> " Yea, quoth Patience, and hente out of his poke
> A piece of the Pater Noster and proffered to us all.
> And I listened and looked what livelihood it were ;
> Then was it 'Fiat voluntas tua' that should find us all.
> 'Have, Actyf,' quoth Patience, 'and eat this when thee hungreth
> Or when thou clomsest for cold or clyngest for drought ;
> And shall never gyves thee grieve nor great lord's wrath,
> Prison nor other pain for—*patientes vincunt*."[1]

Such was Langland's final solution for the disorders of his time. But the English were not a patient people, and the problem of the reorganization of society had become a very serious one towards the close of the Middle Ages, and was perhaps more urgent to men's fears and consciences in the fifteenth century than it had ever been before, or was to be again till our own day. It was a press-

---

[1] Piers Ploughman, passus xvi. 248-255.

ing question for humble folk, for shopkeepers and traders and artisans and journeymen who in the absence of privilege were driven to think of liberty; and in the crowded lanes, the mean workshops, the disorderly market-place, the little thatched Common Hall of the mediæval town, great principles of freedom found their early home, and fought their way to perfection and supremacy. It was not enough that the burghers should create societies of free men—"*gentlemen*," as Piers Ploughman would have said,[1] to whom the great difference that distinguished between man and man was not wealth or poverty, labour or ease, but freedom or bondage. This was the easier part of their task, and was practically finished early in their history. It was a longer and more difficult business to discover how the art of government should be actually practised in these communities, and to define the principles of their political existence. But in these matters also the burghers became the pioneers of our liberties, and their political methods have been handed down as part of the heritage of

[1] "The Jews that were gentlemen, Jesus they despised,
  Both his lore and his law, now are they low churls,
  As wide as the world is woneth (dwelleth) there none
  But under tribute and tallage as tikes and churls.
  And those that become Christian by counsel of the Baptist
  Are franklins and free . . . .
  And gentlemen with Jesus."

(Piers Ploughman, ed. by W. Skeat for Early English Text Society, part iii.; pass. xxii. 34.) I have ventured to give quotations from mediæval writers in modern spelling, as I am here concerned neither with philology nor the history of literature: and there are many to whom the old methods of spelling only serve to obscure the sense.

the whole people. As by degrees the multitude of privileges promised and confirmed left the important towns with no more demands to make, they turned their energies to the work of framing those elaborate and highly artificial constitutions which mark the highest point to which their proud and self-sufficient independence had attained. Instead of tamely accepting the pattern or the theory of its neighbours, every town was making its own peculiar experiment in the art of governing, with a vivacity and a restless ingenuity proper to the culminating moment of their activity.

Meanwhile by a happy coincidence the boroughs were called to take part in the great movement by which the House of Commons was created, at a time when the discipline and experience of local self-government had prepared them to exercise a very real influence in the moulding of the English constitution into its present form. Having for the most part secured their fundamental liberties just before Simon de Montfort in 1265 summoned the middle class to take their share in the work of Parliament, and having steadily strengthened their position during all the thirty years of changing counsels and tentative experiments which followed, they saw the representation of the boroughs definitely established in 1295— the very year after county representation had been at last perfectly acknowledged.[1] If for a time they played apparently a small part in political battles, if the separate action of the borough members is scarcely mentioned,[2] the fact still remains that throughout the

[1] Stubbs, ii. 137-144, 239-244.   [2] Ibid. ii. 560, 671.

century during which the House of Commons was being fashioned [1] members sent from these free self-governing communities formed almost two-thirds of that House. Edward the First sent Parliamentary writs to 166 towns, and in the Parliament of 1399, 176 representatives of boroughs sat by the seventy-four knights of the shire.[2] Silent and acquiescent as they were for a while, there are significant instances to show the steady growth of their importance, and the way in which statesmen had begun to appreciate the new force with which governments had henceforth to reckon.[3] By the close of the fourteenth century their influence was marked; and it was doubtless through its vigorous burghers that the

[1] Stubbs, ii. 332-4.
[2] Ibid. ii. 257; iii. 16.
[3] The former devices for illegal taxation on the King's part broke down when the commons looked so sharply after these matters that no attempt at unauthorised taxation of merchandise was made after the accession of Richard the Second. Stubbs, ii. 574-578. How completely the relation of King and commons had been reasoned out by the people we see in Langland's writings.

"Then came there a King, and ' by his crown,' said,
' I am a king with crown the commons to rule,
And holy Church and clergy from cursed men to defend.
And if me lacketh to live by, the law wills that I take
There I may have it hastelokest; (quickest) for I am head of law,
And ye be both members, and I above all.'

. . . .

' On condition,' quoth conscience, ' that thou conne defend
And rule thy realm in reason right well, and in truth;
Then, that thou have thine asking as the law asketh;
Omnia sunt tua ad defendendum, sed non ad deprehendendum.'"
(Piers Ploughman, passus xxii. 467-472, 478-481.)

House of Commons in the early part of the fifteenth century laid hold of powers which it had never had before, nor was to have again for two hundred years.[1] In the list of petitions and statutes throughout the century in which their influence on legislation was plainly dominant, we may look for the true beginning of democratic government in England.[2] Indeed at a yet earlier time, when the House of Commons was not seventy years old, its power had been already measured and men's imaginations kindled by its mighty destiny. If supreme over all the King kept his state at Westminster,

> "him lord antecedent,
> Both their head and their King, holding with no party,
> But stand as a stake that sticketh in a mire
> Between two lands for a true mark";

if his power was absolute, and he could

> "claim the commons at his will
> To follow him, to find him, and to fetch at them his counsel,"[3]

yet even then Conscience warned the sovereign that to frame a righteous government "without the commons' help it is full hard, by my head";[4] and Reason

> "counselled the King his commons to love,
> For the commons is the King's treasure."[5]

---

[1] Stubbs, iii. 77; Rogers, Agric. and Prices, iv. viii.

[2] See the description of a session of Parliament in Richard the Redeless, passus iii. A.D. 1399.

[3] Piers Ploughman, passus iv. 376, &c.

[4] Ibid. passus v. 176.

[5] Ibid. passus vi. 181. M. Jusserand (Epopée Mystique du Moyen Age, 101–118), justly points out what a typical representative

The whole part however played by the towns in national politics, the degree of influence they exercised, in what ways it differed from that of the aristocratic class, how it affected matters of administration, finance, foreign policy, commercial laws, the strength of the monarchy, and the forms of the constitution—all these questions have still to be investigated. What is perfectly clear is that wise rulers in those days saw the tremendous change that was taking place in the balance of forces in the State, as even the most foolish among them felt that the power of the purse at least was passing from the country magnates to the town merchants;[1] and they gave expression to their convictions by a change in the whole character of their policy. To kings and statesmen the friendship of the burghers even in times of comparative quiet was daily becoming a matter of greater consequence to be bought at their own price. It was no longer the nobles whom they sought to bribe to their interest, but the towns; and as gifts and pensions to Court favourites declined, courtesies and gracious remissions of rent were lavished on the boroughs.[2] From this time, even when the

of common opinion Langland was. Compare the popular manifesto of 1450. (Hist. MSS. Com. viii. 267.) "They say the King should live upon his commons, and that their bodies and goods are his; the contrary is true, for then needed him never to set Parliament and to ask good of them."

[1] The burden of taxation was gradually being transferred from one class to another as subsidies on moveables, and customs on import and export were found more productive and more easily managed. Stubbs, ii. 570.

[2] Reductions of rent are too numerous to give; they occurred everywhere, and were sometimes apparently bought at a considerable price. (See Round's Geoffrey de Mandeville, 366.) Loans

towns had fallen to their lowest estate, their heritage of power was never wholly lost, and through their later humiliation and corruption we may still discover the evidence of their political consequence, since the measure of their influence was in fact the price set on their obedience.

If such a tale of long centuries of national growth ending in a satisfied maturity carries its suggestion of dull monotony, we need only turn to the history of towns in other times and places to discover that in this very monotony is hidden a real element of singularity.

from the towns seem to have been voluntary. In 1435 the Sandwich commonalty refused to lend money to the King; and further excused themselves from sending him soldiers for the defence of Calais, "having all the men they can spare already employed in the service of the Duke of York." (Boys, 672.) A grant to the King was again refused in 1486. (Ibid. 678.) The Norwich citizens got into trouble for instituting a suit to have their loan returned (Blomefield, iii. 147, 152). In 1424 Lynn lent 400 marks, and in 1428 the council agreed that burgesses of parliament should receive from executors of the late king a hundred pounds for a pledged circlet of gold because they could not get more (Hist. MSS. Com. xi. part 3, 161). In 1491 the king was at Bristol, where he had a benevolence of £1,800 (Ricart, 47-48). At the coming of Richard the Third in 1484, York, to gain a reduction of the fee-ferm, agreed to give him 100 marks in a cup of gold, and to the queen £100 in a dish. A list is given of the citizens who subscribed—the mayor giving £20, the recorder £100, and so on. The whole sum subscribed was £437 (Davis' York, 167-9, 174). It would be quite impossible to mention all the loans, but the instance of Canterbury is curious as the first foreshadowing of the national debt. In 1438 £40 was lent to the king, and in 1443 £50; in these cases private individuals advanced the money in various amounts according to their taste for speculation, and probably got certificates promising interest and redemption at par (Hist. MSS. Com. ix. part 1, 139).

The most striking contrast lies perhaps close at hand, in the brilliant and dramatic story of the communes in France—the shortest lived of all the feudal independent lordships in Europe.[1] Of earlier origin than the English, their history goes back to the first part of the twelfth century, fifty years before the movement had effectively begun in England; and the story of their liberties is, taken all together, but a brief tale of some two hundred years, from 1130 to 1330. Their progress was rapid and their decay as swift. Indeed decline had already set in by 1223, at the very time when Norwich, Nottingham, and a number of the greater English towns were just receiving for the first time powers of choosing their own rulers and administering their own justice. In 1280 their condition was almost hopeless,[2] and half a century later the life of the free communities was over and their liberties utterly extinguished, saving always the liberty to carry on trade.

And yet we can only wonder that the attempt lasted for two hundred years, set as they were amid difficulties wholly unknown to English burghers, or with the ghosts or dim reflections of which these at the worst had only to contend in a kind of phantom fight. What were the far-off echoes of foreign conquest or defeat heard on our side of the water, or the report of an occasional local rising, compared to the devastating wars that swept the plains of France, and amid the miseries of which the communes were struggling into life? The necessities of

[1] Luchaire, 288-9.   [2] Luchaire, 64, 137.

war proved fatal to local liberty, and that in more ways than one. If warring kings and lords created independent communities for their own purposes, with the sole idea of forming fortified centres capable of self-defence, such communes could hardly prove strongholds of freedom, and the self-government of the people soon fell in fact before the requirements of military discipline. Sometimes the death of freedom was brought about by more violent methods; and the trembling inhabitants who made their way back from the woods to their ruined homes after a town had been sacked and burned by the enemy, would pray to be disenfranchised that they might thus be delivered from the burdens and dues of a commune which they were no longer able to maintain. Abroad moreover feudalism retained the authority which had been torn from it here by Norman kings, and was yet more dangerous to the burghers than war itself. Against the might of their feudal lord, king or noble or ecclesiastic, they could make in the long run but a sorry fight, and perhaps after a century of desperate struggle for emancipation in which the peasants saw their brethren slain in thousands, their farms devastated, their wealth torn from them, their emigrants driven back starving to plundered homesteads, the outcome of all their misery was finally to gain a few trading privileges by consenting to a charter which once more laid them bound at the feet of their master. Too often the lord avoided open violence by calling political craft to his aid, and devised for his burghers some form of charter which while it admirably suited his own purposes robbed the communal government of any true democratic element and made the name of liberty a mockery. As for the vast number of towns big and little under ecclesiastical dominion, they contended in vain against princes of the Church whose mighty state was measured on the grand scale of the Continent—princes with the Pope always in the background, ready at their complaint to fulminate the decree of excommunication which left all the burghers' goods at the mercy of their lord. Whether the prelate sought to annihilate rebellious serfs with fire and sword, whether with more subtle intention he devised some cunningly delusive form of charter, or contrived to hinder all the operations of free government, to thwart its developement, and to check the spread of its influence, the tragic close was always at hand—political slavery and degradation. Amid the innumerable troubles that compassed the French communes round about, the administrative difficulties, the financial cares, the public bankruptcy of town after town, the evil moments when the king's fiscal officer and the starving people made alliance to destroy the privileges of the burghers, civic freedom failed. Time and fate were allied against the commune, and the issue of the battle was decided before the fight had well begun.

Against the century of growth and the century of decay which made up the record of the French communes, we have to set three hundred years of unbroken prosperity and privilege in which the English burghers added charter to charter and filled their " common chests " with a regularity that knew no check. It is not necessary, however, to assume that Englishmen reached that happy state wholly by virtue of their native superiority; it would perhaps be truer to thank the good fortune of insignificance that so long waited on them. England, in fact, was lagging far away in the rear, where there was little of the noise and dust of battle. It was not there that the idea of municipal liberty was first proclaimed; for in the Dark Ages of riot and disorder and piracy, Celts, Latins, Teutons, all the members of the European brotherhood in fact, found in association their natural succour against danger and aid to labour; and along the great trade routes that traversed Europe the more important societies of men confederated for protection and assistance were formed before ever Englishmen had begun to organize themselves into self-governing communities. In that European drama, everything took great continental proportions; men disputed for tremendous stakes, and in the long battle the mighty lords of the old world were never wholly routed, but still laid their grip on the modern society that was struggling to usher in a new order. In the great fight there were great defeats, such as we have seen in France, and liberty had to begin its course afresh and lead men along new roads in search of freedom and content. But we in our distant island had throughout the Middle Ages all the advantages of obscurity. According to any valid method of determining our place in the European order, whether by yearly income, or size of merchant fleets, or strength of armies, or number of inhabitants, we remained for a time after the loss of Normandy and Anjou unimportant in the eyes of Europe—of little account among the peoples; and as far as popular feeling went ourselves heedless of what went on on the Continent.¹ Tranquil and secure because no one took the trouble to think of us while we were regardless of their quarrels, we were left to learn our lessons as slowly as we would, to lay sure, if lowly, foundations, to practise our skill by safe experiments till our art was mastered. The humble display which we made in our national capacity was repeated in our municipal story. There indeed the tiny dominion of the community, the sparse population, the poor little treasure-box, the solitary "common barge," the handful of militia passing in review with their clubs and forks, present a sorry figure beside the majestic state of the big corporations over sea. But this humble condition was their true security. Set from the first in pleasant places where by conquering kings the lofty had been brought low and the humble lifted up, and where no enemy of invincible strength lay any longer across their path, the burghers might carry on their own business without care. Within the narrow area enclosed by the city wall and ditch, amid a scanty population scarcely bigger than that of a small country town to-day, experiments which would have been impossible on a great scale were tried with every conceivable variety of circumstance and expedient; and the boroughs owed to their early insignificance and isolation a freedom from restraint

¹ M. Jusserand in his Epopée Mystique du Moyen Age has well pointed out that the war with France was royal rather than national. Pp. 7-9, 117.

and dictation in which real political experience became possible.

Thus in England, as elsewhere, the character of the nation and the mould of its political thought were ultimately shaped by outward circumstance; and the forms of our freedom have been profoundly affected by the way which the towns took to liberty, by the manner in which they modified its expression according to the peculiar conditions to which each community was subject, and by the use they made of their power. But since the very existence of the towns as important centres of life, as well as the character of their development, depends on the complete transformation which English society underwent in the later Middle Ages, I venture, before beginning my real story, to give a very brief and rapid sketch of the Industrial and Commercial Revolution in which mediæval England was buried and modern England born.

CHAPTER II

THE INDUSTRIAL REVOLUTION OF THE FIFTEENTH CENTURY

THE history of the fifteenth century has long remained but little known. It is very generally regarded as the "profoundly tragic close of a great epoch," and the historian looks back to the golden age of the thirteenth century as the glorious time of English and of European history—the culminating period to which all the foregoing generations slowly mounted, and from whose heights the later sons of men as slowly and surely declined and went backward. The period of this backsliding is seen as an age altogether wanting in picturesqueness and moral elevation, sunk in materialism, sordid and vulgar, a time of confused and indiscriminate corruption, where "heart and treasure" were linked in ignoble union, and the political demoralization of the people was only matched by their private degradation; and the fifteenth century has long borne the heavy burden of its evil reputation, while its records have been left comparatively undisturbed by inquisitive search.[1] For hackneyed as the period of the Wars of the Roses may seem to the superficial reader, no student has yet adequately studied the secret of the age in which the great revolutions of the next century were being prepared—the age which made possible for England the revival of letters and the reformation, which founded her commercial greatness, which revolutionized her industrial system, which cast away the last bonds of feudalism and laid the foundations of the modern State.

It is indeed true that no great man has made this century illustrious. No general or warrior of

[1] Stubbs, Lectures on Mediæval History, p. 342; Friedman, Anne Boleyn, i. pp. 1-4; Gneist, La Constitution Communale, trans. by Hippert, i. p. 334, &c. "England at the accession of Henry the Seventh was far behind the England of the thirteenth century." (Denton, Lectures on the Fifteenth Century, 120, 118.) "This low and material view of domestic life had led to an equally low and material view of political life, and the cruelty which stained the Wars of the Roses was but the outcome of a state of society in which no man cared much for anything except his own greatness and enjoyment. The ideal which shaped itself in the minds of the men of the middle class was a king acting as a kind of chief constable, who, by keeping great men in order, would allow their inferiors to make money in peace." (Gardiner's Student's History, 330-1.) "The despondency of the English people, when their dream of conquest in France was dissipated, was attended with a complete decay of thought, with civil war, and with a standing still or perhaps a decline of population, and to a less degree of wealth." (National Life and Character, by Charles Pearson, p. 130-1.) "There are few more pitiful episodes in history. Thirty-five years of a war that was as unjust as it was unfortunate had both soured and demoralised the nation." "England had entirely ceased to count as a naval power." As for the burgesses, "if not actively mischievous they were sordidly inert." (Oman's Warwick, 4-11, 67, 133.)

the first rank distinguished wars which were born in iniquity, and kept alive by greed. No gifted statesman left his mark on the government or administration of the country. Among the people themselves interest in national affairs seemed dead; they made revolutions and set up new kings as they were bidden to do, and kept stores of badges of the houses of York and Lancaster alike, to be ready with either sign of loyalty as the fortunes of war turned this way or that;[1] they forgot the stirring political

[1] In Ricart's Calendar in Bristol he enters duly the fact that a battle had been fought and that one side or other was victorious without further comment. He misplaces the date of the murder of Suffolk three years, though he might well have remembered it; and he writes as a sort of after-thought in the margin of his record, "and this year the two sons of King Edward were put to silence in the Tower of London." (Ricart, 40-46.) In 1460 Norwich had its captain and 120 soldiers with King Henry in the north, and all the rest of its available forces had to hurry off to Edward at his accession. (Blomefield iii. 162-163.) The city raised £160 for the coming of Richard the Third to the city, and £140 for the coming of Henry the Seventh. (Ibid. 173-174.) For Nottingham, see vol. ii. There is no mention of Bosworth in Canterbury, and Henry the Seventh was received with the same pomp as former kings. (Hist. MSS. Com. ix. 145.) For Bosworth, where men stood afar off waiting to join the victorious side, see Fabyan, 672-673. The policy of the burghers was the same in this respect as that of the great Churchmen, who were entirely passive in the real crises of the civil war, and so ready to serve every king, that not one of them suffered loss from fidelity to any side. (Rogers' Agricul. and Prices, iv. 9, 10.) The people in general were equally indifferent. "I have read thousands of documents penned during the heat of the strife, and have found only one allusion to the character of the times in the earlier, and one about the later war of 1470-1." (Ibid., 19.) An interesting parallel to the indifference of the

ballads of former generations and sang moral ditties instead. In place of the mighty theologians of an earlier time there came commentators and interpreters of little significance. Nor did a single religious leader or reformer or scholar arise to stir the popular thought or conscience : Lollardy with its questionings and criticisms was still heard of from time to time in the bigger towns and manufacturing districts, but the people generally acquiesced in the demands of the authorized religion and discipline. Literature was well nigh lost as well as the graver kinds of learning. In the beginning of the century one or two nobles had collected libraries and brought tidings of the Renascence in Italy, and later on half a dozen scholars made their way to the Italian universities; but there was neither poet nor scholar to follow the masters of an earlier age. In the fifteenth century the very language in which Chaucer wrote was but half intelligible to the mass of the people, and his tales must have been unknown out of court circles. Men were content with rhymes innumerable—on morals, on manners, on heraldry, on the art of dining, on the rules of thrift and prosperity; and in all our history there is no time so barren in literature as the reign of Henry the Sixth.

Even in a democratic age it is not easy at first sight to recognise where the interest lies of an epoch destitute of all that has made other times illustrious, and whose significance seems to shrink in

trading communities of the fifteenth century during the Wars of the Roses may be seen in the action of the Merchants' Company in the civil wars of the seventeenth century. (Lambert's Gild Life, 177-178.)

comparison with the struggles and victories of the ages that preceded, and the splendid achievements of the age that followed it; and historians finding themselves face to face with so dreary a century may have been tempted to give it a character of its own for grossness, for cruelty, for any distinction whatever which will at least take it out of the range of the absolutely commonplace. But the distinguishing mark of the fifteenth century lies neither in its crime nor in its vulgarity. We must judge this period in fact as a time of transition in many ways extraordinarily like our own. In the centuries between the Great Plague and the Reformation, just as in the nineteenth century, the real significance of our history lies in the advent of a new class to wealth and power, as the result of a great industrial revolution. The breaking up of an old aristocratic order, and the creation of a middle class to be brought into politics and even into "society," the enormous increase of material wealth, the new relation of the various ranks to one another, and the failure under altered circumstances of traditional rules of conduct, the varied careers suddenly opened to talent or ambition, the reproach for the first time attached to incompetence and poverty, the vulgarization of literature and morality which followed on their adaptation to a class as yet untrained to criticism or comparison, the extension of a habit of religion closely related to a plain morality—all these things recall to us many of the experiences of our own days, and may make us more tolerant of the unpicturesque and Philistine element whether then or now. If the chief centre of interest had once lain in the offices of the royal palace it might now be seen rather in the new Town Hall which was being built in almost every borough in England, or in the office where the mayor's clerk was busied in making his copies of Magna Charta or extracts of Domesday, or in translating from the old French the customs and ordinances of the town, or in hunting up the rolls of the itinerant judges; or over the country-side where estates were being sold and bought with the development of a provincial instead of a national nobility and the rise of new men to possess the old acres, and where the quickening of the struggle for life was reflected in the stormy conflicts and significant concessions of the manor courts. The new middle class of shopkeepers and farmers had indeed no chroniclers and no flatterers, for it was long before men could realise how rapidly and completely the weight of influence was being transferred from the old governing class to the mass of the governed, and chroniclers still went on mechanically retailing events now comparatively trivial and unimportant. It was not till the next century that they turned from spinning out these worthless annals to a discussion of matters really important which had by that time forced themselves on the dullest apprehension.

The whole interest of the fifteenth century thus lies in the life of very common folk—of artisans and tradesmen in the towns, and in country parts of the farmers, the tenants of the new grazing lands, the stewards and bailiffs and armies of dependents on the great estates, who did all the work at home while the lord was away at the wars or at the halls of Westminster. If the century produced no great administrator or statesman, it did create a whole class of men throughout the country trained in practical affairs, doing an admirable work of local government, active, enterprising, resolute, public-spirited, disciplined in the best of all schools for political service. If there was no great writer, the new world of the middle class was patiently teaching itself, founding its schools, learning its primary rules of etiquette and its simple maxims of morals, reading its manuals of agriculture or law or history, practising its Latin rhymes, and building up in its own fashion from new beginnings a learning which the aristocratic class had been too proud, too indifferent, or too remote to hand on to it.[1] If no religious revival shook the country, the new society was solving in its own way the problem of helping the sick and poor;[2] it was

[1] See vol. ii. ch. i.
[2] In Lydd corn was given to the poor at Christmas and Easter, and gifts to lepers; payments made from 1480-1485 for Goderynge's daughter, "poor maid," "hosen, shoes, her keep, kertyl-cloth and for making thereof; also in 1490, "paid to the poor man keeping the poor child 12 pence." After a long list of expenses for a thief and making stocks for him and a halter, "paid for one pair of shoes to his daughter 3d.," and "given to the quest of women 4d."; summoned perhaps in reference to the daughter. (Hist. MSS. Com. v. 527, 526.) In Rye sums were paid to the poor on opening the box of maltotes. (Ibid. 494.) For Southampton, Hist. MSS. Com. xi. 3, 112; the steward's book in 1441 contains a list of alms, £4 2s. 1d., given away every week to poor men and women. (Davies, 294.) According to the usual calculation at this time in almshouses of a penny a day for living, this sum would mean that the corpora-

earnest in religious observance, it was framing its English litanies and devising its own plans for teaching the people an intelligent devotion.[1] The burghers

tion paid weekly for the mere subsistence of 140 persons. For Bristol, Ricart's Kalendar, 72-80, 82, &c. For Chester, Hist. MSS. Com. viii. 371. For Romney, Hist. MSS. Com. v. 535-6. The Mayor of Sandwich had to manage the hospitals of S. Bartholomew and S. John, to appoint their officers, to audit their accounts, and administer their estates made up of innumerable parcels of land and houses left by pious people. (Boys, 17-21, 526.) The municipal council of Exeter appointed every year a Warden of the Poor to look after their many charitable foundations. It had charge of Magdalen Hospital, of the Ten Cells Hospital for Poor, founded in 1406 by Simon Grendon, Mayor; the Combrew Almshouse, founded by Sir William Bonville, 1408; and an almshouse founded by John Palmer. (Freeman's Exeter, 175-6.) There was a municipal almshouse in Hereford supported by way of payment to the corporation from ecclesiastical tenants for a share in the city's privileges. (Arch. Ass. Journ. xxvii. 481.) In the fifteenth century bequests by burgesses for these purposes were very frequent and were usually left to the management of the corporation. In all large towns the mayor and aldermen presided over the court of orphans. (Davies's Southampton, 239.) The indications of poor relief by the towns must modify Mr. Ashley's conclusion (Economic History, I. part ii. 338) that "no attempt was made by the State as a whole, *or by any secular public authority*, to relieve distress. The work was left *entirely* to the Church, and to the action of religious motives upon the minds of individuals." It seems difficult to follow in this connexion his distinction drawn between the craft associations which had or had not grown out of religious fraternities (p. 325).

[1] Besides the customary Latin prayers a Norfolk guild used English prayers for Church and State, harvest and travellers, like our Litany. (English Guilds, 111-114.) The play of the Lord's Prayer was performed by a York guild. "They are bound to find one candle-bearer, with seven lights, in token of the seven supplications in the Lord's Prayer." "Also they are

began to perform in the national economy the work which in earlier centuries had been performed by the great monastic societies. The extension of trade and manufacture had fallen into their hands; they were busied in the gathering together and storing up of the national wealth.[1] They gave to labour a new dignity in social life and a new place in the national councils. From the towns came a perpetual protest against war and disorder; throughout the troubles of the fifteenth century, civil war, court intrigues, the tyranny of usurpers and the plots of the vanquished, local raids of private revenge or of land hunger, their influence was always thrown on the side of peace and quietness. Art found in them patrons; illuminators and painters, architects and bell-founders, the makers of delicate shrines and images,[2] engravers of seals, goldsmiths

bound to make, and as often as need be to renew, a table showing the whole meaning and use of the Lord's Prayer, and to keep this hanging against a pillar in the said cathedral church near to the aforesaid candle-bearer." (Ibid. 137–9.) See also Hibbert's Shrewsbury Guilds, 62. For Pecok as "the first author of the Middle Ages who propounded reason as a judge of faith," and one who "might be claimed as at once the forerunner of the Erastian theory of the church, and of the Rationalist interpretation of its theology"; and for the place now given to general councils see Rogers's Agriculture and Prices, iv. 11–13. For the first signs that the revenues of monastic houses were to be devoted to other purposes. (Ibid. 101.)

[1] Agriculture remained stationary during the fifteenth and sixteenth centuries. It was in fact but little changed from the time when Walter of Henley published his treatise until the time when Fitz Herbert wrote his work about 1523 embodying most of the rules which Walter had given before him. The real progress lay not in the country but in the town.

[2] Nott. Records, ii. 143, 145, 167, 179, 121; iii. 21, 29.

and workers in brass, whether of English birth or brought from foreign parts, prospered within their gates; while their harpers and minstrels doubtless had a part in the musical developement of the country at a time when English artists set the fashion of the best music as far as the court of Burgundy.[1] They laid in fact the foundations of a new English society. The men of the New Learning, the men of the Reformation, the men who revealed the New World, were men who had been formed under the influences of the fifteenth century.

All this activity was the outcome of the great industrial and commercial revolution which was passing over the country. Until the middle of the fourteenth century, England had been to Europe what Australia is to-day—a country known only as the provider of the raw material of commerce.[2] At the close of the fifteenth century she had taken her place as a centre of manufactures, whose finished goods were distributed in all the great markets of the Mediterranean and of the Northern Seas. It is no

---

[1] Clément, Jacques Cœur, 196–7. Nicholas Sturgeon was ordered by the Privy Council in 1442 "to go and choose six singers of England such as the messenger that is come from the Emperor will desire for to go to the Emperor." Proceedings and Ordinances of Privy Council, ed. Sir Harris Nicholas, 1834, v. 218.

[2] Mr. Jacobs tells me that he has found no direct evidence of Jews lending to townspeople in the twelfth century; there are only some indications such as that they sought for debtors in S. Paul's; (The Jews of Angevin England, p. 45) and that they claimed to attend the assizes at Bury. (Ibid. 142.) If their business lay, as it seems, with nobles and landowners, it would prove the absence of any demand for capital in the towns.

wonder that during a change which transformed the country from a land of agricultural villages into a land of manufacturing towns, and opened for her the mighty struggle to become the carrier of the world's commerce, the whole energy of her people, thrown into a single channel, should be absorbed in accomplishing their enormous task. Every one was honestly busy in learning either how to make or how to sell, and in conquering the difficulties that beset traders as they strove to push their way into the world's market on equal or, if possible, more than equal terms with competitors who had long held unquestioned supremacy.

From the twelfth century wool had been the one great export of England, and the one great source of wealth for nobles, churchmen, farmers, even kings. So important was its sale that statesmen very early saw the necessity of securing for the national Exchequer a share in the profits of the main national trade; and in aid of the royal treasury they devised in the first half of the thirteenth century a system which was quite peculiar to England, the organization of the Staple.[1]

The Staple was an appointed place to which alone certain goods might be brought for sale, raw materials such as wool, wool-fells, skins, lead, or tin, of which wool was far the most important. Fixed for the first hundred years in some foreign town, generally in Bruges, it was shifted from place to place by Edward

[1] For an account of the Staple see Schanz, i. 327 et seq.; von Ochenkowski, Englands Wirthschaftliche Entwickelung im Ausgange des Mittelalters, 220; Stubbs, ii. 446–8.

the Third, who from 1353 made various experiments as to establishing it in England; but finally about 1390, Calais was decided upon as the most advantageous spot. Thither every dealer had to carry his wares (unless he was ready to pay a high tax to the Crown, or to buy at the King's price a license for free trading); and he must carry them along certain appointed routes only— from Lincoln by St. Botolph, from Norwich by Yarmouth, from Westminster by London, from Canterbury by Sandwich, from Winchester by Southampton, as the government in its wisdom might decide. In a kind of secondary sense these places where the wool was gathered for export thus became towns of the Staple, and certain officers, Mayors and Aldermen of the Staple were appointed to control their trade. The merchants' goods, first weighed at the point of departure, must be weighed again at the port where they were shipped, and sealed with the seal of the Mayor of the Staple, while to check fraud there was an elaborate system of official papers to be sent to the Treasury in London and to the Staple in Calais for every such transaction of weighing and toll-taking. Every possible precaution was taken to maintain the position of the merchants in the European market by rules which practically forced the wool into the hands of foreign and not native buyers, so that English traders complained that their interests were sacrificed to courting the patronage of the Continent. If, for example, the chief Staple town was for any reason moved from over sea to England, native dealers were absolutely forbidden to export any Staple wares, so

that foreigners might be forced or encouraged to come
and take part in the trade. Foreign dealers were
allowed to vote along with them for officials, and so late
as 1445 the English merchants vainly prayed that no
Stapler might take part in election of Mayor or Constable of the Staple unless he had ten sacks of wool
cocketed at Calais.

In thus forcing all the export trade of the country
through one narrow channel the first purpose of the
State was merely to provide a convenient method of
gathering customs into the Exchequer; and in course
of time it further discovered that this trading system
might be used as a weapon against foreign peoples in
case of quarrel. But the very last object of the Staple
organization was the convenience of the traders. Nor
had the merchants themselves any illusions in this
respect. To them the Staple seemed at its beginning
contrary to the liberties of Magna Charta;[1] and a long
experience taught them how its provisions might keep
them shut in between the rapacity of those in authority and the hatred of the farmers who produced the
wool which they sold.[2] They could however still
wring a rich advantage out of superficial calamity
—the advantage to be found in monopoly and corporate privilege—and this was developed with consummate art. The wool trade gathered into their hands
was hedged round with monopolies and regulations,
protected by fixed prices and times of sale. The
concourse of customers at Calais was diligently
maintained; no buyer was allowed to order his work
through a commission house, so that traders might

[1] Schanz, i. 329, &c. [2] Ibid. 657.

be forced to come to the market in person and do their business. By the charter of Edward the Third a Mayor and twenty-four Aldermen chosen by the whole body of merchants absolutely ruled the Staple trade, appointed officers, supervised markets, made regulations as to the treatment of foreigners, the duties of inn-keepers, or the general conduct of business, and administered justice according to the Law Merchant with a sworn jury of foreigners or English or both together, according to the case to be tried.[1] And since the governing body had general control beyond Calais itself over all English merchants, not only in Bruges but throughout Flanders, while they governed in England through their local officers, the power of the Staple extended far and wide and brought all the scattered merchants under one general organization.[2] Formidable through their wealth and power, they could command the support of English kings and Burgundian dukes against rival traders. The profits to be made at Calais tempted the landowners at home,[3] and all who were wealthy enough to pay the required dues and fees flocked into their body, till the great association at last included all rich wool-growers and shut out only the poor farmers and people of no account in the country. Their monopoly was so complete, and their discipline so effective, that they could absolutely dic-

---

[1] Schanz, i. 543; von Ochenkowski, 216-7. For the Law Merchant see Mr. Maitland's Pleas in Manorial Courts (Selden Soc.), p. 137. For Staple Statutes see 14 R. II. cap. 3, 4.
[2] Schanz, i. 332, 338.
[3] See Paston Letters, iii. 166.

tate prices; and a judicious pooling system took away any temptation on the part of the members to break the ranks.[1] At last against the original intentions of legislators they even got into their own hands the carrying of the export trade, and so long as wool remained the chief export of England 80 per cent. of this trade passed through their hands.

But so far as the State was concerned all this elaborate system for the protection of the wool-trade had simply grown out of the fundamental conception of the Staple as a fruitful source of supply for the royal treasury; and this theory was carried out to its logical issues. A fixed sum was demanded from the merchants year by year which they had to pay whether their trade was good or bad; while in their mercantile dealings they were terribly hampered by a host of regulations issued as to the mint in Calais, and invented by financiers who from the middle of the fourteenth century were haunted by alarms as to a possible dearth of gold and silver, and arbitrarily used the Staple as a means of forcing the flow of precious metal into England.[2] Nor was the drain of taxation at all times legal and regular. Merchants paid money down for the protection and favour of the king in reiterated loans or gifts, whether free or forced. The Captain of Calais, as head of the only standing army which the English kings then possessed, advanced a kind of public claim on the Staplers' wealth for the security of his

[1] Schanz, i. 501.
[2] Von Ochenkowski, 202, 210; Schanz, 495–500. Petition of merchants in 1442 to be relieved from these rules refused. Proc. Privy Council, v. 217.

soldiers' pay; and the merchants had many a time good reason to tremble for their wool, and might cry in vain for redress if their whole store was confiscated to pay the soldiers' arrears of two or three years, or if militant lords " shifted with the Staple of Calais " for £18,000 or so for costs of war.[1]

All these burdens however could be borne so long as business prospered in their hands. If a Parliament like that of 1258, or a great statesman like Simon de Montfort, urged that England should herself become an independent and self-supporting centre of manufactures, these seemed as idle words to monopolists dealing in wool with command of the world's market, who saw no need to forsake their easy path to wealth at a moment when the growth of manufactures in the Netherlands opened a vast market for English produce. In the time of Edward the Third it is said that 30,000 sacks of wool were shipped every year from English ports.[2]

But before the reign of Edward had closed, the exporters of wool knew that they had fallen on evil days. Trade began to slip from their grasp. The revenue they paid from their profits to the King's

---

[1] In 1442 the merchants of the Staple of Calais begged that payment should be made to the soldiers for the surety of the merchants' wools. (Proceedings of Privy Council, v. 215, 216.) When the lords seized Calais in 1459, "they shifted with the Staple of Calais for £18,000" to carry on the war with. After Edward's accession, in 1462, the merchants claimed repayment. Edward refused, and after long efforts the merchant who represented them and had borne the chief charges died a ruined man in sanctuary at Westminster (Fabyan, 635, 652-3).

[2] A sack was 364 lbs. of 16 oz. each (Schanz, ii. 569).

Exchequer fell in the few years from 1391 to 1411 to one-fifth of its former value,[1] and was still calculated at this melancholy fifth in 1449. Instead of the thirty thousand sacks which they yearly counted in the fourteenth century, they could not at the close of the fifteenth century collect more than 8,624 sacks, and in the last year of Henry the Eighth even this number had shrunk to under 5,000.[2] Taxes which lay comparatively lightly on them in happy days, fell as an intolerable burden when their warehouses lay empty, and their ranks were thinned by bankruptcy and desertion.[3] At the very moment when all England was being rapidly turned into a land of sheep pastures for the endless production of wool, the great company of the wool traders was finally and irrevocably ruined.

The wool, in fact, was being sold at home, and out of the ruin of the merchants of the Staple the cloth-makers sucked no small advantage. For the great revolution in trade was rapidly being completed—the revolution by which England was turned from being a country whose chief business was exporting wool into a country whose chief business was exporting cloth.[4]

[1] Stubbs, iii. 69, Stat. 27, H. VI. c. 2.
[2] Schanz, ii. 15.
[3] Under the system of paying a fixed sum in good and bad years alike the poor merchants became bankrupt, and in the middle of the sixteenth century the number of wool exporters fell enormously (Schanz, ii. 17). An extremely interesting statement by the Staplers of the causes of their decay is given by Schanz in vol. ii. 565–9.
[4] In the years from 1485 to 1546 general trade had increased by one-third, while the wool trade had decreased by one-third (Schanz, ii. 12).

The people had indeed long manufactured rough cloth for common use.¹ But during the reigns of the three Edwards the idea had constantly gained ground that by working up their own raw material ² Englishmen might easily retain for themselves the profits which foreigners had till now secured, and manufacturers were undoubtedly doing a considerable export trade in the middle of the fifteenth century.³ Half a century later, in 1411, the very year when the subsidy on wool fell to a fifth, broad-cloths are first mentioned in an Act of Parliament; and from this time they became the chief cloths of trade. As though they had been for a while half forgotten by the Exchequer, the exporters of cloth found themselves free from all subsidy tax and only obliged to pay to the indifferent authorities tolls that amounted to less than two per cent. for natives and merchants of the Hanse occupied in the trade, and less than eight per cent. for aliens; and complacently measured this sum with the tolls of the Staplers—the thirty-three per cent. paid by merchants of the Staple, or seventy per cent. by all other traders,⁴ a tax which perhaps explains why in 1424 Parliament had to forbid the carrying of

---

[1] In the Paston Letters there is even in the fifteenth century complaint of the quality of Norfolk cloth, i. 83.

[2] Ashley's Woollen Industry, 39, afterwards expanded in his Economic History, part ii., chap. iii. This book was published after these pages had been printed. Riley's Mem. London, 149–50; Schanz, i. 436–440, 588–9.

[3] The first charter to the company of drapers or dealers in cloth in London was in 1364.

[4] This statement is made by Schanz, i. 441, and his reasons are given, ii. 1–7. 31 H. VI. c. 8.

sheep over sea to shear them there. The manufacturers, too, made alliance with the discontented wool-growers. A farmer who could sell his wool next door, did not trouble to send it with vexatious formalities over sea to Calais; and in course of time the cloth merchants insisted upon laws which gave to them during certain seasons the first choice of the wool before the staplers were even allowed to enter the market.[1]

Under these circumstances trade grew apace. Carracks of Genoa carried English cloths to the shores of the Black Sea; galleys of Venice fetched them to the pits of the Venetian dyers; merchants of the Hanseatic League sold them in the fair of Novgorod; English traders travelled with them to the inland markets of Prussia, and gave them in exchange for casks of herrings in Denmark. At the close of the century the English Merchant Adventurers exported about 60,000 pieces of cloth yearly; and in the beginning of the sixteenth century the cloth dealers boasted that never before in the memory of man was so much cloth sold out of England. The 60,000 bales rose in 1509 to 84,789 pieces, and in 1547 to 122,354;[2] and the dealers claimed further gratitude and admiration of their country for the fact that they had "by their industry" raised by a fifth the price demanded from the foreigner.[3] Meanwhile the manufacturer was also getting hold of the home market, as the great religious corporations and landowners

---

[1] 4 H. VII. c. 11; Schanz, i. 449.
[2] Schanz, i. 11; ii. 17, 18.
[3] Schanz, ii. 571-2.

who had once provided on their own estates for all local wants recognized the new condition of things, and instead of making cloth at home as of old, sent every year far and wide across the country to the great clothing centres to buy material for the household liveries,[1] seeking from one place the coarse striped cloth of the old pattern and from another the goods of the new fashion. The fine black copes of worsted were favourite gifts of benefactors to churches, and a patriotic Norfolk gentleman, after seeing a "tippet of fine worsted which is almost like silk," decided to "make his doublet all worsted for worship of Norfolk."[2]

Nor was the growth of manufacturing enterprise confined to the making of cloth. For a couple of centuries the iron trade had made of the Weald the Black Country of those days, and had stirred the Forest of Dean with the din of its seventy-two moveable forges; and now, what with the metals and what with the coal of the country, "the merchants of England maintain and say that the kingdom is of greater value under

---

[1] In 1472 the prior of Christ Church, Canterbury, buys from a London alderman two pieces of cloth for gentleman's livery, nine for yeoman's, and five for groom's, the price, £39 14s.; from a "raymaker" in New Salisbury he buys similar cloths in 1475 and 1480; again from Hadley, in 1499, he got eighteen pieces, and russet cloths from a Cranbrooke clothier. (Hist. MSS. Com. v. 436–7, 459.) Fastolfe bought cloth for his soldiers at Castlecoombe, Wilts (Paston Letters). The Warden of Merton, Bishop Fitz James, bought for his fellows and himself at Norton Mandeville in Essex. (Rogers' Economic Interpretation of History, 151.)

[2] Paston Letters, ii. 235. 1465.

the land than it is above."[1] In the reign of Edward the Fourth when there was a riot among the Mendip miners, and the Lord Chief Justice went down to "set a concord and peace upon the forest of Mendip," it is said ten thousand people appeared before him at the place of trial.[2] But for all this miners could no longer keep pace with the demands of the country, now that new industries on all sides required metal that had once gone to supply the wants of the farmer only; and though stores were brought from Sweden and Spain, the price of iron increased to double what it had been before the Plague.[3] Shipbuilders at the end of the fourteenth century were fitting out vessels for foreign as well as for English buyers. English gunsmiths began to send out of their workshops brazen guns and bombards superior to anything made in France, and which were said to have given England its success in the French war under Henry the Fifth.[4] A number of towns, big and little, boasted of their bell-foundries,

---

[1] Debate between the Heralds of France and England, probably published from 1458 to 1461, translated by Pyne, p. 61. Published in French by the Société des Anciens Textes Français. In 1454 the commons petitioned that silver mines in Cornwall, Devon, Dorset, and Somerset, should be worked (Schanz, i. 493). For coal see Paston, iii. 363. Nottingham Records, i. 145. In 1307 there were complaints about the corruption of London air by use of coal. Cruden's Gravesend, 84–5.

[2] Hist. MSS. Com. vi. 347.

[3] Rogers' Econ. Interpretation, 276.

[4] Brazen pieces, invented 1340 or 1370, were first used in England at the siege of Berwick, 1405 (Eng. Chron. 1377–1461, p. 184); not known in France so well (Three books of Polydore Vergil's English History, 9–10 Camden Society). For the Lydd

as for example London, Salisbury, Norwich, Gloucester, Bridport, and others.[1] The copper-workers of Dinant had traded with England since the thirteenth century, and in the fourteenth century had an entrepôt at Blackwall; but in 1455 the founders set up their industry in England, stealing away secretly from Dinant to profit by the cheaper labour and ready sale in this country.[2] Flemish experts taught to Englishmen the art of brickmaking, and native builders were setting up throughout the country the first brick houses that had been seen in it since the departure of the Romans.[3] A whole series of industrial experiments proclaimed the enthusiasm with which the people accepted the challenge to secure for themselves the profits of foreign manufacturers. Artificers often more ambitious than skilful tried to establish a native industry of glass painting.[4] Instead of fetching from abroad carpets and the tapestry used

---

gun of 1456 the gunmakers were paid 11s. 8d.; the binding and iron for it cost 18s. "Guns with six chambers" mentioned as early as 1456 in Cinque Port towns. (Hist. MSS. Com. v. xvii.)

[1] Journ. of Archæl. Association, 1871, p. 416; Hist. MSS. Com. vi. 489.

[2] Pirenne, Dinant, 102, 94, 95. In the fifteenth century the Dinant traders sent their wares by Antwerp, not by Damme.

[3] For English brick building see Rogers' Agric. and Prices, iv. 440. First notice of bricks at Cambridge 1449, in London 1453, in Oxford 1461; common in eastern counties before end of fifteenth century. Ibid. iii. 432, 433. The proverb, "as red as Rotherham College," refers to one of the first brick buildings in Yorkshire.

[4] There is good fifteenth century English glass at Malvern and elsewhere. But according to Dugdale English glass was forbidden in the Beauchamp chapel at Warwick.

for churches, manufactories were set up at Ramsey,[1] whence came perhaps also some of the "counterfeit Arras" which adorned the humbler tradesmen's homes. Frames "ordained and made for the making of silk" were at work;[2] lace-makers and ribbon weavers begged the protection of the government; and English workers sent into the market large quantities of the linen called Holland from its first home. The export of raw material fell altogether out of fashion. Traders no longer carried skins over sea undressed to be prepared by foreign labour, but had the work done by English artizans at home. And whereas at the beginning of the fifteenth century merchants brought beer from Prussia to England, at its close they were carrying beer from London to Flanders.[3]

What with the inland and the outland trade, riches gathered into the hands of the merchants with bewildering rapidity, and with results which alarmed

[1] Turner's Domestic Architecture, 98.

[2] Silk manufacture in London in the fifteenth century was carried on by women; their complaints of the Lombard merchants noticed in Act of 1454 (33 H. VI. c. 5). A bill with the royal sign manual prays that the king would grant to Dom. Robert Essex his frames "ordeigned and made for the makyng of sylkes," with their instruments which now "stondith unoccupyed within your Monastery of Westminster," and he will ordain workmen to use them. Temp. Edward the Fourth, Hist. MSS. Com. iv. 1, 177.

[3] Libel of English Policy. (Political Poems and Songs, composed between 1327 and 1483, ii. ed. Wright Rolls Series.) For export of English beer to Flanders, see Fœdera, xii. 471 1492. Beer was a "malt liquor flavoured with bitter herbs," as distinct from ale, made before 1445, though commonly ascribed to a century later.

good conservatives. A statute of Parliament passed in 1455 lamented the good old days when Norfolk and Norwich used to employ only six or eight attorneys at the King's Court, "in which time great tranquillity reigned in the said city and counties." This "tranquillity" was broken by the manufacturing and export trade, for now a body of eighty or more lawyers busily frequented every fair and market and assembly, moving and inciting people to lawsuits, and while having nothing to live on but their attorneyship yet prospered so well that a wise legislature had to order that Norfolk should henceforth as of old have only six attorneys and Norwich two.[1] Nor does it seem that Norwich was exceptionally wicked, even though in Piers Ploughman Covetousness is represented with a "Norfolk nose,"[2] for about the same time we read in Nottingham of twenty-four rolls written within and without with the pleas concerning trading questions of a single year. The whole country in fact shared in traders' profits from king to peasant. It is calculated that in the reign of Henry the Eighth English exports so far exceeded imports as to bring about £50,000 yearly into the country, and the balance of trade inclined yet more strongly in favour of England under Henry the Seventh.[3] Not only did the king lay up vast treasure, but the very goldsmiths' shops in London were reported by a foreign traveller to contain more precious metals than all those of Rome, Milan,

---

[1] Blomfield, iii. 160. 33 H. VI. cap. vii.
[2] Piers Ploughman, Introduction to Text C, xxxi.
[3] Schanz, ii. 35, 36.

Florence, and Venice taken together.[1] So far as the middle class is concerned evidence of accumulating wealth is to be found on every side, and the masses of the people in spite of the drain of war taxation shared in the general prosperity. In the middle of the fifteenth century Chief Justice Fortescue contrasts their state with that of the French commons. "These drink water; they eat apples with bread right brown made of rye. They eat no flesh, but if it be right seldom a little lard, or of the entrails and heads of beasts slain for the nobles and merchants of the land. They wear no woollen but if it be a poor coat under their outermost garment made of great canvas and called a frock. Their hosen be of light canvas and pass not their knee, wherefore they be gartered and their thighs bare. Their wives and children go barefoot; they may in none otherwise live. . . . Their nature is wasted and the kind of them brought to nought. They go crooked and be feeble, not able to fight nor to defend the realm ; nor they have weapon nor money to buy them weapon withal. . . . But blessed be God, this land is ruled under a better law ; and therefore the people thereof be not in such penury, nor thereby hurt in their persons but they be wealthy and have all things necessary to the sustenance of nature." "In France the people salt but little meat except their bacon, for they would buy little salt" unless the king's officers went round and forced every household to take a certain measure, such as they thought reasonable. But "this rule would be sore abhorred in England, as well by the

[1] Italian Relation, 42-3 (Camden Soc.); Schanz, i. 513; Heralds' Debate, 65.

merchants that be wont to have their freedom in buying and selling of salt as by the people that use much to salt their meats."[1]

An industrial revolution on such a scale as this brought a political revolution in its train. The English population, says a writer of about 1453, "consists of churchmen, nobles, and craftsmen, as well as common people."[2] It was a novel and significant division. Traders and manufacturers took their places somewhat noisily beside their fellow politicians of older standing, filling the whole land till it seems for a moment as if nothing counted any more in English life save its middle class—a busy, hard, prosperous, pugnacious middle-class. Slowly emerging from its early obscurity, in this century it had arrived at power definitely, ostentatiously, carrying a proud look and a high stomach, intent on its own affairs, heedless of the Court, regardless of ministers save when it had to bribe them, irreverent to the noble, the "proud penniless with his painted sleeve,"[3] tolerant of ecclesiastics and monks only so long as they could be kept rigidly within their allotted religious functions.[4] Henceforth in the

---

[1] Plummer's Fortescue, 114-5, 132. Compare Bacon's Henry the Seventh, 71-72.

[2] Heralds' Debate, 61, 1453-1461.

[3] Richard the Redeless, passus iii. 172.

[4] Brinklow's Tracts, published in the first half of the sixteenth century, afford interesting illustrations of the type of radical politician formed in the towns. His proposal for a single chamber and the list of reforms sketched out are not more significant than his criticism of parliamentary despotism and inefficiency, "This is the thirteenth article of our creed added of late, that whatsoever the Parliament doth must needs be well done.

workshop and the market-place home politics and foreign affairs were discussed from a new point of view—the interest of the trader and the manufacturer; and the middle and working classes presently began to fling to the winds the old state-craft whose maxims had done service before their advent among the makers of the national policy.

In the matter of our foreign relations we see the drift of public thought and discussion reflected in a pamphlet by which one of the King's ministers, Moleyns, Bishop of Chichester, sought to appeal to the popular imagination and define our right attitude to continental peoples. His Libel (or Little Book) of English Policy, published about 1445, was clearly designed for the vulgar use.[1] Written, as the common taste of the day demanded, in rhyming form where the absence of poetic art and the inspiration of a plain common-sense constituted a double claim on public attention, it made its frank appeal to the prejudice of the stall-holder in the market and of the craftsman who lived by making his homely English wares—men who saw in foreign products articles whose sinful extravagance could only be matched by the worthlessness

and the Parliament, or any proclamation out of the parliament time cannot err.... then have ye brought Rome home to your own doors and given the authority to the King and Parliament that the cardinal bishops gave unto the Pope.... if this be so, it is all vain to look for any amendment of anything." Brinklow's Complaynt, E. E. Text Society, 35. See also pp. 8, 12.

[1] Libel of English Policy (Political Poems and Songs, ii. 157–205. Roll's series, ed. Wright). The Libel was probably written after 1436. The Bishop was murdered in 1450. (Agric. and Prices, iv. 533.)

that distinguished all work not turned out by an Englishman. With vigorous strokes the Bishop sketched the outlines of England's trading interests with every nation in Europe, and at the end of each paragraph passionately drove home his moral. Laying hold of the fundamental axiom that the sole and undivided concern of England in all her foreign relations was the protection of her commerce, he maintained that so long as she kept a firm hold on the narrow seas between Dover and Calais, she might rule the trade of the world. For there all commerce from north to south or south to north had to pass through the strait gate held by her sentinels on either side; so that while an inexorable fate drove the nations into her net, England safely hidden behind her wall of defence, the stormy Channel, need have no care so long as she looked well to her navy and kept it swift to seize her prey and strong to drive her enemies back from looking over the wall. At its very outset the commercial society had thus its Cobden to preach after his kind the doctrine of non-intervention and the kingdom of the seas.

The exponents of a new home policy pressed hard on the heels of the founders of a new diplomacy. About thirty years after the Libel of English Policy, another "Libel" was composed in imitation of the first tract.[1] Less pretentious and elaborate than the first, the new poem was probably the work of some person of less exalted rank, whose converse had been with the working men of the country rather than with merchants of London or peers of the realm and minis-

[1] Wright's Pol. Poems, ii. 282-7. Schanz, i. 446.

ters of the King, and who was far more troubled about our industrial policy at home than our commercial policy abroad. His view of our position was also finely optimistic. For, seeing that foreign traders were bound, whether they would or no, to come to us either for wool or for cloth, and thus depended on England for one of the first necessaries of life, we, who were put in this happy position of universal provider, were clearly "by God's ordinance," destined first to satisfy ourselves, and then " to rule and govern all Christian kings," and make paynims also "full tame";[1] and so "of all people that be living on the ground" were most bound to pray and to please God. The recognition of these inestimable blessings should bring of course its corresponding sense of our duty to sell our goods as dear as we could; to "restrain straitly" the export of wool so that "the commons of this land might have work to the full";[2] and in any case to export only the coarsest wool, on the working of which the margin of profit must be small—but a fifth in fact of what might be made on good material. "The price is simple, the cost is never the less; they that worked such wool in wit be like an ass." Above all, the working men must be protected by law in the conditions of their labour, so that "their poor living and adversity might be altered into wealth, riches,

---

[1] Compare the very similar expression of faith in a modern labour paper. "To this island, small as it is, has been given the work of leading the industrial organization of the world; that is to say, of governing and ordering the affairs of the world." Trade Unionist, Dec. 26, 1891.

[2] Compare Paston Letters, i. 531; Brinklow's Complaynt 11.

and prosperity," and that for the profit of the whole realm. The growth of industry was already bringing in its train a modern theory that "the whole wealth of the body of the realm riseth out of the labours and works of the common people. . . . Surely the common weal of England must rise out of the works of the common people."[1]

From this time therefore the policy of England was to be the policy of a great industrial state. But the new way on which its people were thus striving to enter was not to be a way of good-will at home or of harmony with the nations. Merchant and burgher might remain, as they did, absolutely indifferent to all schemes of mere military aggrandizement[2] such as the conquest of France, so that after the taking of Bordeaux by the French in 1445 not a single cry was raised for the recovery of our lost possessions; and they might rather look for the extension of their

[1] Pauli, Drei volkswirtschaftliche Denkschriften, s. 61, 75.

[2] In 1447 exactions in England were so heavy "as that the minds of men were not set upon foreign war, but vexed above measure how to repel private and domestical injuries, and that therefore neither pay for the soldier nor supply for the army were as need required put in readiness." (Polydore Vergil, 77 Camden Soc.) For interruption of trade by the war, Paston, i. 425-6. Davies' Southampton, 252-3. The Staplers complain that before the war the French bought yearly 2,000 sacks of wool, now only 400 (Schanz, ii. 568). For effect of the war on the salt trade, Rogers' Econ. Interpretation of History, 100. For the wine trade, &c., Schanz, i. 299-300, 643-50. "It cannot be brought to pass by any mean that a French man born will much love an English man, or, contrary, that an English will love a French man; such is the hatred that hath sprung of contention for honour and empire." (Pol. Vergil, 82.)

trade to the bold enterprising genius of trading companies and pirates exulting in freedom from royal interference and military restrictions, and only calling on the State for diplomatic aid in the case where this proved convenient for the winning of a commercial treaty. But the secret of peace was not yet found, nor was the settlement of industrial frontiers to prove simpler than the definition of military borders.

For as yet England had wakened no jealousies simply because she had never been a competitor with other nations; but obvious trouble lay in wait for her people so soon as they were fairly swept into the commercial struggle of the Continent, and introduced by their manufactures to their first real trade disputes. The weaver of the Netherlands, for example, had gladly welcomed the English trader as the inexhaustible provider of his raw material; but it was another matter when the Englishman came as a rival manufacturer laden with bales of cloth, grudging the old supply of wool, and setting up stalls in Flemish markets to seduce away his ancient customers. The Flemish towns had seen an end to their prosperity, and towns in such a case were bitter in negotiations with their rivals.[1] Bruges which in the thirteenth century had 40,000 looms, was at the end of the fifteenth century offering citizenship at a mere trifle to draw back inhabitants to its deserted streets; Ypres, which in 1408 had a population of from 80,000 to 100,000, and from 3,000 to 4,000 cloth-workers, had in 1486 only from 5,000 to 6,000 inhabitants, and twenty-

[1] Schanz, i. 32-33.

five to thirty cloth-factories; and in Ghent matters were little better. Against all the misery of a century of slow death in Flanders—a misery on which the English weaver throve and fattened—the doomed manufacturers set up hasty barriers on this side and on that, taxes and tolls and municipal ordinances and State decrees to shut English cloth out of Flanders, which were met by angry English rejoinders forbidding Flemish cloth in the English markets. Similar difficulties followed everywhere the appearance of the English trader with his goods. The Hanseatic League drove him out of Denmark, and the Teutonic Order banished him from Prussia. Moreover while disputes of manufacturers kept the North in a tumult, commercial quarrels disturbed the South, and English merchant vessels met the Genoese or the Venetians in the seas of the Levant to fight for the carrying trade of the Mediterranean. No limit was set to the pirate wars that raged from Syria to Iceland till a great statesman, Henry the Seventh, made his splendid attempt to discover through international treaties the means of securing a settled order for the new commercial state.

Nor was the question of home politics more easy of solution. Under the steady pressure of public feeling the government was gradually forced out of the early simplicity of its view of regulating commerce as a financial expedient in aid of the Treasury, and began to concern itself anxiously about the protection of industry in the interests of the community. Cloth manufacturers in particular entered on a period of protected security such as the Staplers had never known, when kings became the nursing fathers of their trade, and its prosperity was considered an absorbing charge to the government. But when Parliament began in 1463 (almost the very year in which the second "Libel" appeared) to concern itself very actively with industrial problems,[1] the question of trade legislation had already become extremely complex and difficult. As soon as the village weaver began to make cloth for the Prussian burgher or the trader of the Black Sea instead of for his next door neighbour, the old conditions of his trade became absolutely impossible. The whole industry was before long altogether re-organized both from the commercial and the manufacturing side. The exporting merchants, as we shall see later, drew together into a new and powerful association known as the Merchant Adventurers. Meanwhile the army of workmen at home was broken up into specialized groups of spinners, weavers, carders, fullers, shearers, and dyers. The seller was more and more sharply separated from the maker of goods. Managers and middlemen organized the manufacture and made provisions for its distribution and sale. The clothier provided the raw material, gave out the wool to be made up, and sold again to the draper.[2] And the draper "lived like a gentleman," and sold to the big public, despising the lower forms of trade. Old-fashioned economists and timid conservatives looked on aghast at the accelerating changes,

[1] See the series of statutes with which the reign of Edward the Fourth opens. 4, Ed. IV. c. 1-8. Schanz, i. 447.

[2] Ashley's Wool. Ind. 81-2; expanded in his Economic History, part ii. Schanz, i. 445.

and declared that the country was being brought to certain ruin by the reckless race of its people to forsake handicrafts or the production of wealth, and press wholesale into the ranks of merchants or mere distributors.

With this division of labour and the quickened contest for profits, there started into life rival interests more than enough to break up the whole community into groups of warring factions. The "upper classes" generally, statesmen, treasury officials, nobles, the greater proprietors lay and ecclesiastical—in fact all the wealthy owners of flocks who could enter the company of the Staplers and share their profits—desired an abundant export of wool; while the small farmers and the yeomen, shut out by poverty from the association, and bitterly hostile to the wealthy monopolist, sided with the townsfolk to whom visions of wealth had first dawned in the manufacturing industries and the export of cloth, and who would gladly have kept all the wool of the country at home.[1] Merchants and manufacturers had their own special controversy, for while the foreign trader was boasting of his energy in raising the price of cloth, the middlemen and makers at home, whose whole interest lay in rapid sales, complained that people in the Netherlands would no longer buy English goods owing to the increased cost,

---

[1] Schanz, i. 446. "The caryage out of wolle to the Stapul ys a grete hurte to the pepul of Englond; though hyt be profitabul both to the prynce and to the marchant also." (Starkey, England in the Reign of Henry the Eighth. Early English Text Society, p. 173.)

and that the English towns were thus brought to destitution.[1] Moreover the great London merchants were making a determined effort to force the whole foreign trade of England through their warehouses in London, and to shut all channels of commerce save those provided by themselves;[2] and demanded that all cloth for the Netherlands, that is practically one-third of all the cloth then exported, must be carried by the maker to London, and there sold, as was averred, to the exporting merchants either for credit or below cost price.[3] Here of course they came into conflict with the local dealers who wanted frequent and convenient markets for their wares, and liberty to make their own bargain

[1] Brinklow's Complaynt, E. E. Text Soc. p. 11. Schanz, i. 479, note.

[2] The fellowship of the mercers and other merchants and adventurers living in London " by confederacy made among themselves of their uncharitable and inordinate covetous for their singular profit and lucre contrary to every Englishman's liberty, and to the liberty of the Mart there" made an ordinance and constitution that every Englishman trading with the marts of Flanders or under the Archduke of Burgundy should first pay a fine to the Merchants' Fellowship in London on pain of forfeiture of all their wares bought and sold. The fine was at first half an old noble, and demanded by a colour of a fraternity of S. Thomas at Canterbury, and "so by colour of such feigned holiness it hath been suffered to be taken for a few years past." Finally, however, the London Fellowship raised the fine to £20, then the other merchants began to withdraw from the marts and the cloth trade to suffer. On the complaint of the merchant adventurers living outside London Parliament ordered that the fine should only be ten marks. (12 Henry VII., cap. 6.) For the complaint of the Hull traders against the merchant adventurers of London in 1622 see Lambert's Gild Life, 171-2.

[3] Schanz, i. 342.

with foreign buyers visiting their town; for to the clothier this question of distribution was all-important, since it was in vain for him to increase production by machinery, or by the improved organization of labour, or by division of toil among groups of skilled artizans, unless he could find his profit in a corresponding developement of the means of sale. The exporting merchants had also a quarrel with the artizans, who naturally desired to keep the dressing and finishing of cloth in their own hands, while the merchants insisted on the advantages of a free trade in undressed cloth; in their judgement the cloth-dressers, seeking but their "singular and private wealth," forgot that more men lived by making and selling cloth than by dressing it, and that therefore the rapid developement of exports by carrying out material in the rough to be finished in the Netherlands was really for the enriching of the whole realm.[1] These same dealers, however, looked more leniently on the "singular and private wealth" that went into their own pockets through the profits of the export trade, and also found themselves set at variance with the big public of consumers who were always anxiously on the watch against the raising of prices. At times the manufacturer had his grievances against the municipal authorities, whenever he found himself worried and fettered by the traditional wisdom of Town Councils, who for a variety of reasons of their own wanted to keep the ultimate control over his trade so as to draw a profit for the town. Lastly, the working class had begun to feel difficulties springing

[1] Schanz, ii. 571.

from the new methods of industrial organization, and troubles about wages and prices and the relation of employer to employed assailed the authorities both at Westminster and in the municipal councils. Artificers of all kinds, it was constantly declared, could no longer live of their occupation and were in great misery;[1] in fact, to judge by preambles to Statutes, and the loud complaints as to his condition, the working man believed himself to be in such bad case as to need all the aid of the State to keep him supplied with employment.

This old industrial revolution in short brought with it difficulties which bear to us the familiar look of our own constant and persevering visitors—visitors that force their entrance at every breach in the accustomed order by which trade is fenced round, and that appear as the unwelcome escort of every new form of industrial competition. Moreover, to add to the troubles of the mediæval legislator, the consumer of those days was always insisting on his vested right to the first consideration of the government, as the ultimate dictator for whose benefit the whole colossal structure of trade had been reared, and by whose approval alone it was allowed to remain at that ambitious elevation. With every fresh enterprise of manufacturer or merchant, the problem with which the law-makers had to deal became more subtle and complex. Driven hither and thither by the new conflict of public opinion and the passion of rival interests, baffled by the insoluble problem of how to frame laws which should benefit equally all the

[1] 3 Ed. IV. c. 4.

claimants for its aid, the government hesitatingly felt its way along an ill-defined path, veering from side to side according to the direction of the last impelling force. Even Edward the Fourth had no fixed policy of protection, and passed laws now on this side, now on that, as the imperious necessity of the moment seemed to demand.

But with a rapidly increasing trade, and with a House of Commons three-fourths of whose members were burghers personally concerned in these questions, it was impossible to stand still; and the new industrial legislation gradually became the expression not of the autocratic rule of kings, but of a self-conscious government of the people.[1] A long series of Statutes illustrates this great experiment. The new protection devised by burghers and merchants for the fostering of industry was altogether different from the old protection devised by a Court mainly occupied with the problem of re-filling an empty Treasury. The English manufacturer and the English working man were its recognized charge, and in their interest no measure was considered too heroic and no detail too insignificant, whether the matter in hand was the closing of English markets to a whole people, or the decision of how big a piece of leather it might be well in the interest of the shoemaking trade to allow the cobbler to buy for the patching of an old boot. All native trades were "protected" by laws which declared that none of the wares which Englishmen could manufacture at home might be imported from

[1] Schanz, i. 618-19.

foreign parts, and that none of the raw material they used might be carried out unwrought, or even half finished, to be worked up abroad. The whole people, save a few of the "great estates" and mighty men, must go simply clad in honest goods of English make, and so save themselves from waste, and English workers from poverty. As to the long dispute about admitting foreigners to trade in England, in which the King and the people had ever been in strong opposition, that matter was now more and more regulated according to the desires of the traders. England ceased to be the acquiescent host of guests who, in the vulgar opinion, came to thrive and fatten on her wealth; and a determined resistance was declared against the competition of strangers, till the Hanseatic trader scarcely dared show his face outside the strong walls of his Steel-yard citadel, and the Lombard vainly struggled to protect his last privileges from the assaults of his enemies.

The theory of State protection of industry grew fast, and by the time of Henry the Seventh its triumph was complete, and the foundations of a new national policy were firmly laid—a policy which was to be largely guided by industrial interests and to represent the claims of an elaborate industrial organization established by law and built into vast proportions by international agreement. The new relation of a sovereign to his people in such a State was seen at the end of the century in the first peaceful king of England whose subjects had submitted to his rule, the only English monarch till then who had not been a strong leader in war and who had yet escaped murder or imprisonment at the hands of his people. It has been the singular misfortune of one of our greatest rulers, Henry the Seventh, to be the first sovereign of the modern pattern who ruled over Englishmen, and his memory has in consequence come down to us shorn of all the conventional glory that tradition had until then declared proper to royalty. He has remained in history as we see him in one of his portraits, a dim obscure figure, sadly looking out from the background of a canvas where the big blustering figure of his son, set squarely in front, seems to elbow all virtue save his own out of recognized existence. But in the delicate, careworn, refined face with its suggestion of unrecorded self-effacement, in the penetrating intelligence devoted to the apprehending of the new problems and the infinite labour spent in solving them, in the inscrutable acquiescence with which, "loving to seal up his own dangers,"[1] he carried the burdens that were henceforth to fall to the lot of kings, and the unflinching resolution of his methods, we recognize a new type of royal dignity, and measure the work demanded of rulers who saw the power of mere personal dominion founded on force gradually passing from their hands, and in the changing order of the world were called to take up the leadership of the new commonwealth that was to be.

[1] Bacon's History of Henry the Seventh, 38.

CHAPTER III

THE COMMERCIAL REVOLUTION OF THE FIFTEENTH
CENTURY

A FRENCH proverb of the twelfth century tells us what the world thought in old days of the origin and uses of a navy. " Point de marine sans pelerinages," men said, seeing in pious penitents its means of support, and in the shrines of St. James or St. Peter or the Holy Sepulchre its destinations. Trade in those days avoided the way of the ocean, and followed the well-known land routes across the heart of Europe, and where the land came to an end took the very shortest way over the water to the next point of solid earth.

And slowly as commerce by sea developed in Europe it developed yet more slowly among the English. All goods that came to them from abroad were carried to their shores by powerful confederations of foreign merchants who controlled the great continental trade routes of the north-west. The "men of the Empire" or the Hanse of Cologne, masters of the highway of the Rhine and of Cologne, the great seaport of the

Empire, commanded the whole Eastern trade which then for the most part passed through Germany.[1] The Flemish Hanse of London,[2] which included all the great towns of Picardy and Flanders, and perhaps at one time even Paris itself, carried over sea the wares that were gathered from half of Europe to the great fairs of Champagne. Through these two great companies England first exchanged her wool for certain necessaries such as salt and fish and iron and wood, and for a few luxuries such as spices and silks from the Levant.

And even when commerce swept beyond the narrow seas and passed out of the hands of the men of Cologne and the Flemish Hanse, it was not Englishmen who took their place. If the waterway of the Rhine was forsaken of half its trade as merchants of Northern Italy abandoned the old route across Europe, and instead of sending their goods to the warehouses of Cologne despatched fleets through the Straits of Gibraltar to the ports of the Channel and to Bruges; if the fairs of Champagne languished when armies encamped on its plains and turned them into battle-fields, and the Flemish Hanse of London slowly sank into insignificance—it was only to make way for other competitors of foreign blood. Commerce with the East through the Mediterranean and the Bay of Biscay was

[1] The men of Cologne had a house in London as early as 1157.
[2] Founded before 1240 (Schanz, i. 291-3). Some interesting details are given in Mr. Hudson's Notes on Norwich (Norfolk Archæology, xii. 25 ; see section on madder and woad.) For merchants of Lorraine, Denmark, &c., Liber Custumarum, Nunimenta Gildhallæ Londiniensis (Rolls Series), vol. ii. part 1, xxxiv. &c.

seized by the ships of Florence and Genoa and Venice.¹ The towns of the German Ocean and the Baltic gathered under the banner of Lübeck into a new Hanseatic League² which broke the supremacy of Cologne, claimed the whole carrying trade of the Northern seas, and opened a new line of communication with the Levant. Novgorod became the centre of the Baltic trade, as Alexandria was the centre of the Mediterranean traffic, and the merchants of the Teutonic Hanse offered to the English trader the silks and drugs of the East, with skins and hemp and timber of Novgorod, and the metals of Bohemia and Hungary.

The Mediterranean merchant was the great minister to the growing luxury of mediæval England. "The estates and lords of the realm" and bishops and prelates and parish priests bought from him cloth of gold, rich brocades, vestments of white damask powdered with gold of Venice,³ and precious work of goldsmiths

¹ In the beginning of the fourteenth century (Schanz, i. 113-8).
² See Keutgen, Die Beziehungen der Hanse zu England, 40.
³ Boys' Sandwich, 375; Paston, iii. 436. The foreign trade is illustrated by some of the things in Fastolf's house; the Seeland cloth, i. 481; iii. 405—brass pots and chafferns of French making, i. 481—silver Paris cups, 475; iii. 270-1, 297-8—blue glasses, i. 486—habergeons of Milan, 487—" overpayn of Raines," 489—cloth of Arras, 479—harness from Almayne, iii. 405— German girdles, iii. 270-1—the treacle-pots of Genoa, ii. 293-4, bought of the apothecary. The merchant's marks were especially noted for fear of adulteration. The grocer, or dealer in foreign fruits, also sold hawks, iii. 55-6. In the reign of Henry the Eighth about a dozen shops in London sold French or Milan cups, glasses, knives, daggers, swords, girdles, and such things. Hist. MSS. Com. viii. 93. "A discourse of the commonwealth of this Realme of England."

and jewellers, new-fashioned glass, and many other fine things—articles that "might be forborn for dear and deceivable," grumbled the English dealer in homely goods of native manufacture. The whole luxurious traffic down to the "apes and japes and marmosettes tailed, nifles, trifles, that little have availed,"[1] roused the bitter jealousy of the home trader; and even statesmen foretold with alarm the perils that must come to the nation from a commerce which filled the land with fancy baubles and vanities, and carried away in exchange the precious wealth of the people, their cloth and wool and tin, sucking the thrift out of the land as the wasp sucks honey from the bee. But in spite of the hostility of English dealers needy kings anxious to win favour with the great banking companies of Italy diligently encouraged the trade; and (always in consideration of adequate tolls for privileges) freed merchants who came from beyond the Straits from the vexatious control of the Staple;[2] allowed their vessels to put into port undisturbed at Southampton instead of being forced to go to Calais; and their agents to travel through the country and buy and sell at will.

It was Florence which in the first half of the fourteenth century took the lead in the trade of the Mediterranean with England,[3] and whose merchants

[1] Libel of English Policy; Political Poems and Songs (Rolls Series), ii. 173, 172. Fabyan, 630. See petition of burghers against the Lombards, 1455, in Rot. Parl. v. 334.

[2] Schanz, i. 65. Strangers exporting wool had to pay 43s. 4d. a sack, English merchants only 5 nobles or 33s. 4d. (Fabyan, 594-5).

[3] In 1372 there is a receipt by two of the company of the Strozzi

lent to Edward the Third the money which alone enabled him to carry on the war with France. But when Edward declared himself unable to pay his debts and repudiated the whole of the Florentine loans ruin fell on the city; its trade was paralyzed, and commercial disasters ended in political revolution. Bankers of Lübeck took the place of its financiers as the Rothschilds of the mediæval world; and ship-masters of Genoa seized the commerce which fell from its hands. Though the winning of the port of Leghorn in 1421 brought a fresh outburst of trading activity to Florence,[1] though its merchants established depots and banks and commercial settlements in all the great towns of the North, though cargoes of wool were again shipped to its harbour (one English merchant alone in 1437 selling to an agent of the Albertine Company wool to the value of almost £12,000),[2] the supremacy of the Republic in the Mediterranean trade was never restored.

For its great competitors, Genoa and Venice, were now fairly in the field. Through their station on the Black Sea the Genoese held until the Turkish conquest the chief market in the East for European cloth; and their fleets laden with cloth of gold, silk and spices of the Levant, with alum and mastick from the subject islands of Chios and Phocœa, with the woad of Toulouse, and the wines of Provence, sailed to Southampton

for money from Archbishop Langham. Hist. MSS. Com. iv. part 1, 186.

[1] Clement, Jacques Cœur, 23-4.

[2] For the failure of this company in 1437 and its effect on English traders, see Bekynton's Corres. i. 248-50, 254.

to exchange their cargoes for English cloth, which they sometimes carried back direct to the Black Sea, and sometimes took on to sell at the Flemish markets, and so make a double profit on their journey.[1] For their world-wide business the Bank of St. George was founded at Genoa in 1407, with a system of credit notes of acknowledgement for money deposited which could be transferred from hand to hand.

The great galleys of Venice, however, were formidable rivals of the carracks of Genoa. For Venice, hidden away in the Adriatic, with nothing of its own save salt to offer, showed in perhaps a higher degree than any other Italian State what might be achieved by a lavish system of State protection.[2] It was the State that built its merchant fleets; the State that leased out the vessels every year to the highest bidders for trading purposes; the State that ordered the conduct of their business for the greatest public wealth; the State that protected them from competition by forbidding its citizens to send out their spices by the overland route, or to take in cloth from England that had not been carried in Venetian galleys by long sea. By the authority of its government Venice had been made the emporium of the Mediterranean, and Italian traders obediently carried cloths or tin or bales of skins from England to Venice, and from Venice to Corfu. Fortune favoured the most astute among her wooers, and showered on Venice the coveted blessings of trade. Her ships travelled far, and Italian merchants who had once been only known in England as

[1] Libel of English Policy. Pol. Poems and Songs, ii. 172.
[2] Schanz, i. 124–6.

THE COMMERCIAL REVOLUTION

financial agents employed by the Papal Court to collect the tribute due to Rome, now flocked to the island on business of a very different character. The harbour of Southampton was crowded with galleys, in which cunning tailors sat day and night cutting the bales of material bought into garments, so as to save the export dues on cloth.[1] In the time of Richard the Second a Genoese merchant who had leased the castle as a storehouse for his wares proposed to the King to make of Southampton the greatest trading port of the west, and he might well have carried out his promise if the London merchants had not prudently sent a messenger to murder him at his own door.[2] Notwithstanding the inhospitable and grudging welcome given by London itself the Lombards found means by the King's help to maintain a thriving settlement, and in the fifteenth century the Venetian Consuls gathered letters for the regular mail to Venice once every month.[3]

What the Venetians were to the commerce of the Mediterranean that the merchants of the Hanseatic League were to the commerce of the Baltic and the German Ocean. A double strength had been given to the confederation of towns which Lübeck had drawn under its banner by its union with the Teutonic Order—an order which had originated in Bremen and Lübeck and then settled on the Baltic to create the trading pros-

---

[1] Hist. MSS. Com. xi. 3, p. 11, 87. 11 H. IV. c. 7. Yarn and unfulled cloths paid only subsidy—finished cloths paid also customs and measuring tax. Schanz, i. 448, note.
[2] Davies' Southampton, 254.
[3] Denton's Lectures, 192 ; Paston Letters, iii. 269.

perity of Danzig and Elbing. These Prussian cities, while they owned the Grand Master of the Order of Teutonic Knights as their feudal chief, were still dependent on Lübeck.[1] And with them were joined a multitude of towns so imposing in their very numbers alone that when the ambassadors of the Hanseatic League in England in 1376 were asked for a list of the members who made up their vast association, they answered scornfully that surely even they themselves could not be supposed to remember the countless names of towns big and little in all kingdoms in whose name they spoke.[2] Under the strangely diverse lordship of Kings, Dukes, Margraves, Counts, Barons, or Archbishops, they found a link in their common union in the Holy Roman Empire, and ever counted England, cut off from that great commonwealth, as a "foreign" nation.[3]

In war or in commercial negotiations this mighty confederation, with its members disciplined to act together as one body, dealt proudly as a nation on equal terms with other peoples, and in the strength of its united corporation it was in fact a far more formidable force than the jealous and isolated Republics of the South. Denmark was laid at its feet by a triumphant war. Norway was held in complete subjection. It forced the English traders in the North

[1] Pauli's Pictures, 126-132.　　　　[2] Keutgen, 41.
[3] Keutgen, 41. Dinant was the only town outside German-speaking countries that belonged to the Hanseatic League. It entered the League in the middle of the fourteenth century as a sort of external member—only *sharing its privileges in England* and never voting in its assemblies—tolerated rather than holding its right by formal grant. Pirenne, Dinant, 97-102.

Sea to bow to its policy and fight at its bidding. So powerful was the League in the fourteenth century, that when Edward the Third had ruined the banks of Florence it was the merchants of Lübeck who became his money-lenders; they were made the farmers of the English wool-tax; they rented the mines of the northern counties and the tin-works of Cornwall.[1] The whole carrying trade of the northern seas lay in their hands. It was vessels of the Hanse that sailed from Hull or from Boston to Bergen with English wares and brought back cargoes of salt fish;[2] that fetched iron from Sweden, and wine from the Rhine vineyards, and oranges and spices and foreign fruits from Bruges; and that carried out the English woollen cloths to Russia and the Baltic ports, and brought back wood, tin, potash, skins, and furs. Within the strong defences of their Steel-yard[3] on the banks of the Thames by London Bridge, the advance guard of the League lived under a sort of military discipline, and held their own by force of the King's protection against the hatred of London traders and burghers, which now and then burst into violent riots.

Thus throughout the fourteenth century it was strangers who held the carrying trade to England along the two great commercial routes—the passage by Gibraltar to the harbours of Italy and thence to Alexandria, and the passage by the Sound to the Baltic ports and so to Novgorod. All the profits of transit as of barter were secured by alien dealers who travelled from village to village throughout the coun-

[1] Keutgen, 5, 30.   [2] Keutgen, 14–18.
[3] For a description of the Steel-yard see Pauli's Pictures.

try in search of wool or cloth to freight the foreign vessels that lay in every harbour—vessels bigger and better built for commerce than any of which England could boast.[1] Moreover, the English government was content to have it so, and Kings who wanted to build up alliances for their foreign wars, or to replenish their failing treasury at home, in all commercial regulations showed their favour mainly to foreign traders and left the native shipowner to do as best he could for himself. Once, indeed, in the reign of Richard the Second, a solitary attempt was made to encourage the shipping industry, and the first Navigation Act passed in England ordered " that none of the King's liege people do from henceforth ship any merchandise in going out or coming within the realm of England but only in ships of the King's liegance."[2] This Act, however, after the fashion of the time, was only to be in force for a few months; and after very brief experience Parliament wisely decided that the law need only be obeyed when " the ships in the parts where the said merchants shall happen to dwell be found able and sufficient . . . and otherwise it shall be lawful to hire other ships convenient."[3] With this the experiment of State protection came to an end for the next century; and against the great

[1] The ordinary size of French ships seems to have been 1,000 or 1,200 tons. (Heralds' Debate, 51-2.) Cannyngs, of Bristol, had in his little fleet vessels of 900, 500, or 400 tons. (Cruden's Gravesend, 131.) The " Harry Grace à Dieu," built at Woolwich, 1512, was of 1,500 tons, and cost £6,472. (Ibid. 143-9.)

[2] 1382; 5 Richard II., Stat. 1, c. 3. See Schanz, i. 360, for the scope of this law.

[3] 6 Richard II., Stat. 1, c. 8.

confederations and State-protected navies of the Continent English merchants were left to wage singly as best they could their private and adventurous war.

English shipping, indeed, so far as it existed at all, may be said to have existed in spite of the law. There was no navy whatever in any national sense. A few balingers[1] and little coasting vessels lay in the various ports—some of them belonging to private merchants, some to the town communities—and when the King wanted ships for the public service, whether it was to fish for herrings for his household or to fight the French, he simply demanded such vessels as he needed in any harbour, kept them and their crews waiting on his will for weeks or months, sent them wherever he chose, and laid all costs on the town or the owner's shoulders.[2] Moreover, the unlucky merchant forfeited his ship to the Crown for any accident

---

[1] A small war vessel with probably about forty sailors, ten men-at-arms, and ten archers. Nott. Rec. i. 444.

[2] Southampton had to keep a ship, "le Grâce de Dieu," at its own expense for the king's service. In the last year of Henry the Sixth its master received from the mayor £31 10s. 0d. In the first year of Edward the Fourth the mayor paid for the victualling and custody of the ship £68 5s. 10d. In 1470 there was a great deal of difficulty about the matter. The king ordered certain payments to be made for the ship which the town for some months absolutely refused to carry out. The sheriff at last stepped into the breach and paid the sums due from money in his own office, and the next year the town was forced by the king to refund what he had spent. Three successive sheriffs were in difficulties about this dispute between the king and the town. They made payments as best they could, and were afterwards given indemnity for the sums they spent. (Hist. MSS. Com. xi 3, 98–100; Davies, 77. See also H.M.C. xi. 3, 215–16, 188–191, 221–2; Ibid. iv. 1, p. 426, 429–31; Ibid. v. 517–18, 521, 494;

that might happen on it—if a man died, or fell overboard, or if it struck another vessel or touched a rock. The masters might suffer ruin, or in mere self-defence give up the owning of ships, and the sailors might forsake the sea and turn to other occupations to escape being impressed for war : government interference to regulate wages only sent men to take service at more tempting pay in foreign boats.[1] We cannot wonder that towards the end of the fourteenth century it seems to have been thought more profitable under these conditions to make ships for others than to own them, and that builders were selling their vessels to aliens, and these aliens "by reason of the excessive profits thence arising have often sold the same to the enemies of the realm."[2] Henry the Fifth, indeed, proposed to build up a royal navy, but his plans were cut short by his death and his ships sold under Henry the Sixth, and matters went on as before.[3]

Boys' Sandwich, 663; Nottingham Records, i. 196; Paston Letters, ii. 100-105; Rot. Parl. i. 414, ii. 306-7.) Full accounts of the making of a barge in Ipswich in 1295 are given in Hist. MSS. Com. ix. 257-8.

[1] Schanz, i. 356-7, 362, 367. On page 357 he quotes from a petition of the commons in 1371 (Rot. Parl. ii. 306-7) to prove that the one result of the foreign policy of Edward the First was the *narrowing of town franchises*, and consequent decline of the navy. If the petition is read to the close the passage seems to be merely a piece of fine writing to arrest attention, and the town franchises are not mentioned again when the king asks to have the real grievances stated. In the second petition (Rot. Parl. ii. 332) the gist of the complaint is that foreign merchants are allowed to sell and buy in England, which is represented as a loss of all their franchises.

[2] Hist. MSS. Com. v. 501.

[3] Edward the Fourth made one futile attempt to revive the

English traders, however, did not sit down idly to wait for State protection.[1] Already in the middle of the fourteenth century a new life was stirring in the sea-ports, and before long every one of them began to send its contingent to the host that went out for the conquest of the sea. Towns big and little were creating or strengthening their fleets, made up either of the "common barges" of the community, or the private ships of their trading companies. Shipbuilding was dear in England from the want of wood in the country as well as of iron suitable for the purpose, and cost, if we may believe a contemporary observer, twice as much as in France.[2] So poor communities like Lydd that could not afford big ventures made shift by hiring vessels from Britanny, Sandwich, or London, and fitting them out as economically as might be, with an old wine-pipe sawed in half to serve for a bread barrel.[3] On the other hand, prosperous ports like Lynn added large sums year after year to the town budget for shipping.[4] A far poorer place, Romney, spent £73 on its common barge in 1381; in 1396 another was bought and fitted out for £82; and a third in 1400 at over £40; while a few years later yet another ship was procured for the Bordeaux trade. These vessels sailed to Scotland and

protection of English shipping, but the Act only lasted three years. (3 Ed. IV. c. i.)

[1] Schanz, i. 328.
[2] Heralds' Debate, 51-2.
[3] Hist. MSS. Com. v. 528. See the hiring out of the London barge; loss by accident from tempest or enemies to fall on the commonalty; Mem. Lond., 478.
[4] Hist. MSS. Com. xi. 3, 215-16, 221-2, 188-191.

Newcastle and Norfolk and the ports of the Southern coasts; or to Ireland for wood, to Amiens for sea-coal, to Britanny for salt, to Flanders for the wares of the Levant, to Southern France for cargoes of wine, and oil, and wood. In 1400 "the new barge" carried forty-two tuns of wine from Rochelle; in 1404 it brought forty tuns besides oil and wood, and in a later voyage carried fifty-six tuns.[1] Everywhere the trading temper laid hold upon the people. In Rye, where the inhabitants had been wont to pay their yearly oblations punctually on the 8th of September, there came a time when so many of them were abroad, some attending fairs, some fishing in remote seas, "that Divine worship is not then observed by them as it ought to be, and the due oblations are withheld and hardly ever paid;" and the day of offering had to be changed.[2]

The more important side of the movement, however, was the growth of private enterprise as shown in the associations of merchants formed in all the bigger

---

[1] Hist. MSS. Com. v. 534–540.

[2] Hist. MSS. Com. v. 496. Rye kept its own "schipwrite," John Wikham, who had the freedom of the town for sixteen years while building the ships of the port, and at last left in 1392 with a glowing testimonial from the mayor and barons of Rye. Along with other towns it had made profit by selling ships to aliens, which might afterwards be used by the enemies of England, and a proclamation was sent to Rye in 1390 forbidding such sales. For the export of eggs from Norwich in 1374, as well as butter and cheese and corn, and possibly oysters, see Hudson's Norwich Leet Jurisdiction (Selden Society), 62, 63, 65. The practice of forestalling, carried to so great an extent as is here and elsewhere described, doubtless implied buying for the foreign market.

towns for trading purposes. Already in the time of Richard the Second there was a "Fellowship of Merchants" in Bristol who directed the whole foreign trade and the import of foreign merchandise, and who even then did business on a very considerable scale, for when in 1375 Bristol ships laden with salt were captured and burnt in the Channel the losses were set down at £17,739. Before fifty years were over their trading vessels were known in every sea from Syria to Iceland. The richer merchants built up by degrees little fleets of ten or twelve vessels varying from 400 to 900 tons; and one of them, William Cannynges, an ancestor of Lord Canning, who in 1461 had ten ships afloat (one *The Nicholas of the Tower* from whence came Suffolk's headsman), employed 800 seamen and 100 carpenters, masons, and artificers.[1] Nor was Bristol singular in its activity. The Guild of Merchants at Lynn rivalled that of York. "With the Divine assistance, and the help of divers of the King's subjects," John Taverner of Hull in 1449 built a great "carrack" on the scale of the mighty ships of Genoa and Venice. Far and wide the movement spread till the brief tale of 169 merchants which had been counted up by Edward the Third when he wanted to borrow money from them, expanded towards the close of the fifteenth century into a company of more than 3,000 traders engaged in sea-commerce alone.[2]

[1] Hunt's Bristol, 74, 94–96.
[2] Schanz, i. 328. For St. Mary's Gild in York see Hist. MSS. Com. i. 109, 110. This "mystery of Mercers," or "Community of Mercers" in York formed into a body with a governor

From whatever town they came these traders with foreign ports were all alike known to the men of the fourteenth century by one significant name—the Adventurers. For since there was but one protected industry in England, the Staple, every merchant who was not a Stapler was a free Adventurer. All trade that lay outside the Staple was for his winning.[1] Bound to no place or company or government or laws, he was left to discover for himself a corner in the world's market, and to protect himself on sea and land. A perfectly indifferent State gave him no help in his first ventures to become the carrier of English commerce, and vouchsafed no encouragement to shipbuilder or master by offers of special favours or grants of reduced tolls on a first voyage.[2] He sailed out of port into a sea of peril. Pirates of all nations, Vitalien Brüder in the Baltic and the North Sea, Likedelers of Calais,[3] Breton cruisers, vigorous monopolists of the Hanse, outraged merchants of the South burning for

in 1430—in fact, became a company of Merchant Adventurers. (Gross, ii. 280.) The Shipmen's Guild of Holy Trinity in Hull drew up its constitution in 1369, but got its first royal grant in 1443. The Merchant Guild of S. George also dates from the fifteenth century. (Lambert's Guild Life, 128-131, 156-161.)

[1] In 1422 a writ was issued by the Privy Council to permit a Bristol merchant to take two vessels laden with cloth, wine, salt, and other merchandise not belonging to the Staple. The cloth and wine were to be sold, and meat, hides, salmon, herrings, and fish to be bought, and the salt used for salting these provisions. Proc. Privy Council, ii. 322-3.

[2] When Taverner built his ship for the Mediterranean trade he got no reduction of tolls, but had to pay the high export dues fixed for foreigners. Schanz, i. 367.

[3] Keutgen, 79 ; Plummer's Fortescue, 232-3.

vengeance, lay in wait on every quarter of the horizon. In 1395 Norfolk traders were robbed of £20,000 "by the Queen's men of Denmark, the which was an undoing to many of the merchants of Norfolk for evermore afterwards;"[1] and frequent and piteous were the complaints that went up to the Privy Council from English shippers begging redress and protection as outrage followed outrage.[2] But a State which was without any organized naval force was powerless to establish order. Whether it gave the charge of keeping the peace on the high seas to the merchants themselves, or to the Staplers, or by special commission to the Admirals[3] of the coast, or to a committee of lords, or to the foremost among the offenders, the Captain of Calais himself, its experiments were equally

[1] Eng. Chron. 1387-1461, 113. French pirates "whirling on the coasts so that there dare no fishers go out," (Paston Letters, iii. 81) behave "as homely as they were Englishmen." (Ibid. i. 114-116.)

[2] For the frequent disputes in the reign of Henry the Fourth see Hist. MSS. Com. v. 443. In 1419, when some Bristol merchants had seized vessels belonging to the Genoese, the King sent a messenger to choose for him a portion of the prize, for which, however, he promised honestly to pay the merchants. Proc. Privy Council, ii. 267. The mayor of Lynn attended by two proctors travelled with the King's embassy to Bruges in 1435 "for the worship of the town" as its representative to declare the wrongs done to Lynn merchants "by the master of Pruce and his subjects and by them of the Hanse." Hist. MSS. Com., xi. 3, 163; Polydore Vergil, 159; Davies' Southampton, 252-3, 275, 475.

[3] Stubbs, ii. 314, iii. 57, 65; Plummer's Fortescue, 235-7. From time to time money was collected for the protection of trade; (Nott. Rec. ii. 34-36). In 1454 Bristol gave £150 for this purpose—the largest sum given by any town save London. (Hunt's Bristol, 97-8.)

vain. In self-protection town barges and merchants' ships sailed in companies under an admiral of their own choosing, armed to the teeth like little men of war against the enemy, and even carrying cannon on board as early as 1407, before any kind of hand-guns had been invented.[1] If when disaster overtook them their masters appealed for compensation to the government they did not wait solely on the State for redress; and English rulers seem to have been often less perplexed to bring a remedy to their sufferings than to conciliate the great foreign confederations whose anger had been roused by their swift and violent retaliation. There were indeed probably no more formidable pirates afloat than these English cruisers themselves, for they were hard fighters who took a prompt revenge; and among foreigners at all events they won the reputation of using their shipping for no other purpose than to harass all trade of other peoples in the narrow seas, and "obstruct the utility of commerce throughout all Christendom."[2]

Under these conditions we can easily understand that throughout the century whenever the question of the English navy emerges in Rolls of Parliament

[1] Rymer's Fœdera, viii. 470.
[2] Debate of Heralds, 49. In 1488 a letter from London to the money-changer Frescobaldo, at Venice, told that Flanders galleys which left Antwerp for Hampton fell in with three English ships, who commanded them to strike sail, and though they said they were friends, forced them to fight. Eighteen English were killed. But on the complaint of the captain of the galleys the King sent the Bishop of Winchester to say he need not fear, as those who had been killed must bear their own loss and a pot of wine would settle the matter. Davies' Southampton, 475.

and Statutes and official statements, we have a contemporary picture drawn in the gloomiest colours.[1] Statesmen heap up details to show how badly the merchant service fulfils its vague functions as a royal navy. Ship-owners bring their loud complainings to prove how ill they have been used by the State. Each side burns to waken the other to a sense of its duty, and talk of the decay of English power by sea might be pressed into the service of either, while the loss of Southern France and the temporary blow which this gave to English shipping was used to point the argument on both sides. The sea was our wall of defence, it was said; but now the enemy was on the wall and where was our old might of ships and sailors? The very Dutch were laughing at our impotence, and when they insolently jested at the ships engraved on the coins of Edward the Third and asked why we did not engrave a sheep on them instead, the pun was felt to inflict a deep wound on the national honour.[2]

Such judgements, however, should be read in the light of the records which tell us what English ships afloat upon the sea were actually doing in those days. For at this very time the unofficial Englishman seems to have been boasting that his people possessed a greater number of fine and powerful ships than any other nation, so that they were "kings of the sea;"

[1] See Libel of English Policy, Pol. Poems and Songs, ii. 164–5 For complaints in 1444 and 1485 see Rot. Parl. v. 113.

[2] Libel of English Policy, Pol. Poems and Songs, ii. 159. Capgrave de Illust. Henricis, 135. A man at Canterbury was accused in 1448 of saying that the king was not able to bear the fleur-de-lys nor the ship in his noble. (Hist. MSS. Com. v. 455.)

[3] Heralds' Debate, 17.

and if the boast was a little premature it lay on the whole nearer to the truth. Even now the fleets of the Adventurers were going forth to the conquest of the seas, and their enterprise marks one of the great turning points in our history. It was in fact during this century that England raised herself from the last place among commercial peoples to one of the first. At the close of the fourteenth century, as we have seen, English merchandise was mostly borne in foreign ships; a hundred years later, English vessels carried more than a half of all the cloths exported from the country, and about three quarters of all other goods,[1] and the Navigation Act that had failed under Richard the Second was put in triumphant operation by Henry the Seventh.[2]

It was in the Northern Seas that the real stress of the battle lay. There from a very early time bands of roving adventurers went cruising from harbour to harbour to discover what spoils of trade the orthodox merchants of the Staple or the Hanse had left ungathered, and how the fertile resources of the lawless free-trader might be used to shatter these stately organizations. When the older merchants concentrated themselves in Bruges and Calais the free lances of trade sought out the neglected markets of Brabant and Holland. Driven from the marshes of Middleburg they turned to Antwerp which the Staplers had forsaken. Scarcely had the Hanse merchants under the

[1] Schanz, ii. 27.
[2] 4 H. VII. cap. x.; Schanz, i. 368-9. Encouragement was also given to building of English ships—as for example by remission of tolls on the first voyage (Schanz, ii. 591).

stress of their Danish wars withdrawn from Bergen than the Adventurers forthwith slipped into their place, set up their own Staple, gathering goods there to the value of 10,000 marks, and for years fought steadily against fire and sword to hold their own.[1] If the Baltic towns fell behind the western members of the League in maritime enterprize, the Adventurers' fleets flocked to their harbours, so that three hundred of them were seen in the harbour of Danzig alone, carrying dealers in cloth ready to spread their wares in every market town of Prussia. They pushed their way into the fish-markets of Schonen, offering bales of cloth instead of money[2] for salt herrings, and rousing the alarm of the Hanseatic merchants there also. By the close of the fourteenth century they had so prospered in the world on all sides that they professed to look on large branches of trade as their own exclusive property, and to make a grievance of interference with their profits by other "meddling merchants who were not content with their own business in which they had been brought up and by which they were well able to live."

This was the beginning of a new stage in their history. The Adventurers now proposed to enter the decent ranks of recognized associations, and exchange their roving wars for the more formal aggressions of a chartered company; and at their prayer Henry the Fourth granted them in 1406, for their better ordering and for their protection from other "meddling merchants," a charter by which they took as their official

[1] Keutgen, 55, etc.   [2] Ibid. 54.

title their old name of the Merchant Adventurers.[1] The grant included all dominions over-sea, and allowed them to wander where they would in the wide world, and to draw within their ranks all the Adventurers of England.[2] As yet their organization was loose and free, and was in fact no true incorporation as a Guild. But it marked the passing away of their free and stormy youth. From this time privileges came to them from all sides by English grants, by gifts from foreign towns, by protection of the rulers of various countries. Finally in 1446 they received a new charter of privileges from the Duke of Burgundy [3] by which their tolls were fixed, full protection assured to them, and an organization provided which lasted for the next century. So confident did they become of their power, that when Henry the Seventh at his accession raised the tolls required of them they refused to pay, and he did not dare to enforce the order.[4] Seeing indeed in their success the triumph of English commerce, he remained their steady supporter, confirmed their privileges,[5] and when at Calais they desired greater centralization and a stricter discipline, he gave them a regular organization after the pattern of the Staplers under Edward the Third, with governors and a council of twenty-four assistants.[6] Amid all their successes it was little wonder

[1] Schanz, i. 332; ii. 575. A list of the charters granted to them follows, ibid. 575-8. See also treaty given, ibid. 159.
[2] Ibid. i. 339, 340.   [3] Ibid. ii. 162.
[4] Ibid. i. 340.   [5] 1500; Schanz, ii. 545-7.
[6] In 1505. Henry VII. issued regulations for the Merchant Adventurers. They might meet *in Calais* to elect governors; and they were at the same time to elect a council of twenty-four called "assistants," who were to have jurisdiction over

that there came a time when they themselves forgot the free audacity of their adventurous youth. In their maturer years, as the vehement assertors of monopoly and State protection, they cast behind their backs the very remembrance of their lawless predecessors, and for a braver pedigree they traced their greatness back to ancestors made respectable by a fabled charter from King John himself, and boasted of Aldermen clothed in scarlet who were supposed to have borne rule over them in good old times in Antwerp.

The legend was the product of a time when Antwerp was in fact the capital of the Merchant Adventurers—the home and centre of their trade. For there in the fifteenth century they entered on an inheritance which had been left waste when the merchant princes of the Staple had finally retired to Calais, and had thus practically abandoned all direct trade between Antwerp and England to private hands. The Adventurers soon solved the question of who was to carry it on.[1] In 1407 the

all members and power to make statutes, and to appoint officers both in England and in Calais to levy fines and to imprison offenders. The council filled up its own vacancies. Every merchant using the dealings of a Merchant Adventurer was not only to pay its tolls and taxes, but must enter the fellowship and pay his ten marks. The Calais officials were to proclaim the marts whenever required to do so. The Adventurers might appoint their own weighers and packers, and have nothing to say to the royal officers. (Schanz, ii. 549-553.)

[1] Schanz notes the settlement in Antwerp as one of the most critical turning points of English industrial and commercial history (i. 339). The movement had well begun in the fourteenth and early part of the fifteenth centuries, but the real influx of English traders was from 1442-4 (ibid. i. 9). For the treaties

city gave them a House in perpetual succession. Three of their merchants sat in the Toll-hall with the toll-keepers of the borough to see justice done to their brethren. Known among the people as "the nation,"[1] they early showed their power, and in the first half of the fifteenth century privileges in the English trade were more and more withdrawn from the native traders of the Netherlands, and gathered into their own hands. They used their powers to the full, governed firmly, ordered the whole English trade with the Low Countries, dictated what fair was to be attended, and ruled the prices, in spite of the loud remonstrances of the unlucky natives.[2] At the great marts held in the Netherlands four times a year[3] "they stapled the commodities which they brought out of England, and put the same to sale,"[4] and by 1436 they could boast that they bought more goods in Brabant, Flanders, and Zealand[5] than all

with the Duke of Burgundy in 1407 concerning English traders in Flanders, Rymer's Fœdera, viii. 469-78.

[1] Schanz, ii. 577, 581, 582.
[2] Ibid. i. 343, 344.
[3] 12 Henry VII. c. 6.
[4] Wheeler, Treatise of Commerce, 19, 23.
[5] "Déjà au quinzième siècle les Écossais avaient à Veere en Zélande un dépôt pour leurs marchandises, administré par un 'Conservator.' Sir Thomas Cunningham remplit cet office jusqu'à sa mort en 1655, et ce ne fut que le 28 novembre, 1661 (sic), que Sir W. Davison en fut chargé; il demeura de temps en temps à Amsterdam, où il eut des querelles à l'occasion des impôts municipaux. Plus tard, il eut des différends avec le pasteur épiscopal Mowbray, qui par suite fut déplacé, et enfin avec les Écossais de Veere eux-mêmes. En 1668 Davison fit un traité avec la ville de Dordrecht, pour y transporter les affaires

other nations, and that if their merchants were withdrawn it would be as great a loss to the French trade as though a thousand men of war were sent into the country.[1] The growing jealousy of the manufacturers in Flanders indeed threatened at times to cut off their entire business; and as they were the first to bear the rising storm of commercial rivalries, so again and again they were brought within sight of ruin by the laws passed on either side the water forbidding all import or export trade.

For in their desperate attempt to save the Flemish weavers from ruin the Dukes of Burgundy forbade dressers to finish English cloth, or tailors to cut it in the Netherlands, and laid heavy penalties on any man

d'Écosse; mais comme les Écossais ne voulurent pas s'y conformer, Davison fut contraint de prendre son congé en mai 1671; Veere resta le dépôt du commerce écossais. Consultez encore l'ouvrage très rare. "An account of the Scotch Trade in the Netherlands, and of the Staple Port in Campvere. By James Yair, Minister of the Scotch Church in Campvere. London, 1776." (Œuvres Complètes de Huygens. Amsterdam, 1893. Note on a letter from R. Moray to Huygens, Jan. 30, 1665.)

[1] Libel of English Policy. Pol. Poems and Songs, ii. 180, 181. See Hist. MSS. Com. x. 4, 445–6. William Mucklow, merchant at London, sent commissions to his son Richard at Antwerp; a Richard Mucklow was warden of S. Helen's, Worcester, either in 1510 or 1519 (446). An account book of Wm. Mucklow, merchant, "in the Passe Mart at Barro, Middleburg, in the Synxon Mart at Antwerp, in the Cold Mart and in Bamys Mart," in 1511 records sales of white drapery and purchase of various goods —a ball battery, fustian, buckram, knives, sugar, brushes, satin, damask, sarsenet, velvet, pepper, Yssyngham cloth, spectacles, swan's feathers, girdles, "socket," treacle, green ginger, ribands, brown paper, Brabant cloth, pouches, leather, buckets, "antony belles," "sacke belles," sheets, &c.; and the names of the vessels in which the goods were shipped.

in Flanders who was seen dressed in woollen stuffs of English make;[1] but still the cloth came in, smuggled by speculating dealers from Antwerp, or scattered broadcast by licensed merchants who had bought from the authorities leave to evade the law.[2] Once in consequence of political disputes [3] the Adventurers had to migrate to Calais, and see the legal trade with the Low Countries given to the Easterlings, a sight which "sore nipped their hearts;" but first in "disordered" fashion, then lawfully, they were soon back at their old occupations.[4] With the steady support of Henry the Seventh, whose whole policy was directed to develope the trade with Burgundy and bind England and the Netherlands into a united commercial state, their prosperity was assured; and before the close of the century Antwerp, after two hundred years of struggle for supremacy in trade, took its place as the great centre of commerce [5] in the Netherlands, while its rival Bruges sank into utter poverty and decay. When at last after many chances and changes, the English won in 1506 through Henry the Seventh free trade in cloth throughout all the dominions of the Archduke Philip save Flanders, they actually found themselves better off in the Netherlands

[1] Rot. Parl. iv. 126; Schanz, i. 443-445. For English reprisals, 27 H. VI. cap. i.; 28 H. VI. cap. i.; 4 Ed. IV. cap. 5.
[2] Schanz, ii. 191-3, 203-6. Negotiations were still going on in 1499 as to the trade disputes between Henry the Seventh, the Archduke, and the Staple at Calais (Schanz, ii. 195-202). The main point in dispute was allowing English cloths to be cut in the Netherlands for making clothes.
[3] In 1493; Schanz, i. 17, 18.   [4] Schanz, ii. 582-5.
[5] Ibid. i. 7-11.

than the native merchants, paid less tolls than they, and were in a position whence they might easily overrun the country with their wares and finally destroy its decaying cloth industry.[1]

From their central stronghold in Antwerp the Merchant Adventurers further maintained a lively war to right and left, on the one side with the Staple at Calais, on the other with the Hanseatic League.

It was practically the jealousy of the Staplers that had first driven the Adventurers from Bruges, and no sooner did they feel their strength than they prepared to make their ancient enemies pay the penalty for old wrongs. Towards the merchants of the Staple the very character of their trade from the first forced them into a militant attitude. Shut out from all interest in the sale of wool, their fortune rested solely on the manufacturing industries, and the more weaving at home was encouraged the greater were their gains.[2] And since the wool merchants proceeded both to claim and to practise the right of exporting and selling cloth as well as wool, they became in a double sense obnoxious to their rivals. Now, however, the Adventurers could fight from the vantage ground given them by their new position as a chartered company. Out of their acknowledged right to demand tolls on the sale of cloth in their marts, they deduced by a liberal interpretation of their powers the right to require from each trading Stapler in addition to the ordinary tolls an entrance fee or hanse of ten marks, by payment of which he became a freeman of the Adven-

[1] Schanz, i. 31, 32.   [2] Ibid. i. 339.

turers' Company and was made subject to their laws and courts,[1] and if he refused to pay they seized his wares, or imprisoned him till he gave the "hanse."[2] Wealthy merchants of the Staple who had taken their wares to Middleburg might find themselves thrown into prison among felons and murderers infected with odious diseases; the resolute Adventurers refused bail, and quietly ignored royal letters of remonstrance.[3] Already in 1457 the Staplers complained bitterly to the English King and to the Duke of Burgundy, that under colour of letters patent and charters, their enemies so vexed them both in their goods and persons as to threaten them with utter ruin.[4] But the decision of Henry the Sixth that the Adventurers were asserting unjust claims which were strictly forbidden for the future [5] scarcely interrupted the battle, and the same series of complaints and aggressions was brought in 1504 before the Star Chamber, by whose judgement the Adventurers were again forbidden to go beyond their right of levying tolls. But if the law was against them they had on their side their own inexhaustible activity, their unscrupulous audacity, their large self-confidence, and the weakness of the dying company of the Staple. Six years later when the Staplers again summoned them before the King for their "crooked minds and froward sayings" and lawless deeds of violence, they answered with uncompromising contempt. The Staplers, they allowed, might have certain privileges

[1] Schanz, i. 345; ii. 561, 562. [2] Instances, Schanz, ii. 557, 558.
[3] Ibid. ii. 564. [4] Ibid. ii. 543.
[5] From Antwerp Archives; Schanz, ii. 539-43.

in Calais—but as to talking of rights in Burgundy, that in their opinion was absurd to urge after the removal of the Staple thence. Outside Calais the Staplers had no rights. With regard to their claim to exclusive jurisdiction over their members, "that article might have been left out of their book, for why every reasonable man knoweth the contrary." In spite of such "reasonable men," however, once more the law was proclaimed to be against them; but as they knew well the law was powerless to set up again the ruined company of the Merchant Staplers.[1]

With the second and more formidable army arrayed against them, the merchants of the Hanseatic League, the war of the Adventurers had to be carried on with greater circumspection. Through a couple of centuries the doubtful conflict was maintained on every sea and

[1] In November, 1504, the Staplers and Adventurers appeared before the Star Chamber. The Staplers pleaded a charter which declared them free from the jurisdiction of the Adventurers. The Star Chamber decided that every Stapler who dealt or traded as an Adventurer was to be subject to the courts and dues of the Adventurers: and every Adventurer dealing as a Stapler in like manner to be subject to the Staple (Schanz, ii. 547). This decision seemed to imply the ruin of Staplers, but the next year it was explained that the authentic interpretation was simply that "the merchants of the Staple at Calais using the feate of a Merchant Adventurer passing to the marts at Calais should *in those things* be contributories to such impositions and charges" as the Adventurers had fixed (ibid. 549); and that they could not be compelled to join the Adventurers' company. In 1510 Henry the Eighth repeated the decree of Henry the Seventh that the Adventurers must not force Staplers to join their body (555). For the pleadings before the Star Chamber under Henry the Eighth see Schanz, ii. 556-564.

in every port from Danzig to Iceland. For the first hundred years things went ill for the Adventurers. The League monopolized the whole commerce between the Scandinavian kingdoms and England;[1] drove out the English from Schonen, the centre to which all the fishers of the Baltic and North Seas gathered for the salting, packing, and selling of their fish;[2] harassed them with fire and sword in Bergen, the Staple town of the north,[3] scattering them at one time by starvation, at another by decrees of expulsion; banished them from the Prussian towns belonging to the Teutonic Order which they were "destroying" with their cloth,[4] and sought to ruin their trade by issuing an order that no merchant of the Hanse should buy English cloth outside England itself. When the League waged war with Denmark and Norway in 1368-9 to confirm its mastery of the Northern Seas, it dragged the English traders at its heels into the fight, and at its close threw them off without a thought.[5] It gave a scornful answer to demands made by Parliament under Edward the Third and Richard the Second that the tolls exacted from Hanseatic traders for exporting goods from England should be increased; and retorted by a decree that all trade with England should be utterly broken off, thus shutting the great market at Elbing to the English merchants who had made it the centre of their trade with Russia and the towns of Prussia.[6]

[1] Schanz, i. 249. [2] Keutgen, 42, 51-54.
[3] Schanz, i. 251. [4] Keutgen, 30, 81. [5] Ibid. 44, &c.
[6] Pauli's Pictures, 172, 185. Keutgen, 10-43. Richard the Second complained to the Grand Master that traders were forced

The English traders, however, took all misfortune with the hardihood and exuberant courage of youth. Help from their own government was beyond hoping for, so long as conquering kings like Edward the Third and Henry the Fifth were bound hand and foot to the great mercantile houses of Lübeck and the Hanse towns by the loans raised from them to carry on the French wars; while Henry the Fourth, who, before he came to the throne, had been in Danzig and seen the troubles of the English merchants there,[1] and who in his anxiety to win the support of the trading class, was persistent in negotiations to improve their position, had not the power to give effect to his desires. The Adventurers, therefore, could only follow the one obvious course open to them, and kept up a steady brigandage on the seas and a series of opportune attacks on the enemy's out-posts. They held on

to carry their cloth to Elbing instead of Danzig (ibid. 72). In 1388 three citizens of London and York were sent to Marienberg with an interpreter to make a treaty of commerce with the "general master of the house of S. Mary of Teutonia." (Hist. MSS. Com. i. 109.) In 1397, however, trade with the Easterlings was practically stopped. The English imposed enormous duties on German imports; the Germans forbade traffic in English cloth. For the negotiations carried on by Henry the Fourth see Literæ Cantuarienses, iii. xxviii.-xxxi., and the various letters on the subject. The English colony in Danzig increased greatly after the peace of Marienberg. (Schanz, i. 231.) In 1392 more than 300 English came into Danzig to carry corn. (Keutgen, 71.) But the resistance of the Danzig burghers to English trade was strenuous. They were less jealous of the Netherlands manufacturers, and the Teutonic Order in the fifteenth century sent to Dinant for the rough cloth needed for the Baltic trade. (Pirenne, Dinant, 97; Keutgen, 81-83.)

[1] Pauli's Pictures, 135-8.

desperately at Bergen,[1] and stoutly clung to the formal right which Henry the Fourth had given them to organize themselves under consuls in Norway, Sweden, or Denmark, for the carrying on of their trade.[2] Fishing boats which were shut out from the Baltic or from Bergen sailed on to Iceland, where, as the island was the private property of the King of Norway (who was himself the servant of the League) and was allowed to receive no ships save the King's, or those licensed by the King, opportunities for illegal trade were abundant and profits large. A frugal people, needy and remote, eagerly welcomed smuggled goods from England in exchange for their fish; and the smugglers carried on a rough business—outlaws and daring men of their company plundered and killed and stole cattle and desolated homesteads, and bartered after their own self-made laws.[3] It mattered nothing to them that Henry the Fifth, in obedience to the League, forbade the trade, or that in a storm of 1419

[1] 8 H. VI. c. 2; Proc. Privy Council, iv. 208; Schanz, ii. 170.
[2] In 1425 there were letters from Henry the Sixth to the King of Dacia, Norwegia, and Swecia, concerning the merchants of Lynn who traded with the parts of North Berne; (Hist. MSS. Com. xi. 3, 203). In 1427 he wrote to the English merchants "in partibus Prucie, Dacie, Norweie, Hanse, and Swethie commorantes," to assemble in a sufficient place, elect governors and make ordinances for self-government in mercantile matters, and for reasonable punishment of any merchants disobedient (203). At times the English even forced compensation from the Hanse merchants for outrages (Schanz, i. 250). In 1438 rye was brought from Prussia "by the providence of Stephen Browne," the mayor, at a time of famine in England, when a bushel of corn was sold for 3s. 4d., and the people were making bread of vetches, peas, beans, and fern-roots. (Fabyan, 612.)
[3] Schanz, i. 254.

twenty-five English ships were driven on the coast of Iceland in three hours. Bristol men found their way to its shores by help of the compass, leaving for us the first record of its use in England, probably in 1424; and about 1436, in a year when the English had been expelled from Bergen, so many vessels sailed to Iceland that they could get no return cargo, and half of them had to come empty home.[1] But the northern trade was not all violent or lawless. English merchants bought double licenses from the English and the Norwegian kings, which allowed them to carry on a regular traffic; and in the middle of the fifteenth century one of the Bristol merchants, Cannynges, had in his hands the chief trade with northern Europe. Not only were his factors established in the Baltic ports, but his transactions with Iceland and with Finland were on so great a scale that when in 1450 all English trade with these regions was forbidden in virtue of a treaty with the King of Denmark, Cannynges was specially exempted on account of the debts due to him there by Danish subjects, and for two years he had a monopoly of the trade.[2]

Meanwhile the Adventurers watched their oppor-

[1] Libel of English Policy. Pol. Poems and Songs, ii. 191. The bailiffs and community of Chepstowe did trade with Iceland and Finmark. (Proc. Privy Council, iv. 208.) In 1426 Lynn forbade trade with Iceland to its inhabitants and the whole community sent a petition against the trade to the King's Council. (Hist. MSS. Com. xi. 3, 160.)

[2] Hunt's Bristol, 94–6. In 1491 fishing-smacks starting for Iceland had to get leave to sail, after finding surety that they would not carry more grain nor any other forbidden thing than sufficed for their own food. Paston Letters, iii. 367–9.

tunity to carry the war nearer home, for the League, already weighted with the effort to maintain its monopoly before the rise of Scandinavian powers and the consolidation of the Duchy of Burgundy, was further troubled within its own ranks by divided counsels.[1] In the reign of Henry the Sixth, therefore, the English renewed among other claims their old demand that the Hanseatic merchants should no longer be favoured at their expense, but should be treated like any other foreigners and forced to pay the same tolls on wine and wool. There was a chance of success, for Lübeck and the western towns finding in their strength and self-reliance arguments for a policy of peace with England, were generally for amicable compromise; though the eastern towns led by Danzig, weaker at sea and peculiarly sensitive to any increase of money burdens, preferred fighting to submission with its apprehended dangers.[2] The party of violence won the day and a fierce maritime war followed with open hostilities and reprisals and law-suits and endless negociations. On one occasion the English seized a fleet of 108 sail returning to Lübeck and Riga, and the men of the Hanse retaliated by laying hands on rich English prizes. Trade was so ruined that Henry the Sixth declared himself unable to pay to the Count Palatine the dowry of his aunt Lady Blanche, because there were now no dues and customs coming into his Treasury from the German merchants.[3] At last the

[1] Keutgen, 30.
[2] Ibid. 84-5, 70-71. For these negotiations see Rymer's Fœdera, x. 656-7, 666-70, 753. Bekynton, i. 215.
[3] In 1439. Bekynton's Corres. i. 183-4.

dispute came to a climax in 1469, when the English quarrelled with the German traders in London, summoned them before the courts and imposed a fine of £13,520,[1] while members of the Steel Yard were thrown into prison, and the corporation nearly broken up.[2] The answer of Bremen, Hamburg, and Danzig was given in a fleet which gathered against England under the leadership of Charles the Bold. But just at this moment came the English revolution by which Edward the Fourth was driven out of the country, and all the great trading bodies, the Hanseatic League, and the Flemish and Dutch corporations, seeing the danger which threatened their commerce from the new political situation, cast aside minor quarrels and united to set Edward again on the throne.[3] Such a service

---

[1] "Whereof the payment was kept secret from writers" (Fabyan, 657.)

[2] The fortunes of Memling's Last Judgement now at Danzig give a curious illustration of this war and the trade complications of the time. Ordered at Bruges through the Florentine agents there (the Portinari), probably by Julian and Lorenzo de Medici, the picture could not be carried to Florence on account of this war begun in 1468. At last in 1473 it was sent off from Sluys in a British-built ship, which had been bought by English merchants as a French prize, chartered by Florentines in Bruges for a voyage to London, registered in the name of the Portinari, commissioned by a French captain, and navigated under the Burgundian flag for greater security against capture. It was, however, taken off Southampton by a privateer sailing under the Danzig flag and commanded by a noted captain Benecke. In spite of a bull issued by Sixtus the Fourth the cargo was sold at Stade and the picture brought by the owners of the ship to Danzig. (Crowe and Cavalcaselle, Early Flemish Painters, 257-260.)

[3] Henry the Sixth, on the other hand, brought the help of the Genoese. Possibly the excessive price of fish mentioned in the

demanded a great reward; and in 1474 a treaty was signed at Utrecht, by which the Hanse was given back all its earlier privileges, and secured in possession of its Guild Hall and Steel Yard in London, and its houses in Boston and Lynn. The Adventurers who made a bold demand that the Easterlings should renounce the right of carrying out wool or wool-fells from England can scarcely have expected to succeed; but they at least gained some measure of peace for their colony in Danzig.[1]

The Hanseatic League, however, had now come to an end of its triumphs. From this time the English pressed them hard. A law which forbade the import of silk and the export of undressed cloths struck a heavy blow at their trade. Then came the order that Rhine wine must only be carried in English ships. Officials used their infinite powers of annoyance with hearty good will, and the merchant who landed with his goods, harassed first by the relentless officers sitting at the receipt of custom, and then thwarted in every possible way by the Mayor and corporation,[2] was at last driven by public abuse behind the walls of the Steel Yard, so that in 1490 a member of the Hanse dared scarcely show himself in the streets of London.

Meanwhile the great confederation of Commonwealths itself showed grave signs of falling asunder. The bigger towns that no longer needed the protection of the association were quite ready to forsake it, and in

---

Paston Letters in 1471 may have been caused by the political troubles (iii. 22, 254).

[1] Schanz, i. 172-9; ii. 388-396. Pauli's Pictures, 185-7.
[2] Schanz, i, 186.

1501 began to refuse to bring their cloth to the Staple at Bruges, and to look for freer conditions of trade. At the same time the monopoly of the League was being threatened on all sides. The Prussian and Livonian towns treated them as enemies. A Dutch fleet competed with them in the Baltic. A Danish trading company had risen to dispute their monopoly in Denmark. The Swedes shut them out. The Norwegians made intermittent experiments at independence. At last in 1478 came the worst calamity that could befall their trade, the capture of Novgorod by the Muscovites, with the destruction of its free government and the ruin of its position as one of the commercial capitals of the world.

With the demolition of the League factory, the loss of all its possessions in the city, and the whole dislocation of the Eastern traffic, the supremacy of the Hanseatic Confederation was shattered, as the supremacy of the Italians in the Southern trade had been shattered half a century before by the conquest of Alexandria. English Adventurers naturally saw in every fresh trouble that assailed their rivals a new argument for aggression, and welcomed in Henry the Seventh a leader equal to the great occasion. Never had they found a better friend, or one who so finely interpreted the popular instinct of his time. How completely his determination to strengthen by every means in his power the position of the Adventurers in Antwerp against the Hanseatic traders at Bruges, and to bind England and Burgundy together into a united commercial state, fell in with the needs and temper of his people was strikingly shown after a two years' interruption of commerce with the Low Countries caused by the affair of Perkin Warbeck, when a burst of popular joy hailed the renewal of trade, and the wild enthusiasm of the people gave to the treaty of 1496 which restored the old kindly relations the high-sounding name of the *Intercursus Magnus*.

The big name has, as usual, imposed a little on later generations, and greater treaties have gone unnoticed for want of an equally pompous title. At first, indeed, amid the political disquiet and the trade depression which marked the early years of his reign, Henry went to work slowly and patiently, and in 1486 even confirmed the Utrecht treaty of 1474 which ensured a number of privileges to the Hanse. But this policy of peace was only assumed for a brief space while he was making ready for war. In 1486 he renewed the commercial treaty made by Edward with Britanny in 1467.[1] The real campaign, however, may be said to have opened by the Navigation Act of 1489, when the shipping trade was definitely taken under State protection. And what that State protection implied was at once shown in a series of commercial treaties with almost every trading country of Europe, whether its traffic lay in the northern or the southern seas. Building up on every hand alliances against the Hanseatic Confederation he steadily drew to himself the friendship of the Scandinavian peoples tired of the domination of the League. In 1489 he sent an embassy (two of the deputation being Lynn merchants), to make terms for a com-

[1] Schanz, i. 294.

mercial alliance with Denmark and Norway, and won from the Northern powers freedom of trade for the English in Denmark, Norway, and Iceland, with the right to acquire land, to form corporations and choose aldermen, and to be under special protection of the Danish King.[1] To defeat the pretensions of Danzig he turned to the Livonian towns, and by treaty with Riga attempted to secure a Russian trade which might open the way of Novgorod and the East to English Adventurers—an attempt which however was frustrated a few years later.[2] A conference was held in 1491 at Antwerp with the Hanseatic envoys, whom Henry with diplomatic insolence kept idly waiting for four weeks till the messengers he had sent to Denmark with friendly proposals of a treaty as unfavourable as possible to the interests of the Hanse, returned with their answer. The promise of this inauspicious opening for the League was amply fulfilled in the long negotiations which lasted at Antwerp from 1491 to 1499, and in which the foreigner was consistently humbled before the triumphant Merchant Adventurer, all his compromises rejected so far as they tended to limit the freedom of the English trader, and the League compelled to accept terms ruinous to its interests and disastrous to its great tradition of supremacy.[3]

---

[1] Schanz, i. 257.   [2] Schanz, i. 237–42.
[3] For the negotiations between the Easterlings and the English merchants, see Schanz, ii. 397-430 ; i. 179–201. In 1498 Archduke Philip, seeing the utter ruin into which Bruges had fallen, tried to revive it by ordering that all foreign merchants should do their business there only, by improving the harbour, *and by*

The story of these Antwerp negotiations gives us a true measure of the place gained during the last hundred years by the Merchant Adventurers in the North, where, having dealt the last blows to the ancient company of the Staple, and broken the power of the Hanseatic League, their fleets now sailed triumphantly on every sea. And yet this was but half their work; for the North was a small thing to win unless they could also load English vessels with the cargoes of the East and the tribute of the great commercial cities of the Mediterranean. Until the middle of the fifteenth century the trade of the eastern Mediterranean had been altogether carried on by Italians.[1] It was only in 1432 that the French merchant Jacques Coeur (the stories of whose wealth and power read like fables beside the modest doings of our native traders), had sent out some ships to take part in the Eastern trade; and the Levant was not really opened to Western merchants till 1442, when the Venetians were driven out of Egypt and the monopoly of the

making it the Staple for English cloths in Flanders. (Schanz, i. 26-27.) In 1501 Philip made Bruges a Staple where English cloth might be sold in Flanders under strict conditions. (Ibid. ii. 203-6.) In 1506 Henry won from the Archduke the right to sell cloth by the yard and to have the manufacture of it finished in all his dominions except Flanders. (Ibid. i. 31.)

[1] The friendly way in which the English merchants even in 1405 looked on Genoese traders is illustrated in the story told by Fabyan (571), of three carracks of Genoa laden with merchandise plundered by English lords. The Genoese merchants made suit to the King for compensation, and meanwhile borrowed from English merchants goods amounting unto great and noble sums. When their suit was seen to be in vain they made off with their spoils "to the undoing" of many merchants.

Italians broken up. It was very soon after that a Bristol merchant, Sturmys, fitted out probably the first English ship that visited the Eastern shores of the Mediterranean. But the new inheritors of the East were received with bitter jealousies. Rival vessels fought for the spoils and carried off the booty like common pirates; and the Genoese traders in their anger seized Sturmys' ship on its return voyage and robbed it of its cargo of spices and green pepper. He reckoned his loss at 6,000 francs, and on his complaint to the government all the Genoese merchants in London were thrown into prison until they should give bonds for the payment of this sum.[1]

The question of the Mediterranean was thus vigorously opened. In London, indeed, the Italians might securely reckon on hard treatment. Merchants just beginning to feel their strength, half-ruined Staplers, London shopkeepers and manufacturers, all alike hated their Italian rivals with a common hatred, and were crying out for the most decisive measures against foreign competition. Less careful than their King of nursing political alliances[2] in view of foreign wars and complications, the traders boldly proposed a bill in the Parliament of 1439 to forbid the Venetians from carrying any wares save those of their own manufacture—a measure which if it had passed would have

[1] Hunt's Bristol, 97-8.
[2] For the anxiety as to the friendship of powerful maritime states see the French boast of the alliance of Spain and Genoa; Heralds' Debate, 59. It is interesting to notice that both Edward the Fourth and Henry the Seventh preferred Florence to Venice. Disputes about the Venetian wool trade under Henry the Sixth are mentioned in Bekynton's Corresp. i. 126-9.

practically annihilated the whole Venetian trade to England. Their next proposal was a law to forbid selling anything to the Genoese or carrying anything to their port. Steadily supported as the Lombards were by the King against the people, they nevertheless saw their privileges from this time limited step by step; and once after the persecution of 1455 in London even attempted to leave the capital for ever. The great days of their trade monopoly were gone. Edward the Fourth and Richard the Third laid heavy burdens on them. Henry the Seventh kept them dependent on his arbitrary will for a very slight increase of freedom, such as he might see fit to grant from time to time, tried to limit their gains, and in the very first year of his reign forbade them to carry French woad or wine, or silk goods, and further hindered them in the export of wool.

At this time the population of the Venetian Republic was bigger than that of all England, and English traders had a good many other affairs on their hands beside their quarrel with Venice. The dispute, nevertheless, did not languish. No sooner were Henry's regulations proclaimed in 1485 than English merchants set sail for Crete, bought up the stores of malmsey there,[1] and carried them off to the Netherlands under the very eyes of the Venetian captains. Venice passed a law against such traffic, and in the stress of anxiety as to the English competition took to building better ships to maintain her own carrying trade; while England retorted by setting up a mono-

[1] The price of wine had been raised in England by new rules about measures.

poly of her own wool in revenge for the Venetian monopoly of wine.

Meanwhile, the quick-witted Florentines, driven out of traditional routine by the intensity of the long competition for supremacy, had begun to doubt the value for them of the old policy of naval protection which the city had shared with Venice and Genoa; and had frankly adopted in 1480 a system of free-trade. In Constantinople and Egypt Florence began again to hold her own against Venice and to win back command of Eastern markets, and she eagerly welcomed English wool merchants to her port at Pisa.[1] In 1485, the year when England entered into the lists with Venice, these had become so numerous and powerful a body that a consul was appointed over them; and five years later, Henry made a commercial treaty with Florence which was one of the most remarkable acts of his reign. By its provisions English merchants undertook to carry every year to Florence sufficient wool to supply all the Italian States save Venice, and in return they were given every privilege their hearts desired.[2] The only resource left to the Venetians was

[1] A pilgrim to Rome in 1477 got letters in London on the bank of Jacobo di Medici. (Hist. MSS. Com. vi. 361.)

[2] 1. English merchants might trade freely with Florence in all kinds of wares of home or foreign origin.

2. The Florentines promised to buy no wool save from English ships. The English on their side were bound to carry yearly to Pisa an average quantity for all the Italian states save Venice. In Pisa they were to have all the privileges of inhabitants and to have land for a building.

3. The English were to be free from personal services and from taxes which might be raised on trade.

4. The merchants might form a corporation in Pisa.

to forbid that any wine should be shipped from Crete to Pisa, so that English vessels which went out laden with wool finding no return cargo should be driven to sail home empty. Henry immediately set such heavy import duties on malmsey in England that the Venetians, seeing their wine-trade on the point of ruin, bowed at last to the inevitable. The victory of the English merchants was finally proclaimed when Henry in 1507 only consented to renew the charter that gave Venetians rights of trade in England on condition that they bound themselves to do no carrying trade between the Netherlands and England, but to leave that to the Merchant Adventurers.[1]

Meanwhile, in all the ports visited by English ships between the Mediterranean and the Channel the same buoyant spirit of successful enterprise vanquished every obstacle. Englishmen had always traded much with their fellow-subjects in Aquitaine. From the days of St. Thomas Canterbury had dealings with the wine-growers of the south.[2] Ships of Bordeaux were

5. Quarrels between Englishmen to be settled by their own head. Quarrels between an Englishman and a foreigner to be decided by the municipality and the English consul. Criminal cases by the municipality alone.

6. The English to share all advantages the Florentines might win by trading treaties.

7. The wishes of the English to be considered in all new privileges granted in the Florentine dominions.

8. The English King was to allow no stranger to carry wool out of England. The Venetians only might carry 600 sacks.

9. The wool was to be of good quality and well packed. (Schanz, i. 126-137.)

[1] Schanz, i. 119-142; 7 Henry VII. c. 7.

[2] An interesting account of this is given in Hist. MSS. Com. v. 461.

known in every port of the Channel, and in 1350, 141 vessels laden with wine sailed thence to London alone,[1] while the early wealth of Bristol had been created by the cargoes of wool carried from its port to feed the Gascon manufactories, and the casks of wine sent back to fill its cellars. Conditions so pleasant for the Bristol burghers were rudely changed when in 1445 Bordeaux fell into the hands of the French, and English traders instead of being the masters had to go humbly at the bidding of the men of Bordeaux with a red cross on their backs, doing business only in the town, or going into the country under the guardianship of a police agent. But if the burghers of the later fifteenth century cared nothing for the re-conquest of the French provinces, on the other hand they were determined not to lose their trade. The wool dealers, shut out of Bordeaux, turned to the North, to Rouen and Calais, changed their wool there for the wine of Niederburgund, and so started the woollen manufactures of Normandy, while those of Bordeaux declined. By a succession of commercial treaties [2] and by the Navigation Act of 1489, which shut out Gascon ships from the English wine trade, Henry secured for English merchants in Bordeaux such adequate protection that the efforts of Louis the Twelfth to limit their freedom of trade by passing a Navigation Act of his own were utterly vain. The Bordeaux citizens, filled with impotent rage,

[1] Schanz, i. 298.
[2] In 1475, 1486, and 1495. (Schanz, i. 299–304.) In 1475 a proclamation in Cinque Ports forbade Englishmen to buy Gascon wine of an alien. (Hist. MSS. Com. v. 494.)

watched the English traders going up and down the land, 6,000 to 8,000 of them, as they averred, armed with sticks, and scouring the country for wine.

The ports of Spain and Portugal also were visited by increasing numbers of English vessels on their way to the Mediterranean, and old trading alliances were renewed with countries whose harbours were such valuable resting places.[1] There had long been commercial treaties with Castile and Catalonia, who competed for the profits to be won by carrying to England Spanish iron and fruits along with the wine and woad of neighbouring lands. But Henry the Seventh took the occasion of the negotiations for the Spanish marriage in 1489 to stipulate anew for freedom of trade and protection of English ships; while at the same time the English merchants asserted that by the new Navigation Act the whole export trade was now their exclusive right, and under the plea that their ships could not make the voyage to Spain unless they had a certainty of coming back well laden, forbade the carrying of Toulouse woad and Gascony wine in Spanish ships. By this time the Englishman had as usual roused the fear and hatred of the native merchants, and the Spaniards violently resisted the new policy. Heavy tolls were imposed on either side to ruin the trade of the other, and in one season eight hundred English ships were sent home empty from Seville because the patriotic Spanish dealers with one accord

---

[1] An interesting trace of foreign connections is given in the will of Wm. Rowley, who left money to a parish church and a nunnery at Dam in Flanders, and to two places in Spain. (Hist. MSS. Com. v. 326.)

refused their wares to the enemy. Again fortune came to help the pertinacity of the Adventurers. In 1492 Spain drove the Jews and Moors from her shores. But their business simply fell into alien hands waiting to receive it, and the hated English merchants flocked to Spanish harbours now swept of their old rivals, and sailed back to England laden with the gold of the New World.[1]

Nor was the good chance that favoured them in Portugal less wonderful. With the traders of Lisbon and Oporto England had entered into a commercial treaty in the middle of the fourteenth century—a treaty which was altered in 1386 to include the whole of Portugal.[2] But by some happy destiny whose favours strewed the path of English traders, they asked and obtained in 1458 a revision of old agreements so as to secure the utmost advantage for their own interests, and all this had been completed just before the discovery of the Cape route gave to Portugal its enormous naval importance and threw Eastern commerce into a new channel. The quarrel with Venice inspired the English with increased ardour in their friendship for the new masters of the spice trade; and when Portuguese dealers invited English merchants to make their bargains for Eastern wares in Lisbon instead of journeying to Venice, these gathered in such numbers to the new emporium of Indian goods that their own shipping failed to carry the wealth offered to

[1] Schanz, i. 275-7.

[2] Ibid. i. 285-90. The Portuguese were among those who were allowed to export woollen cloths under Henry the Sixth. (Proc. Privy Council, v. ii. 11.)

them and the merchants had to hire Portuguese vessels.[1]

Thus it was that in the face of the powerful confederations that held the trade of the Northern and the Southern Seas English merchants were laying violent hands on the commerce of the world. They had vanquished their rivals in the north, while in the south they had firmly planted themselves in every important trading port along the western coast of Europe, and competed with the Italian Republics not only for their own carrying trade but for that of the Netherlands as well. If in the reign of Edward the Third practically the whole of the foreign commerce of England was carried in foreign vessels, in the reign of Henry the Seventh the great bulk of the trade had passed into English hands. British merchants were to be found in every port from Alexandria to Reykjavik, and wherever they touched left behind them an organized and firmly established trade. As we have seen, their battle for supremacy in commerce had in its beginnings been fought by free-traders and pirates warring against the orderly forces of organized protection; but the final victory was awarded to them in their later stage of a company of monopolists sustained and cherished by the State. The question, indeed, of how far protection contributed to the success of the English or to the loss of the foreigner is far from being a simple one. For

---

[1] Notices of English trade with Portugal in the second half of the fifteenth century may be found in the complaints of the merchants; Schanz, ii. 496-524. For Portuguese in Lydd in 1456, Hist. MSS. Com. v. 521.

in its first stages the work done by protection may possibly consist for a time mainly in the *abolition* of privilege, and this process may pass by very slow and imperceptible degrees to its last stage, that of *conferring* privilege. It is, therefore, hard to decipher the lesson when we are studying a commerce where protection has but begun its work in conflict with a commerce when that work is perfected. In the history of the later fifteenth century, moreover, the problem is yet further complicated by the present working of those vast forces which make or unmake the fortunes of continents, and before which the wisest policies of States, policies of protection or of free-trade or of any other elaborate product of human intelligence, are powerful as an army of phantoms.

CHAPTER IV

THE COMMON LIFE OF THE TOWN

WE who have been trained under the modern system have forgotten how people lived in the old days, when the necessity of personal effort was forced home to every single member of the fellowship of freemen who had life or liberties or property to protect. For in spite of the vigour and independence of our modern local administration every Englishman now looks ultimately for the laws that rule his actions, and the force that protects his property, to the great central authority which has grown up outside and beyond all local authorities. He is subject to it in all the circumstances of life; whether it exercises wholly new functions unknown to the middle ages; or takes over to itself powers which once belonged to inferior bodies, and makes them serve national instead of local ends; whether it asserts a new direction and control over municipal administration; or whether, instead of replacing the town authorities by its own rule, it upholds them with the support of its vast resources and boundless strength. By whatever right the State holds its manifold powers, whether by inheritance, or purchase, or substitution, or influence, or the superiority of mere might, he feels its working on every hand. It is to him visibly charged with all the grand operations of government.

But to a burgher of the middle ages the care and protection of the State were dim and shadowy compared with the duties and responsibilities thrown on the townspeople themselves. For in the beginnings of municipal life the affairs of the borough great and small, its prosperity, its safety, its freedom from crime, the gaiety and variety of its life, the regulation of its trade, were the business of the citizens alone. Fenced in by its wall and ditch[1]— fenced in yet more effectually by the sense of danger without, and the clinging to privileges won by common effort that separated it from the rest of the world—the town remained isolated and self-dependent. Within these narrow borders the men who went out to win the carrying trade of the world learned their first lessons in organization, and acquired the temper by virtue of which Englishmen were to build up at home a great political society

[1] In Piers Ploughman a graphic illustration is taken from the mediæval borough thus isolated and protected.

"He cried and commanded all Christian people
To delve and dike a deep ditch all about unity,
That Holy Church stood in holiness as it were a pile.
Conscience commanded then all Christians to delve,
And make a great moat that might be a strength
To help holy Church and them that it keepeth."
—Pass. xxii. 364–386.

and to conquer abroad the supremacy of the seas—the temper which we recognize in an early confession of faith put forth by the citizens of Hereford as to the duties which a man owed to his commonwealth and to its chief magistrate. "And he to be our head next under the King, whom we ought in all things touching our King or the state of our city to obey chiefly in three things—first, when we are sent for by day or by night to consult of those things which appertain to the King or the state of the city; secondly, to answer if we offend in any point contrary to our oath, or our fellow-citizens; thirdly, to perform the affairs of the city *at our own charges, if so be they may be finished either sooner or better than by any other of our citizens.*"[1] Public claims were insistent, and under the primitive conditions of communal life, in small societies where every man lived in the direct light of public opinion, no citizen was allowed to count carefully the cost of sacrifice, or stint the measure of his service, when the welfare of his little community was at stake. His duties were plainly laid down before him, and they were rigidly exacted. According to the accepted theory it was understood that all private will and advantage were to be sacrificed to the common good, and Langland speaks bitterly of the "individualists" of his day.

> "For they will and would as best were for themselves,
> Though the King and the commons all the cost had.
> All reason reproveth such imperfect people."[2]

---

[1] Journ. Arch. Assoc. xxvii. 461.
[2] Piers Ploughman, passus iv. 386.

I. The inhabitants of a mediæval borough were subject to a discipline as severe as that of a military state of modern times. Threatened by enemies on every side, constantly surrounded by perils, they had themselves to bear the whole charges of fortification and defence. If a French fleet appeared on the coast, if Welsh or Scotch armies made a raid across the frontier, if civil war broke out and opposing forces marched across the country, every town had to look to its own safety. The inhabitants served under a system of universal conscription. At the muster-at-arms held twice a year poor and rich appeared in military array with such weapons as they could bring forth for the King's service; the poor marching with knife or dagger or hatchet; the prosperous burghers, bound according to mediæval ideas to live "after their degree," displaying mail or wadded coats, bucklers, bows and arrows, swords, or even a gun. At any moment this armed population might be called out to active service. "Concerning our bell," say the citizens of Hereford, "we use to have it in a public place where our chief bailiff may come, as well by day as by night, to give warning to all men living within the said city and suburbs. And we do not say that it ought to ring unless it be for some terrible fire burning any row of houses within the said city, or for any common contention whereby the city might be terribly moved, or for any enemies drawing near unto the city, or if the city shall be besieged, or any sedition shall be between any, and notice thereof given by any unto our chief bailiff. And in these cases aforesaid, and in all like cases, all manner of men abiding within the city and suburbs and liberties of the city, of what degree soever they be of, ought to come at any such ringing, or motion of ringing, with such weapons as fit their degree."[1] At the first warning of an enemy's approach the mayor or bailiff became supreme military commander.[2] It was his office to see that the panic-stricken people of the suburbs were gathered within the walls and given house and food, that all meat and drink and chattels were made over for the public service, and all armour likewise carried to the Town Hall, that every inhabitant or refugee paid the taxes required for the cost of his protection, that all strong and able men "which doth dwell in the city or would be assisted by the city in anything" watched by day and night, and that women and clerics who could not watch themselves found at their own charge substitutes "of the ablest of the city."[3]

If frontier towns had periods of comparative quiet, the seaports, threatened by sea as by land, lived in perpetual alarm, at least so long as the Hundred Years' War protracted its terrors. When the inhabitants had built ships to guard the harbour, and provided money for their victualling and the salaries of the crew, they were called out to repair towers and carry cartloads of rocks or stones to be laid on the walls "for defending the town in resisting the king's

[1] Journ. Arch. Assoc. xxvii. 466.

[2] "And we use that during the siege if the bailiff be an unable and impotent man or unlearned, to choose us one other for the time being; but not a far-dweller unless by the pleasure of the commonalty." (Ibid. 488.) See Proc. Privy Council, iv. 217.

[3] Journ. Arch. Assoc. xxvii. 463, 488.

enemies."[1] Guns had to be carried to the church or the Common House on sleds or laid in pits at the town gates, and gun-stones, saltpetre, and pellet powder bought. For weeks together watchmen were posted in the church towers with horns to give warning if a foe appeared; and piles of straw, reeds and wood were heaped up on the sea-coast to kindle beacons and watch-fires. Even if the townsfolk gathered for a day's amusement to hear a play in the Court-house a watch was set lest the enemy should set fire to their streets—a calamity but too well known to the burghers of Rye and Southampton.[2]

Inland towns were in little better case. Civil war, local rebellion, attacks from some neighbouring lord, outbreaks among the followers of a great noble lodged within their walls at the head of an army of retainers, all the recurring incidents of siege and pitched battle rudely reminded inoffensive shopkeepers and artizans

[1] In Rye there was a tax "from every stranger, as though from a prisoner taken, payment of his finance for his ransom, and when he has entered the fortresses of the port for his passage thence, 3s. 4d.; he having to pay towards the building of the walls and gates there what pertains to the common weal of the town." (Hist. MSS. Com. v. 490.) For the strengthening of Canterbury wall against the French, (ibid. ix. 141.) It had twenty-one towers and six gates, and mayors in 1452 and 1460 left money for the gates. (Davies' Southampton, 62-3, 80, 105. Hist. MSS. Com. xi. 3, 167.)

[2] Hist. MSS. Com. v. 518-24, 492-3. The Common House at Romney was only provided with bows until in 1475 a gun was laid on it. Burgesses were sometimes driven from towns by the excessive charges of war and of watch and ward. (Owen's Shrewsbury, i. 205.) For Southampton, see Davies, 79, 80, Chester, Hist. MSS. Com. viii. 370.

of their military calling. Owing to causes but little studied, local conflicts were frequent, and they were fought out with violence and determination. At the close of the fourteenth century a certain knight, Baldwin of Radington, with the help of John of Stanley, raised eight hundred fighting men "to destroy and hurt the commons of Chester"; and these stalwart warriors broke into the abbey, seized the wine and dashed the furniture in pieces, and when the mayor and sheriff came to the rescue nearly killed the sheriff.[1] When in 1441 the Archbishop of York determined to fight for his privileges in Ripon Fair he engaged two hundred men-at-arms from Scotland and the Marches at sixpence or a shilling a day, while a Yorkshire gentleman, Sir John Plumpton, gathered seven hundred men; and at the battle that ensued, more than a thousand arrows were discharged by them.[2]

Within the town territory the burghers had to serve at their own cost and charges; but when the King called out their forces to join his army the municipal officers had to get the contingent ready, to provide their dress or badges, to appoint the captain, and to gather in money from the various parishes for the

[1] Hist. MSS. Com. viii. 370. In 1399, when the master-weavers and tradesmen came armed to the cathedral and led an attack on "William of Wybunbur and Thomas del Dame and many of their servants called journeymen in a great affray of all the people of the city against the peace of the Lord King." Ibid. 367. See also Paston Letters, i. 408; Hist. MSS. Com. iv. 1, 432.

[2] Plumpton Correspondence, liv. lxii.

soldiers' pay, "or else the constables to be set in prison to abide to such time as it be content and paid."[1] When they were sent to a distance their fellow townsmen bought provisions of salt fish and paniers or bread boxes for the carriage of their food,[2] and reluctantly provided a scanty wage, which was yet more reluctantly doled out to the soldier by his officer, and perhaps never reached his pocket at all.[3] Universal conscription proved then as now the great inculcator of peace. To the burgher called from the loom and the dyeing pit and the market stall to take down his bow or dagger, war was a hard and ungrateful service where reward and plunder were dealt out with a niggardly hand; and men conceived a deep hatred of strife and disorder of which they had measured all the misery.[4] When the common people dreamed of a brighter future, their simple hope was that

[1] Davies' York, 183. For the directions given about the gathering of troops, see ibid., 152–157. For cost of arms and maintenance of troops to towns, see Stubbs ii. 309. Hist. MSS. Com. ix. 143.

[2] Hist. MSS. Com. xi. 7, p. 171.

[3] The authorities of York decreed that the soldiers sent on a Scotch campaign should be given their wages for the first fourteen days, and the captain should have in his pocket the money for the second fortnight. The troops struck, however, and insisted on having the whole twenty-eight days' pay before they started, and the town had at last to give in as the only way of getting the expedition started. (Davies' York 132–7.) The soldiers, once paid, often did no more than start on their journey and then "straggle about by themselves" with their pay in their pockets. (Paston Letters ii. 1–2.)

[4] Eng. Chronicle, 1377–1461, pp. 71, 83, 90, 109.

every maker of deadly weapons should die by his own tools; for in that better time

"Battles shall never eft (again) be, ne man bear edge-tool,
And if any man [smithy] it, be smit therewith to death." [1]

II. Nor even in times of peace might the burghers lay aside their arms, for trouble was never far from their streets. Every inhabitant was bound to have his dagger or knife or Irish "skene," in case he was called out to the king's muster or to aid in keeping the king's peace. But daggers which were effective in keeping the peace were equally effective in breaking it, and the town records are full of tales of brawls and riots, of frays begun by "railing with words out of reason," or by "plucking a man down by the hair of his head," but which always ended in the appearance of a short dagger, "and so drew blood upon each other." [2] For the safety of the community—a safety which was the recognized charge of every member of these simple democratic states—each householder was bound to take his turn in keeping nightly watch and ward in the streets. It is true indeed that re-

[1] Piers Ploughman, passus iv. 478, 479.
"'Therefore I counsel no King any counsel ask
At conscience if he coveteth to conquer a realm,
For should never conscience be my constable
Were I a king y-crowned, by Mary,' quoth Meed,
'Nor be marshall of my men where I most fight.'"
—Passus iv. 254–8.

[2] In Canterbury, any man drawing a knife was fined or imprisoned forty days. (Hist. MSS. Com. ix. 172.) In Sandwich if any one wounded another with a sword or knife he might choose one of three punishments, a fine of 60s. to the commonalty, imprisonment for a year and a day, or to have his hand perforated with the weapon by which he had inflicted the wound. (Boys 502.)

luctant citizens constantly by one excuse or another sought to escape a painful and thankless duty: whether it was whole groups of inhabitants sheltering themselves behind legal pretexts; or sturdy rebels breathing out frank defiance of the town authorities. Thus in Aylesbury, according to the constable's report, one "Reygg kept a house all the year till the watch time came. And when he was summoned to the watch then came Edward Chalkyll 'fasesying' and said he should not watch for no man and thus bare him up, and that caused the other be the bolder for to bar the King's watch. . . . He saith and threateneth us with his master," add the constables, "and thus we be over 'crakyd' that we dare not go, for when they be 'mayten' they be the bolder." John Bossey "said the same wise that he would not watch for us"; and three others "lacked each of them a night."[1] But in such cases the mayor's authority was firmly upheld by the whole community, every burgher knowing well

[1] Parker, Manor of Aylesbury, 20-21. "Also I complain," said one of them pitifully, "upon James Fleccher for fraying of my wife about 10 o'clock in the night and I ready for to go to bed, standing scolding at my door bidding me come out of thy doors an thou dare with his dagger in his hand ready to break the king's peace." The prudent constable, however, refrained from coming out and was content to appeal to the next court; "he is coming and therefore I beseech you of peace of his godabery." In Canterbury one of the watchmen called to a person "walking out of due time" to know wherefore he walked there so late. "The suspect person gave none answer, but ran from thence into St. Austin's liberty and before the door of one John Short they took him. And the same John Short came out of his house with other misknown persons and took from the said watchmen their weapons and there menaced them for to beat contrary to the oath of a true and faithful freeman." (Hist. MSS. Com. ix. 174.)

that if any inhabitant shirked his duty a double burden fell upon the shoulder of his neighbour.

III. All inhabitants of a borough were also deeply interested in the preservation of the boundaries which marked the extent of their dominions, the "liberties" within which they could enforce their own law, regulate trade, and raise taxes. Century after century the defence of the frontier remained one of the urgent questions of town politics, insistent, perpetually recurring, now with craft and treachery, now with violence and heated passion breaking into sudden flame. Every year the mayor and corporation made a perambulation of the bounds and inspected the landmarks;[1] the common treasure was readily poured out if lawsuits and bribes were needed to ascertain and preserve the

---

[1] "The freemen of the borough of Huntingdon have this week been engaged in the observance of a curious and ancient local custom. With their sons, the whole of the freemen of the borough have assembled in the morning in the Market-place. The skull of an ox borne on two poles was placed at the head of a procession, and then came the freemen and their sons, a certain number of them bearing spades and others sticks. Three cheers having been given, the procession moved out of the town and proceeded to the nearest point of the borough boundary, where the skull was lowered. The procession then moved along the boundary line of the borough, the skull being dragged along the line as if it were a plough. The boundary holes were dug afresh, and a boy thrown into each hole and struck with a spade. At a particular point, called Blacktone Leys, refreshments were provided, and the boys competed for prizes. The skull was then again raised aloft, and the procession returned to the Market-place, where three more hurrahs were given before it broke up." (From the Pall Mall Gazette, September 16th, 1892.) In Hythe Holy Thursday was the day of perambulation. (Hist. MSS. Com. iv. i. 432.) For Canterbury in 1497 see Hasted's Kent, iv. 399–401.

town's rights; and if law failed, the burghers fell back without hesitation on personal force. In Canterbury the town and the convent of Christ Church were at open war about this question as about many others. The monks remained unconvinced even though the mayor and council of thirty-six periodically " walked the bounds," giving copper coins at the various turning points to " divers children " that they might remember the limits of the franchise, while they themselves were refreshed after their trouble by a " potation " in a field near Fordwich. At one time the quarrel as to the frontier raged round a gigantic ash-tree—the old land-mark where the liberties of the city touched those of Fordwich—which was in 1499 treacherously cut down by the partizans of Christ Church; the Canterbury men with the usual feastings and a solemn libation of wine set up a new boundary stone. At another time the dispute shifted to where at the west gate of the town the river wound with uncertain and changing course that left frontiers vague and undefined. A low marshy ground called the "Rosiers" was claimed by the mayor as under his jurisdiction, while the prior asserted that it was within the county of Kent; and for thirty years the question was fought out in the law courts. On July 16th, 1500, the mayor definitely asserted his pretensions by gathering two hundred followers arrayed in manner of war to march out to the Rosiers. There certain monks and servants of the prior were taking the air; one protested he had been "late afore sore sick and was walking in the field for his recreation"; another had a sparrow-hawk on his fist, and the servants declared they were but peaceful haymakers; but all had apparently gone out ready for every emergency, for at the appearance of the enemy bows and arrows, daggers, bills, and brigandiers, were produced from under the monks' frocks and the smocks of the haymakers. In the battle that followed the monks were beaten, and the citizens cut down willows and stocked up the dyke made in the river by the convent; and boldly proceeded the next day[1] to other outrages. The matter was brought to judgement, and a verdict given against the mayor for riot—a verdict which that official, however, lightly disregarded. It was in vain that the prior, wealthy and powerful as he was, and accustomed to so great influence at court, appealed to the Star Chamber to have the penalty enforced, for no further steps were taken by the government. It probably judged wisely, since in such a matter the temper of the citizens ran high; and the rectification of frontiers was resented as stoutly as a new delimitation of kingdoms and empires to-day.

IV. Resolution in the defence of their territory was no doubt quickened by the sense which every burgess shared of common property in the borough. The value of woodland and field and meadow which made up the "common lands" was well understood by the freeman who sent out his sheep or cows to their allotted pasture, or who opened the door of his yard in the early morning when the common herd went round the streets to collect the swine and drive them out on the moor till evening.[2] The men of Romney did not count grudgingly their constant labour and cost

[1] Hist. MSS. Com. v. 434.
[2] History Preston Gild, 41, 42; Hist. MSS. Com. iii. 345; Nottingham, Records, i. 150-151, 268, 164-165.

in measuring and levelling and draining the swamps belonging to their town and protecting them from the encroachments of "the men of the marsh" beyond, for the sake of winning grazing lands for their sheep, and of securing a "cow-pull" of swans or cygnets for their lord the archbishop[1] when it was desirable "to have his friendship." In poor struggling boroughs like Preston, in large and wealthy communities like Nottingham, in manufacturing towns like Worcester with its busy population of weavers, in rich capitals like York, in trading ports like Southampton where the burghers had almost forgotten the free traditions of popular government, the inhabitants never relaxed their vigilance as to the protection of their common property.[2] They assembled year after year to make sure that there had been no diminishing of their rights or alienation of their land, or that in the periodical allotments the best fields

---

[1] Hist. MSS. Com. v. 519.

[2] For common pasture and closes see short account in Rogers' Six Centuries of Work and Wages, i. 89-90, taken from Fitzherbert's Treatise. In 1484 a great riot broke out in York on the question of the common lands. The King had begged the council to make an order that a close which belonged to S. Nicholas, but was common from Michaelmas to Candlemas, should be "closed and several" for the use of the hospital if the commons would agree to the same. The order was made, but a few days after Michaelmas, when the close was not thrown open as was customary, the citizens met in a "riotous assembly or insurrection" which led to interference of the King. (Davies' York, 190-198.) In Winchester (1414) John Parmiter was punished for accusing the mayor of intending to sell the Coitebury mill without consent of the citizens. (Kitchen's Winchester, 171.) For other instances see Vol. II. "Democracy in the Towns," Note A.

and closes had not fallen to the share of aldermen and councillors; and by elaborate constitutional checks, or if these failed, by "riotous assembly and insurrection," they denounced every attempt at encroachment on marsh or pasture.

V. So also in the case of other property which corporations held for the good of the community—fisheries, warrens, salt-pits, pastures reclaimed from the sea, plots of ground saved in the dry bed of a river, building sites and all waste places within the town walls, warehouses and shops and tenements, inns and mills, the grassy slopes of the city ditch which were let for grazing, the towers of the city walls leased for dwelling-houses or store rooms, any property bequeathed to the community for maintaining the poor or repairing the walls or paying tolls and taxes all this corporate wealth which lightened the burdens of the taxpayer was a matter of concern to every citizen. The people were themselves joint guardians of the town treasure. Representatives chosen by the burghers kept one or two of the keys of the common chest, which could only be opened therefore with their consent.[1] Year after year mayor or treasurers were by the town ordinances required to present their accounts before the assembly of all the people " in our whole community, by the tolling

---

[1] At Worcester the common coffer which contained the city deeds and moneys was fastened with six locks; three keys were kept by the bailiff, an alderman, and a chamberlain, chosen by the " Great Clothing," or the council of " the twenty-four above;" the other three by a chamberlain chosen by the " Low Election " or the council of " the Forty-eight beneath," and by two "thrifty commoners." Eng. Gilds, 377.

of the common bell calling them together for that intent"[1]—an assembly that perhaps gathered in the parish church in which seats were set up for the occasion at the public expense.[2] There the people heard the list of fines levied in the courts; of tolls in the market, or taxes taken at the gates or in the harbour; of the "maltodes," or sums paid on commodities for sale; of the "scot" levied on the property of individuals; of the "lyvelode" or livelihood, an income tax on rates or profits earned. They learned what means the corporation had taken of increasing the common revenue; whether it had ordered a "church-ale," or an exhibition of dancing girls, or a play of Robin Hood;[3] what poor relief had been given in the past year;[4] what public loans with judicious usury of over ten per cent., it had allowed, as when in Lydd "the jurats one year lent Thomas Dygon five marks from the common purse when going to the North Sea, and he repaid the same well and trustily and paid an increase thereon seven shillings;" or they were told whether the Town Council

[1] In case of error or fraud, or if the bailiff refused to make answer to complaints of the burghers, he was brought before the court of his fellow-citizens "and he shall make satisfaction as the commonalty shall think fitting." Journ. Arch. Ass. xxvii. 462.

[2] In Romney the town paid every year to have seats put in the church of S. Lawrence on the day of the Annunciation. (Hist. MSS. Com. v. 546.) In the same way town accounts at Rye were made up and audited in the church at the end of the year. (Ibid. v. 494.) Lydd in 1471 "spended in the church upon the bailly and jurats when they enquired what lyvelod men have in Lydd two pence." (Ibid. 525.)

[3] Hist. MSS. Com. i. 106, 107.   [4] See p. 41, note 2.

proposed to do a little trading for the good of the community; and how a "common barge" had been built with timber bought at one town, cables and anchors at another, pitch and canvas at a third; and how, when the ship was finished, the corporation paid for a modest supply of "bread and ale the day the mast was set in the barge," before it was sent out to fish for herrings or to speculate in a cargo of salt or wine, for the profit of the public treasury.[1]

Lessons in common financial responsibility had been early forced on the burghers everywhere by the legal doctrine that the whole body might be held responsible for the debt of one of its members, while each member on his part was answerable for the faults of his fellows, whether singly or collectively. Thus when Norwich failed in paying debts due to the King in 1286, the sheriff of Norfolk was ordered to enter the liberty and distrain twelve of the richer and more discreet persons of the community;[2] and when the rent of

[1] Hist. MSS. Com. iv. 1, 438. The Hythe barge brought back three lasts of herrings which were sold for £12. In 1409 Romney Jurats got 6s. increase upon white salt bought for the community. (Ibid. v. 537.) If a corporation was in need of money it could always fall back on loans from rich townsmen, who were willing to lend even on long credit. In 1455 or 1456 one Canterbury merchant lent £13 6s. 8d., which was needed for a gift to the queen, then travelling on pilgrimage, and he was only repaid in 1464. Three leading men, who advanced large sums to do honour to Edward the Fourth on his first coming to the city in 1460, waited four or five years for their money. (Ibid. ix. 139-140.) In Lynn the loans to the corporation were on a very great scale according to the ideas of the time, and the municipal debt, entirely raised on the spot, was as permanent and as progressive as that of a modern town.

[2] Madox, Firma Burgi, 159. See also in 1322, when the

Southampton was in arrears, one of its burgesses was thrown into the Fleet in London.[1] Under such a system as this the ordinary interest of citizens in questions of taxation and expenditure was greatly quickened. The municipalities were stern creditors. If a man did not pay his rent for the King's ferm the doors and windows of his house were taken off, everyone in it turned out, and the house stood empty for a year and a day or even longer before the doors might be redeemed in full court, or before it passed to the next heir.[2] But it was probably rather owing to the happy circumstances of the English towns than to the vigilance of the burghers that there is no case in England of a disaster which was but too common in France—the disaster of a borough falling into bankruptcy, and through bankruptcy into servitude and political ruin.

VI. In the town communities of the middle ages all public works were carried out by what was in fact forced labour of the whole commonalty. If the boroughs suffered little from government interference neither could they look for help in the way of state aid or state loans; and as the burgher's purse in early days was generally empty he had to give of the work of his hands for the common good. In Nottingham "booners"—that is the burgesses themselves or

---

missing ferm was to be levied of the bailiffs' goods, chattels, and lands, and, if this did not suffice, of the goods of the citizens. Documents pr. 1884. (Stanley v. Mayor, &c., 24.) See Note A at the end of chapter.

[1] Davies, 111, 37.
[2] Eng. Gilds, 362-363; Nott. Records, i. 267.

substitutes whom they provided to take their place—repaired the highways and kept the streets in order.[1] The great trench dug at Bristol to alter the course of the Frome was made "by the manœuvre of all the commonalty as well of Redcliffe ward as of the town of Bristol.[2] When Hythe in 1412 sent for a Dutch engineer to make a new harbour, all the inhabitants were called out in turn to help at the "Delveys" or diggings. Sundays and week days alike the townsmen had to work, dining off bread and ale provided by the corporation for the diggers, and if they failed to appear they were fined fourpence a day.[3] In the same way Sandwich engaged a Hollander to superintend the making of a new dyke for the harbour; the mayor was ordered to find three workmen to labour at it, every jurat two, and each member of the Common Council one man; while all other townsmen had to give labour or find substitutes according to their ability. The jurats were made overseers, and were responsible for the carrying out of the work; and so successfully was the whole matter managed that in 1512 the Sandwich haven was able to give shelter to 500 or 600 hoys.

Forced labour such as this could of course only be applied to works where skilled artificers were not

---

[1] Records of Nottingham, iv. 449. Afterwards a paviour was appointed who was paid, or partly paid, by a toll taken for corn "shown" for sale in the market. This tax, known as "shewage" or "scavadge," gave rise to our later word scavenger (iv. 453). Rules for keeping streets clean in Southampton. (Gross, ii. 223.)

[2] Ricart, 28. 1240 A.D. For carrying great stones for the quay and walls of Rye. Hist. MSS. Com. v. 492, 493.

[3] Hist. MSS. Com. iv. 1, 434.

necessary; but occasions soon multiplied when the town mob had to be replaced by trained labourers, and we already see traces of a transitional system in the making of the Hythe harbour, where the municipality had to engage hired labour for such work as could not be done by the burgesses.[1] But undertakings for which scientific skill was needed sorely taxed local resources, and the burghers were driven to make anxious appeals to public charity. In 1447, when Bridport wanted to improve its harbour, collectors were sent all over the country to beg for money; indulgences of forty or a hundred days were promised to subscribers by archbishops and bishops; and a copy of the paper carried by one of the collectors gives the sum of the masses said for them

[1] One man received £30 10s. in various sums, 3s. 4d. a rod for nineteen rods, 1s. 8d. a rod for 106 rods, and 12d. a rod for 380 rods. (Hist. MSS. Com. iv. 1. 434.) For forty years the men of Romney fought a desperate battle with the sea and the changing bed of the Rother to preserve the harbour on which their prosperity depended. In 1381 they spent nearly £9 on making a sluice (Boys' Sandwich, 803); there were heavy payments for it again in 1388, and in 1398 John Roan was brought over from Flanders to take charge of it. The commons turned out in 1406 for "digging the common Rie," or bed of the Rother, and in 1409 were again busy "digging the watercourse." In 1410 Gerard Matthyessone was brought over from Holland to make the sluice at a cost of £100; in 1412 over £44 was spent on it besides clothing for Gerard and his household; and in 1413 payments were still being made to him. A few years later in 1422 his place was taken by another Dutchman, Onterdel, who seems to have finished the work, for after this there are only charges for slight repairs. Their improvements remained the model for neighbouring towns, and when Lydd was occupied in works of the same kind its citizens came to study the jetty at Romney.

in the year as amounting to nearly four thousand : " the sum of all other good prayers no man knoweth save only God alone."[1] The building and repairing of bridges as being also work that demanded science and skilled labour involved serious cost. When the King had allowed the bridge at Nottingham to fall into the river, he generously transferred its ownership and the duty of setting it up again to the townspeople; who appointed wardens and kept elaborate accounts and bore grievous anxiety, till finding its charges worse than all their ordinary town expenses they at last fell to begging also. So also the mayor of Exeter prayed for help in the matter of the bridge there, which had been built by a wealthy mayor and was "of the length or nigh by, and of the same mason work as London Bridge, housing upon except; the which bridge openly is known the greatest costly work and most of alms-deeds to help it in all the west part of England."[2] Such instances reveal to us the persistent difficulties that beset a world where primitive methods utterly failed to meet new exigencies, and where the demand for technical

[1] Ibid. vi. 495–7. A messenger went as far as Kent and Essex to gather alms for making the harbour. He collected groats, pence, fleeces of wool, broken silver and rings, a dish full of wheat, malt, or barley, a piece of bacon and so forth; and got a man to help him who swore before the canons of Christchurch that he would be true, but declared he must have a crucifix and writing as sign of authority, and got a goodly crucifix with beryl set therein and a new suit of clothes, and then made off with his booty.

[2] Shillingford's Letters, 141, 142. Rec. Nottingham, i. 183. For Rochester, Eng. Chron. 124; Hist. MSS. Com. ix. 76. For London see Lit. Cantuar. iii. 169.

quality in work was beginning to lead to new organizations of labour. Meanwhile the burghers had to fight their own way with no hope of grants in aid from the state, and little to depend on save the personal effort of the whole commonalty.

VII. The townspeople all took their part not only in the serious and responsible duties of town life but apparently in an incessant round of gaieties as well. All the commons shared in supporting the minstrels and players of the borough. The "waits" (so called from the French word guet) were originally and still partly remained watchmen of the town, but it was in their character of minstrels, "who go every morning about the town piping," that they were paid by pence collected by the ward-men from every house.[1] Every town moreover had its particular play, which was acted in the Town Hall, or the churchyard, before the Mayor and his brethren sitting in state, while the whole town kept holiday. In 1411 there was a great play, *From the Beginning of the World*, at the Skinner's well in London, " that lasted seven days continually, and there were the most part of the lords

[1] Boys' Sandwich, 673, 676, 684. The town council of Lynn decreed in 1431 "that the three players shall serve the community this year for 21s., and their clothing to be had of every house;" but two years later the players demanded an increase of their "reward," and a grant was made to each of them of 20s. and their clothing, in return for which "they shall go through the town with their instruments from the Feast of All Saints to the following Feast of the Purification." (Hist. MSS. Com. xi. 3, p. 162-3.) In Canterbury four minstrels were appointed every year, and each one was given a silver scutcheon worth 100s.—a badge which was returned at the end of the year to the city chamberlain.

VOL. I. L

and gentles of England."[1] At Canterbury the chief play was naturally *The Martyrdom of S. Thomas.* The cost is carefully entered in the municipal account books—charges for carts and wheels, flooring, hundreds of nails, a mitre, two bags of leather containing blood which was made to spout out at the murder, linen cloth for S. Thomas' clothes, tin foil and gold foil for the armour, packthread and glue, coal to melt the glue, alb and amys, knights' armour, the hire of a sword, the painting of S. Thomas' head, an angel which cost 22d., and flapped his wings as he turned every way on a hidden wynch with wheels oiled with soap. When all was over the properties of the pageant were put away in the barn at S. Sepulchre's Nunnery, and kept safely till the next year at a charge of 16d. The Canterbury players also acted in the *Three Kings of Cologne* at the Town Hall, where the kings, attended by their henchmen, appeared decorated with strips of silver and gold paper and wearing monks' frocks. The three "beasts" for the Magi were made out of twelve ells of canvas distended with hoops and laths, and "painted after nature"; and there was a castle of painted canvas which cost 3s. 4d. The artist and his helpers worked for six days and nights at these preparations and charged three shillings for their labour, food, fire and candle.[2]

[1] Chronicle of the Grey Friars of London (Camden Society), 12.

[2] Hist. MSS. Com. ix. 147-8. A most interesting example of an English play is given in the "Common-place book of the fifteenth century," ed. by Miss Toulmin Smith, pp. 46-9, the play of Abraham and Isaac. The vivacity, the pathos, the dramatic movement, the strong human interest, are very remarkable.

Minstrels and harpers and pipers and singers and play-actors, who stayed at home through the dark winter days "from the feast of all Saints to the feast of the Purification," to make music and diversion for their fellow citizens, started off on their travels when the fine weather came, and journeyed from town to town giving their performances, and rewarded at the public expense with a gift of 6s. 8d. or 3s. 4d., and with dinner and wine "for the honour of the town."[1] It was an easy life—

"Some mirth to make as minstrels conneth (know),
That will neither swynke (toil) nor sweat, but swear great oaths,
And find up foul fantasies and fools them maken,
And have wit at will to work if they would."[2]

Entries in the town accounts of Lydd give some idea of the constant visits of these wandering troops, and of the charges which they made upon the town treasure.[3] Players from Romney came times without number, others from Rukinge, Wytesham, Herne, Hamme, Appledore, Stone, Folkestone, Rye; and besides these came the minstrels of the great lords, the King, the Duke of Somerset, the Duke of Buckingham, Lord De Bourchier, Lord Fiennes, the Earl of Warwick, the Duke of York, Lord Arundel, Lord Exeter, Lord Shrewsbury, the Earl of Pembroke, Lord Dacres, etc. ; all of whom doubtless the town dared not refuse to entertain, but "for love of their lords lythen (listen to) them at feasts."[4] Besides this Lydd had its own

[1] Hist. MSS. Com. v. 516–527.
[2] Piers Ploughman, pass. i. 34–38.
[3] Hist. MSS. Com. v. 518, &c.   [4] Ibid. pass. viii. 98.

special plays, *The May* and *The Interlude of Our
Lord's Passion*, and the whole town would gather on
a Sunday to hear the actors, while watchmen were
paid to keep guard on the shore against a surprise of
the French. Its players seem to have set the fashion
in the neighbourhood; the Romney Corporation
" chose wardens to have the play of *Christ's Passion*,
as from olden time they were wont to have it," and
paid the expenses of a man to go to Lydd " to see the
original of our play there," besides giving the Lydd
players a reward of 20s. for their performance.[1]

Other wanderers too knocked at the gates of Lydd
—" the man with the dromedary," a " bear-ward," or
the keeper of the King's lions travelling with his men-
agerie and demanding a sheep to be given to the lions ;
archers and wrestlers from neighbouring towns whom
Jurats and Commons gathered to see, and supplied
with wrestling collars and food for themselves and their
horses, as well as a " reward " at the public expense.[2]
Besides bull-baiting, Lydd, doubtless, like other towns,
had its occasional " bear-baiting." There were the
Christmas games and mumming, and the yearly visit
of the " Boy Bishop "[3] of S. Nicholas who came from
Romney to hold his feast at Lydd. And there was
the universal festival of the " watch " on S. John's
Eve, when Lydd paid out of its common chest for the
candles kept burning all night in the Common House,
and for the feast—not a trifling expense if we may

[1] Hist. MSS. Com. v. 540, 541, 544, 552, 548, 549.
[2] Ibid. xi. 7, 172-4.
[3] " Two Sermons of the Boy Bishop at S. Paul's " have been
published by the Camden Society, 1875.

judge by the case of Bristol where the crafts who took part in the watch divided among them ninety-four gallons of wine.[1]

This festival was observed everywhere, but other local feasts were arranged according to local traditions. In Canterbury every Mayor was bound " to keep the watch" on the Eve of the Translation of S. Thomas. " And in the aforesaid watch the Sheriff to ride in harness with a henchman after him honestly emparelled for the honour of the same city. And the Mayor to ride at his pleasure, and if the Mayor's pleasure be to ride in harness, the Aldermen to ride in like manner, and if he ride in his scarlet gown, the Aldermen to ride after the same watch in scarlet and crimson gowns." The city was to be lighted by the Mayor finding " two cressets, or six torches, or more at his pleasure," every Alderman finding two cressets, and each of the Common Council with every constable and town clerk one cresset. In Chester the great day for merry making was Shrove Tuesday, when the drapers, saddlers, shoemakers and many others met at the cross on the Roodeye, and there in the presence of the Mayor the shoemakers gave to the drapers a football of leather " to play at from thence to the Common Hall." The saddlers at the same time gave " every master of them a painted ball of wood with flowers and arms upon the point of a spear, being goodly arrayed upon horseback accordingly." The whole town joined in the sports, and everyone married within the year gave some contribution toward their funds.[2]

To these festivities we must add the yearly pageants

[1] Eng. Guilds, 430.   [2] Hist. MSS. Com. viii. 363.

of the Guilds—whether of the great societies like the Guild of St. George at Norwich,[1] whose Alderman in scarlet robe followed by the four hundred members with their distinguishing red hoods, marched after the sword of wood with a Dragon's head for the handle which had been presented to them by Henry the Fifth; —or of the Corpus Christi Guild which evidently played a political part in the life of every great town. In York it is said to have had in the sixteenth century nearly fifteen thousand members, and at its great pageant, the Mayor and Town Council "and other worshipful persons" joined in a common feast, and sent wine and fruits at the public expense to great nobles and ladies in the city, till perhaps supplies ran out and the town was "drunken dry."[2] The Craft Guilds also, whether voluntarily or by order of the Corporation, had their pageants, acting the same play year after year.[3]

It has been commonly supposed that the English people had in the later middle ages a passion for pageantry and display, which was one of the strongest forces in maintaining their guild organization. But

[1] See vol. ii.

[2] Davies' York, 43, 77; Eng. Guilds, 141-3. The expenses that fell on a town at a royal visit were exceedingly heavy. (Davies' York, 69.) For Canterbury, Hist. MSS. Com. ix. 140-151.

[3] In 1415 there were fifty-seven crafts in York, each of which had its special play. (Davies' York, 233-236; English Guilds, 141-3; Hist. MSS. Com. i. 109.) Plays were given over to certain trades to act. *Abraham and Isaac*, for instance, was given to the slaters in Newcastle, the bowyers and fletchers in Beverley, the weavers in Dublin, the parchminers and bookbinders in York, the barbers and wax-chandlers in Chester. (Commonplace Book, ed. by Miss Toulmin Smith, 47-8.)

towards the end of the fifteenth century at least it becomes less and less clear that the freewill of the craftsmen had much to say to the maintenance of these public gaieties, or that they felt any enthusiasm for amusements which yearly grew more expensive and burdensome.[1] There were places where the crafts, whether through poverty or economy, neglected to spend a due proportion of their earnings on the public festivals, and in one town after another as popular effort declined the authorities began to urge the people on to the better fulfilment of their duties. In 1490 a complaint was made in Canterbury that the Corpus Christi Play, the City Watch on S. Thomas' Eve, and the Pageant of S. Thomas had fallen into decay. Some Mayors indeed " in their year have full honourably kept the said watch ; " but others had neglected it, and " all manner of harness within the city is decayed and rusted for lack of the yearly watch." It was therefore decreed that every Mayor should henceforth " keep the watch," and that the crafts who apparently hoped to escape from the heavy charges of these plays by declaring themselves too poor to be formed into a corporate body, should forthwith be grouped together into a sort of confederation or give up their bodies for punishment.[2] In the same way when the tailors of Plymouth were incorporated in 1496, they had to bind themselves to provide a pageant every year on Corpus Christi Day for the benefit of the Corpus Christi Guild,[3] and so on in many

[1] The prices charged by players and minstrels seem to have risen considerably between 1400 and 1500. For a growing economy, see Hist. MSS. Com. iii. 345.   [2] Ibid. ix. 173.
[3] Ibid. ix. 274. For the Worcester rules of 1467, see English Guilds, 385, 407-8.

other towns. Occasionally indeed the Corporation took a different and more merciful line; for the Mayor and Sheriffs of Norwich petitioned the Lords and Commons to pass an Act or Order to prevent Players of Interludes from coming into the city, as they took so large a share of the earnings of the poor operatives as to cause great want to their families, and a heavy charge to the city,[1] and Bridgenorth got an order from Elizabeth that the town might no longer pay players or bear-wards; whoever wanted to see such things must see them "upon their own costs and charges."[2]

On the whole it is evident that long before the Reformation, and even when as yet no Puritan principles had been imported into the matter, the gaiety of the towns was already sobered by the pressure of business and the increase of the class of depressed workers. It was not before the fanaticism of religion, but before the coming in of new forms of poverty and of bondage that the old games and pageants lost their lustre and faded out of existence, save where a mockery of life was preserved to them by compulsion of the town authorities. And the town authorities were probably acting under pressure of the publicans, and licensed victuallers. Cooks and brewers and hostellers[3] were naturally deeply interested in the preservation of the good old customs, and it

[1] Hist. MSS. Com. i. 103–104, no date.
[2] Ibid. x. 4, 426.
[3] The York hostellers contracted in 1483 to bring forth yearly for the next eight years a pageant of their own, *The Coronation of Our Lady.*

was in some cases certainly this class, the most powerful in a mediæval borough, who raised the protest against the indifference and neglect of the townspeople for public processions and merry-making, because "thereby the victuallers lose their money, and who insisted on the revival of these festivals for the encouragement of trade. Probably where the crafts were strong and the votes of the working people carried the day, the decision turned the other way.

VIII. All the multitudinous activities and accidents of this common life were summed up for the people in the parish church that stood in their market-place, close to the Common House or Guild Hall. This was the fortress of the borough against its enemies— its place of safety where the treasure of the commons was stored in dangerous times, the arms in the steeple, the wealth of corn or wool or precious goods[1] in the church itself,[2] guarded by a sentence of excommunication against all who should violate so sacred a protection.[3] Its shrines were hung with the strange new things which English sailors had begun to bring across the great seas—with "horns of unicorns," ostrich eggs, or walrus tusks, or the rib of a whale given by Sebastian Cabot. From the church tower the bell rang out which called the people to arm for the common defence, or summoned a general assembly, or proclaimed the opening of the market.[4] Burghers

[1] A small fee was sometimes paid to the parson when the church was used as store-house for grain or wool as in case of Southampton. Roger's Agric. and Prices, ii. 611.
[2] Paston Letters, iii. 436.
[3] Hist. MSS. Com. v. 306. York Ritual.
[4] The belfry where the clock hung played so important a part

had their seats in the church apportioned to them by the corporation in the same rank and order as the stalls which it had already assigned to them in the market-place. The city officers and their wives sat in the chief places of honour; next to them came tradesmen according to their degree with their families honour-ably "y-parroked (parked) in pews," where Wrath sat among the proud ladies who quarrelled as to which should first receive the holy bread;[1] while "apprentices and servants shall sit or stand in the alleys." There on Sundays and feast-days the people came to hear any news of importance to the community, whether it was a list of strayed sheep, or a proclamation by the bailiff of the penalties which had

in the communes of France that the right to have a belfry and a town hall were given by charter when the commune was established, and were taken away when it was suppressed (Ordonnances des Rois de France, vol. xi., cxlii., cxliii.), and the bell-tower often formed the town prison. In England, on the other hand, the town clock and the assembly and curfew bells in almost all cases were set in the tower of the parish church, and the ringers paid by the corporation.

[1] Piers Ploughman, passus vii. 144. In Totnes in the thirteenth century there is a long list of entries such as these:— "Alice wife of Walter Cochela sits above the seats of Walter rustic;" "Nicholas son of Henry has his seat by common purchase;" and so on. And down to recent times the mayor, who by tradition represents the head of the Merchant Guild, was charged with appointing seats in the church to the inhabitants. (Hist. MSS. Com. iii. 242–3.) In Liverpool, "according to ancient custom," the city officers and their wives had special seats in S. Nicholas, and after them the householders; "apprentices and servants shall sit or stand in the alleys." (Picton's Liverpool, ii. 53, 54, 57.) For allotment of seats in the parish church see Toulmin Smith, The Parish, 2nd Edition, 1857, 441.

been decreed in the manor court against offenders.¹ The church was their Common Hall where the commonalty met for all kinds of business, to audit the town accounts, to divide the common lands, to make grants of property, to hire soldiers, or to elect a mayor. There the council met on Sundays or festivals, as might best suit their convenience; so that we even hear of a payment made by the priest to the corporation to induce them not to hold their assemblies in the chancel while high mass was being performed.² It was the natural place for justices to sit and hear cases of assault and theft; or it might serve as a hall where difficult legal questions could be argued out by lawyers. In the middle of the fifteenth century when the Bishop and the Mayor of Exeter were in the height of a fierce contest about the government of the town they met for discussion in the cathedral. "When my lord had said his prayers at the high altar he went apart to the side altar by himself and called to him apart the mayor and no more, and there communed together a great while." And on this common ground the dean and chapter on the one side and the mayor and Town Council on the other, attended by their respective lawyers, fought out the questions of law on which the case turned.³

[1] In Cumberland stray sheep were proclaimed at the church on Sunday. At Rotherham the penalties decreed in the manor court were commonly ordered to be published by the bailiff in the church. (Hunter's Doncaster, ii. 10.) In 1462 the king's judges sat to hold trials in the Grey Friars' Church at Bridgewater for cases of assault and theft. (Hist. MSS. Com. iii. 316.)
[2] Hist. MSS. Com. v. 537. Romney. Ibid. iv. 1, 436.
[3] Shillingford's Letters, 48, 94. For the church of S. Nicholas

In fair time the throng of traders expected to be allowed to overflow from the High Street into the cathedral precincts, and were "ever wont and used . . . . to lay open, buy and sell divers merchandises in the said church and cemetery and special in the king's highway there as at Wells, Salisbury and other places more, as dishes, bowls, and other things like, and in the said church ornaments for the same and other jewels convenient thereto."[1] In a draft presentation to a London vicarage of 1427 there is a written memorandum with an order from the king that no fairs or markets shall be held in sanctuaries, "for the honour of Holy Church."[2] Edward the First had indeed forbidden such fairs in his Statute of Merchants, but such an order was little in harmony with the habits and customs of the age; and if there was an occasional stirring of conscience in the matter, it was not till the time of Laud that the public attained to a conviction, or acquiesced in an authoritative assertion, that the church was

Romney, 1422, see Hist. MSS. Com. v. 542. In Dover barons of Cinque Ports met at the church of S. James. (Ibid. v. 528, 538.) For Rye, Ibid., 499. The meetings of the town council in Southampton were probably first held in the church of S. Cross or Holy Rood, where the assembly bell and curfew bell hung; and so closely did the idea of the town life come to be connected with this spot that when a town hall was built in the fourteenth century the church was moved further back that the hall might stand on its exact site. As late as 1470 the mayor and his brethren met in the parish church to settle a question of town business.

[1] Shillingford's Letters, 93. Report on Markets, 25. Fairs forbidden on Sundays and feast days; 27 Henry VI., cap. 5.

[2] Hist. MSS. Com. v. 436.

desecrated by the transaction in it of common business.[1]

In the middle ages however the townspeople were connected with their parish church after a fashion which has long been unknown among us. They were frequently the lay rectors; they appointed the wardens and churchwardens; they had control of the funds, and the administration of lands left for maintaining its services and fabric; sometimes they laid claim to the fees paid for masses.[2] The popular interest might even extend to the criticism and discipline of the rector; so that in Bridport an enquiry of the bishop as to whether his chaplain, "a foreigner from Britanny," was " drunk every day " was held in presence of " a copious multitude of the parishioners," and twelve townsmen acted as witnesses.[3] If a religious guild

[1] It is interesting to note the scientific experiments of "Doctor Wren" in the tower of old S. Paul's, described in a letter from Moray to Huygens, Sep. 23, 1664. Œuvres Complètes de Huygens. Amsterdam, 1893, vol. v.

[2] The mayor and jurats of Rye had the nomination of the chaplain of S. Bartholomew's. (Lyons, ii. 367.) For Sandwich Boys, 672-3. The Bridgewater burgesses were lay rectors of the church. (Hist. MSS. Com. iii. 312.) For the Wells corporation, Hist. MSS. Com. i. 106. At Dartmouth the parish church was built by the mayor; and a dispute began between mayor and vicar who was to have fees for masses; fresh dispute raised every thirty years from that time till 1874, when it had come to a question of pew rents, and a compromise was made. In Andover the custodians of the cemetery were chosen by the people (Gross, ii. 331). "If any person shall be a water bearer in Totnes he shall cry the hour of the day and shall carry the holy water every Sunday throughout the whole ville of Totnes." (Hist. MSS. Com. iii. 344.) Payment was often made for sermons. (Hist. MSS. Com. v. 549. Davies' York, 77.)

[3] Hist. MSS. Com. vi. 495. For the presenting of parish

had become identified with the corporation, the town body and the Church were united by a yet closer tie. The corporation of Plymouth, which on its other side was the Guild of our Lady and St. George, issued its instructions even as to the use of vestments in St. Andrews, ruling when "the best copes and vestments" should be used at funerals, and how "the second blue copes" only might be displayed at the burial of any man who died without leaving to the Church an offering of twenty shillings.[1]

The people on their side were taxed, and heavily taxed, for the various expenses of the Church.[2] Sergeants sent by the Town Council collected under severe penalties the dues for the blessed bread and "trendilles" of wax, or "light-silver" for the lights burned beside dead bodies laid in the church; and the town treasury paid for "coals for the new fire on Easter Eve."[3] If a church had to be repaired or rebuilt the

priests and clerics by the town juries see Cutts' Colchester, 129. "And also the parish priest of St. Peter's for over assessing of poor folks and men's servants at Easter for their tythes and other duties." (Nott. Rec. iii. 364.) In 1476, when the chaplain of Old Romney Church was arraigned for felony, "according to the custom of the Cinque Ports, for his acquittance it is assigned that he shall have 36 good and lawful men to be at the Hundred Court next to come at his peril." Hist. MSS. Com. vi. 544. See ch. v. p. 175, note.

[1] Hist. MSS. Com. ix. 272.

[2] For the rise of the new parish administration, Gneist i. 282-5; ii. 21.

[3] Hythe, Hist. MSS. Com. iv. 1, 432. Bridport, Hist. MSS. Com. vi. 495; Andover, Gross, ii. 345. In Lynn all houses leased for 20s. a year were bound to supply the blessed bread and wax for S. Margaret's, and the most elaborate rules were drawn up to regulate the contributions which were to be paid by tene-

pressure of spiritual hopes or fears, the habit of public duty, the boastfulness of local pride, all the influences that might stimulate the common effort, were raised to their highest efficiency by the watchful care of the corporation. All necessary orders were sent out by the mayor, who with the Town Council determined the share which the inhabitants were to take in the work; and in small and destitute parishes where the principle of self-help and independence was quite as fully recognized as it was in bigger and richer towns, real sacrifices were demanded. Men gave their money or their labour or the work of their horse and cart, or they offered a sheep or fowls, or perhaps rings and personal ornaments.[1] In the pride of their growing municipal life the poorest boroughs built new towers and hung new chimes worthy of the latest popular ideals. The inhabitants of Totnes were so poor that in 1449 there were only three people in the town who paid as much as twentypence for the

ments lying together, or by various tenements under one roof. In case payment was refused the common sergeant, or any officer sent by the mayor, might levy a distress and carry off the tenant's goods to the Guild Hall to be kept till he had made satisfaction or paid a fine of 20s. (Hist. MSS. Com. xi. 3, 161.) Payments for the holy fire are frequent. (Hist. MSS. Com. iv. 432, v. 549.) Sometimes fines for breach of trade laws went to church uses. (Gross, ii. 331, 345.) In Rye, if any animal got into the churchyard the owner paid 3s. 4d. to fabric of church. (Hist. MSS. Com. v. 489.)

[1] In Bridport the bequests for the church from 1450 to 1460 consist of such things as a brass crock, a ring, small sums of money, and more often one or two sheep or lambs. Hist. MSS. Com. vi. 494. Manorial Pleas (Selden Soc.), 150. Hist. MSS. Com. x. 4, 524, 529, 531. Gross, Gild Merchant, ii. 345.

tax of half-tenths and fifteenths for the King. But since Totnes had four new bells which had been anointed and consecrated in 1442, it decided that the old wooden belfry of the parish church should be replaced by a new stone tower. A master mason was appointed in 1448, and "supervisors" were chosen to visit the bell towers of all the country round and to make that at Totnes "according to the best model." The proctors of the church provided shovels and pickaxes, and the parishioners were called out to dig stones from the quarry; every one who had a horse was to help in carrying the stones, "but without coercion," while "those who have no horses of their own are to work with the horses of other persons, but at their own cost." Last of all an ordinance was made that the mayor, vicar, and proctors of the church should go round to each parishioner and see how much he would give to the collection on Sundays for the bell tower, and those who contributed nothing were to have their names entered on a roll and sent to the Archdeacon's Court.[1] When St. Andrews at Plymouth was enlarged the town authorities decided that the money should be collected by means of a yearly "church-ale." Taverns were closed by order of the council on a certain day, and every ward of the town made for itself a "hale" or booth in the cemetery of the parish church. All inhabitants of the wards

[1] Hist. MSS. Com. iii. 345, 346. When Hythe set up its new steeple in 1480 the twelve jurats headed the list of subscriptions, the greatest sum given by them being 10s. Then came the commons giving from 20s. down to 1d., that is, a day's subsistence. (Ibid. iv. 1, 433.)

were commanded to come with as many friends and acquaintances as possible "for the increasing of the said ale," and to bring with them "except bread and drink such victual as they like best"; but they must buy at the "hale" "bread and ale as it cometh thereto for their dinners and suppers the same day." After ten years of these picnics in the churchyard the new aisle of St. Andrews was finished at a cost of £44 14s. 6d.[1]

In the midst of this busy life—a life where the citizens themselves watched over their boundaries, defended their territory, kept peace in their borders, took charge of the common property, governed the spending of the town treasure, laboured with their own hands at all public works, ordered their own amusements, the mediæval burgher had his training. The claims of the commonwealth were never allowed to slip from his remembrance. As all the affairs of the town were matters of public responsibility, so all the incidents of its life were made matters of public knowledge. The ancient "common horn" or the "common bell"[2] announced the opening of the market, or the holding of the mayor's court, or called the townspeople together in time of danger. Criers went about the streets to proclaim the ordinances of the community, and to remind the citizens of their duties. From the church

[1] Hist. MSS. Com. ix. 273. Money was collected for the church at Yaxley, in Suffolk, in 1485 and the following years, by a similar custom of the yearly "church ale," the usual amount contributed from each householder for his bread and drink being about 4s. or 5s. (Ibid. x. 4, 465.)   [2] Boys' Sandwich, 784.

stile or in the market-place they summoned men to the King's muster, or called them to their place in the town's ship or barge; or if danger from an enemy threatened, warned the citizens "to have harness carried to the proper places," or "to have cattle or hogs out of the fields." They exhorted the people "to leave dice-playing," "to cease ball-playing and to take to bows;" to shut the shops at service time; "to have water at men's doors" for fear of fire. The crier "called" any proclamation of the King in the public places of the town; he declared deeds of pardon granted to any criminal, or proclaimed that some poor wretch who had taken sanctuary in the church had abjured the kingdom and was to be allowed to depart safely through the streets. Perhaps the "cry" was made that a prisoner had been thrown into the town gaol on suspicion, and accusers were called to appear if they had any charge to bring against him; or it was announced that the will of a deceased townsman was about to be proved in the court-house, if there were any who desired to raise objections; or there was proclamation that a burgher had offended against the laws of the community and was degraded from the freedom of the town, or perhaps banished for ever from its territory. At other times players and minstrels would pass through the market-place and streets "crying the banns" of their plays. The merchant, the apprentice, the journeyman, the shopkeeper, gathered in the same crowd to hear the crier who recorded every incident in the town life or brought tidings of coming change. News was open. public, without distinction of persons.

Where the claims of local life were so exacting and so overpowering we can scarcely wonder if the burgher took little thought for matters that lay beyond his "parish." But within the narrow limits of the town dominions his experience was rich and varied. While townsmen were forced at every turn to discover and justify the limits of their privileges, or while controversies raged among them as to how the government of the community should be carried on, there was no lack of political teaching; and all questions "touching the great commonalty of the city" for whose liberties they had fought and whose constitution they had shaped, stirred loyal citizens to a genuine patriotism. Traders too, intent on the developement of their business, were deeply concerned in all the questions that affected commerce, the securing of communications, or the opening of new roads for trade, or the organization of labour. In such matters activity could never sleep; for the towns anticipated modern nations in the faith that the advantage of one community must be the detriment of another, and competition and commercial jealousy ran high.[1] Never

---

[1] In 1327 a violent quarrel broke out between Sandwich and Canterbury. The convent was put to great inconvenience, and the prior wrote to "the mayor and bailiff of Sandwich" asking to be allowed to buy food and wax, as they had been put to great straits. The Sandwich men agreed on condition that the monks should in no manner relieve or give supplies to the Canterbury citizens. (Lit. Cantuar. i. 248-254.) There was great jealousy between Norwich and Yarmouth. Yarmouth was made a Staple town in 1369, in spite of all the efforts of Norwich. In 1390 Norwich paid large sums to have the wool staple at Norwich again. (Blomefield, iii. 96, 113.) In the fifteenth century

perhaps in English history was local feeling so strong. Public virtue was summed up in an ardent municipal zeal, as lively among the " Imperial Co-citizens " of New Sarum[1] as among the " Great Clothing " of bigger boroughs. In those days indeed busy provincials but dimly conscious of national policy found in the confusion of court politics and the distraction of its intrigues, or in the feuds of a divided and bewildered administration, no true call to national service and no popular leader to quicken their sympathies. Civil wars which swept over the country at the bidding of a factious group of nobles or of a vain and unscrupulous King-maker left, and justly left, the towns supremely indifferent to any question save that of how to make the best terms for themselves from the winning side, or to use the disasters of warring lords so as to extend their own privileges.[2] Meanwhile in the

Yarmouth set up a crane, which the Norwich men forced it to take down again.

[1] 1478. Hist. MSS. Com. xi. 3, 88.

[2] The towns were not wholly untouched by the struggle but their interest was very languid. Many, like London, were divided in sympathy. (Polydore Vergil, 106 ; English Chronicle, 1377–1461, 20-1, 67, 95 ; Fabyan, 638.) During this queasy season the Mayor of London feigned him sick and kept his house a great season. (Ibid. 660; see also Warkworth's Chronicle, 12-22.) Bristol and Colchester were Yorkist (Hunt's Bristol, 97-100, 102; Cutts' Colchester, 131-2). For Nottingham see vol. ii. The chief interest was probably felt in Kent and Sussex. (English Chronicle, 1377-1461, 84, 91-4.) Canterbury was against Cade and Lancastrian in sympathy (ibid. 84-95 ; Hist. MSS. Com. ix. 140-3, 168, 170, 176-7) ; but in 1464 entered in its accounts presents to the brothers of the king " nunc." The city suffered severely. The Cinque Ports went generally for Warwick and York. Lydd sent Cade a porpoise to London, and

intense effort called out by the new industrial and
commercial conditions and the reorganization of
social life which they demanded, it was inevitable
that there should grow up in the boroughs the
temper of men absorbed in a critical struggle for ends
which however important were still personal, local,
limited, purely material—a temper inspired by private
interest and with its essential narrowness untouched
by the finer conceptions through which a great
patriotism is nourished. Such a temper, if it brought
at first great rewards, brought its own penalties at last,
when the towns, self-dependent, unused to confederation for public purposes, destitute of the generous
spirit of national regard, and by their ignorance and
narrow outlook left helpless in presence of the revolutions that were to usher in the modern world, saw the
government of their trade and the ordering of their
constitutions taken from them, and their councils
degraded by the later royal despotism into the
instruments and support of tyranny.

NOTE A.

There are many instances of the responsibility of individual citizens for costs of various kinds which were the charge of the whole borough. In 1212 the townsmen of Southampton got hold of the King's money that came from Ireland, and two bailiffs and six principal men were charged with its payment to the King. (Madox Firma Burgi, 158.) A bailiff of Chichester was fined in 1395 for not attending at a session of the peace, and as he had no lands and

a letter to have his friendship in case he succeeded. (Hist. MSS. Com. v. 518, 520, 523, 525.) For Romney, ibid. 543, 545; Rye, ibid. 492–4; Sandwich, Boys, 676.

chattels to seize for the debt, two citizens were charged with the payment of the fine. (Ibid. 187.) In 1256, when Warwick had to pay a fine of forty marks to the King for a trespass, the sheriff was ordered to raise the fine both from the townsmen and from all men of the suburb, both within and without the liberty, who did merchandise in the city of Warwick. (Ibid. 183.) In 1431 the bailiffs of Andover were held responsible for various escapes from prison. They were declared insolvent and the charge thrown back upon the town. The townsmen, however, pleaded that two of the officers charged had quite enough goods and chattels either in the town or in the country to pay themselves, and as for the third they had never chosen him. (Madox, 210. Other instances, ibid. 182, 184, &c.; Hist. MSS. Com. ix. 173.) In 1456 the Mayor and Common Council of Leicester agreed that all actions brought against them in the King's Court by the bailiff should be paid for by the whole town. (Hist. MSS. Com. viii. 422.)

This method of raising money was never a popular proceeding, and in almost every case where there is an account of goods seized from a community or guild for the payment of ferm or fine, the sheriffs seem to make the return that these goods remain on their hands for want of buyers. (Madox, 188, 212, 214, 217, 218.) It is evident that the responsibility of the private citizens was almost extinguished in later times (see Madox, 217), at least in some cases—a fact which may be referred to "the mayor and burgesses" replacing for official purposes "the community," and being licensed to hold *corporate* property.

It is necessary to distinguish between the responsibility for the *borough* expenses and the responsibility for the *trading* debts of the burghers. In the latter case the "community" was also responsible, but the guarantee was strictly confined to burghers and not shared by inhabitants. For the inconvenience to which burghers were subject by being seized for debts whereof they were neither debtors nor pledges, see Derby. (Rep. on Markets, 58.) Mr. Maitland points out that the doctrine that traders form a society in which each member is answerable for the faults of the others, which is shown in early charters, was gradually wearing out, and in 1275 a law was passed that no Englishman could be distrained for any debt unless he was himself the debtor or the pledge, though possibly this law still left members of a community in the position of pledges. But long before this law was passed all the bigger towns had already obtained charters to the same effect. See the charter of Norwich in 1255. "We have granted, and by this our Charter confirmed, to our beloved citizens of Norwich, that they and their heirs for ever shall have this liberty through all our land and power, viz. that they or their goods found in whatever places in our power shall not be arrested for any debt of which they shall not be sureties or principal debtors." (Stanley v. Mayor, Norwich Doc. 1884, 7.) In 1256 goods belonging to the Norwich freemen were arrested for the debts of others that were not free at Boston fair. Norwich however produced its charter of the year before, making their goods free from arrest for any debt unless they were the principal debtors, *or the debtors were of their society.* (Blomefield, iii. 50, 51.)

Mr. Maitland (Select Pleas in Manorial Courts, Selden Society, ii. 134-5) in discussing this question of the trading guarantee points out the difference between the responsibility of the "communitas" and of the "cives" or "burgesses" of a town, showing that the "communitas" did not form a juristic person, while "the citizens" of a town could sue and be sued collectively by a common name. He thinks that the "communitas" may mean the merchant guild "though not perhaps in all cases a duly chartered guild." Of this there is no proof, and many serious difficulties lie in the way of accepting the hypothesis. In the case of Leicester, where there was a merchant guild, it is never mentioned, the responsibility lies on the "members of the community of Leicester," (p. 145-7) and Thomas pleads, not that he was not in the merchant guild, but that he was from Coventry. So also "the whole community of Norwich" is spoken of in exactly the same way, but in Norwich there was *no* guild merchant, (p. 149, 152. See also on this point Hudson's Mun. Org. 36. Notes on Norwich in the Norfolk Archæology, xii. "The city and feudalism.") In Nottingham, John Beeston (p. 153-4) brings a counter-charge against the community of Stamford, (p. 159); he was probably one of the very numerous licensed traders of Nottingham and not a burgher. (Nott. Rec. ii. 102-4, 240-4; iii. 349-52.) It is important to notice the words of the charter by which in 1255 the Nottingham burghers had obtained freedom from arrest, "except in case the debtors are of their commune and power, having whereof their debts may be wholly or partly satisfied, and the said burgesses shall have failed in doing justice to the creditors of the same debtors." (Nott. Rec. i. 41.) For Wiggenhall, (Select Pleas, pp. 157–8.) The mutual responsibility must be considered in connection with the inter-municipal treaties (see Vol. ii. ch. iii.) which were always drawn up in the name of "the community" at this early time, and never at *any* time in the name of the guild merchant. I have suggested in vol. ii. (see Norwich, Lynn, Nottingham, Southampton) another meaning of "communitas," which seems to me to apply also to the instances here mentioned by Mr. Maitland.

CHAPTER V

THE TOWNSPEOPLE

No dispute has raged more fiercely in this century, not only in England but throughout Europe, than the dispute as to what qualifications should make a man fit to take part in the government of his state. The possession of property in land, a fixed yearly income, birth into a certain rank, a standard of age, some degree of education—these and other tests of merit have been applied in the hope of securing that every active citizen shall be distinguished by a fitting capacity, whether proved by his own attainments or guaranteed by the virtues or the prosperity of his ancestors. But the anxieties and cares of great states in this matter are only the repetition on a grand scale of the perplexities that beset the humble communities who first tried to solve the problem of how a society of freemen could best rule themselves. In the early "communitas" of the village or town out of which the later chartered borough was to grow —a community which possessed common fields or customary rights of common over surrounding meadows, and which had doubtless found some regular system for the management of its own affairs [1] —the obvious course was to count as the responsible men of the township the land-holders who had a share in the common property; and when the community had received the charter which made it into a free borough the same system was naturally continued. Those who owned a house and a certain amount of land, measured according to the custom of the borough, formed the society of burghers,[2] and

[1] The agricultural tenants and labourers on a manor were accustomed to elect from among themselves a "Provost" to be head over them and to stand between them and their lord, whom they were pledged to obey in all things, and who on his side undertook to answer for them to their master. Bound by the closest ties of mutual responsibility, their fortunes were inseparably connected. If the lord suffered any loss, small or great, by the tenant's fault, the provost had to pay the value, recovering it afterwards as best he could from the servant who was to blame; and on the other hand if the damage had come through the provost's neglect, and he had not of his own property the wherewithal to make it good, all those of the township who elected him had to pay for him; and hence people and lord alike in self-protection upheld the rule that the provost must be no stranger of doubtful character or property, but chosen "from their own men," and that "by election of the tenants." (Walter of Henley, edited by E. Lamond, Husbandry, 65.) It is easy to see the similarity between the simple methods of rural government and the organization of municipal independence under an elected mayor. An admirable illustration is given in Mr. Maitland's Manorial Pleas, Selden Society, 161–175.

[2] A citizen of Preston was obliged to show a frontage of twelve feet to the street; in Manchester or Salford he was bound to own at least an acre of land. Custumal in Hist. of Preston Guild, 75. Thomson's Mun. Hist. 165; Gross, i. 71, note.

to the townspeople, as to Swift centuries later, the definition of law was "the will of the majority of those who have the property in land." Equality of possessions brought with it equality of civil rights, and each community formed a homogeneous body whose members were all subject to the same conditions and shared in the same interests. When the burgher's life was over, the son who inherited his property appeared before the bailiffs within forty days, to deliver up to them his father's sword and take the freeman's oath;[1] and the common life went on undisturbed by the intrusion of any foreign element, vagrant, restless, encroaching.

But such simple conditions of life, only possible in a stationary agricultural society,[2] disappeared when industry and commerce brought their revelation of new standards of prosperity. In the course of a very few generations there was scarcely a trace left of that primitive relation of equality out of which the early equality of rights had sprung. As the country folk migrated in increasing numbers from manor and village to the town [3] old rigid distinctions

[1] Ipswich, Hist. MSS. Com. ix. p. 244. Otherwise he was not allowed to be of the common council of the town.

[2] At Bury S. Edmunds there were seventy-five tradesmen of various kinds, bakers, tailors, shoemakers, &c., who were bound to cut corn in harvest, the services being commuted for a rent called reap silver when the place became a borough. At Battle, under Henry the Second, 115 burgage tenements were occupied by tradesmen who had to work in the meadows or at the mill, but were called burgesses "on account of the superior dignity of the place's excellence." Rep. on Markets, 17, note.

[3] From examination of the names of the Norwich inhabitants in the Conveyance Rolls, Mr. Hudson thinks it certainly within

were swept away, and the simplicity and uniformity of the burgage tenure was completely broken up. In Liverpool, for example, the burgages originally established by John were already in the fourteenth century divided into small fractions one-eighth or even one-forty-eighth part of their original size;[1] and the amount of land held by owners of property in Nottingham in the fifteenth century varied so much that the taxes levied on them were in some cases as high as £3 14s. 7½d., in other cases as low as a farthing.[2] The owners of capital began to thrust out the owners of land; the shopkeeper replaced the agriculturist, the tradesman and the artizan exercised a new power, as the boroughs quickly adapted themselves to the changing conditions

the mark to assume "that the city of Norwich, towards the close of the thirteenth century, had attracted within its sheltering walls natives of at least four hundred Norfolk, and perhaps sixty Suffolk, towns, villages, and manors." Notes on Norwich, Norfolk Archæology, vol. xii. p. 46.

[1] Picton's Mun. Rec., i. 10-12. For the survival in Wareham of these burgages of various sizes, Hutchins' Dorsetshire, i. 77. Henry the First of England gave charters to some of his towns in Normandy early in the twelfth century, by which the burgess was obliged to own a house, and was originally granted three acres and a garden, but with the right of creating other burgesses by giving up to them a part of his land. Flach, Origines de l'Ancienne France, ii. 347-8.

[2] In Nottingham a subsidy roll in 1472 gives a list of the 154 owners of freehold property in the town, headed by one the tenth of whose property was assessed at 74s. 7¼d.; then came one whose tenth was worth 67s. 7¼d.; six others paid sums from 30s. to 20s.; and a great number paid from 5s. to 2s. At the bottom of the list came three men whose tenth was assessed, one at 1¼d. and one at ¼d. Nott. Records, ii. 285-297.

of the time and opened one door after another for the bringing in of new members whose wealth or whose skill might benefit the community. The ownership of land still carried with it its ancient rights.[1] But the son of a freeman who himself owned no land might be made a burgher in his father's lifetime. Aliens might buy the franchise. Craftsmen were admitted into the circle of the citizens.[2] Recruits from every class and from every nation pressed into the ranks of burgesses. There were foreigners from Bordeaux or from Flanders or from Lisbon,[3] and Irishmen in abundance, in spite of occasional outbursts of hostility in which Irish burghers were deprived of their freedom, " till they bought it again with the blood of their purses, and with weeping eyes, kneel-

[1] The old feeling about burgage property is shown in the custom of Nottingham that when a man sold land his nearest heirs might redeem it if they made an offer in the Guild Hall within a year and a day of the sale to pay to the buyer the price he had given; and they might thus redeem even if the buyer refused to accept their offer. Cases of a messuage and a butcher's booth thus redeemed (Nott. Rec. i. 70, 100). See also at Dover (Lyon's Dover, ii. 274). In Lincoln and Torksey no burgess could sell his burgage tenement save to a burgess or a kinsman without leave (Rep. on Markets, 35). The mayor and jurats of Rye might compel a tenant to keep his house in proper order, "at the request of him that is in the reversion." (Lyon's Dover, ii. 362.)

[2] For London rules in 1319 see Lib. Cust. 269-70.

[3] As, for example, John de Ypres at Romney (Hist. MSS. Com. v. 542. Ibid. iv. i. 427). Foreigners no longer lived separately, as in towns of the Conqueror's time, but tended to become completely united with the English in customs and law. See Nott. Rec. i. 109; Norwich documents, printed 1884, in the case of Stanley v. Mayor, p. 1.

ing on their knees, besought the mayor and his brethren of their grace."[1] No limit was set, whether of race, or occupation, or descent, or wealth, if they "are born in the city and be of good report, and if their presence may be profitable to the city as well as for his wisdom, as also for any other validity or worth known to the citizens."[2] The new society took in alike traders, agriculturists, bondmen looking for freedom,[3]

[1] Ricart, The Mayor of Bristol's Kalendar, Camden Society, 41. In 1439 two severe ordinances were passed by the Bristol Council that no Irishman born might be admitted to the Council by the Mayor under penalty of £20 each from the Mayor and from the Irishman. In Canterbury also the Irish were busy and unpopular traders (Hist. MSS. Com. ix. 173). When Irishmen were ordered out of England in 1422, burgesses and inhabitants of boroughs of good reputation were excepted. (Statutes 1st Henry VI. cap. 3.)

[2] Journ. Arch. Ass. xxvii. 468. There was constant communication between various towns about the character of new settlers who offered themselves, and the testimonials preserved to us show how careful the towns were in such matters. (Hist. MSS. Com. vi. 488. Piers Ploughman, edited by Skeat, Part iii. passus iv. 108–116.) No one of illegitimate birth might be a burgess. Nott. Rec. ii. 66.

[3] A bondman born could in many if not in most towns win the freedom of the city, as in Norwich where serfs were admitted to the franchise; but it is clear that here certainly mere residence without admission to citizenship was no protection against the claims of a feudal lord. (Norf. Arch. vol. xii.; Hudson's Notes on Norwich, Sec. xi.) It is most probable that the common phrases of "dwelling in the town a year and a day, and holding land in it and being in lot and scot," or of being "in the Merchant Guild," or of "remaining in the town *without challenge*," were in fact equivalent to having been received as burghers; and in such cases emancipation was won not by a year's residence but by a year's citizenship. In Norwich a serf had to produce his lord's license. (Hudson's Leet Jur. in Norwich, Selden Soc.

parish priests,[1] merchants who owned eight or ten ships and employed over a hundred workmen; small masters with but a single journeyman or perhaps two; artizans just released from apprenticeship and enrolled as members of some craft gild; rich folk who held several burgages, and men who rented a tiny shop. Everywhere the town communities were fast outgrowing the old simple traditions of common acquaintance and friendship, and throughout the fifteenth century the seals of the frequent new comers were so unfamiliar to their fellow citizens that deeds of sale had constantly to be brought to the

lxxxv.-vi.) For a similar instance of feudal claims urged by a lord over his serf dwelling in a city, see Owen's Shrewsbury, i. 133. Compare the references given by Gross, i. 30. There were exceptions, as in London, where men who held land in villeinage of the Bishop of London were not allowed in 1305 to be freemen of the City (Riley's Mem. 58-9). And after the Peasant Revolt some towns withdrew the privilege (Hist. MSS. Com. i. 109).

[1] A chaplain and four parsons of churches in Norwich were presented before the Leet Court of Norwich for various offences in 1292, in 1374, and in 1390. One of them had occupied himself with a large brewing business, another traded as a wool merchant, and two were charged with not being citizens. There were in all towns plenty of "clerici" who were citizens. (Hudson's Norwich Leet Jurisdiction, Selden Soc. pp. 45, 63, 65, 76.) For burgages owned by parsons and clerics in Southampton, Hist. MSS. Com. xi. 3, 65, 70, 71, 75, 81. In Romney, where "the freedom" seems to have meant more than the right to trade, it was given to the vicar and others. (Hist. MSS. Com. v. 540, 542, 546-7.) Monks and heads of religious houses were, according to Dr. Gross, excluded from citizenship (i. 66) though given rights of trade; but from the Charter Rolls, John, 1215, it appears that in Bridgewater the brethren of the Hospital of S. John were to be capable of taking up burgages in the town and to have the

Mayor for the addition of his seal of office to overcome hesitation and distrust.[1]

The hospitality of the corporations differed from place to place. Sometimes a borough threw its gates wide open and welcomed any new comer who would but choose one of the half-dozen avenues to citizenship that lay before him,—who would buy land, or marry a free woman, or pay the fixed price for his freedom, or serve his apprenticeship to a trade, or accept the franchise as a gift from the community; while a neighbouring town, looking on aliens with jealousy and hesitation, would close its doors and cling to some narrower system of enfranchisement

same liberties within and without the town as burgesses. This instance, has been kindly given to me by Miss Greenwood from her study of the muniments of the town; she adds that in the documents at Bridgewater there are many instances of houses and market-stalls being held by clergy. In all the bills of sale *stalls in High Street* are named burgages, and a law-suit shows that a wool-stall there was sold to the abbot of Michelney. For Ipswich, Gross, ii. 123; and Andover, ibid. 321. Local customs doubtless differed. The Guild Merchant at Lynn allowed no " spiritual person " to work on their quay—that is, to trade there (ibid. ii. 166)—a circumstance which reflects the greater credit on the hermit who about 1349 lived in the Bishop's marsh by Lynn and set up at his own great cost a certain remarkable cross of the height of 110 feet, of great service for all shipping coming that way (Blomefield viii. 514). When the burgesses of Totnes admitted the abbot and convent of Buckfastleigh into the Merchants' Guild, so as to make all their purchases like the burgesses, all sales that they might attempt to make " by way of trading " were excepted. Hist. MSS. Com. iii. 343.

[1] In Bristol; Hist. MSS. Com. v. 327. In Rye, " by the Common Seal of the Barons of the Ville of Rye;" ibid. v. 513, 499. For the old custom of sealing through rush rings see ibid. ix. 234–5.

which kept its ranks pure from foreign blood, and
its burghers free from anxieties of competition.[1] Each
community in fact had full liberty to order its own
political experiment. In the matter of choosing
their fellow burgesses, of framing their own society
and fixing the limits of its growth, the citizens knew
no law and recognized no authority beyond their
own,[2] and enjoyed herein a measure of independence
unknown in continental countries where a powerful
feudal system still barred every road to freedom.

[1] For the various ways of winning municipal freedom see First
Rep. of the Commissioners on Mun. Corporations, 1835, 19, and
especially the table given on page 93. Even towns as closely
connected as the Cinque Ports differed much in their willingness
to admit new burgesses. The freedom of Sandwich might be
acquired in six ways—by birth, by marriage with a free woman,
by buying a free tenement, by seven years' apprenticeship, by
purchase, by gift of the Corporation. In New Romney freedom
could only be acquired by birthright in the male line, and grant
of the Corporation; while in Hythe all children born after the
father's admission to freedom were entitled to the freedom, and
daughters could convey it upon their marriage (Boys' Sandwich,
787, 796, 799, 812, 821). The same differences existed in other
towns. See Davies' Southampton, 140; Boase's Oxford, 48;
English Guilds, 390; Freeman's Exeter, 142; Hereford, Journ.
Arch. Ass. xxvii. 471, 468.

[2] Leet Jur. in Norwich, Selden Soc. xxxvii. I have
met with but one instance in which the King interfered—
when Edward the Second by Royal Letters Patent granted the
right of burgesses at Southampton to John de London of
Bordeaux, and in 1312 extended them to his wife and children.
(Davies, 190.) Henry the Fourth granted to the Archbishop of
Canterbury the right to trade in Ipswich; but this right carried
with it no political privileges in the town. (Hist. MSS. Com.
ix. 246.) For the granting of franchises by French kings, see
Luchaire, Les Communes Françaises, 56–7.

When a new comer who desired to be "franchised for a free man, ... and fellow in your rolls"[1] was accepted by the commonalty he was summoned before them in a public court, "having with them the common charter of the city; and then the steward shall take the book, and bid them lay their right hands thereon, commanding all those that are standing by, in the behalf of our Lord the King, to keep silence," and the oath of obedience to the King and fidelity to the customs of the town was administered,[2]— perhaps, as at Winchester, the "oath to swear men to be free, kneeling on their knees."[3] The candidate had further to find two or more good men as pledges that he would "observe all the laws;"[4] and to pay the customary fees, which varied with the caution or the poverty of the borough from three shillings to five pounds; while a poor corporation like Wells was content to receive its payments in wine or gloves or wax when money was scarce.[5]

[1] Piers Ploughman, passus iv. 111, 114.
[2] Hereford; Journal Arch. Ass., xxvii. 468.
[3] Gross, ii. 257.
[4] Totnes, Hist. MSS. Com. iii. 342, 343. Preston Guild Rolls. xvi., xix. In Nottingham one pledge was required in the fourteenth century; generally two in the fifteenth century. See Nott. Records, i. 285-7, ii. 272, 302, iii. 58, 80, 84, 90, 102.
[5] In 1397 the burgesses of Preston paid sums varying from 3s. to 40s. (Preston Guild Rolls, xvi.-xix.) In Exeter an artificer had to pay 20s., a merchant whatever the Mayor chose to ask (Freeman's Exeter, 142). In Canterbury freemen were admitted in the fourteenth century for 10s.; in 1480 the sum had risen to 40s. (Hist. MSS. Com. ix. 144). See also Hereford (Journal Arch. Ass., xxvii.). In the sixteenth century

The new burgess was then required to give security to the town for payment of taxes or any other municipal claims by proving that he had either a good yearly revenue or a tenement, or by at once building himself a house.[1] A wooden framework was put together either on some building ground or perhaps in a vacant space in the open street,[2] and was then carried to the new site. The interstices were quickly filled up with plaster, and the little tenement was complete. A couple of rough benches and one or two pots and a few tools served as furniture, and the new burgess entered into possession and began life as a citizen householder. Henceforth he was bound to live within the walls of the borough, for his franchise was forfeited if he forsook the town for a year and a day.[3] Over the house, which was the town's security for rent and taxes, the municipality kept a watchful eye: if it became ruinous and dangerous to the passer-by it

the jury of the Mickle Tourn of Nottingham presented a request that every foreigner should henceforth pay £10. (Nott. Rec. iv. 170-1. Wells, Hist. MSS. Com. i. 106.) In Dover the payment was "put into the common horn" by the new freeman (Lyon's Dover, ii. 306).

[1] In Preston the rule was that if he had received for his burgage "a void place" he must set up a house on it within forty days; in other towns, as in Norwich or Hereford, he was allowed a year and a day. (Custumal of Preston, given in Hist. of Preston Guild, 74. Hudson, Municipal Organization of Norwich, 27. Journ. Arch. Ass. xxvii. 468.)

[2] In Preston regulations had to be made to prevent builders blocking up a street by temporarily fixing in it the framework of a house. (Hist. Preston Guild, 47.)

[3] Carlisle Mun. Records, Ed. Ferguson and Nansen, 63-4.

was thrown down at the owner's cost, or if needful at the cost of the commonalty; if through neglect or poverty it fell into decay the next heir and the commonalty together could compel him to put it in order or give it up.[1] Once or twice a year the burgher had to appear at the Portmote or Borough Court to prove his presence in the town, and to take his necessary part in the duties of the court.[2] An unwavering loyalty and public spirit was demanded of him, and the loss of "frelidge," as they said in Carlisle, avenged any breach of public duty, such as a refusal to help the Mayor in keeping the peace, clamour and undue disturbance at the election of town officers, revealing the counsels of the Common Assembly, resistance in word or deed to the municipal officers, contempt of the Mayor's authority, or any offence for which the punishment of the pillory or the tumbrill was adjudged.[3] For such things the burgher was "blotted out of the book of the bailiff"; and the forfeiture of his freedom was declared by open proclamation of the common crier, or by sound of the town bell, or by having his name written up

[1] Journ. Arch. Ass. xxvii. 472, 475; Lyon's Dover, ii. 362.
[2] Gross, ii. 276. Custumal, Preston Guild, 75. Hist. MSS. Com. viii. i. 426.
[3] In Hereford the freeman who lost his position for perjury could never recover it save by the special favour of the commonalty, "and by the redemption of his goods and chattels at least for twice as much as he gave before." Any citizen who had been sentenced to the pillory, tumbrill or the like, "by that means let him lose his freedom; but afterwards by the special favour of his bailiff and the commonalty he may be redeemed." (Journal Arch. Ass., xxvii. 468, 481.)

on a Disfranchised Table in the Guild Hall,[1] so that all the town should know his shame. In Preston those who betrayed the municipal confidence or exposed the poverty of the town were not only deprived of the franchise, but their toll was taken every day as of forsworn and unworthy persons who could not be trusted beyond the passing hour.[2]

It was no mean advantage to be a burgher in those days, when nearly all material benefits and legal aids and political rights were reserved for the favoured classes, and when it was the towns that opened for the working man and the shopkeeper a way to take their place too among the people of privilege. The burghers, of course, shared alike in rights of common and of pasturage on the town lands, of fishing in the town waters,[3] of the ferry across the stream or

[1] English Guilds, 403.
[2] Also at Andover; Gross, The Gild Merchant, ii. 320, 324. Public disapproval was held to be a powerful motive. In Hereford if a plaintiff brought a writ of right for the possession of a tenement into the court and the defendant refused to appear at the court, "there ought to be taken from the tenement demanded one post and to be brought unto the court and delivered to the bailiff; and the second time two; and the third time three; and *this to be done always towards the street, in reproach to him, and to the noting of his fellow-citizens;* and if he shall not come, the house ought to be thrown down, by taking one post towards the street, and so forward and forward until the whole house be thrown down to the ground." (Journal Arch. Ass., xxvii. 481-2.)
[3] A copy of the Charter of Manchester, granted 1301, is given in Baines' History of County of Lancaster ii. 175-6. A comparison of the special privileges of the burgesses with those in the Preston custumal illustrates the variety in the customs of different towns. (Cutts' Colchester, 169-170. Davies' Southampton, 111.)

sea channel, and so forth; but their pre-eminent privilege was the right to trade. If ordinary inhabitants were allowed to buy and sell food or the bare necessaries of life, all profitable business was reserved as the monopoly of the full citizen.[1] Protected from the intrusion and the competition of the alien,[2] he paid a reduced toll for his merchandize at the entrance of the town; his stall in the market was rented at a lower price than that of the stranger; he had the first choice of storage room in the Guild Hall for his wool or leather or corn; the town clock which tolled the hour when the market might begin, struck for the burgher an hour or two earlier than for strangers and visitors.[3] If a travelling merchant brought his wares to the town the citizen might claim the right of buying whether the owner wished to sell or no, and might insist on a share in the profits of any mercantile venture.[4] He alone might keep apprentices, and become a master in his craft. If he travelled out-

---

[1] See von Ochenkowski, Die wirthschaftliche Entwickelung im Ausgange des Mittelalters, 66. Stubbs' Charters, 107, 159. The monopoly was sometimes the privilege of the Merchant Guild. "So that no one who is not of that Guild shall make any merchandise in the said town, unless with the will of the merchants." (Hist. of Preston Guilds, Custumal, 73. Gross, ii. 122, 127, 129.) In other towns where we do not hear of a Merchant Guild it belonged to the whole body of burgesses. (Hist. MSS. Com. iv. 1, 425.)

[2] An alien living in Romney paid double Scot to the town. (Lyon's Dover, ii. 332.)

[3] English Guilds, 392, 384. Lyon's Dover, ii. 332.

[4] Boys' Sandwich, 521. Lyon's Dover, ii. 365, 366, 367, 386; Pleas in Manorial Courts, Selden Soc. 137.

side his own town for the purpose of trade he carried privilege with him everywhere, and confidently claimed freedom from " pontage " and " passage " and " pesage " and " shewage,"—that is from tolls for crossing bridges, for passing into a town, for the weighing of goods, for showing merchandize in the market,[1] —and from a host of similar imposts. Wherever he went he was shielded by the protection of his fellow citizens ;[2] if he had an action for debt in any other town he was granted common letters from the Mayor and Jurats to assist him in his suit;[3] if any wrong was done him they enforced compensation, or they avenged his injuries by confiscating the goods of any merchants within their walls who had come from the offending town.

[1] An Act to prevent Mayors from levying shewage from denizens. Statutes 19 Henry VII., Cap. 8.

[2] " The Mayor of the city of York and his brethren made great instance" to Lord Surrey to see that their fellow citizen, Thomas Hartford, bower in Norwich, should not be annoyed by Thomas Hogan, a shoemaker. (Paston Letters, iii. 366.) This protection however was only given on the condition of his renouncing all other aid. The mayor of York and his brethren aldermen in 1488 were applied to by Sir Robert Plumpton to protect some " servants and lovers " of his dwelling in York from annoyance by certain York citizens. The mayor answered in the name of himself, the aldermen, and the common council, that these dependants of Plumpton's had been franchised and sworn to keep the customs of the city of York, that they were therefore bound to show any variance or trouble to the mayor " and to none other, and he to see an end betwixt them." The mayor plainly intimates that these men must either go home and live under the protection of their master there, or else if they stay in York must submit their affairs to the mayor alone " as their duties had been." (Plumpton Correspondence, 57–58.)

[3] Hist. MSS. Com. iv. 1, 425.

Legal safeguards and privileges moreover fenced him about on every side. He could only be impleaded in the courts of his own town, and any fellow citizen who brought an action against him outside the borough might be disgraced and disfranchised;[1] while the King himself could not summon a burgher to appear before his judges at Westminster, save on the plea that there had been "lack of justice" at the first trial in the court of his own town. No "foreigner" might meddle in any legal inquiry in which their houses and property were concerned;[2] while, on the other hand, every citizen from twelve years old could serve on juries for the town business.[3] Peculiar favours were extended to the burgher,[4] as at Worcester where there were special provisions to protect him from any wrongful fine by the bailiff,[5]

---

[1] Preston Guild Rolls, xxiv.; Freeman's Exeter, 144; Hist. MSS. Com. ix. 241, 242, 246. For instances of royal pressure brought to bear on the town courts, see Proc. Privy Council, ii. 152; Hist. MSS. Com. xi. 3, 97, 99, 100, 102, 104.

[2] There was a hot dispute on this question between Wycombe and the Abbot of Missenden under Edward the First, and the jury was finally formed of seven burgesses and five foreigners, "thus saving to the said burgesses their liberty aforesaid." (From Pleas de Quo Warranto, Bucks, Rot. i. Edw. I., 1286. Parker's Hist. of Wycombe, 23–4.) [3] Parker's Hist. of Wycombe, 12.

[4] Especially in matters of debt and arrest. Stubbs' Charters, 107. In Romney a burgess might recover money owed to him by a stranger in the town by himself going, in the absence of the bailiff, to make distraint on the stranger's goods under the sole condition of delivering the distraint to the bailiff. (Hist. MSS. Com. iv. 1, 425. For Rye see Lyon's Dover, ii. 358; Boys' Sandwich, 449. See also for the difficulties of aliens, Hist. MSS. Com. ix. 243.)

[5] English Guilds, 391; Hist. MSS. Com. ix. 170–1. Henry the

and the city sergeant had to do any legal business required of him at reduced fees; or at Canterbury, where special formalities of trial assured to him a more exact and careful justice; or at Sandwich, where he could be tried only before the mayor, and could not be summoned before his deputy like a common stranger.[1] Everywhere he could claim the right of being separated from the common criminals and imprisoned in some tower or room in the Guild Hall used as the Freeman's prison.[2]

But all these privileges were far from being a free gift to be enjoyed in idle security; and to each individual burgher the franchise practically meant a sort of carefully-adjusted bargain, by which he compounded for paying certain tolls by undertaking to

Second granted to burgesses of Wallingford that if his provost impleaded any one of them without an accuser, he need not answer the charge. (Gross, ii. 244.) See Newcastle, Stubbs' Charters, 107. The importance of these provisions is obvious if the custom of Sandwich was common. There the mayor might arrest and imprison any one whom he chose as a "suspect." After some time the prisoner was brought from the castle to the Mastez and a "cry" made to ask if there were any one to prosecute him. If no one appeared he was set free on giving security, but if he could find no security he might at the mayor's will be banished for ever from the town. The bailiff could not arrest on suspicion as the mayor did. (Boys' Sandwich, 687, 466-7.) For mediæval notions of punishment see the sentence of the King in Piers Ploughman, pass. v. 81-82—

"And commanded a constable to cast Wrong in irons,
There he ne should in seven year see feet ne hands."

[1] Hist. MSS. Com. ix. 170-1. Boys' Sandwich, 445 and 443. In Winchester the freeman was summoned three times to the court, others only once. (English Guilds, 360.)
[2] English Guilds, 391. Hist. MSS. Com. ix. 152.

do work, and work which might be both costly and laborious, for the community. The body of citizens was but a small one, and every man in it was liable at some time or other to be called on to take his part in the public service. Taxation for the town expenses, watch and ward, service on juries, the call to arms in defence of the borough, were incidents as familiar as unwelcome in every burgher's life; but a more serious matter was the summons to take office and serve as mayor or bailiff or town clerk or sergeant or tax-collector or common constable—offices not always coveted in those days, when the mayor was held personally responsible for the rent of a town which was perhaps vexed with pestilence or wasted with fire; when treasurers had to find funds as best they could for too frequent official bribes or state receptions of great lords or court officers; when bailiffs had to meet the loss from failing dues and straitened markets;[1] when the boxes of the tax-collector were left half empty through poverty, or riots, or disputed questions of market-rights;[2] and when the constable was "frayed" day and night by sturdy men, dagger in hand, ready to break the King's peace.[3] Many modes of escape were tried. The inhabitants would refuse to take up the franchise, or they would leave the town for a time;[4] an elected officer would

[1] In Norwich the bailiffs were liable to such heavy expenses in bad years that in 1306 it was ordained that they could only be compelled to serve once in four years. (Blomefield, iii. 73. Ordinances in Hist. of Preston Guilds, 12.)
[2] Hist. MSS. Com. ix. 145.
[3] Parker's Manor of Aylesbury, 20, 21.
[4] Hist. MSS. Com. v. 536-541.

plead a vow of pilgrimage to "S. James in Gallice;" or an influential burgess might obtain letters patent from the King which granted him freedom from serving any municipal office during his life.[1] But generally a heavy fine compelled the submission of a refractory citizen, and in the last resort the community would apply for a writ against him from the Privy Council.[2] The town allowed no excuses, and everywhere the citizens were forced by stringent laws to take on them the offices to which they had been elected by their fellows. In Lydd an order was made in 1429 that any one who had been appointed by the bailiff or jurats to take any journey on town business should pay a fine if he refused without reasonable cause.[3] In the Cinque Ports generally if a citizen who had been elected as mayor or jurat declined to serve, his house was pulled down;[4] or as at

[1] Davies' Southampton, 168. In 1422 a Winchester burgess paid £10 to be free of holding any office save that of Mayor for the rest of his life. Another paid five marks to be freed from ever taking the office of bailiff. (Gross, ii. 259-260.) In Lynn, when a man was chosen jurat, "he took time till the next assembly to bring ten pounds into the Hall, or otherwise to accept the burden." (Hist. MSS. Com. xi. 3, 167.) Fine for refusal to go to Yarmouth as bailiff of Cinque Ports, and payment to substitute (Ibid. v. 541). In 1491 an Act was passed forbidding the burgesses of Leicester to refuse the Chamberlainship. Sixty years later another Act ordered them not to refuse the Mayoralty. By Acts of 1499 and 1500 members who absented themselves from the Court of Portmanmote at Whitsuntide and Christmas were fined. (Ibid. viii. 426.) In Canterbury certain powers were exempted by writ from serving on juries, 1415. (Hist. MSS. Com. ix. 169.)

[2] Shillingford's Letters, xxiii.   [3] Hist. MSS. Com. v. 527.
[4] Lyon's Dover, Custumals, vol. ii. 267, &c.

Romney the bailiff with the whole community went to his dwelling, turned himself, his wife, his children, and all his household into the street, shut the windows and sealed the door, and so left matters until "he wished to set himself right by doing the said duty of jurat." In Sandwich again, "if a person when elected treasurer will not take upon him the office he shall not be permitted to bake or brew, or if he does bake or brew the commons may take his bread and beer to their own use till he accepts the office."[1] At the worst, however, the burgher might thankfully remember that his public duty practically ceased at the wall and moat that bounded the town, and that when he had paid down his money towards the buying of the town charter he was at least safe from the danger of being sent as tax-collector or constable or juror anywhere throughout the country round.[2]

The privileges and duties of the free citizen remained, however, the endowment of the few. That larger conception of the common rights of man which had begun to make its way in the boroughs, was checked and hindered at every turn by the complicated

---

[1] Hist. MSS. Com. iv. 1, 425; Boys' Sandwich, 679, A.D. 1493. Gross, The Gild Merchant, ii. 276.

[2] The charter of Edward the Fourth to Colchester declared that the burghers should never be appointed against their will in any assizes or any quests outside the borough; nor to any post of collector of taxes or aids, or of constable, bailiff, &c., nor should they be liable to any fine for refusing these posts. (Cromwell's Colchester, 257.) The Winchester people paid a sum about 1422 "to excuse every citizen of the city from being collector of the King's money within the county of Southampton." (Hist. MSS. Com. vi. 602.)

conditions of town life, by the jealousy of established settlers as to new comers, the exclusive temper which the crafts had begun to show, the terror of the trader before free competition, the imperfectly developed authority of the corporations over the space within the town walls, where it had failed to break the barriers of feudal custom and the claims of ecclesiastical corporations. Howsoever the towns widened their borders, there was still a growing population which lingered just outside the circle of free citizens, shut out by one cause or another from full municipal liberty. Settlers came who did not care to burden themselves with the duties and charges of citizenship; there were dwellers in churchyards and tenants of ecclesiastical estates, who carried on their business within the town liberties but remained without the town jurisdiction; landowners from outside the walls brought their corn and wool to the town market; traders came from time to time with wares to sell; there were apprentices and journeymen, escaped bondmen, and country-folk coming to look for work. As all of these alike needed the protection of the town, so the town needed their services; and by degrees their respective duties and rights were laid down in charters, in ordinances, or in friendly compacts.

I. Thus it came about that below the ranks of the burgesses, themselves secure in their municipal supremacy, were ranged orders of men more or less highly favoured according to their degree. First came the inhabitants who had paid for special rights of trade in the town, or were admitted as members of the Merchant Guild. In times of commercial prosperity when wandering dealers and artizans were attracted to some thriving borough for trading purposes they went to swell this class of independent inhabitants, subject to the jurisdiction of the town courts, but taking no part in its politics;[1] so that it occasionally happened, as in Norwich and Worcester, that the town refused to harbour this body of irresponsible inhabitants and passed a law ordering them to become citizens.[2] When on the other hand trade declined and poverty settled down on the town, as in Romney and Winchester, the failing fortunes of the people were marked by a steady decrease of the class of "advocantes," or those who would "avow" themselves freemen, and inhabitants who in their distress refused or renounced the franchise,[3] were driven into the ranks of the politically unfree.

II. So long as the trading inhabitants owned the jurisdiction of the town courts their presence brought no serious difficulty to the ruling authorities. But within the town walls there were other groups of men who lay beyond this jurisdiction, and

---

[1] Thus in Hythe there was a privileged body who were not of the franchise, but were still apparently subject to the town jurisdiction, and excused by a writ called Dormand from Hundred Court and Shire Court and inquests. See also Preston Guild Record, xii., xvi., xx., xxix.

[2] English Guilds, 394. Blomefield, Hist. of Norfolk, iii., 80.

[3] Hist. MSS. Com. v. 544—545. At one time when Preston was much distressed, it was ordained that decayed burgesses unable to pay their yearly taxes should not lose their freedom because of poverty. (Thomson's Mun. History, 104. Custumale in Hist. of Preston Guild.)

held an ambiguous position which was the source of many a quarrel for ascendency and many a struggle for license in the course of the fifteenth century. These were the tenants and dependants of bishop or abbot, of some lay lord, or of the king's castle—men who lived within the liberties of the borough and who had the right of trading in the town, but who were bound to do suit and service at the courts of their own special lord.[1] To some extent they were forced to recognize the mayor's authority, since their rights of trade were guaranteed by his protection, and since he yearly reminded them of his power to levy taxes on all property within the liberties of the borough. But their obedience was grudging and their loyalty was cold. The mayor could not awe them by a summons to his court, or enforce his demands with threat of pains and penalties; he could scarcely terrify them into submission with his sergeant and a few constables. By degrees, it is true, the tenants of the king's castle or of feudal lords became merged in the general body of the inhabitants. But the tenants of ecclesiastical estates[2] were maintained by lords who were bound by every tradition of their order never to yield up the least jot of authority to the secular power, and least of all to the secular power as represented by groups of upstart drapers and fishmongers and weavers whose humble shops and booths leaned against the walls of the abbey or the priory, and whose pretensions, loud and noisy though they might be, were perhaps a century or so old at the best. The ecclesiastical

[1] See ch. x. [2] See ch. xi.

tenants therefore remained everywhere an alien body, no true partakers in the life of the town, and when supported by a powerful bishop or abbot determined to crush the pretensions of a struggling borough they proved a serious danger to municipal unity, and one which the authorities found themselves powerless to conquer till the Reformation settled the question for ever.

III. There was another class of privileged traders, —those who lived altogether outside the town,[1] who knew nothing of its courts, and bore none of its charges. We find everywhere these country traders under various styles and with various privileges according to the town's discretion and convenience. Sometimes the citizens sold rights of trade to cultivators of the surrounding lands and occasional visitors to fair or market, and nobles and landowners were ready to give large yearly payments for freedom of the market and for the right of having granaries in the town. Peasants who owned a plot of land just outside the borough increased their scanty store by learning some little handicraft or doing a small trade in the town; or craftsmen settled down beyond the boundaries to escape the town dues and live more cheaply. At first the settlement of workmen and traders at their gates may have seemed a matter of small consequence, but as time went on the danger which was hidden in these communities of free-traders became apparent. The manufacturer or dealer was able by one device or another to protect himself against

[1] See vol. ii., The Town Market.

the enterprising man of the suburbs who came in with his cheaper goods; it was the journeymen of the towns who failed before the stress of the battle, driven back from their poor entrenchments by the masses who pushed forward on all sides to contest with them admission into the lower ranks of industry where the scantiest skill sufficed to earn a bare subsistence.

IV. Last of all came the non-burgesses, who had neither any share in the government, nor any rights to rent a stall in the market, nor to own shop or workroom in the town. These formed an obscure company of workers without records or history. They counted among their number ancient burghers who had fallen into low estate and could no longer pay their burgage dues, as well as the poor who had never prospered so far as to buy a tenure or citizenship. But they were not all necessarily poor or miserable.[1] Rich merchants came from foreign parts to settle for four or eight months at a time, as the law might allow them, and bought and sold within the four walls of the room which the Town Council had ordered in some inn as their dwelling-place, with the host standing at their elbow to witness every bargain. Foreign workmen sometimes came to settle, like the Flemish weavers in Bristol, or the Dutch makers of canals and sluices whom we find in the towns of the southern coast. Companies of tilers or builders

---

[1] The non-burgesses of Lynn, the "Inferiores," were men of substance and formed an important body, whose struggles for a re-distribution of power fill the annals of the town in the fifteenth century.

gathered in towns where stone houses were becoming the fashion, or where the Council had issued an order that within the next few months every house must provide itself with roof and chimney of brick or tiles.[1] The seaports had their uncertain element of sailors, "shipmen that had nought, and cared never an they were once on the sea whether they come again or not," and who at Yarmouth formed a riotous population, so that it was said that "no thrifty man would live in it."[2] Labourers from the country came in to win freedom from serfage. Others came to look for higher wages, and the hope which town life held out to the enterprising and the ambitious; so that in 1405 an Act of Parliament declared that the fields were deserted, and the "gentlemen and other people of the nation greatly impoverished" by the labourers seeking apprenticeship in towns, "and that for the pride of clothing and other evil customs that servants do use in the same."[3] Children came, constantly as young as seven, never older than twelve—when they were expected to begin the work of life just as at that age their brothers of a better station took on themselves the duties of citizenship, for "every poor man that hath brought up children to the age of twelve year waiteth then to be holp and profited by

---

[1] English Guilds, 386, 399.   [2] Paston Letters, ii. 293.
[3] 7 Henry IV. cap. 17. The coming of country apprentices into towns, though forbidden by Richard II. and Henry IV., was afterwards permitted in London, Bristol, and Norwich. (Statutes 8 Henry VI. cap. 11; 11 Henry VII. cap. 11; 12 Henry VII. cap. 1).

his children."¹ Thenceforward they had to fight their own way, looking for assistance not to their fathers but to their patrons, "whence it proceeds that, having no hope of their paternal inheritance, they all become so greedy of gain that they feel no shame in asking almost 'for the love of God,' for the smallest sums of money; and to this it may be attributed that there is no injury that can be committed against the lower orders of the English that may not be atoned for by money."²

But if apprenticeship ever brought with it "pride of clothing," the poor working class of the towns fared roughly and worked hard among artizans who "hold full hungry house," who know "long labour and light winning," who taste no wine from week to week, whose bed has no blanket, and on whose board no white bread ever comes."³ Once this rough living and rougher toil had been a sure way of entering into the privileges of municipal freedom. But even in the fourteenth century this was no longer the case. The poorer burghers opposed the admission of new comers to share their common lands, and insisted on selling the franchise dearly. The crafts had already begun to form themselves into close companies, and by prohibitive fines shut out all save the descendants of their own members; while at the same time the custom was growing up that the town franchise should be given

---

[1] Paston Letters, iii. 481. Apprentices in London and Bristol might not be *under* seven years old. Ricart, 102.
[2] Manners and Meals, xv.
[3] Piers Ploughman, Passus x. 206—207, 253-4.

only to those who were enrolled in a craft or trade guild; and strangers therefore found the way barred against them; they could neither become masters in their craft nor burgesses in their town, and went to swell the general mass of journeymen and serving men. Moreover the Peasant Revolt had carried with it widespread terror, and from that time some towns, as for instance York and Bridgenorth, refused to allow any born bondman, whatever his estate, to receive the freedom of the city. Thus from one cause or another groups of men were formed in the midst of every town who were shut out from the civic life of the community, and whose natural bond of union was hostility to the privileged class which denied them the dignity of free citizens and refused them fair competition in trading enterprise. The burghers yearly added to their number half a dozen or perhaps even a score of members wealthy enough to buy the privilege, while the increase in the unenfranchised class, which had begun very early in the town life, proceeded by leaps and bounds; till presently the old balance of forces in the little state was overthrown, the ancient constitution of a free community of equal householders was altogether annulled and forgotten, and a comparatively small class of privileged citizens ruled with a strong hand over subject traders and labourers to whom they granted neither the forms nor the substance of liberty.

CHAPTER VI

THE PROBLEM OF GOVERNMENT

Bridport

THE comfortable independence in which the townspeople of the fourteenth and fifteenth centuries had stoutly entrenched themselves, was the reward of a couple of centuries of persistent effort, in which they had steadily laboured at their double work of emancipation, freeing themselves on the one hand from the feudal yoke, and on the other from political servitude. No independent life of the community could arise so long as the inhabitants of a town acknowledged an absolute subjection to their feudal lord, and bore the heavy burdens of services and taxes which, however they might differ according to the usages of the several manors, weighed upon the people everywhere with persistent and intolerable force. The lord might destroy their industry by suddenly calling out the inhabitants to follow him in a warlike expedition, or demanding services of forced labour or laying on them grievous taxes; his officers could throw the artizan or merchant into his prison, or ruin them by fines, or force upon them methods of law hateful and dangerous to their conceptions of a common life; as he claimed supreme rights over the soil it was impossible for the burgher to leave his property by will; and on the tenant's death officers visited his house and stables and granaries to seize the most valuable goods as the lord's relief. It was necessary to gain his consent before any new member could be admitted into the fellowship of citizens; and without his permission no inhabitant might leave the borough to carry on his trade elsewhere. He could forbid the marriage of children arranged by the fathers, or refuse to allow a widow to take a new husband and so make him master of her house and freeman in her town. He fixed the market laws and the market tolls. He forced the people to grind at his mill and bake at his oven.

If therefore the burghers were ever to develope commerce, or gather wealth, or form an organized society, or keep order in their streets, it was before all things necessary that serfs should be made into freemen; and the first object of the town communities was to find deliverance by purchase or negociation from those tyrannous usages by which their masters pressed most heavily on them. Vexatious feudal obligations were commuted for fixed payments in one town after another as their inhabitants grew rich and independent. A bargain was made, for instance, with the lord of Preston that he should no longer summon any burgess to follow him on a warlike expedition which lasted more than one day nor imprison on any accusation whatever a townsman who found sureties; and he was forced to sell or renounce the right of compelling the people to carry their corn to the lord's mill or oven or kiln, and to allow any householder who chose to build an oven on his own ground.[1] The burgher everywhere became the acknowledged guardian of his own children and might betroth them at his pleasure; the right of widows to re-marry was secured against any interference from without; and absolute security was given to every citizen that under no circumstances could his tenement or plot of ground be claimed by any superior lord.[2] When the burgesses of Hereford were asked by a neighbouring town to give an account of their constitution they proudly dwelt upon the freedom they had won. "We do not use," they say, "to do fealty or any other foreign service to the lord of the fees for our tenements, but only the rents arising out of the said tenements; because we say that we hold our tenements by the service of burgage, or as

[1] Custumal in History of Preston Guild, 73–78. As late as the time of James I. lords here and there were fighting to keep up old customs. An action was brought by a lord against a townsman of Melton for not baking his bread at the lord's oven; "and the action," wrote the steward, "is like to prove frequent, for the lord's court there is scarce able to preserve his inheritance in this custom of baking." Lives of the Berkeleys, ii. 342-3.

[2] If a Preston burgher died suddenly, neither lord nor justices might seize his lands, which passed on to the next heir; only if he had been publicly excommunicated they were to be given in alms. Custumal. Hist. Preston Guild, 77. Compare Luchaire 248.

burgesses, so that we have not any other lord between our lord the king and us." "And we do not so use," they add, "to give any heriot nor mortuary to any one at the death of any of the citizens dying within the said city or suburbs, for any of his tenements." Moreover "we say that every citizen of the city or suburbs may give and assign their tenements freely and quietly as well in health as in sickness, when and to whomsoever they please, whether those tenements are of their inheritance or of their purchasing or getting, without any malicious detracting of their lord, so that they be of such an age and no less, that they know how to measure a yard of cloth, and to know and tell twelve pence."[1]

In these ways and in many others by which personal freedom was checked and thwarted, the rights of the feudal lord were irresistibly swept away by the pressure of growing societies of active traders and artizans.[2] But the need for political emancipation was

[1] Journ. Arch. Assoc. xxvii. 471. The age was sometimes fixed at twelve, sometimes at fourteen. (Hist. MSS. Com. ix. 244.) The burgher had no power to leave by will any lands he held outside the town liberties, which must pass to the heir appointed by the common law. For the frauds to which this might give rise, see Hist. MSS. Com. x. 3, 87-9. Wills bequeathing land were read publicly in the borough courts (Nottingham Records, i. 96), and there enrolled by the mayor as a Court of Record. The muniments of Canterbury show that from this right the mayor went on to claim probate, possibly following the example of Lynn. The claim was perfectly illegal, but was energetically pressed.

[2] Birmingham, which under Henry the Eighth had 2,000 houselings, and was said to be "one of the fairest and most profitable towns to the King's highness in all the shire" (English

no less urgent; and here the way to liberty was neither simple nor easy. A very hierarchy of powers held the path. The authority which the lord of the manor did not assume was exercised by the sheriff of the county; and where the authority of the sheriff ceased the supreme right of the king began. All government and jurisdiction were divided among powers in high places; and whatever privileges the

Guilds, 247-9), only counted in Doomsday nine heads of families. In 1327 these had risen to seventy-five. The burghers first won the lightening of feudal dues, when Birmingham was freed from ward and marriage, heriot and relief, so that if a burgess died the lord could only take his best weapon—a bill or a pole-axe—or forty pence. (Survey of the Borough and Manor of Birmingham, 1553. Translated by W. B. Bickley, with notes by Joseph Hill, pp. xii., 108.) The bailiff and commonalty rented the stalls in the market from the lord, and leased them out by their constables to the townsfolk, fishmongers, butchers, and tanners, and in this way secured complete control of the town market (pp. 60-61), where burgesses were exempt from toll, while strangers free of the market paid a small sum, and those not free a larger amount. After the Plague a "free burgage by fealty" grew up, with an oath to observe the customs and services of the manor. The normal holding of the villein seems to have been forty-five acres, that of the cotters less (pp. xii., xiii. See Rogers' Agric. and Prices, i. 12, 298). As population increased new pastures in the foreign were leased out for a term of years at an annual rent, and while the increase of perpetual free tenures thus ceased the alienation of the whole domain was prevented (pp. xiv., 74, 102). Though the town was not made a borough by royal grant, it had even in the thirteenth century secured an independent life, called itself a borough and elected its officers (pp. 60-1, 108-9). Its public acts were done under the style of "bailiff and commonalty" or "bailiff and burgesses." See also Manchester Court Leet Records, 12, 14, 169, 170. For examples of the first privileges which the townspeople sought to win see the "customs" of Newcastle under Henry I., Stubbs' Charters, 106-8.

burghers might secure must be won here a little and there a little, bought for money, or snatched amid the distresses and calamities of their masters, or held as the reward of importunate persistence, the tribute to successful craft, the recompense of some timely service rendered.

The case of Bridport illustrates the life of any provincial town in early times whose burghers still served many masters.[1] It was a busy little trading community in the thirteenth century. Hemp was grown in its fields which was sent to Plympton to be made into rope yarn, returned to Bridport to be woven into ropes, and then sent back again to Plympton for sale, or fashioned at home into the girths, horse-nets, and reins for which the Bridport men were famous. The inhabitants had won a considerable measure of self-rule. They elected the two bailiffs who were at the head of their local government, presided in the little town court, and doubtless regulated the market and controlled the trade. These two had under them under-bailiffs, cofferers, and constables; and were assisted by twelve jurors chosen every Michaelmas, who yearly perambulated the town to watch over its boundaries, and who had charge of the "parish cheste" or coffin and the parish bier, and of the pillory, whipping post, and cucking stool. Twelve men were also chosen to conduct any business in which Bridport was concerned. At the visits of the king's justices they were summoned with the clerk in council to assist in the business of the court; they represented their fellow

[1] Hist. MSS. Com. vi. 491, et seq.

burgesses if any question was called for trial before the sheriff's court at Dorchester, or if a dispute arose with the bishop, or a settlement had to be made with the convent at Abbotsbury.

I. The powers of the burgesses however were shut up within the narrowest limits. At every moment of their lives some authority from without stepped in with rigorous control and ceaseless exactions. The Lord of the Manor (who in this particular case was the king) owned the soil of the town; therefore his Steward kept the Law Day,[1] judged the petty offences of the townsmen, summoned them before him to see that each was properly enrolled under the system of frankpledge, and swept their fines and forfeitures into the lord's coffers.[2]

II. Bridport further owed obedience to the officers of the shire. The coroner [3] came to make inquisition in case of mysterious or violent death or of fire, judged the cause, seized forfeited goods or chattels, and assessed the fines. The sheriff of the county exercised a jurisdiction which extended over the most

[1] For the injuries that might be inflicted on a community by a lord's reeve, see Select Pleas in Manorial Courts, Selden Society.

[2] If the lord of the soil held the town as a market-town, and not as a borough, the inhabitants had to attend the Sheriff's tourn, where their petty offences were judged by him or his deputy. In all cases which were not specially exempted they had to appear also twice a year at the court of the shire for view of frank pledge and for judgment of their more serious crimes. Manchester Court Leet Records, 14.

[3] The coroner was an officer elected in full county court, and was charged with guarding the interests of the Crown. His intrusion in the towns was much resented.

important affairs of the community, and touched at every point the daily life of the burghers. That his supervision might be constant and effectual, he was accustomed to appoint a deputy or under-sheriff to represent him on the spot, generally some man of importance in Bridport itself, who living in the centre of the town could keep a close watch on its affairs and manage them with a more exact control. It was the sheriff's business to keep order, and guard against breaches of the king's law. At stated times he called the town bailiff and constable to appear at his court at Dorchester; crimes which lay beyond the control of the manor court were brought to judgment before him and fines, or the gifts that averted fines,[1] reminded the burghers of his power. As head of the shire forces he ordered at his own will the muster-at-arms of the townsmen, and in times of disturbance called out the levies for the king's service; he fixed the number of archers and fighting men; he regulated the contribution of bows and arrows, of hemp and cord, of corn or wine or fish. Year by year he assessed and levied the royal taxes,[2] and collected the rent due from the borough to the king's exchequer. Payments were not made in money in such a town as Bridport; so when the rent day came near the sheriff or his deputy first drew up a list of oxen and other goods which

---

[1] When a robber from Bridport escaped from the town prison a set of girths or horse-nets was sent by the town to Dorchester to mitigate the sheriff's anger.

[2] For abuses in appointing tax collectors, see Paston Letters, i. li.

were to be given up by the various inhabitants and ultimately sold on the Monday after Palm Sunday for the ferm. Meanwhile this list was handed over to the charge of the "bailiff-errant," who travelled from town to town with his clerk and groom[1] on the business of the shire; and certain citizens were made responsible for the safety of the cattle and goods until the appointed day. The choice of goods to be taken from each person, the chance of accident before the day of sale, the naming of citizens who were to bear the charges of making good any possible loss, the various fortunes of the auction and of the prices it might bring, the skilful calculations necessary to ensure that however much the profits might exceed the needed sum they should never fall short of it—all these things created at every turn new chances of corruption, new hopes of profit to those in authority, and new prospects of ruin to those under the law.[2] The division of powers between the sheriff and his deputies, and the practical impossibility of fixing any responsibility or of calling any one of them to account, left the inhabitants mere creatures at mercy, subject to varied and fortuitous hardship; while on the other hand the art of government became to every one concerned in it a mere business of self-preservation. When John in 1216 sent a commission to collect the ferm of Northampton which had fallen into arrears, the commissioner was informed that the king could not afford payment either for himself or for his servants, and that he must there-

[1] Hist. MSS. Com. vi. 491.
[2] See Round's Geoffrey de Mandeville, 361-3.

fore provide as best he could for their salaries and provisions out of the arrears of the ferm which he was sent to collect.[1] Such a system quickened zeal on the part of officials, if it did not lighten the troubles of the people. In those days every officer in the scale, from the sheriff to the constable, subject to the claims and exactions of his immediate superior, could only indemnify himself by exercising a corresponding pressure on those below him, and passing on the tradition of fraud and tyranny.

It would be hard to say whether the sheriff's position as tax-gatherer, as judge, or as recruiting officer and military leader, gave him the largest opportunities for extortion and tyranny; but so long as every office that he held added new pretences for arbitrary interference, the townspeople were driven to win his favour by frequent gifts, whether to himself or to his wife, which indeed his deputies were strict in levying when voluntary action proved tardy. He generally required a "year gift" from towns under his control, either to induce him not to come within their liberties, or to remind him to "shew his friendship" to the inhabitants in their necessities;[2] and it was a common custom, when money fell short, to make collection by means of a "scot-ale,"[3] and summon the townsfolk to a drinking feast where

---

[1] Close Rolls, I. p. 273, 1216.   [2] Nottingham Records, i. 46.

[3] This appears in the records of Gloucester. The scot-ale was a very common method of collecting money for other purposes. See Malmesbury, Gross, ii. 172, Newcastle (183), Wallingford (245), Winchester (253), Cambridge (358). It was an article of inquiry for Justices Itinerant in 1254. (417) Stubbs' Charters, 258-259.

they were bound to contribute a supply of provisions, and to spend a certain sum at the ale-booths set up for the day, while the proceeds of the whole entertainment went into the sheriff's pocket. Modes of extortion, however, might vary infinitely. In Canterbury the sheriff once broke down the only bridge over the river, and so kept it for three months, while he put a ferry boat on the water which the people were forced to use and pay for on his own terms.[1] The confessed superiority of these officials in the arts of fraud and tyranny was proclaimed by the universal fear and hate which followed them—passions which break out in the popular ballads where by a traditional touch the people's hero, Robin Hood, is endowed with the hatred of all sheriffs; and which stir the heart of the writer of Piers Ploughman as he pictures these officers in the foremost place wherever there is a gathering of the servants of corruption, and in his parable of the Lady Meed travelling to the Court tells how it was a sheriff who was appointed to bear her softly in a litter from Assize to Assize with tenderest care for her safety, since "sheriffs of shires were shent (undone) if she were not."[2]

III. The sheriff however was but the deputy of the crown, and the sovereign rights of the King lay behind and above all subordinate authority whatever.

[1] Hundred Rolls, i. 49, 55. The jurors of Bridgenorth complained in 1221 that the sheriff's bailiffs and the men of the country had committed to them the duty of following the trail of stolen cattle through their town and fined them if they failed, whereas they could not follow a trail through the middle of the town. Select Pleas of the Crown, Selden Society, 113.

[2] Piers Ploughman, Pass. iii. 59, 177, iv. 172.

When a royal messenger rode through the gates of a town the officers of the lord of the manor and of the shire alike acknowledged a higher law; and such messengers were not rare. The sheriff's accustomed rule was set aside whenever judges from Westminster sat in the church or the Guild Hall to administer the justice of the King's Court. Sometimes the king's escheator came to investigate into lapsed estates, to ascertain whether any socage tenants had died, and claim the customary fines.[1] From time to time Court officials "carrying the mace of the lord the king" appeared to announce statutes or ordinances made in Parliament; or came as unwelcome commissioners to ask for benevolences and loans. The king's clerk of the market[2] might ride into the town with a troop of horses and followers carrying weights and measures signed with the sign of the exchequer; he would call

[1] For the profits to be made in this business and its opportunities of fraud, see Winchelsea (Rot. Parl. i. 373). Sometimes the escheator divided the fines levied between himself and the King; in other cases the office was farmed out and the King took a fixed sum leaving the escheator a free hand to do what he pleased. In the towns the office was finally given to the mayor at a fixed salary. The Mayor of Norwich received as escheator £10; that is, an equal salary to that which he received as Mayor (Blomefield, iii. 179). As Mayor of the Staple he was given £20. (Ibid. iii. 94.)

[2] He was forbidden by Richard the Second to ride with more than six horses, or tarry long in a town. (Statutes, 13 Richard II. 1, cap. 4, and 16 Richard II., cap. 3.) In 1346 the King by charter freed Norwich from "the clerk of the market of our household," so that he should not enter the city to make the assay of measures or weights, or any other duties belonging to his office. (Norwich Doc., pr. 1884, case of Stanley v. Mayor, &c., p. 26.) For clerk of the market in Calais, Lives of Berkeleys, ii. 198.

for all the town measures, test them by his models, see that the false ones were burned, and then claim a fresh relay of horses to carry him on to his next stage. If the sovereign chose he might send an officer under the assize of arms to "sit at Bridport to array the men" and call for archers for the king's service; or in case of need the king's "harbinger" or "sergeant-at-arms" came to judge how many soldiers should be billeted on the inhabitants. In time of rebellion or civil war,[1] suspicion of disaffection might fall upon the town, and then commissioners travelled from London to hold a special "inquisition" on the spot.

IV. All these officers represented the king as supreme head of the law; but other messengers came from the court, as unbidden and unwelcome as the last, who claimed for the sovereign a tribute which belonged to his personal dignity and state. When the monarch travelled he carried his own law with him; wherever he went the steward and marshal of his house had jurisdiction for twelve miles to be counted from the lodging of the king;[2] and their authority superseded all other law whether of the borough or the shire. The marshal demanded such supply of horses as was necessary for the king or his messengers;[3] the

[1] Hist. MSS. Com. v. 545.
[2] Statutes, 13th Richard II., 1, cap. 3.
[3] In Rochester "the King's hackney-men" took oath to be ready at all times, early and late, to serve the King's Grace with able hackney horses at the calling of the Mayor, and to provide at all times for any man riding on the King's message, and to give information to the Mayor in case any hard-driven hackney-man in the town "purloin or hide any of their able hackney horses

purveyors and larderers and officers of the household levied provisions on all townsfolk,[1] save the few who had been lucky enough to gain the king's grant of protection,[2] seized what they needed of their corn and bread and salted meats, called out the inhabitants for forced labour, billeted the crowd that made up the royal train on the various householders,[3] and in fact governed at their own will any town through which the king passed. A happy obscurity and distance from the court could alone preserve a little borough like Bridport from exactions of royal travellers; and its people might bear with resignation a poverty and insignificance which at least protected them from evils

in any privy places, whereby the King's service may be hindered, prolonged, or undone." (Hist. MSS. Com. ix. 287.) For Romney see Lyon's Dover, ii. 341. In some towns certain innkeepers had letters patent to require horses and carts for the King's service. The right was greatly abused, and such patents declared void by Statute. (28 Henry VI. cap. 2.)

[1] For purveyors, Rogers' Agric. and Prices, 1., 119, 166. Brinklow's Complaint, 19, 20. Rot. Parl. i. 400. At Lynn the King's Larderer would claim ships to go out fishing for the King's provisions, or perhaps to carry 5,000 fish for the King's household. (Hist. MSS. Com. xi. 3, 188-9.) As late as 1493 it was necessary for Canterbury (which had been freed by charter from these exactions in 1414) to get a "breve" from Henry the Seventh to give its inhabitants a summary means of resisting the demands of the King's Purveyors. (Ibid. ix. 168.) For seizing of carts, see Nottingham Records, i. 118. The King's cart-takers in the seventeenth century, Hist. MSS. Com. v. 407.

[2] Instances in Chester, 1282, Hemingway's Chester, i. 132.

[3] Among the Bristol liberties was one that no burgess nor inhabitant of Bristol shall against his will receive none host into his house by lyverance of the King's Marshall. (Ricart, 24.)

of so great magnitude to poor and over-tasked workers.

V. There was yet another form in which the power of the crown pressed upon the inhabitants of a borough. Privileges granted by the king might be withdrawn at his caprice ; and the burghers lay absolutely at his mercy for all the liberties and rights which they enjoyed. At the beginning of every reign the confirmation of their charters, and the affixing of the new king's seal, had to be won by such payments and bribes as the officials in high places judged that the burghers could afford.[1] The king might at any moment raise a question as to the value of their charters ; or he might make some public revolution

[1] Instances of the necessity for new grants and confirmations and the heavy consequent expenses are too numerous to quote. In Canterbury £36 was paid in 1460 for a new charter, and other payments connected with the same business were made in the following year. In 1472 messengers were sent to London for the obtaining again of a charter of liberties. Two years later an envoy rode to London to treat with the Treasurer, Lord Essex, about a writ of proviso touching the liberties of the city, and a grant was then made, probably in return for heavy payment, which confirmed a recent restoration of ancient privileges. A magnificent supper given to Lord Essex expressed the gratitude of the city. In 1474 the city paid for a proviso to confirm the restorations of their liberties. In 1475 there was an investigation *in camera* of the charters and muniments concerning the bounds of the liberty; and in 1481 payments were made to friends and patrons who had helped them with the King in preserving the liberties of the city. At the accession of Henry the Seventh it became necessary to buy renewal and confirmation of the charter, and this was completed in 1487. In 1490 the Mayor conferred with Cardinal Morton on the renewal and extension of the liberties of the city. (Hist. MSS. Com. ix. 140 *et seq.*, 170.) See Romney, Ibid. v. 534–5, 537, 539, 543–4.

or local disturbance the occasion for a revision or a threatened withdrawal of ancient "customs."[1] When their rights were menaced the townsmen had but one resource, and hastily met together, as in the case of Bridport, to order by the "common assent" that reins and horse nets should be provided at the public cost and sent to London, for "furthering the common business."

For the whole of this complicated system of administration was kept in working order by a generous system of bribes—bribes given largely and openly, registered in the public accounts, and granted indifferently to any official, great or small, who might be induced by a timely gift to "show his friendship." Towns won the renewal or the preservation of their chartered rights by offerings to king or queen, to chancellors and bishops and great officers of the household, with whom they interceded by the aid of a "cow-pull" of swans or cygnets or heronshaws, a porpoise, a store of dried sprats, or a cask of wine. "The law is ended as a man is friended," said the wise folk of the fifteenth century, and if any legal question arose the town could only "have a verdict" when due "courtesies," as they were called, were prepared for justices and their clerks, barons of the exchequer and sheriffs and counsel and attorneys, besides any sums required to pay a "friendly" jury.[2]

[1] Writ of inquisition as to privileges of Cinque Ports. (Hist. MSS. Com. vi. 544.) The instance of charters forfeited on these grounds are very frequent.

[2] In Southampton a hogshead of Gascony wine was given "by common consent" to the sheriff to have his friendship in the

If the king sent pressing and overwhelming demands for money, a deputation of leading burghers would hurry up to Westminster, carrying gifts and bribes to the Clerk of the Rolls and the usher of Parliament as a peace offering.[1] Or some gracious patron might be persuaded to divert from the town "a quest of the Admiralty, that it would not come thither as was intended to come."[2] When men were called out for war the community would consult by what gifts or "courtesies" it might arrange "to have pardoning that we should not ride up so many men as the said warrant commanded."[3] At the appearance of the King's harbinger or sergeant-at-arms the first thought was to collect a sum which might induce their formidable guest to limit the number of troops billeted on the town, or even to march them away altogether.[4] In the same way if a messenger appeared bearing part of the body of a traitor who had been executed, which by the King's orders

return of a jury. In 1428 a sum of 13s. 4d. was paid for returning "friends of the town" on a jury to settle a question which had arisen between the King and Southampton as to which was to have the goods and chattels of a felon who had run away. (Hist. MSS. Com. xi. 3, 140, 142.) See also Ibid. v. 518.

[1] Hist. MSS. Com. v. 539. The Lieutenant of Dover, who settled the amount and division of benevolences required from the Cinque Ports, had also his offerings from the various towns that they might be well dealt with. (Ibid. v. 527.)

[2] Ibid. v. 528. These courts on the sea-shore meant considerable expense in fees and feasts.

[3] Hist. MSS. Com. v. 491. In 1474 money was given by Canterbury to Kyriel, that he might excuse the city from sending men and ships to the war. (Ibid. ix. 143.)

[4] Ibid. v. 518, 522.

was to be set up on the gate of the borough, the inhabitants would give him a present to carry on his burden to some other town.[1]

Counted among the usual incidents of government, and reckoned in the ordinary expenditure of the municipality, the payment of such bribes was to all concerned merely the customary mode of defraying some of the expenses of administration;[2] and the public sense acquiesced in a prudent and necessary method of carrying on the affairs of state. Gifts to great officials were not tokens of servitude required only from dependent towns, but a tribute levied as rigorously from the free boroughs. The bribes demanded were not less in number; the main difference was that they went into different pockets. Thus the offerings required from Canterbury when its municipal existence was most vigorous and self-dependent, were naturally on a scale unexampled in a little place such as Bridport.[3] The gifts of the town were scattered far and wide; a pike to a London lawyer, wine to Master John Fineux the justiciar, a conger eel to the Dean of Windsor, wine to the chancellor of the Archbishop of York, payments to the Bishop of Winchester that the city might "have his mediation," gifts to Cardinal Beaufort to win his help

[1] Hist. MSS. Com. v. 543. Three and fourpence, and 18d. for a pair of boots as a reward.

[2] See in Winchester the gifts to the coroner's clerk, to jurors at the Pavilion, to the King's taxers, to the wife of the Sheriff, to the Bailiff of the Soke of Winton, and so on. (Hist. MSS. Com. vi. 595-605.)

[3] Hist. MSS. Com. xi. part 3, 138-149. The expenses at Lynn were very great. (Ibid. 218-225.)

when it was proposed to change the municipal constitution, offerings to the Bishop of St. David's—who nominally got a double supply, one present being provided for the Episcopus Menevensis and another for the Episcopus de Seynt Taffey[1] to " have their friendship" with the King in the anxious days of 1483. Royal dukes and court officers, bishops, chamberlains; notaries, clerks of the Rolls, knights who had access to the palace, sheriffs, judges of the king's court, were sumptuously feasted, and messengers knocked at the doors of their lodgings laden with pheasants, cygnets, capons, rams, oxen, geese, with Rhenish wine, wine of Tyre, claret, muscatel, and red wine and white by thirty or fifty gallons at a time. In the revolutionary times of 1470 the citizens were unluckily associated with the party of Henry the Sixth, and for years after their wealth was lavished in buying back the favour of the court. The Duchess of York, who had once been accustomed to receive her tribute of Rhenish wine, red wine, and wine of Tyre, visited the city in 1471, when her son was in difficulties; but the prudent citizens now only offered the poor lady " for bread 12*d*." On the other hand when Edward was again triumphant officers and commissioners of the king of every degree accepted pheasants, geese, capons and red wine. The burghers presented to the Duke of Clarence a load of claret and capons which it took four men to carry. Soon after when the King's

---

[1] Doubtless a scribe's error for Llandaff. (Hist. MSS. Com. ix. 145.) The Bishop of St. David's writes that "in many great cities and towns were great sums of money given him which he hath refused."

Chamberlain came to Canterbury, he was given his dinner at the "Swan," one of the inns belonging to the corporation, where he feasted off "a wild beast called a bukk" which had been brought from Westenhanger; and after the dinner eight men carried a peace-offering to his inn, two swans, two fat capons, four capons, four pheasants, fifty-six gallons of red wine, and half a gallon of muscatel; and shortly after another tribute was sent up to him in London.[1]

But behind this customary system of bribes and gifts lay the deep and permanent trouble of perpetual uncertainty and dread. Everywhere authority came home to the unhappy subjects as a mere matter of arbitrary and violent caprice, and the main function of government as that of rough extortion and successful pillage; while the recognition of privilege on every side blotted out all sense of equality before the law, and the weak, knowing all their helplessness, were as anxious to buy the commodity of protection, as the powerful, conscious of their might, were willing to make a gain of it. Canterbury sought the patronage of leading people in the county or the court;[2] Norwich profited, so long as he was in favour, by the protection of Suffolk; York gratefully recognised the services of the Duke of Gloucester. When he

[1] Hist. MSS. Com. ix. 141-3.

[2] At the important meeting in 1474, when the constitution of the town was reaffirmed, William Haute, the lord of the manor of Bishopsbourne (four miles away), who was then patron of the town, was put at the head of the list before even the five aldermen, the sheriff, or any town officers, as establishing and ordaining the town ordinances. Poynings, Browne, Guildford, were at different times patrons of the city.

passed through the city, an order was sent out by the corporation that every alderman and council man in livery, and every member of any craft in his best array, should go out to meet him at the gate—the commoners being in their places by the early dawn, at three of the morning, the grand people an hour later in consideration of their rank. In 1482 the Duke acted as mediator between the city and the King in the matter of the election of a mayor, and the council agreed that in regard of "the great labour of the good and benevolent lordship," that he "have at all times done for the weal of this city," the whole community should join in giving him "a laud and thank;" and the aldermen dressed in scarlet, with the Council of Twenty-four in murrey or crimson, attended at the mayor's house to present the Duke with a gift of all kinds of wine and fish, and lead a procession of the whole commonalty to his lodging at the Friar Austins.[1]

Patronage and protection, however, were dearly bought at all times, and at any moment their price, determined by the reckless habits of a lord, or the necessity of a king, or the greed of a sheriff, might be raised so as to bring years of confusion to municipal finances. Demands sudden and irregular, which no wisdom could calculate beforehand and no prudence could avert, wasted the substance of the people; and thrifty burghers learned to measure their progress to independence by their success

[1] Davies' York, 128-9, 123-5. For an interesting instance of beneficent protection in 1605, see Hibbert's Influence and Development of Guilds, p. 95.

in limiting the pleas which the great could urge as reasons for levying toll and tribute on their labour. The love of liberty was forced on them by the practical needs of life. A people long used to hardship, dependent on the capricious mercy of their masters, subject without appeal to impositions laid on them by the stronger hand, they learned by daily experience that government by laws made without their own consent, and administered by officers imposed on them against their will, was the very definition of slavery. By a rude experience of alien officials they were effectually taught that the first necessity of a free community was the right of choosing its own governors, that the control of life and goods and the responsibilities of any office of honour and profit and trust in the town should no longer be entrusted to strangers, but committed into the hands of their own fellow citizens, of whose fidelity, patriotism, and credit they could assure themselves. It was impossible that all the fortunes of their commerce should hang on the will of some distant master whose faculty of ruling them in all their concerns rested on the mere superiority of power; and traders everywhere demanded authority to order their own business, and rule their markets. The inhabitants of a town could not claim the property in their own borough till they had secured the right of holding it directly from the crown at a yearly rent which they themselves should pay into the exchequer at Westminster;[1] and even then their

[1] The election of a Mayor as a responsible person through

privileged existence was a mere matter of royal caprice till they found means to have the corporate succession of the borough legally recognized.[1] Their municipality was threatened with financial calamities unless they could win exemption from the Statute of Mortmain, and obtain the right of holding property for the town's good.[2] The bondage under which they lay to the sheriff[3] and tax-gatherer could only be broken when they were given full powers to assess and collect all their own taxes.[4] Vexed and impoverished by journeys to

whom the King could deal with the town was probably often connected with the settlement of the fee-farm rent. In Liverpool the first mention of a Mayor is in 1356, the very next year the fee-farm was granted to the Mayor and others on behalf of the burgesses for ten years. (Picton, Municipal Records of Liverpool, i. 13-15.)

[1] As against the idea of Merewether and Stephens, that charters of municipal incorporation only began in 1439, Dr. Gross points out that such a charter occurs in 1345, that in the time of Edward the First the technical conception of municipal incorporation was familiar, and that long before the judicial conception came into being the borough had a real corporate existence, and exercised all the functions of a corporate body. (Gild Merchant, i. 93, &c.)

[2] In 1391 the Statute of Mortmain was extended to cities and boroughs. (Statutes, 15 Richard II., cap. 5.) Even when license to hold land was granted by the Crown the amount was strictly limited, and the power of refusal or of limitation was a serious consideration to the town.

[3] According to Mr. Round, London found means of annexing the shire of Middlesex instead of asking to be separated from it. (Geoffrey de Mandeville, 347-373.)

[4] We have a hint of a troublesome mode of interference with the municipal taxation in an incident in Norwich in 1268, when "the lord the King commanded all his bailiffs that, *for a fine*

distant courts for justice, harassed by the interference in their most private affairs of some far-off governor, forced in every recurring emergency to carry appeals for justice or petitions for favour to an alien power separate from all their interests, they urged the claim that right should be done to the burghers in their own courts and by their own officers as of the very essence of any true liberty. "We are the citizens of our lord the king," said the burghers of Hereford, " and have the custody of his city for us and for his heirs and for our heirs, and we ought not to go out of our city for the recovering of our debts, for divers dangers and misfortunes which might happen to our wives and children ; and if we ought to spend our goods and chattels in parts afar off, by impleading and labouring for that, by that means and the like we shall be impoverished ; and being made poor, we shall not have wherewith to keep the city, and so disinheritance by such ways would easily fall upon our children."[1] And as the burghers claimed that each community should have absolute control over its members for the peace and order of the commonwealth, so they were resolute that no powerful patron, within or without the borough, should on

of £10, which Margaret the Taneresse of Norwich made with the same lord the King, he granted to her such liberty that for the whole time of her life she should be quit from all his tallages in the town of Norwich .... for whatsoever cause they may be made. And he commanded that they vex not the aforesaid Margaret contrary to this his grant." (Norwich Documents, pr. 1884, 9.) In any case where the tallage was a fixed sum due from the town some one else would have to pay Margaret's share.   [1] Journ. Arch. Ass. xxvii. 478.

any plea whatever venture to aid or " maintain " a townsman who had offended against the municipal law, " because by such maintainers or protectors a common contention might arise amongst us, and horrible manslaughter be committed amongst us, and the loss of the liberty or freedom of the city to the disinheritance of us and our children; which God forbid that in our days by the defect of us, should happen or fall out in such a manner."[1] From the first they were forced to look beyond the question of mere personal regard, seeing how deeply legal forms of procedure affected their common life as a separate society, and they had their grave reasons of state for insisting that the older forms of administering justice in their courts should be maintained, and trial by combat rejected and abolished from among them, " by reason of perpetual enmity of us the parents and of our children, which might turn to the ruin or perdition of the city and other innumerable accident dangers."[2] In the same way

[1] Journ. Arch. Ass. 479. Hist. MSS. Com. ix. 241–2. Statute of Maintenance, 13 Richard II., Stat. 3. For the jealousy of the towns as to any inhabitant relying for protection on a lord outside, see p. 183, note 2.

[2] Journ. Arch. Ass. xxvii. 482. For a duel in Leicester in 1201, see Select Civil Pleas, Selden Society, p. 33. Judicial combat in Fordwich with an alien had to take place in the middle of the river Stour, the alien standing up to his middle in the water, while the Fordwich man apparently fought from a boat tied to the quay, with an instrument called an "ore," three yards long. (Hist. MSS. Com. v. 442.) In 1200 " the citizens of Lincoln came and produced the king's charter which witnesses that none of them need plead outside the city walls except the king's moneyers and servants, and that they need not fight the duel

they were driven to realize the necessity of having some share in deciding on the laws by which they were to be governed, and which might have the gravest results to their little state ; as, for example, when the people of Leicester petitioned for a charter from Henry the Third to do away with the ancient usage of " borough English," and grant the right of inheritance to the eldest son, since owing to defective heirs and their weakness, the town was falling into ruin and dishonour.[1]

because of any appeal." An accused man answered the charges against him " word by word as a free citizen of Lincoln," and " according to the franchise of the town " waged law with thirty-six compurgators. (Select Pleas of the Crown, Selden Society, p. 39.) For compurgation in Sandwich in 1493, Boys, 680.

With old forms of trial old forms of punishment were allowed to survive. In Sandwich, if a man failed to clear himself by compurgation of a charge of homicide or theft he was condemned to be buried alive in a place called the Thiefdown at Sandown. (Ibid. 465.) Felons were also drowned in a stream called "the Gestling"; but in 1313 a complaint was made that the prior of Christchurch had diverted the course of the stream, and that criminals could not be executed in that way for want of water. (Ibid. 664.) At Dover and Folkestone a thief was killed by being thrown from a cliff, and at Winchelsea was hanged in the salt marsh. (Lyon's Dover, i. 231.) In others of the Cinque Port towns when a thief was taken his ear was nailed to a post or cart-wheel and a knife put in his hand, he had to free himself by cutting off his ear, to pay a fine, and to forswear the town. In 1470, 12d. was paid "for nailing of Thomas Norys his ear." (Hist. MSS. Com. v. 525, 530.)

[1] Hist. MSS. Com. viii. 407. Nottingham retained the old usage till after the fourteenth century ; Records, i. 175. Exeter till 1581 ; Freeman's Exeter, 119. The question may have partly turned on the form of government adopted in the town and the work required of the common assembly in which the burghers voted.

All these privileges and exemptions were matters of negociation between the borough and the king or the lord of the manor to be bought for money, or for political support, or for loans in time of need.[1] The people everywhere simply won such advantages as time and opportunity allowed, and secured benefits which were measured by the grace of the king, or by the price they could afford to pay, or by the show of resistance they could make to their lord. Nor was there anything startling or revolutionary about the first beginnings of independent municipal life. The town assemblies which discussed and inaugurated a new constitution transacted their business with a completeness and accuracy of methodical routine which might kindle the sympathy of a Town Council of modern Birmingham. In the organization of "meetings" the mediæval Englishman seems to have had nothing to learn, and the doings of the people of Ipswich when they got their first charter from King John in 1200 carry us into the quiet atmosphere of a board-room where shareholders and directors of some solid and old-established company assemble for business with the decorum and punctuality of venerable habit.[2] The charter granted those essential privileges which were

[1] It has been argued (Gneist, Constit. Communale, tr. Hippert, i. 263 ; v. 275) that the State created local government in the towns as a method of developing better administration, and that it was therefore only accidentally and as a secondary consequence that independence and local liberties came in the wake of this administrative system. The facts, however, of their story make it perfectly clear that municipal liberties were of natural growth, and sprang out of local needs rather than out of Court statecraft.

[2] Gross, i. 23 ; ii. 115.

recognized by all boroughs as of the very first importance—the right henceforward to deal in financial matters directly with the Exchequer, and no longer act as a mere fragment of the shire through the sheriff; to be free of tolls on trade throughout the kingdom, and have a Guild Merchant with all its commercial privileges; to carry out justice according to the ancient custom of the borough; and to elect each year from among themselves officers to rule over the town, who being thus appointed by common consent could only be removed from office by the unanimous counsel of the whole people. The charter was given on May 25, and in the following month a general assembly of the burghers was summoned. At this meeting they first elected the chief officers for the year, the bailiffs and coroners, and then proceeded to decide by common counsel that a body of twelve "Portmen" should be appointed to assist them; and three days later these too were formally chosen through another and more complicated system of election by a select body of citizens named for the purpose. Having taken an oath faithfully to govern the borough and maintain its liberties, and justly to render the judgments of its courts, the new officers then caused all the townsmen to stretch forth their hands towards the Book, and with one voice solemnly swear from that hour to obey and assist them in guarding the liberties of the town. Twelve days after this they met to ordain the most necessary rules for the administration of the town. Two months were then spent in drawing up "Ordinances" which were finally solemnly read to the whole people assembled in the church-yard, and received their unanimous consent. And lastly a month later, on October 12, the organization of the Merchant Guild for the regulation of trade was completed and its officers elected; the newly made Common Seal[1] was inspected; and the community ordered that a record of all their laws and free customs should be written for perpetual remembrance in a roll to be called Domesday. And thus with all the grave ceremony which befitted the dignity of a new republic, Ipswich started on its independent career as a free borough.

[1] The seals of English towns of the thirteenth, fourteenth, and fifteenth centuries were of finer workmanship than any in Europe. They generally represented a fortress or walled town, a ship, a patron saint, or heraldic arms, but it is interesting that in no case is the figure of the Mayor used to typify the borough save in the London seal, where he stands among the corporation and citizens. Sometimes a bridge is given, as at Barnstaple; in two or three cases the Guild Hall.

CHAPTER VII

BATTLE FOR FREEDOM

(1.) *Towns on Royal Demesne*

So auspicious a beginning of municipal life as was granted to Ipswich did not however fall as a matter of course to the lot of every English town, nor was political liberty by any means an inevitable consequence of favourable commercial conditions, or necessarily withheld from boroughs in a humbler way of trade. In a society where all towns alike depended upon some lord of the manor who owned the soil and exercised feudal rights over his tenants, that which mainly determined for each community the measure of independence it should win, and the price which its people should pay for liberty, was the form of lordship to which it was subject. By the decisive accidents of position and tenure the fate of the town was fixed, rather than by the merits or exertions of the burghers.

First among the boroughs in number and importance were those in "ancient demesne"—that is, boroughs which held directly from the king, and were therefore reckoned as being a part of the national property, such as Canterbury, York, Winchester, Southampton, Yarmouth, Nottingham, Gloucester, and so on. A second group was formed by the towns which belonged to a lay noble, like Morpeth, Berkeley, or Leicester; or were held by him as a special grant from the king, as Barnstaple or Liverpool. Finally there were the towns on ecclesiastical estates, whether they were the property of a bishopric like Lynn, which was under the Bishop of Norwich, Wells under the Bishop of Wells, Romney and Hythe under the Archbishop of Canterbury; or whether they owed suit and fealty to a convent, as the towns of Reading and St. Albans, which belonged to the abbots of those monasteries respectively, Fordwich to St. Augustine's at Canterbury, Weymouth to St. Swithun's at Winchester.[1] In all these various groups the towns were equally willing to relieve their feudal superior, king or lord or bishop, of the cares of government, and the only question was how far the king would go in supporting these demands, or how far the noble and ecclesiastic could be compelled to acquiesce in a re-distribution of feudal jurisdiction and privileges in favour of traders and "mean" people.

Happily for the national wealth and freedom the great majority of towns in England, and almost all those of importance, were part of the royal demesne, and the king was lord of the soil. Fenced in by privi-

[1] A few towns, in the case of some members of the Cinque Ports, depended on another borough.

leges which had been devised to protect the interest of the King, and which they gradually found means to transform into institutions for the protection of their own interests, the burghers on ancient demesne were bound into one fellowship by the inheritance of a common tradition and common immunities;[1] and regarding their towns as the very aristocracy among the boroughs, enjoyed a self-conscious dignity such as the Great Powers of Europe might feel towards the less favoured minor States. There is the ring of a haughty spirit in the answer sent by the men of Hereford when the people of Cardiff begged for a copy of their "customs" to help them in deciding on the constitution of their own government. "The King's citizens of Hereford," they say, "who have the custody of his city (in regard that it is the principal city of all the market towns from the sea even unto the bounds of the Severn) ought of ancient usage to deliver their laws and customs to such towns when need requires, yet in this case they are in no wise bound to do it, because they say they are not of the same condition; for there are

---

[1] For the position of tenants on ancient demesne, see Vinogradoff, Villainage in England, ch. iii. Mr. Maitland (Select Pleas in Manorial Courts, ii. 99, &c.) gives an account of King's Ripton, a manor on ancient demesne, whose tenants when transferred to the Abbey of Ramsey were always fighting with their new lords as to the services due from their holdings. "The privileged nature of the tenure had engendered a privileged race, very tenacious of its land and of its customs" (p. 105). The study of the way in which the customs of ancient demesne affected the later constitution of the boroughs lies outside my subject, and is therefore merely indicated.

some towns which hold of our Lord the King of England and his heirs without any mesne lord ; and to such we are bound, when and as often as need shall be, to certify of our laws and customs, chiefly because we hold by one and the same tenure ; and nothing shall be taken of them in the name of a reward, except only by our common town clerk for the writing and his pains as they can agree. But there are other market towns which hold of divers lords of the kingdom wherein are both natives and rustics of ancient time, who pay to their lords corporal service of divers kinds, with other services which are not used among us, and who may be expelled out of those towns by their lords, and may not inhabit in them or be restored to their former state, but by the common law of England.[1] And chiefly those and others that hold by such foreign services in such towns are not of our condition ; neither shall they have our laws and customs but by way of purchase, to be performed to our Capital Bailiff as they can agree between them, at the pleasure and to the benefit of the city aforesaid." [2]

I. Singular advantages, indeed, fell to the lot of towns thus happily situated on the national estate. The King was a Lord of the Manor too remote to have

[1] Vinogradoff, Villainage in England, 89. Compare the claim of Bristol to be "founded and grounded upon franchises, liberties, and free ancient customs, and not upon common law." (Ricart's Kalendar, 2.) For its liberties, see p. 24–5.

[2] As a matter of fact the various towns of this kind which applied to Hereford for any information as to its customs on any point had to pay one hundred shillings for the answer vouchsafed to them. (Journ. Arch. Ass. xxvii. 470.)

opportunity for overmuch meddling, and too greatly occupied with affairs of state to concern himself with the details of government in his numerous boroughs.[1] County magnates might cling passionately to the right of holding local courts as sources of power, and yet more important sources of wealth; but such rights were of small consequence to a powerful sovereign, who as supreme head of the law could call up criminals to his own judgement seat from every court in the country.[2] Confidence of supremacy made him careless to put it to the test by abrupt assertions of authority, as private owners, apprehensive and uncertain, might be tempted to do; and in his indifference to small uses of power and devices for paltry gain, he held loosely to rights that brought much trouble and little profit.[3] So long as his yearly

[1] There was constant watchfulness on both sides as to their rights. In 1400 the bailiffs of Ipswich granted land for the building of a mill for the benefit of the corporation; the King's officers declared the grant to have been made without the royal licence, and the mill was seized for the King. On the other hand, when the sheriff of the county arrested a felon in the liberties of Ipswich and put him in the King's jail, the bailiffs required that he should be given up to them. (Hist. MSS. Com. ix. 231, 246.)

[2] That is on the plea of lack of justice in the borough court. In 1401, when the citizens of Canterbury were summoned by the Crown to appear at Westminster about a breach of the statutes for the regulation of the victualling trades, they pleaded that by their charter they could not be called to answer civil suits out of their own city. (Hist. MSS. Com. ix. 167.)

[3] In 1299 the amercements ordered by the Leet Court of Norwich amounted to £72 18s. 10d; the amount accounted for by the collectors was £17 0s. 2d. (Hudson's Leet Jurisd. of Norwich, Selden Soc. xl.) Where there was profit to be made the King

ferm was punctually paid,[1] he was ready to grant to the townsfolk leave to gather into their own treasury the petty sums collected at the borough or manor courts,[2] or to make their mayor the king's escheator; and while he thus won their gratitude and friendship he lost nothing by his generosity. In surrendering local claims for a fixed payment, he not only relieved himself of the charge of salaries to a multitude of minor officials, but he had no longer to suffer from the loss of fines and dues and forfeitures

was, however, always on the alert. In Piers Ploughman, Passus v., 169, he complains bitterly of the lawyers; "through your law I believe I lose my escheats!"; and it was often late before he made the mayor escheator. In 1492 two Scotch priests were arrested in Ipswich for treasonable talk, and the King granted their chattels to one of his own serjeants. The bailiffs sent the Town Clerk to Henry to represent that the forfeited goods of felons rightly belonged to the town; to which the King answered that he would not for a thousand pounds infringe in the least degree their charters, but that the community had really no right to these particular chattels, since the priests, being Scotch and not the King's subjects, could not fairly be accused of treason, and had a perfect right to talk as they chose. On this plea he kept the goods. (Hist. MSS. Com. ix. 247.)

[1] This was strictly enforced, and the town charter forfeited if the rent fell into arrears. (Madox, 139, 161-2.) The towns therefore made careful provision for the discharge of the debt, sometimes setting apart a mill or some valuable property for its payment (Madox, Firma Burgi, 251-2; Hist. MSS. Com. ix. 198-9; Nott. Rec. i. 313), or assigning certain tolls or customs; (Shillingford's Letters, 92); or collecting it as rent from house to house. (Custumal in Hist. Preston Guild, 75.)

[2] When the ferm of Carlisle was raised from £60 to £80 the citizens were granted, as a help towards its payment, all fines inflicted by the King's judges within their walls. (Hist. MSS. Com. ix. 198, 200.) See also Norwich Documents, 16, 17.

which were nominally levied for the King, but which had a constant tendency to find their way into the pockets of the town officers or the tax-collectors rather than into his exchequer. In many cases, moreover, he may have gained considerably by the price which he demanded for his favours; and the royal accounts possibly give a very inadequate record of the number of special gifts of money and yearly annuities paid by boroughs to the King in return for liberties granted to them.[1]

II. As lord of the manor, therefore, the King was a liberal master, always ready to arrange a compromise with his tenants as to vexatious feudal claims. But he was equally ready to listen to their prayers for freedom from the control of officers of the Shire and the Hundred. So long as it was to the benefit of the central authority to break up and weaken provincial governments, to curtail the powers of the sheriff, to confound ambitious designs of local magnates, and shatter pretensions on the part of the nobles which might tend to strengthen hereditary enemies of the crown, so long the townspeople might count on the sovereign's support in the struggle for independence. In questions therefore that arose as to rival jurisdictions, in claims put forward by a borough

[1] Thus the Nottingham men paid 13s. 4d. a year to Henry the Sixth, at least from 1454, for liberties granted them. There is no entry of this in the King's accounts, and the only evidence of it is in the Nottingham Records (iii. 133). The loyal theory of Hereford was that "our goods and chattels are to be taken and taxed at his pleasure, saving unto ourselves a competent quantity for our sustentation and tuition of our city." (Journ. Arch. Ass. xxvii. 471.)

against neighbouring lords for rights of navigation or pasturage or fishing, in all disputes which were carried in the last resort to the arbitration of the king, his sympathy, especially if a fitting " courtesy " was offered by the burghers, was with his borough.[1] Powers won from local governments or from feudal lords were divided between the King and the municipality; and under shelter of the royal authority large rights of local self-government were rapidly gathered into the burghers' hands. Functions once exercised by the bailiff of the hundred and the sheriff of the county were handed over to the mayor; he collected the fee-ferm, held the view of frankpledge, levied taxes,[2] mustered the men-at-arms, and presided over civil and criminal courts.

III. Nor was there any serious difficulty as to the exercise of the sovereign rights of the crown. To the King it mattered little whether he sent a special deputy direct from the court, or whether he delegated powers to the mayor, and used him as an official immediately responsible to the crown; while on the other hand such a change meant much present solace to the townsfolk. A compromise was therefore easily brought about between the monarch and the people. The mayor was invariably appointed as the King's Clerk of the Market, the

[1] Nott. Rec. i. 225, 227, 413, 421.
[2] The agreement made in the fourteenth century which fixed the tenths and fifteenths for the towns at a permanent fixed sum, made it easy for the King to give over to local officials the levying of this tax without fear of injury to the Exchequer. (Stubbs, ii. 599, 600.)

Measurer and Gauger at the King's Standard, the Manager of the King's Assize; he became the representative of the sovereign in the most important charges of administration, as one of the King's Justices[1] in the town, as Admiral,[2] as Mayor of the Staple. Administrative changes such as these left the power of the sovereign untouched and cost him nothing; while on the other hand the central government was by this means provided with a ready-made staff of trained officials,—a staff which the King could not possibly have created,[3] nor paid out of his empty exchequer even if he had been able to create it—but which had become absolutely essential for carrying out the supervision of local

---

[1] Blomefield, iii. 137.

[2] The Admiral and his deputy had jurisdiction over everything done on the sea and the great rivers up to the first bridge. (13 Richard II. St. 1, cap. 5; 15 Richard II., cap. 3; Blomefield, iii. 103; Davies' Southampton, 239-40.) In 1487 the commonalty of Ipswich by a covenant with the King bound themselves to take surety of every owner, master, or purser of every English ship to twice the value of the ship, that the mariners should keep the peace on the sea; that if the surety by any means became less than twice the value of ship, tackle, and victuals, new security should be taken; and that the town should strive to arrest every robber and spoiler in the sea or the streams thereof. (Hist. MSS. Com. ix. 259-60.) In 1463 a charter was given to the corporation of York, constituting them the King's justiciaries for overlooking and preserving the main rivers of Yorkshire. For the expenses and difficulties which this involved, see Davies' York, 59-63, 82, &c.

[3] As an illustration of his difficulties, see the statute allowing sheriffs and escheators to remain for four years in office, because owing to pestilence and wars there was not a sufficiency of persons to occupy these offices. (9 Henry V. St. 1, cap. 5.)

affairs at a time when such supervision was growing more important every day, from the point of view both of the King and of the people. The towns on their side, relieved by the new system from miseries[1] under which they had suffered, readily forgot distinctions between laws made by them and made for them, so long as these were administered by officers of whom they were allowed the election and control.[2]

IV. Finally if the towns suffered from the officers of the royal household, a remedy was easily granted them. The sovereign found no personal

[1] In the lack of officials to carry out the regulations for the control of trade a number of private people got royal letters appointing them surveyors and correctors of victuallers in various cities and boroughs, and freely used their privileges for extortion and oppression, and the taking of heavy fines and ransoms; their patents were gradually withdrawn; and in 1472 an Act was passed that all such letters and patents should be void, and that the duty of searching and surveying victuals should rest wholly with the mayor or bailiff. (12 Edward IV. cap. 8.)

[2] In this matter the King was not allowed to interfere. In 1489 there was a dispute in Leicester between the Town Council and the Commons about the election of a Mayor. The matter was referred to the King, who issued a precept under the seal of the Duchy of Lancaster, showing that it was as Lord of the Manor and not as King that he interfered. He set aside both candidates and reappointed the last Mayor. The next year the question was settled by Act of Parliament. (Thomson, Mun. Hist., 84.) For authority exercised by Parliament see Norwich (Doc. Stanley v. Mayor, &c. 30.) When the citizens applied in 1378 to the King and Council for a renewal of their ancient liberty that no stranger should have power to buy or sell by retail, they were answered that it would not be valid "without Parliament"; they therefore pray for a grant by charter.

inconvenience in transferring the duties of these officers to the governors of the boroughs themselves; and the mayor or bailiff became the King's Steward, and Marshal of the King's Household in the borough. In short, as the towns advanced to independence, all manner of powers and responsibilities were heaped together on their chief officer, with no clear discrimination between his various and oddly mingled functions. Men did not pause to ask which of his masters the mayor at any given moment was serving, whether he was acting as head of the city government to carry out the burghers' will, or as the officer appointed by the sovereign to execute his laws;[1] and nice questions as to the exact division of authority which had really taken place were so manifestly irrelevant in presence of the harmonious concentration of all power in a single hand, that jealousies and suspicions on both sides were allayed, to the great furtherance of peace and concord. To the mediæval poet who drew a picture of Love as " the leader of our Lord's folk in Heaven," standing as a " mean " or mediator of peace, there was one obvious comparison—

[1] See Hudson's Leet Jur. in Norwich, Selden Soc. xxvii. xc. "For he doth represent to us the body of our King." (Journ. Arch. Ass. xxvii. 462.) See the proclamation of the London Mayor : "We do command, on behalf of our Lord the King, that no dyer or weaver shall be so daring," &c. (" Memorials of London," p. 309.) An illustration of how the King's law and the town law ran side by side may be seen in the fines for the breach of certain rules, as, for instance, the rule against liveries, which had to be paid both to the King and to the town. (English Guilds, 388-9.)

even "as the mayor is between the King and the commons."[1]

The history of the royal boroughs, therefore, so far as their relations with the King are concerned, reduces itself into a long list of favours asked and given. Frequent troubles of state no doubt stimulated the generosity of sovereigns; and times of political disturbance and revolution proved occasions when the towns rose into independence through the necessities of kings, who confirmed old franchises and granted new ones, and "right largely made charters thereof, to the intent to have the more goodwill and love in their land."[2] The civil wars under Henry the Second,[3] the money difficulties of Richard and John, the troubled minority of Henry the Third, the disorders under Edward the Second, the commercial policy of Edward the Third, the political insecurity of Henry the Fourth after his seizure of the throne, the financial needs of Henry the Fifth, the tumults and fears of the reign of Henry the Sixth, the anxiety of Edward the Fourth to conciliate the kingdom,—all these were so many heaven-sent opportunities for the burghers to win new instalments of local liberty; while the two periods of reaction brought about by the fear of the Peasant Revolt under Richard the Second, and the nervous apprehensions of Richard the Third, were themselves made use of by the governing class in the boroughs to confirm and tighten their authority.

[1] Piers Ploughman, Passus ii. 156, 157.
[2] Warkworth's Chronicle, 2.   [3] See Gross, ii. 245.

So monotonous indeed is the record of the burghers on the royal demesne, all moving together along the same well-beaten road to independence, winning the same privileges, even winning them at the same time,[1] that a brief statement of liberties secured by any single city will serve to illustrate the general history of all.

Up to the time of Henry the Second Norwich enjoyed certain liberties and privileges, but its citizens were practically feudal servants of the King, who appointed their governors, took the profits of their courts, and looked on the city as a private possession of his own. Their true freedom began with the charter granted them in 1194 by Richard the First.[2] They were to have the customs of London; the burgesses might not be summoned to answer any plea outside the city; they were henceforth to elect their own Provost, "such as may be fitting to us and to them;" and they were allowed to hold their city at a ferm rent of £108 a year, which they themselves, instead of the sheriff, should collect and pay to the Exchequer. For the confirmation of their rights, "and for having the city in their hand," the Norwich people paid 200 marks.[3] From this time the provost took

---

[1] The instances of similar grants made to various towns at almost the same date are too numerous to give, but they would form a striking list.

[2] Charter of Lincoln the same year; that of Winchester, 1190. (Stubb's Charters, 257–8). Nottingham and Northampton in 1200 (ibid. 301–3). The system of government adopted at Norwich was followed or imitated a little later by the neighbouring towns of Yarmouth and Colchester.

[3] Norwich Doc. Stanley *v.* Mayor, &c. p. 3. In the great

the place of the officer formerly appointed by the King, presided over the Borough Court in the Tolbooth and possibly held the view of frankpledge, and paid the fines of the courts into the city treasury. The sheriff of the county, however, still held a higher court, the *Curia Comitatus*, within the enclosure of the castle, where he exercised criminal jurisdiction, and jurors made the presentments ordered by the assize of Clarendon.[1]

But this power of the sheriff only lingered on for a few years. In 1223 a new arrangement was made between the citizens and Henry the Third. Norwich consisted of four distinct divisions which had been naturally formed out of the four hamlets created by the first settlers and which had by degrees become united into a single town:—*Conesford*, where the earliest comers gathered round the ford

---

majority of cases this grant was made once for all; but occasionally it was renewed from time to time. Thus Henry the Sixth in 1437 gave the mayor and burgesses of Bristol a lease of the town and its profits for a term of twenty years. In 1446 he granted a new lease for sixty years. In 1461 Edward the Fourth renewed the lease, not for a term of years, but for ever. (Seyer's Charters of Bristol, 105.) The ferm was granted in the same way for a term of years in the case of Dunwich, a royal town, where it was let out to the highest bidder. Here, however, the collection of rent was peculiarly uncertain from special circumstances (Madox, 235-8, 241); and in 1325 Dunwich, ruined by the filling up of its port, prayed to have the town taken into the King's hand and a guardian appointed. (Rot. Parl. i. 426.) For the inconvenience of this letting out to the highest bidder, see Madox, 251.

[1] Hudson, Municipal Organisation in Norwich, 20; Leet Jur. in Norwich, Selden Society, xvi. lxxii.

over the river, protected by the stream on one side, and on the other by the mound on which the castle stood in later days; the *Westwick*, whose name shews its later foundation, and which lay on the further side of the fortifications, within the bend of the river; the *Magna Crofta* or big field of the castle, lying below the entrenchments midway between Conesford and Westwick, which was made at the Conquest into a new ward, Mancroft Ward; and the *Ward-over-the-Water* on the further bank of the river, somewhat cut off from the rest of the town.[1] For the government of these "leets," as the divisions came to be called, it was decided in 1223 that the burghers should elect four bailiffs, one for each district.[2] There was no longer to be any provost, since the bailiffs were to take his place in joint government of the town, and were further to take over the criminal jurisdiction hitherto exercised by the sheriff in his court at the castle. From this time therefore most of the social, commercial, and criminal affairs of the city lay in the burghers' own hands.

The four bailiffs, however, had still no control over the castle and its entrenchments, nor over a wide reach of land that lay along the river, stretching past Conesford and Mancroft and Westwick—land owned by the prior and convent; nor had they any authority over the cathedral, the priory, and the bishop's palace that lay within Westwick, nor over property owned by them or by other ecclesiastical bodies which

[1] Hudson's Notes about Norwich, Norfolk Arch. vol. xii. p. 25.
[2] In 1288 the four bailiffs presided over the courts of these leets. (Hudson, Municipal Organisation, 16, 21.)

penetrated into the heart of the city; while on the other hand tenants of castle and prior and bishop were all making their profit out of the city trade, and enjoying its peace and protection. Therefore the next claim of the burghers necessarily was that the King should give to the municipality authority to tax for the common expenses all inhabitants alike, under whatever lord they held; and in 1229 they obtained a royal grant that all "who should partake of the liberties which we have granted to the said citizens of Norwich .... shall be taxed and give aid as the said citizens;" and that "if anyone has withdrawn from their customs and scots, he shall return to their society and custom, and follow their scot, so that no one shall be quit therefrom."[1] There was no trifling with the municipal authority in this matter; in 1236 and 1237 when the tenants of castle and prior attempted to resist the claim on their moneys, the sheriff was ordered to summon them before him to show by what right or warrant they claimed acquittance from payments to the city treasury; and again in 1276, when the tenants of the castle refused to pay their share of taxes, the case was brought before the barons of the exchequer, and an order came from Westminster that the sheriff was forthwith to levy the sum due and hand it over to the city.[2]

Henry the Third granted many other favours " to our beloved citizens of Norwich," feeling perhaps the

[1] Norwich Doc., Stanley *v.* Mayor, &c., p. 5.
[2] Ibid. 6, 8, 10. Blomefield, iii. 46, 62.

advantage of their friendship amid the increasing troubles of his reign; and the burghers of Norwich certainly, like those of Winchester, took sides with him in the war against Simon de Montfort.[1] In 1253 they had been allowed to enclose their city with a ditch.[2] In 1255 (twenty years before a general law was passed to this effect for all Englishmen), they were freed from arrest for debt of which they were not sureties or principal debtors. And in 1256 Henry granted a charter which ordered that the "citizens shall answer at our exchequer by their own hands for all debts and demands .... and that no sheriff or other bailiff of ours shall henceforth enter the city aforesaid to make distresses for any debts;" which decreed further that all merchants who shared in the Norwich liberties and merchandises were to pay the city taxes "wheresoever they shall make their residences;" and which ordained lastly that "no guild shall henceforth be held in the aforesaid city to the injury of the said city."[3] The sheriff was thus finally shut out from all land or houses held by the citizens; and absent merchants were subjected to their lot and scot.

From Edward the First the citizens in 1305 obtained the right to hold the Leet of Newgate in Norwich, which the King had "lately recovered against the Prior of Holy Trinity"; and further paid a fine down, and promised to pay £10 yearly into the Exchequer

---

[1] The convent sided with De Montfort. For the state of affairs in the city, see Blomefield, iii. 52, &c.

[2] Blomefield, iii. 49.

[3] Norwich Doc., Stanley v. Mayor, &c., 7.

for ever, for a charter granting that they should
not be impleaded outside the city; that they should
not be convicted by any foreigners but only by their
co-citizens, save in matters touching the King or the
whole commonalty; that the bailiffs should have
power to assess tallages and other reasonable aids "by
the assent of the whole of the commonalty, or of the
greater part of the same" for the protection and advantage of the city, and to make "reasonable distresses"
for the levying of these tallages as was done in other
cities; and that they should hold the Leet of Newgate
which the Crown had "lately recovered against the
Prior of Holy Trinity."[1] Further the burghers remembered a trouble into which they had fallen in
the case of a thief who had stolen some cloth and
brought much sorrow on the city; for having fled
to the church of St. George he finally escaped out
of it though the door was guarded by four parishes,
who were all fined for their lax vigilance; then being
caught and condemned by the bailiffs and commonalty
he was condemned to be hung, but at his burial found
to be still alive, and the man who had cut him down
was thrown into prison; and lastly the bailiffs were
accused of illegal action in hanging him "without any
man's suit and without capture in the act," and of
"taking up thieves and malefactors for trespasses
done outside the city and executing judgement on
them in the city," and the city liberties had been
seized into the King's hands, and a royal officer set to
rule over them.[2] So the burghers in 1307 presented

[1] Norwich Doc., Stanley v. Mayor, &c., 16, 17.
[2] Ibid. 10–12.

a petition that the right of infang theof and outfang theof, which they had used at all times "whereof memory runneth not," might now be definitely inserted in their charter. Further, since the sheriff "by malice" still found means on one excuse or another to arrest a citizen from time to time—and this though the Norwich people had the return of all manner of writs[1] so that neither the sheriff nor any foreign bailiff had any right to meddle with them—they required of the King that at their demand every citizen thus seized should be delivered over to them out of the hands of the alien. Likewise they prayed that so long as a burgher lived in the city he should never be required to attend any foreign court whatever by reason of any foreign tenure he might hold; and that no foreign tenement should give the right to sheriffs or foreign bailiff to summon him to be in juries or inquests outside the city. Lastly, as a protection against any danger of forfeiting their franchise by failure to pay the ferm rent, they asked permission for the corporation to hold in perpetual possession certain lands and houses the profits of which might be set apart for the rent.[2]

Under Edward the Third the sheriff of the county was deprived of his last plea for interference within the city walls. Up to this time he had still collected rents and taxes and done justice for the tenants of the Castle Fee; and the ditches of the

---

[1] This meant that it was the town bailiff who was to return the certificate of what he had done in execution of a writ addressed to him, instead of this being returned, as formerly, by the sheriff. [2] Norwich Documents, 16, 18.

Castle and the Fee, thus freed from city rule, had been made a sort of refuge for felons and malefactors flying from the jurisdiction of the city officers. All this, however, was in 1346 handed over to the bailiffs, and the sheriff was in no wise to interfere.[1] Moreover, in consideration of the cost to which the citizens had gone in enclosing the city, they were set free for ever from the jurisdiction of the clerk of the market of the King's household.[2] Norwich was further given its own Admiral, who sailed about in the "admiral's barge," and who held admiralty courts and administered its law.[3] In 1331 it became a Staple town, and its mayor was made a mayor of the Staple, with a salary of £20 and a seal given by the king.[4]

Meanwhile the Norwich people had been gradually perfecting their own internal system of government—a system which will be described in a later chapter—and in the difficulties of Henry the Fourth they found opportunity to complete their work. A sum of £1,000 given to the King, besides heavy fines paid in bribes on all sides, secured in 1403 a charter which finally guaranteed to them the constitution of their choice.[5] Norwich was made into a county of itself. A mayor was appointed, who was given supreme rights of juris-

[1] Norwich Documents, 25.   [2] Ibid. 26.
[3] Blomefield's Hist. of Norfolk, iii. 103.
[4] Ibid. iii. 81, 94-5. In 1393 the corporation was granted shops and houses held of the King and worth £10 yearly, the profits of which were to be spent on repairing the walls and towers. For this licence they had to pay the King £100.   Norwich Documents, 32.   [5] Ibid. 33-37.

diction in the city, and received from the King himself a sword which was to be carried before him with the point erect, along with the gold or silver maces borne by the serjeants-at-mace. The four bailiffs were replaced by two sheriffs, also elected by the burgesses, who were charged with matters concerning the interests of the crown which had formerly been the business of the bailiffs, and were responsible for the yearly rent of the city. The mayor was appointed the King's escheator, and thus the last office which had been reserved in alien hands was given over to the municipality. Finally in token of the consummation of the municipal hopes the old seal of the bailiffs was abolished to make way for a new city seal.

Norwich was but one among a number of boroughs whose inhabitants quietly and steadily gathered to themselves the liberties that made them free, for in the fellowship of towns holding of the King under a uniform tenure throughout the "ancient demesne," the list of privileges granted to any one became the model for its neighbours near and far.[1] With orderly progression, unbroken by any of the violent and dramatic incidents that indicate a time of conflict, all the bigger towns won by gradual instalments complete local independence. Such changes of method as we observe are simply changes made necessary by new national legislation, such as the form of incorporation required after the Statute of Mortmain,[2] or the right to elect Justices of the

[1] Gross, i. 240–267.
[2] Report on Municipal Corporations, 1835, pp. 16–17. Gross, i. 94, note 1.

Peace when one power after another had been given to these officers by law.[1] We do not distinguish seasons of plentiful harvest and periods barren of all growth; in one century as in another Kings stooped to accept the "courtesies" offered, and granted the favours solicited. Nor do we find records of advantages hastily given and timidly withdrawn; or, until the reign of Richard the Third,[2] is there any suggestion of anxiety on the part of Kings to check or limit the free action of the boroughs.[3] Up to that time rulers of the state seem to have had no apprehension of peril to public order, of jeopardy to trading interests, of injury to the ad-

[1] This change was evident from the time of Richard the Second, when the powers of the Justices were rapidly enlarged. See Statutes, 12 Richard II. cap. 10; 13 Richard II., 1, cap. 8; 13 Richard II., 1, cap. 13; 13 Henry IV. cap. 7; 2 Henry V. cap. 4; 2 Henry V., 1, cap. 8; 2 Henry VI. cap. 12; 2 Henry VI. cap. 14; 2 Henry VI. cap. 18; 6 Henry VI. cap. 3; 18 Henry VI. cap. 11.

[2] Southampton, Hist. MSS. Com. xi. 3, p. 104. Cases of interference occur in the unpublished records of Coventry. For Romney see Lyon's Dover, 313. In 1489 there was some such trouble in Leicester (Thompson, Mun. Hist., 84). And in 1512 there is another instance in Nottingham (Records, iii. 341-2). From the time of Richard the Third there seems evidence of the growth of a new anxiety in the central government about the democratic movement in the boroughs, and a determination to reserve power in the hands of a small corporation. An earlier instance may perhaps be found in the Exeter quarrel from 1477 to 1482 (English Guilds, 305, &c.); and in York in 1482 (Davies, 122-4).

[3] There were many cases in which a town's privileges were forfeited, whether for arrears of rent (Madox, 139, 161-2) or for other causes (154-5, 157). The franchises of Nottingham

ministration of justice, of possible usurpations by the municipalities which might bring them into collision with the ordered forces of the world; and for three hundred years statesmen freely allowed the growth of municipal ambition, and gave full scope for the developement of all the various systems of local self-government. The full importance of these facts only becomes clear when we turn to the history of the towns that were under subjection to other lords

were twice forfeited for some unknown cause—in 1283 for three years (Records, i. 56), and in 1330 for a short time. (Ibid. 102.) In the same year Edward the First seized the franchises of Derby because of exactions of the Merchant Guild, but restored them on payment of a fine. (Gross, ii. 53.) For the case of Sandwich (Boys, 661, 676). Ipswich charter withdrawn, 1285; regranted, 1291. (Hist. MSS. Com. ix. 230, 239, 243.) Chester in 1409. (Hemingway's Chester, i. 137.) The liberties of Carlisle were forfeited for a short time for some irregularity in the town courts in the thirteenth century. (Gross, ii. 38.) Southampton lost its freedom in 1276 and 1285, and again in the next century for letting the French into the town. (Davies' Southampton, 33, 35, 79.) Norwich suffered several times; for its attack on the Priory in 1272; for an accusation of having exceeded its powers in punishing crime in 1286; for riots about the election of mayor in 1437; and for Gladman's insurrection in 1443. (Stanley v. Mayor, &c., Norwich Doc., 9–12. Proceedings, Privy Council, v. 45. Hist. MSS. Com. i. 103.) In these cases a royal officer was appointed to rule the town; and the complaint of Scarborough, when Edward the Second in 1324 deprived it of the right of direct payment to the Exchequer, shows how a town suffered when its ferm was leased out. (Rot. Parl. i. 423.) The loss of liberty was always temporary, lasting from a few months to five or six years, and had no political significance as in France, where it formed part of a settled policy and had results which to the English mind seem of peculiar importance in the history of constitutional development.

than the nation itself; and compare the peaceful negotiations by which matters were arranged between the royal boroughs and the State, with the violence of feeling aroused when the misgivings and alarms of private owners were brought into the controversy.

CHAPTER VIII

BATTLE FOR FREEDOM

(2) *Towns on Feudal Estates*

ON the King's lands, as we have seen, the interests of the monarch never came into collision with the interests of his burghers, and the townsfolk found an easy way to liberty. From time to time they presented a petition for freedom, brought their gifts to win the sovereign's favour, and joyfully carried back to their fellow citizens a new charter of municipal privileges. But the condition of the towns that belonged to noble or baron was doubly depressed from the standpoint of their happier neighbours. Of secondary importance alike in numbers, in wealth, or in influence, as compared to those on royal demesne, they for the most part never emerged into any real consequence; while their lord had every reason to oppose the growth of independence in his boroughs, and lacked nothing for its complete suppression but the requisite power. New franchises were extorted from his weakness rather than won from his good will, and where acquiescence in the town's liberties was not irresistibly forced on him his opposition was dogged and persevering.

The dispute was none the less intense because under the conditions of English life the controversy between the town and the feudal lord was limited within a very narrow field; for the burghers saw well how the lord's claims to supremacy might permanently fetter an active community of traders, and on this point townspeople fought with a pertinacity determined by the conviction that all their hopes of prosperity depended on victory. To manufacturers and merchants the rule of an alien governor was fatal; trade died away before vexatious checks and arbitrary imposts, and enterprising burghers hastened to forsake the town where prosperity was stunted and liberty uncertain, and take up citizenship in a more thriving borough. Success and emancipation went hand in hand; for the effects of a maimed and imperfect freedom were always disastrous and far-reaching, and there is not a single instance of an English town which remained in a state of dependence and which was at the same time prosperous in trade.

One or two instances will be enough to show the extent and character of the traders' claim for "liberties." The burghers of Totnes, who had been fined for having a Guild by Henry the Second, had no sooner succeeded in securing its authorisation from John than they at once made it a weapon of offence, and a formidable weapon too with its roll of more than three hundred members, against their lord's control of the town market and of the shopkeepers. The Guild claimed the right to admit non-residents to their company, so that these might freely trade without paying any tribute to the lord for one year, after that giving six pence annually; and pretended to have authority to test weights and measures without orders from the lord's bailiff; to hold the assize of bread and ale and receive fines; and apparently to deal out justice for petty offences. These usurpations of his rights were discussed between the lord and his tenants with riots and contentions, in which the lord proved victorious in 1304, forcing the burghers to submit on every point in which the Guild tried to bring in customs which lay beyond the ancient rights of the community. They were forbidden to admit to the Guild anyone who had not a house in the town, and non-residents had to take oaths before his bailiff to pay a yearly fine to the lord. No trial of weights and measures could take place till orders had been issued to the Seneschal of the Guild by the lord's bailiff; when the trial came on bailiff and town provost sat beside him in the Guildhall to hear the charges, and even then all false or suspected measures were to be kept by the provost till the lord's next court. On the other hand the bailiff might hold a trial of measures whenever he judged that he could do the business better. So also the assize of bread was given to the lord's bailiff sitting with the provost of the town; all suspected bread and weights were to be seized by him, the offenders to be fined in the lord's court, all punishments by tumbril or pillory inflicted by his orders, and all proceeds of fines given over to him.

Lastly when small thefts and riots were to be judged
the bailiff sat by the town officers and as many
burgesses as chose to come, and took his share in the
proceedings—though occasionally in his absence the
town officers might act by common consent of the
community.[1]

Such was the comparative helplessness of a community which, with all its tenacity of purpose, could
neither urge custom nor tradition on its side in
pleading for independent rights. In the borough of
Barnstaple, on the other hand, which had been
granted by the King [2] to Sir John Cornwall and his
wife the Countess of Huntingdon, we have an instance
of the immense advantages possessed by a town which
though now in private ownership, inherited the
tradition of privilege which its people had won as
tenants of ancient demesne.[3] In 1423 the Mayor,

[1] Gross, ii. 235-243.

[2] Occasionally a borough was granted to a great noble or
court favourite; but more commonly as time went on the grant
merely meant giving a charge on the rent of the town. Thus
before 1339 Preston had been granted at various times to
neighbouring lords. In 1361 John of Gaunt held the manor,
but long before this the rights of the lord were so reduced that
they are practically never mentioned in the history of the town.
(Hewitson's History of Preston, 7-8.) For the troubles to which
the nobles' claims to rent might lead, see Davies' Southampton,
112. Edward the Fourth granted the ferm of Bristol to the
Queen for her life. The treasurer of the King's chamber declared
it had been assigned to him in payment of a debt and brought
an action for it against the Bristol sheriff. Bristol proved the
money had been paid to the Queen and gained the case, 1465.
(Madox, 227-8.)

[3] In 1273 Henry de Tracy held the borough from the King in
chief at a ferm of about £5 14s. 2d. There were 36 tenants

Aldermen, and capital burgesses drew up a list of byelaws for the good government of the borough, which apparently stirred the apprehensions of its lords. For a few years later, reviving ancient traditions of feudal authority in a suit against the borough, they complained that the mayor and burgesses had of their own authority admitted as "Burgesses of the Wynde" "foreign" merchants and victuallers who merely visited the town; and had turned to their own use the fines from denizens pertaining to their lord; that they had taken the correction of bread and ale, and unlawfully seized fines and tolls; that they would not suffer his officers to take custom after ancient usage from the people of Wales for their merchandise; and that they even seized fines belonging to him for heaps of rubbish in the streets. Moreover they did not render the suit and service due to the lord's court from all the inhabitants of the borough, for without his leave they themselves held a court every Monday, and instead of coming to every court of the lord's steward they did not come oftener than twice a year;

whose rent amounted to 23s. 8d. and some tenants in a suburb who paid an uncertain rent, but generally about 6s. 8d. A market was held every Friday which yielded in tolls to the lord about £3 a year, and a yearly fair gave 10s. Fines, reliefs, &c., came to about 13s. 4d. a year. The wealth of the town increased after the building of the "Long Bridge" in 1280 over "the great hugy, mighty, perylous, and dreadful water named Taw," and the increase of the cloth trade about 1321. Towards the close of the fourteenth century the legacies and accounts show that the burghers were laying up considerable wealth and doing a thriving trade. Hence probably the dispute as to the claim to profits. Hist. MSS. Com. ix. 206-213. See also case of Bridgewater, ibid. iii. 310-14.

nor would they suffer the lord's officers to make attachments in the borough at the Nativity of Our Mother after the ancient custom. In other words the townsfolk, just like the people of Totnes two hundred years before, were bent on regulating their trade and spending the money collected in their courts and markets; but they were happier than they of Totnes in being able to claim that all these so-called usurpations were ancient rights of the burgesses, by virtue, as they said, of a charter granted by King Athelstan 500 years before. As this charter however had unluckily been "casualiter amissa," the town had to fall back on the verdict of an inquisition held about 1300 as to the usages and franchises to which it was entitled, and the payments which were due by the mayor and commonalty in place of old feudal services. Here the Barnstaple men held their own successfully, and in 1445 they secured a charter from Henry the Sixth, "for accommodation of the burgesses in doing their business quietly," which confirmed to them the fullest rights of self-government.[1]

The struggle of the boroughs with their feudal lords was however a matter of little significance in England, where since the Conquest feudalism from the point of view of the noble had so unsatisfactory a record. Fallen from the high estate of his brethren on the Continent, despoiled of his might by one strong king after another, he saw himself condemned to play in England a comparatively modest part, and from his

---

[1] They even claimed the right of infang theof and outfang theof, and to be impleaded only in their own court. Hist. MSS. Com. ix. 206.

less exalted plane was even constrained to assume in his relations to burghers and traders a conciliatory, almost at times a deprecating tone, not because he was lacking in "a high and pompous mind," but simply because his fortunes had sunk low. Hence the conflict in England was of a very different character from the conflict abroad. Fashions of careful ceremonial indeed long preserved the traditional sense of impassable barriers set between the dignity of the great whose daily needs were supplied by the labour of others, and the low estate of those who had to depend upon their own toil. "Whensoever any nobleman or peer of the realm passed through any parish, all the bells were accustomed to be rung in honour of his person, and to give notice of the passage of such eminency; and when their letters were upon any occasion read in any assemblies, the commons present would move their bonnets in token of reverence to their names and persons." Burghers and journeymen with an irreverent laugh at men "evermore strutting who no store keep,"[1] gathered to see the noble go by "in his robe of scarlet twelve yards wide, with pendent sleeves down on the ground, and the furrur therein set amounting unto £20 or better," while a train of followers crowded after him anxiously holding up with both hands out of the filth of the mediæval streets the wide sleeves made to "slide on earth" by their sides, and eagerly watching lest the ladies should forget to admire "the plaits behind;" and the busy mockers of the market-

[1] Rich. Redeless, ed. Skeat, Early English Text Society, Text C, Pass. iii. 177, &c.

place guessed that tailors and skinners must soon carry their cloths and skins out into the fields if they would find space enough to cut out robes like these.[1] But the fine garments and leisurely state of the great folk, the hollow ornaments of a vanquished feudalism, were matters of little significance; the forces of the future lay rather with the crowd of workers to right and left—with the men who watched the brave procession sweep by, and then gathered in their Common House to decree that any burgher who put on the livery of a lord, or accepted his maintenance and protection, should be blotted out of the book of burgesses, and driven from their marketplace and assembly hall, and "that he come not among them in their congregations."[2]

For the moment, indeed, the noble class was as it were thrown aside by the strong current of the national life, nor could the handful of families that held half the soil of England and the lesser baronage who followed in their train be recovered of their impotence, of their impoverishment of intellect and decay of force, even by the greatest landholder and the most typical member of their body, Warwick the

---

[1] Book of Precedence, E. E. Text Society, 105–108. Langland in Richard the Redeless describes the noble who "keepeth no coin that cometh to their hands, but changeth it for chains that in Cheap hangeth, and setteth all their silver in samites and horns;" and

"That hangeth on his hips more than he winneth
And doubteth no debt so dukes them praise."

Richard the Redeless, Passus iii. 137–40, 147–8.
[2] Journ. Arch. Ass. xxvii. 467. Nott. Rec. ii. 425.

Kingmaker. Sated with possessions, forced into a position of leadership mainly by the imposing list of his great relations and the surprising number of his manors—a patriot who consecrated his services to the cause of a faction and the unrestrained domination of a family group of blood relations—a general who never got beyond an already antiquated system of warfare, devoid according to public rumour of personal courage, deserted in a crisis by the one organised military force in the public service—a commander with all the ready instincts of the common pirate—a statesman made after an old ancestral pattern, who had learned his politics a couple of centuries before his time, and to the last remained absolutely blind to the great movements of his own day—an administrator who never failed at a critical moment to put in jeopardy the most important national interests—an agitator restless for revolution, but whose influence in the national counsels was practically of no account when there was a pause in mere fighting —it is thus that Warwick stands before us, a consummate representative of his demoralized class.

The conditions under which the great landowners were living at this time were indeed singularly unfavourable. With the new trade they had comparatively little to do,[1] and the noble, with his throng of depend-

---

[1] The landowner of the fifteenth century was usually a mere landlord subsisting on his rents and not interested in the produce of the soil except as a consumer. He was only occasionally a trader. (Rogers' Agriculture and Prices, iv. 2; see Berkeleys, i. 365-6; ii. 23; Paston, i., lxxxviii-ix., 416, 430, 431, 454; ii. 70, 106; iii. 430; Hist. MSS. Com. viii. 263; iv. 1, 464.) The

ents and his show of state, was really living from hand to mouth on the harvests from his fields and the plunder he got in war.[1] After the fashion of the time the treasure of the family was hoarded up in his great oak chests; splendid robes, cloth of gold, figured satins, Eastern damasks and Sicilian silks, velvets and Flemish cloths, tapestries and fine linen, were heaped together with rich furs of marten and beaver. Golden chains and collars of "the old fashion" and "the new," rings and brooches adorned with precious stones, girdles of gold or silver gilt by famous foreign makers, were stored away in his strong boxes, or in the safe rooms of monasteries, along with ewers and goblets and basins of gold and silver, pounced and embossed "with great large enamels" or covered with silver of "Paris touch."[2] But the owner of all this unproductive treasure scarcely knew where to turn for a little ready money. The produce of the estate sufficed for the needs of the household, and if the lord was called away on the king's service, or had to

really important classes were the new proprietors who rented land for trading purposes.

[1] See Fastolf, Paston Letters, i. 187-8.

[2] Treasures were apparently stored in different quarters for greater security. See Fastolf's stores at Caistor. (Paston Letters, i. 416, 473-475; S. Benet's, 468, 508; S. Paul's, London, 493; Bermondsey, 474; White Friars, Norwich, ii. 56.) The religious houses had their reward in the form of benefactions for which masses were sung for the donor. (Hist. MSS. Com. iv. i. 461.) In the Paston house there was stored away over 16,000 ounces of silver plate, nearly 900 yards of cloth, about 300 yards of linen, and coats and hats without number. See also Hist. MSS. Com. vii. 537; viii. 93; Berkeleys, ii. 212. Plumpton Corresp. 10-11, 13, 37.

attend Parliament, a supply of oats was carried for the horses " to save the expenses of his purse"; and an army of servants rode backwards and forwards continually to fetch provisions from fields and ponds and salting tubs at home, so that he should never be driven to buy for money from the baker or at the market.[1] The crowd of dependents who swelled his train, easily content to win an idle subsistence, a share of booty in time of war, "maintenance" in the law courts, and protection from all enemies, either received no pay at all, or accepted the most trifling sums—a few shillings a year when they could get it, with a "livery" supplied like their food from the estate.[2] For money which was scarce everywhere was nowhere so scarce as in the houses of the landed proprietors, who amid their extravagant display found one thing always lacking—a few pounds to pay an old debt or buy a new coat. Sir John Paston, the owner of broad estates in Norfolk, was forced more than once to pawn his "gown of velvet and other gear" in London to get a few marks; when it occurred to him to raise money on his father's

---

[1] Berkeleys, i. 167.

[2] John of Gaunt retained Rankyn d'Ypres to dwell with him for peace and war for the term of his life, granting him board and twenty-five marks a year from the ferm of Liverpool, *in time of peace*. (Picton's Municipal Records of Liverpool, i. 16.) For the management of a great house with the giving out of wool for spinning and weaving and accounts audited by a master clothier, see Berkeleys, i. 167; Hist. MSS. Com. v. 330; Denton's Lectures, 293; Paston, ii. 354-5; Hist. MSS. Com. x. 4, p. 297. Often they supplied their own livery. (Brinklow's Complaynt, 45; Paston, ii. 139.)

funeral pall, he found his mother had been beforehand with him, and had already put it in pawn. During an unwonted visit to Westminster in 1449, the poor Lady of Berkeley wrote anxiously to her husband, one of the greatest landowners in England, "At the reverence of God send money, or else I must lay my horse to pledge and come home on my feet"; and he managed to raise £15 to meet her needs by pawning the mass book, chalices, and chasubles of his chapel.[1] So also the Plumptons, in Yorkshire, were in perpetual money difficulties; servants were unpaid, bills not met, debts of £2 10s. and £4 put off from term to term, and at last a friend who had gone surety for a debt of £100 to a London merchant was arrested. "Madam," a poor tradesman writes to Lady Plumpton, "ye know well I have no living but my buying and selling, and, Madam, I pray you send me my money." One of the family tried in vain to get a friend to buy him some black velvet for a gown. "I pray you herein blame my non-power, but not my will," the friend answers from London, "for in faith I might not do it but if I should run in papers of London, which I never did yet, so I have lived poorly thereafter."[2] When times grew pressing the country families borrowed freely from their neighbours and relations; no one, even the sister of the Kingmaker, felt any hesitation in pleading poverty

[1] Lives of the Berkeleys, ii. 63.
[2] Plumpton's Correspondence, 13, 20-1, 41, 71, 72, 97, 99, 148, 194, 206, 187, 198-9. The abbot of Fountains had to write a severe letter to order that a wine-seller in Ripon shall be paid

as a reason for being off a bargain or asking for a loan;[1] and those who were in better case lent readily in the hope of finding a like help themselves in case of difficulty.[2] Year by year debts accumulated, till the owner's death allowed the creditors to open his coffers and scatter his treasured stores, when the "array, plate, and stuff of the household and of the chapel" scarcely sufficed to meet the legacies and bills, the charities deferred, and the masses required for his soul's safety.[3]

There were indeed instances in which the growing poverty of the nobles opened an easy way for the emancipation of the towns, since it was sometimes possible, under the pressure of poverty or bankruptcy, to convince the lord of a borough, even though he had but such a measure of good wit in his head

"As thou shouldest mete of a mist from morn till even,"[4]

that the balance of profit lay on the side of freedom. For to some extent the difficulties of the landowners arose from the fact that on their estates the commuta-

for a tun of wine. (Ibid. 62.) For courtiers who "paid on their pawns when their pence lacked," Richard the Redeless, Pass. i. 53-4; Paston Letters, ii. 333-5, 349-50; iii. 99.

"Butt drapers and eke skynners in the town
For such folk han a special orison
That florisshed is with curses here and there
And ay shall till they be payd of their gere."

Book of Precedence, Early English Text Society, 107.

[1] Paston Letters, iii. 326, 194, 219, 358.
[2] Ibid. iii. 6-7, 20, 23, 24, 35, 46, 49, 114-5, 219, 258.
[3] Lives of the Berkeleys, ii., v.; Brinklow's Complaynt, 40.
[4] Richard the Redeless, Pass. iii. 172.

tion for feudal services, or dues to be rendered for the holding of land, had been settled in early times when money was scarce and demands for profit modest, and these charges remained fixed when prices were rising and when the need of ready money was keenly felt.[1] But while the lord could look for no increase from his lands, a new source of profit had been opened to him in the boroughs on his estate. He could find money surely and easily by leasing out rights of trade, collection of tolls, and other privileges to the townspeople. In the middle of the thirteenth century the mayor and burgesses of Berkeley obtained from their lord freedom from all kinds of toll which he either demanded or might demand of them;[2] and in the fourteenth century he rented to them the tolls of the wharfage and of the market, and received larger profits from this transaction than he gained from all the rent of the borough.[3]

---

[1] Berkeleys, i. 159.

[2] Lives of the Berkeleys, i. 130. A charter given by Baldwin of Redvers to Plympton, 1285, grants the same rights as the citizens of Exeter had from the King, except that Baldwin's serfs, if they lived in the borough, might not be granted its liberties without his leave. (Madox, Firma Burgi, 42.) The King could grant a number of privileges which were beyond the power of any other lord—such as freedom from tolls throughout the kingdom, exemption from the sheriff's jurisdiction, freedom from interference of royal officers, and so on; and the matter of tolls was so important that towns on private estates were practically obliged to get a royal charter as well as a charter from their lord. Compare the charters given in Stubbs' Charters, 105; and Gross. ii, 136; with royal charters such as those in Stubbs' Charters, 103; and Nott. Rec., i. 1. See also Hist. MSS. Com. ix. 273.

[3] Berkeleys, i. 341.

The weakest corporation moreover had a persistence and continuity of life which gave it incalculable advantages in the conflict with individuals subject to all the chances and changes of mortality. For the nobles indeed the fight with the town was in many ways an unequal one. Driven hither and thither by urgent calls of war or of the King's business, the lord was scarcely ever at home to look to his own affairs. In the frequent absences of the masters of Berkeley, perpetually called away by "troubles of state," when the King summoned them to his aid whether for civil war or war of conquest,[1] the neighbouring towns of Bristol and Gloucester found opportunity to escape from their control; and the march of the baron and his retainers from Berkeley was a subject of much greater gladness to the townsmen of Bristol than to the lord of the castle himself; for "the household and foreign accounts of this lord," we are told, "reveal a marvellous unwillingness in him to this Scottish war, dispatching many letters and messages to the King, and other lords and favourites about him, for excuses."[2] When, as a reward for his services, one of the Berkeleys was given the custody and government of the town of Gloucester,[3] he was also charged with the government of Berwick, and was moreover called away whenever the King found himself in military difficulties; so that the Gloucester burgesses cannot have had much to fear from him. The care of the

---

[1] Berkeleys, i. 226, 228.
[2] Ibid. i. 183-185.   [3] Ibid. i. 227

great estates, in fact, was constantly left to the women of the house and to stewards, while the master, pressed by ambition, or quite as often by the driving necessity of getting money, was fighting in Wales or Scotland, or was looking for plunder in France, or for place at court. For three generations the lands of the Pastons in Norfolk were managed by the capable wives of absentee landlords—of the judge who must have spent most of his time in London or on circuit; of his son the sharp London lawyer; and of his grandson, Sir John, the gay young soldier who hovered between London and Calais, and whose only care for his property was to press anxiously for its rents. The story of the Plumpton family was much the same. One of the Plumptons spent his last years and died in France; and no sooner did the young Sir William reach his majority in 1426, than he also left his Yorkshire estates and set off to join the French campaign.[1]

On the noble class too fell the heavy consequences of the rebellions and civil wars of which they were the main supporters. If the lord died in battle his estates might pass to a minor; if he died on the scaffold they passed to the crown; or long imprisonment might thwart his best laid plans for strengthening his hold over his boroughs. The young Lord Maurice of Berkeley, for instance, was drawn into rebellion against Edward the Second, and died in prison four and a half years later. During the whole time that

---

[1] Plumpton's Correspondence, l-li.

he held his estates he was only in freedom for four months; and his eldest son, who was imprisoned with him, was not set at liberty till some months after his father's death.[1] Meanwhile the towns were always quick to make their profit in such times of disturbance and revolution, as for example when the Earl of Devonshire was attainted by Edward the Fourth after the battle of Towton for his support of the Lancastrian cause, and the citizens of Exeter seized so favourable an opportunity to claim the restitution of a suburb stretching down to the riverside which the earls had held to strengthen their hold on the navigation of the Exe.[2]

Nor was the lord's position made more hopeful by the furious feuds between noble and noble which distracted the provinces in the fifteenth century, and the incessant lawsuits by which the landowners sought to mend their fortunes. In 1463 James Lord of Berkeley made an agreement with the Countess of Shrewsbury that they would have no more battles at law; for he was then sixty-nine, and she fifty-two, and neither of them since their ages of discretion had "enjoyed any three months of

[1] Berkeleys, i. 233-236, 272, 280. Compare the story of Sir William Plumpton, who fought at Towton on the losing side. He was brought before the chief justice in York and gave a bond for the payment of £2,000 before next Pentecost, and failing to procure it had to give himself up a prisoner at the Tower. He obtained a pardon, was released from his bond in 1462, and had new letters of pardon in 1463, but was still unable to return home till 1464, after he had been through a new trial and been acquitted. (Plumpton's Corres. lxvii-ix. 30.)

[2] Freeman's Exeter, 166-7.

freedom from lawsuits."[1] Nor did they wage their fight in the law-courts only, but carried on an open war by which Gloucestershire had been distracted since 1421, and which proved one of the most deadly of the many provincial conflicts of the fifteenth century. Appeased at intervals to break out again with renewed force, and with the usual incidents of hangings and finings and imprisonments and ransomings, it finally culminated in 1470 in a pitched battle on Nibley Green, where the Berkeleys triumphantly maintained their cause at the head of about 1,000 fighting men, and Lord Lisle, the son of Lady Shrewsbury, who led the enemy's army, was killed. To country folk and traders this feud of the nobles carried with it, we are told, " the ill-effects and destructions of a petty war, wherein the borough town of Berkeley, for her part, saw the burning and prostration of many of her ancient houses, as her old rent which till that time was £22 by the year and upwards, and by those devastations brought down to £11 and under, where it sticketh to this day, without recovery of her ancient lustre or greatness."[2] Such a strife was by no means singular or without parallel, and the histories of Norfolk, Yorkshire, Derbyshire, or Lancashire have their records of similar outrages. Exeter was thrown into alarm by a great fight on Clistheath in 1453 between the Earl of Devon and Lord William Bonvil where

[1] Berkeleys, ii. 95. Compare the expenses of Fastolf in a lawsuit of ten years, the costs of which were recorded in a roll of seven skins. (Hist. MSS. Com. iv. 1, 461.)
[2] Berkeleys, ii. 65–73, 75, 84, 103–116.

many persons were grievously wounded and much hurt done : "the occasion whereof was about a dog ; but great displeasure thereby came to the city, where presently after the fight the Lord Bonvil sheltered himself, which the Earl took amiss, thinking it had been so done by the city in some displeasure to himself." [1]. The mere instinct of self-protection naturally drove the towns to detach their interests from nobles whose alliance brought disaster and ruin to simple traders, and in every borough statute after statute forbidding the inhabitants to wear the "livery"[2] of any lord whatever, testified to the determination of the towns to cut off from the great people of the country round every possibility of stirring up faction within their borders.

[1] Freeman's Exeter, 164; Paston, i. xcviii, 350–1; Proceedings of the Privy Council, v., xc–xci.; vi. lxxviii–ix. In 1437 a commission of inquiry into felonies and insurrections in Bedford could not be held because Lord Grey, to whom the town belonged, appeared with a strong armed force, and was met by Lord Fanhope ready to oppose him with another army. (Proceedings of Privy Council, v., Preface xv–xvi.) Account given by witnesses before Privy Council, v. 35, 39, 57. Fresh troubles in 1442, v. 192.

[2] For the evils of liveries and maintenance under Richard the Second, see Richard the Redeless, Pass. i. 55 &c., ii. 74 &c., iii. 309 &c. The wearing of liveries was forbidden in Shrewsbury lest "when any affray or trouble fall in the said town each man having livery would draw to his master or to his fellow and not to the bailiffs." (Owen, i. 217.) From the towns these evils seem to have been rigorously and effectually banished by ordinances from 1309 (Freeman's Exeter, 165, 143) throughout the two following centuries. (Hist. MSS. Com. v. 557; Eng. Gilds, 385, 388–9, 393, 333; Hist. MSS. Com. xi. 3, page 16.) The cases of trouble which occur are rare. (Nott. Records, ii. 384; iii. 37, 344–5. Hist. MSS. Com. viii. 415. Hunt's Bristol, 103–5.)

But if boroughs in the ownership of a private lord might secure advantages through his poverty, his misfortune, or his weakness, their position was one of essential inferiority as compared with towns on the public demesne.[1] In the story of Liverpool we have a curious illustration of the fortunes of a borough whose lot it was to fall at one time into the charge of the state, and at another to be thrown into the hands of a noble—and whose vicissitudes at last left it in a sort of indeterminate condition

---

[1] Leicester shows the comparatively slow growth of freedom in one of the most favoured towns dependent on a great lord. Its great charter given by Edmund Crouchback in 1277, and translated into English under Henry the Sixth, was mainly concerned with the ordering of legal procedure for the burghers; and it was not till 1376 that the town bought from its earl the right to appoint its own bailiff, and to receive the annual profits of its courts, and various other dues and fines. The town property was simply a tenement, a chamber, and a small place yielding a few pence yearly till 1393, when it was allowed to hold a little property for the repair of the bridges; and not till 1435 were the mayor and the corporation given the right to acquire lands and rents for the sustenation of the town and mayoralty. (Hist. MSS. Com. viii. 404, 412, 413, 414. Thompson, Mun. Hist., 74. A pamphlet on the Origin of the Leicester Corporation by J. D. Paul gives a translation of Crouchback's charter.) Doncaster belonged to the family of De Mauley till the middle of the fifteenth century, when it passed for a few years to the Duke of Northumberland, and in 1461 was taken into the possession of the Crown. Edward the Fourth made it a free borough and gave it a common seal. Henry the Seventh in 1505 granted to the corporation all the property which the Crown had acquired at Doncaster on the attainder of Percy in 1461, and for a yearly rent of £74 13s. 11½d. secured to it the rights which had belonged to the ancient feudal lords. (Hunter's History of the Deanery of Doncaster, i. 13-15.)

where it owed a deferential obedience to patrons or masters on every side.

Liverpool, which had been granted by Henry the Second to the constable of Lancaster Castle, was resumed in 1207 by John, who granted it a charter of trading privileges. A new charter of Henry the Third, in 1229, gave it a guild merchant and hanse, with freedom from toll, and the rights of a free borough; and on the very next day after this grant Henry gave the lease of the fee-farm to the burgesses for four years at £10 a year.[1] The true foundations of municipal independence were thus laid. The town had its common seal; one of its two bailiffs was apparently elected by the people, and charged with the collecting of tolls for the ferm; and the busy trade with Ireland at that time, and the later advantage of a secure place of embarkation for troops, which became very important as the harbour of Chester silted up, promised prosperity. In the same year, however, the town was granted away by the King to the Earl of Chester, then passed in 1232 to the Earl of Derby; and in 1266 was given to Edmund Crouchback, Earl of Lancaster, and under the Lords of Lancaster Liverpool remained till a century later, when in 1361 it passed by marriage to John of Gaunt.

All hope of freedom for Liverpool died away under its new lords. The grant of the ferm was not renewed for over a hundred years; and at an enquiry of "Quo Warranto" in 1292 under Edward the

[1] Picton's Municipal Rec. of Liverpool, i. 1–4.

First "certain men of the Borough of Liverpool came for the commonalty, and say that they have not at present a bailiff of themselves, but have been accustomed to have, until Edmund the King's brother impeded them, and permits them not to have a free borough." Wherefore they claim only "that they may be quit of common fines and amercements of the county, &c., and of toll, stallage, &c., through the whole kingdom," for "as to the other liberties" which they used to have "the aforesaid Edmund now has them." They quote charters to show that their ancient liberties had been held direct from the crown, and the court decided that "Edmund hath usurped and occupied the aforesaid liberties," and ordered him to appear before it; but no action seems to have been taken against him, and for forty years he and his successors went on themselves collecting the tolls.[1] At last in 1356 the lord Henry allowed the townsmen to elect a mayor every year, and the next year the first Duke of Lancaster (father-in-law of John of Gaunt) leased the ferm to the mayor and others to hold for the burgesses for ten years,[2] and Liverpool was thus restored to the same position in which the King had put it a hundred and thirty years earlier. But even now its limited privileges rested simply on

[1] Picton's Municipal Rec. of Liverpool, i. 5-7.
[2] Ibid. 13, 14, 16. From this time leases of the ferm were very numerous and were constantly granted to one or more individuals; between 1354 and 1374 Richard de Aynesargh and William Adamson, who were often mayors, took such leases for several terms. (Picton's Memorials of Liverpool, ii. 54.)

the will and caprice of the lord; he might give the lease of the ferm with the right of collecting tolls for the rent to the mayor, or an ex-mayor, or whomever he would; he might grant it for a year, or for ten years, or he might take it all back into his own hands. As a matter of fact questions of convenience and profit seem to have made it advisable to leave the collections of taxes mainly with the town officers. When John of Gaunt granted his lease, at the request of the "honest and discreet men of the burgesses" the articles were embodied in a patent "to ourselves, to the mayor, and to the bailiffs,"[1] and in his time the lease was commonly granted for ten years.[2]

However some of the evils of such a system might be mitigated by the prudence of rulers bent on securing the utmost possible profits from their subjects, there was no real guarantee of freedom or security to the people. But when at the death of John of Gaunt in 1399, the Duchy of Lancaster was united to the crown, there was a new gleam of hope. The ferm of Liverpool, like that of Leicester, was now again paid to the King; an effort seems to have been made to abolish the old uncertain[3] system, and in 1421 Henry V. granted the

[1] Picton's Mem. of Liverpool, i. 35-36. [2] Ibid. i. 27-28.

[3] In 1413 the burgesses presented a petition complaining that their privileges were infringed upon by the shire officers coming into the borough and holding courts by force, by which "the said burgesses are grievously molested, vexed, and disturbed, to the great hindrance and detriment of the said borough and the disinheriting of the burgesses." It was declared on the other side, that the mayor and bailiffs had held the King's Courts without authority and received the tolls and profits. It is not

fee-farm for one year to the corporation, while an inquiry was held as to the value of the property and the terms of its tenure since the time of John of Gaunt. The King's death however stopped the proceedings, and the rising fortunes of the town were extinguished by the two great families who were from this time definitely settled down on it.[1]

For Liverpool was now hemmed in between two rival fortresses. Sir John Stanley with an army of followers was encamped in a great square embattled fort, with subordinate towers and buildings forming three sides of a quadrangle, the whole planted on the river edge, and commanding both the town and the Mersey, where the Stanleys' ships were moored, and whence they set sail for their new kingdom, the Isle of Man.[2] Sir Richard Molyneux, as hereditary Constable, held

known how the case ended. Ibid. i. 31-2. Picton's Mun. Records, i. 20.

[1] The revenue from Liverpool in 1296 was £25 : it then had 168 inhabited houses. (Picton's Mem. of Liverpool, i. 20.) In 1342 the personalty of the burgesses taxed was £110 13s. 3d., that is, the average personalty of each was about one mark (25). The revenue in 1327 was £30; in 1346 it was £38 (26), and remained the same in 1394 (31). In 1444 it was reduced to £21; in 1455 to £17 16s. 8d.; and under Edward the Fourth to £14 (36-7). In 1515 an inquiry was made as to the decay of the revenue (38), and the Act of 1544 put Liverpool in the list of towns which had wholly fallen into decay (45). Two plagues, one in 1540, another in 1548, probably carried off half its population (47); and in 1565 it had but 138 inhabited houses, and probably seven or eight hundred inhabitants, and twelve vessels navigated on an average by six men each (55). There were five streets under Edward the Third, and seven under Elizabeth (62).

[2] Fortified in 1406. Picton's Mun. Records, i. 21, 22.

the King's castle a little further along the river, with its area of fifty square acres defended by four towers, and surrounded by a fosse thirty yards wide, much of which was cut in the solid rock.[1] When a quarrel broke out in 1424 between the lords of these rival fortresses, Stanley collected a multitude of people in the town to the number of 2,000 or more, for he declared that Sir Richard Molyneux "will come hither with great congregations, riots, and great multitude of people to slay and beat the said Thomas (Stanley), his men and his servants, the which he would withstand if he might." On the other hand Sir Richard had gathered his forces near the West Derby fen, "and there on a mow within the said town we saw the said Sir Richard with great congregations, rout and multitude to the number of 1,000 men and more, arrayed in manner as to go to battle, and coming in fast towards Liverpool town." A pitched battle was only prevented by the sheriff of the county, who hastened to the rescue at the head of his forces, and succeeded in seizing first Stanley in his tower, and then Molyneux as he rode towards the town.[2]

Such scenes of riot and disorder were fatal to the prosperity and municipal hopes of Liverpool; but there was no escape from their unwelcome patrons. Both the great houses fought for York; and in return

---

[1] A little thatched building in the High Street which had to serve as toll house, town hall, and gaol, but the greater number of criminals were imprisoned and judged in the Stanley and Molyneux Castles. Picton's Memorials, ii. 25–6.

[2] Picton's Mem. of Liverpool, i. 32–3.

Edward the Fourth granted to Stanley the borough of Liverpool and other estates formerly belonging to the Duchy of Lancaster; while Molyneux was made chief forester of West Derby, steward of West Derby and Salford, and constable of Liverpool castle. Richard the Third again gave to the Stanleys large grants in Lancashire, and confirmed the Molyneux people in their offices,[1] and Henry the Seventh favoured their claims. The lords were great and important people in those days, and the little town of no account. Its independence died away, and the troubles of the ferm revived in their old bad form. The question of the lease was never settled, but in any case it passed out of the hands of the corporation. From 1495 it was for many years granted to David ap Griffith, who when he became mayor in 1502 had it renewed to him. Henry the Eighth leased it in 1525 and 1529 to his widow and son-in-law for terms which were to expire in 1566. In 1537, however, it was let to Thomas Holcraft, who sublet it to Sir William Molyneux. The mayor and corporation under Edward the Sixth declared the authority of the Molyneux family to be illegal, and claimed under the old lease granted to Griffith. For many years they fought obstinately in the case, holding perhaps that the house of their old mayor more nearly represented the town and its interests than the house of Molyneux; and one of them was thrown into prison for his resistance under Mary.[2] The ferm was not finally granted to the corporation till 1672; and Liverpool was for a

[1] Picton's Mem. of Liverpool, i. 36, 37.
[2] Ibid. i. 37, 38, 46, 48–9.

couple of centuries so sorely tried by the necessity of keeping well with the two great families that overawed it as well as with the Chancellor of the Duchy of Lancaster,[1] whether in the collecting of its scanty taxes or the choosing of its burghers for Parliament, that the history of its civic developement long remained of no importance.[2]

[1] Picton, i. 63.
[2] As an illustration of the reverse process, showing the impulse given to municipal liberty when a borough was transferred from private ownership to the State, see the case of Sandwich (Ch. XII.).

CHAPTER IX

BATTLE FOR FREEDOM

(3) *Towns on Church Estates*

THE towns on ecclesiastical estates form a distinct group, whose lot was materially different from boroughs on ancient demesne or on feudal lands. All lay property was subject only to laws and customs which had been ultimately determined by the necessities of social or political expediency, and which, dealing with secular possessions for secular purposes, were capable of being unmade as they had been made. But the towns which were reckoned among ecclesiastical estates lay under the special conditions that governed those estates, where religious and supernatural influences had been forced into the service of material wealth, and the attempt was made by spiritual authority to fix fluctuating political conditions into perpetual immutability. Prelates of the Church professed to rule with a double title, not only as feudal lords of the soil, but as guardians of the patrimony of S. Peter, holding property in trust for a great spiritual corporation, and exercising an authority maintained by formidable sanctions. If the watchwords of property are always impressive, among lay folk they are still open, under sufficiently strong pressure, to reasonable discussion; and it is admitted that temporal rights may be plausibly exchanged for others more expedient, or may be fairly bartered away as a means of buying a continued and secure existence. The Church, however, by a fruitful confusion of the terms ecclesiastical and religious, assumed to hold property by another tenure than any temporal owner; girt round about by tremendous safeguards to which the lay world could not aspire, and leaning on supernatural support for deliverance from all perils, it could the better refuse to discuss bargains suggested by mere political expediency.

The difficulty of reconciling this assumption of permanent and indivisible supremacy with the actual facts of life became very apparent with the passage of the centuries, when from a variety of causes it was no longer possible for the clerical order to maintain the place it had once held as the advanced guard of industry and learning, and its tendency was to sink into the position of a parasite class, producing nothing itself, but clinging to the means of wealth developed by the labour of a subject people. With the wisdom born of experience the Church was ready to give to its tenants all trading privileges, and any liberties that directly made for the accumulation of wealth;[1] but the flow of its liberality was suddenly

[1] See charter to Beverley; Stubbs' Charters, 105; Lambert's Gild Life, 73-6, York; Stubbs' Charters, 304, Salisbury; Gross' Gild Merchant, ii. 209-10.

dried up when townspeople proposed to add political freedom to material gain, nor was it likely to be quickened again by the crude simplicity with which the common folk resolved the question of the lordship of canons and monks.

> "Unneth (scarcely) might they matins say,
> For counting and court holding;"
>   .   .   .   .   .   .
> "Saint Benet made never none of them
> To have lordship of man nor town." [1]

The rising municipalities on the other hand, even if they had a history but a century or two old, were endowed with all the young and vigorous forces of the modern world; nor is there a single instance of a town where a lively trade went hand in hand with a subservient spirit, or where a temper of unconquerable audacity in commercial enterprise did not throw its exuberant force into the region of government and politics. With all their abounding energy, however, burghers had still to discover that freedom might be won anywhere save at the hands of an ecclesiastical lord.[2] If Norwich received from the bounty of

---

[1] Pol. Poems and Songs (Rolls' Series). Ed. Wright, i. 327, 334.
[2] The Church always showed itself exceedingly hostile to the formation of communes. The synod of Paris in 1213 denounced the "synagogues (c'est-à-dire' ces associations) que des usuriers et des exacteurs ont constituées dans presque toutes les cités, villes et villages de la France, appelées vulgairement communes, qui ont établi des usages diaboliques, *contraires à l'organisation ecclésiastique et tendant au renversement presque complet de la juridiction de l'Église.*" (Luchaire, 242. See especially pp. 235-50.)

Kings one privilege after another in quick succession till its emancipation was complete, its neighbour Lynn, equally wealthy and enterprising, but subject to the Bishop of Norwich, was fighting in 1520 to secure just such control of its local courts as Norwich had won for the asking three hundred years before. The royal borough of Sandwich had been allowed to elect its mayor and govern itself for centuries, while Romney, also one of the Cinque Ports but one which happened to be owned by the Archbishop of Canterbury, did not gain the right to choose its own mayor till the time of Elizabeth, and was meanwhile ruled by any one of the archbishop's squires or servants whom he might send as its bailiff, and forced to adopt any expedient by which while under the forms of bondage it might win the practice of freedom. A dozen generations of Nottingham burghers had been ordering their own market, taking the rents of their butcheries and fish stalls and storage rooms, supervising their wool traders and mercers, and admitting new burgesses to their company by common consent, while the men of Reading were still trying in vain every means by which they might win like privileges from the abbot who owned the town. Everywhere the same story is repeated, with varying incidents of passion and violence. The struggle sometimes lasted through centuries: in other cases it was brought to an early close. Some boroughs won a moderate success, while others wasted their labour and their treasure for small reward. In one place ruin settles down on the town, in another gleams of temporary success kindle new hopes, in a third the dogged fight goes on with monotonous persistence; but everywhere anger and vengeance wait for the day of retaliation, when monastery and priory should be levelled to the ground.

I. There was a distinct difference in the lot of towns under the control of a bishop, and others which were subject to a convent. Burghers who owed allegiance to a bishop had to do with a master whose wealth, whose influence, whose political position, whose training, made him a far more formidable opponent than any secular lord. On the other hand he probably lived at some distance from the borough, and, charged as he was with the administration of his bishopric and the estates of the see, besides all the business of a great court official occupied in weighty matters of state, he had but limited attention to give to its affairs. As the see passed from hand to hand, a resolute fight with an over-ambitious borough which was begun by one bishop might die away under the feebler rule, the indifference, or the wiser judgement of his successor. In the case therefore of towns on episcopal estates, if the struggle was arduous and costly, still its issue was not irrevocably determined beforehand, and the burghers might hope for at least partial victory. But the emancipation of the townsmen was long deferred, and in the fifteenth century there were boroughs where the bishop's hand still pressed heavily on the inhabitants.[1]

[1] The Bishop of Salisbury by a royal charter of 1304 got the right to tallage the townspeople of Salisbury, while the burghers

One of the greatest trading towns in England gives such a record of ceaseless contention carried on to win rights which had been peacefully granted long before to every prosperous borough on the royal demesne. The Bishop of Norwich had been lord of Lynn since its earliest history.[1] It is true that about 1100 A.D., one Bishop Herbert made a grant of the Church of S. Margaret and the little borough that lay around it—between Millfleet and Purfleet—to the monks of Norwich. But the land beyond these boundaries still belonged to the see. Lying as it did at the mouth of the Ouse, and forming the only outlet for the trade of seven shires, Lynn was destined to be one of the great commercial

were given municipal privileges the same as those of Winchester. In 1305, however, the burghers, rather than pay tallage to the bishop, surrendered their municipal privileges to the King, and promised to give up to him their common seal. (Rot. Parl. i. 174-6.) But in the composition made the next year between the lord bishop and the citizens, those who had shared in the revolt and had not made their submission were utterly separated and removed from privileges of trade or government. (Gross, ii. 209-10.) In 1396 there was again a quarrel between the bishop and the citizens, and the case was carried to the King's Council, when the mayor and commonalty entered into a recognizance to the King in £20,000 to behave well to the bishop, and two hundred of the citizens entered into recognizances to the bishop, each one in the sum of £1,000. In the agreement, however, certain provisions were made to prevent the ecclesiastics from taking advantage in any way of this treaty. (Madox, 142.)

The Commons in giving the grant of 1435 pray that no prelate may be a collector, adding that the dioceses of bishops and the neighbourhood of abbeys were greatly oppressed by ecclesiastical lords. (Rogers' Agric. and Prices, iv. 164.)

[1] Our Borough, by E. M. Beloe, 1-3.

ports of the east coast, and the bishops proved good stewards of their property. As population outgrew the Lynn of older days, with its little market shut in between the Guildhall and S. Margaret's where the booths then as 'now leaned against the walls of the parish church, and its tangle of narrow lanes leading to the river side, houses began to reach out over the desolate swamp that stretched to the north along the river side. Under the energetic rule of the prelates the sea which ebbed and flowed over the marsh was driven back, and a great wall raised against it, 340 feet long and nine feet thick at the base; while another stone wall ran along the eastern side to protect the town from enemies who might approach it by land. In the second half of the twelfth century the "Bishop's Lynn" rose on the newly won land along the river bank, with its great market-place, its church, its Jewry, its merchant houses; and soon in the thick of the busiest quarter by the wharves appeared the "stone house" of the bishop himself, looking closely out on the "strangers' ships" that made their way along the Ouse, laden with provisions and merchandise.

Lynn was now in a fair way to become the Liverpool of mediæval times. Under King John its prudent bishop obtained for the town charters granting it all the liberties and privileges of a free borough, saving the rights of its lords;[1] and then at once proceeded by a bargain with the convent at Norwich to win back for the see the whole of the lay

[1] Hist. MSS. Com. xi. part 3, 185-6.

property in the old borough, leaving to the monks only the churches and spiritual rights. Once more sole master of the town, his supremacy was only troubled by the lords of Castle Rising who, by virtue of a grant from William Rufus, claimed half the profits of the tolbooth and duties of the port, while the bishop had the other half. In 1240 however an exact agreement was drawn up between prelate and baron as to their respective rights; and the bailiffs of both powers maintained a somewhat boisterous jurisdiction over the waters of Lynn,[1] collected their share of dues paid by the town traders on cargoes of herrings, or on the wood, skins, and wine they imported from foreign parts, and in their own way made distresses for customs, plaints, and so forth. Thus Robert of Montault, in the time of Edward the Second, set up a court under his own bailiff at one of the bridges, and caused the merchants "rowing and flowing to the said town of Lynn with their ships and boats, laden as well with men as with merchandise," to be summoned, distrained, and harassed, "both by menacing them with hurling of stones that they come to land and tarry, and by extorting heavy fines from them," till at last in despair the traders gave up their business, and sold all their ships and boats. And when the exasperated burghers in their turn set upon these alien officers in 1317 and threw Robert himself into prison,[2] this out-

[1] For the troubles of the mayor and community in trying to carry out the King's laws in the presence of this divided jurisdiction, see Rot. Parl. i. 331.

[2] There had been trouble the year before which Robert's soft

break only brought upon them new calamities, for they were condemned by the King's judges to make atonement for their crime by paying to the offended lord within the next six or seven years a fine of four thousand pounds; which was practically equal to the confiscation of the whole of the municipal expenditure for about thirty years. Soon after this, however, the rights of the lords of Rising were sold to the Queen Dowager Isabella and passed through her to Edward the Third; so the rough and ready methods of their bailiffs came to an end.[1]

The power of the bishop on the other hand was still untouched. He held the Hall Court through his steward; and held further the Court Leet and view

---

words failed to dissipate. "Know, dear friends," he writes, "that I am surely concerned for your trouble, and if I could give you ease or alleviation of your trouble I would do it most readily, but assuredly, dear friends, I am at present in such misfortune of money that .... wherefore I pray you, my dear friends, that you put me in possession of my moneys as speedily as you can, since of a truth I can no longer dispense with them which much troubles me. And with respect to the wrong that was done to my bailiff, you have sent me word that the parties are in agreement. Know you that though peace be made between them the contempt done to me is not redressed, wherefore, I pray you, dear sirs, that you will take order amongst yourselves that amends may be made to me for the aforesaid contempt. Adieu, dear friends! May he give you happy and long life!" Hist. MSS. Com. xi. part 3, 241–4.

[1] For the King's bailiffs, see the petition in 1382 to the Lord Chancellor for relief from extortionate demands of the bailiffs of the Tolbooth. The bailiffs were perhaps not to blame; in 1396 and 1397 they had to pay 20 marks of silver out of receipts to the Duke of Britanny; in 1398, 10 marks to the Duke of York; in 1400, 8½ to the Duke of Lancaster. Ibid. 244–5.

of frankpledge; and owned the Tolbooth Court. There was indeed a mayor,[1] but his authority was small, for the bishop who had been eager to grant his burghers the privileges of trade [2] was less eager to see them set up any real self-government. Owing his post to the bishop's approval and nomination, if the mayor failed in obedience or respect his place might be at once forfeited. His power of levying taxes was limited and subject to his lord's control, nor could he make distress for sums levied on the commonalty. He was not charged with the custody or the defence of the town; it was the bishop who had command of the town gates, who could order them to be shut at his own will, and with a following of men-at-arms could enforce the order.[3] What was far more important, the bishop on the plea of protecting the poor from tyranny had withdrawn from him the power of compelling inhabitants to take up the franchise, and by thus establishing in the borough a population dependent on himself had permanently divided its forces.[4]

As in other towns, however, so here the Guild Merchant proved itself a most powerful organization for the winning of local independence.[5] Lynn was already in the thirteenth century becoming one of the richest towns in the country, and the mayor was supported by a Guild as masterful and as

---

[1] The charter of 1268 granted the right to elect a mayor in accordance with the former charter of the bishop. Hist. MSS. Com. xi. part 3, 186, 246; Gross, ii. 158.
[2] Gross, ii. 165.   [3] Gross, ii. 155; Paston Letters, ii. 86–7.
[4] Gross, ii. 155–6.   [5] See Vol. II., Chap. XIV.

wealthy as any in England. When once the question was raised whether he or the bishop was really to command within its gates, two equally matched and formidable forces were brought into play; and a war of two hundred years was conducted on either side with violence and craft, and remained of doubtful issue to the last. The bishop narrowly watched every effort made by the mayor to enlarge his powers or exalt his state; and the mayor was no less jealous of the pretensions of his lord. In the course of many experiments in the making of constitutions for its government, Lynn was again and again torn with disputes, and harassed by the difficulties of rightly adjusting the powers of its various classes; and in every constitutional struggle the bishop interfered anew, and often almost dictated the final settlement. The burghers treated him as occasion served. Constant gifts were offered to soften his heart. A pipe of red wine, a vessel of Rhine wine, portions of oats with a sturgeon, pike and tenches, formed one of these peace offerings;[1] at another time it would be a costly gift of wax. But what they gave with one hand they were ready to take away with the other; and when chance happily favoured them appropriated without scruple a house, 100 acres of land and twenty acres of pasturage which the bishop held in right of his church of Holy Trinity at Norwich.[2] As disputes grew hot, now over one point, now over another, prelate and town alike called the king's authority to their aid. If a sea-wall was washed away by a high tide, the

---

[1] Blomefield, iii. 163. [2] In 1403. Blomefield, viii. 531.

burghers would cry to the Privy Council to compel the bishop to rebuild it;[1] or they would demand justice against him on the plea that he had usurped their own officers' right to hold the Leet Court and the Tolbooth Court. The decision of the crown was given sometimes on one side, sometimes on the other; or the sovereign might for a time take the disputed authority into his own hands. But it was inevitable that the final gain should fall to the king, whose authority was strengthened by every appeal to his supreme jurisdiction; while lesser profits came to the court by the way—gifts to high officials and great people, and to the royal judges when they came to hold their assizes in the Guild Hall, and the town lavished its treasures in costly dinners and varied wines and presents to them and to their clerks.

From the beginning of the fourteenth century we can trace the progress of the long strife as the town gradually perfected its municipal organization. First came the necessary financial precautions. In 1305 the Guild established itself more firmly by a charter which secured to it all its lands and tenements; and the mayor obtained power to distrain for sums levied on the commonalty.[2] Then at an assembly held in the Guildhall in 1314 authority was given to twenty-six persons to elect twelve of the more sufficient of the town to make provision for all

[1] Proceedings of Privy Council, vol. i., 167 (1401).
[2] Hist. MSS. Com. xi. 3, 186-7. In 1307 the mayor and community got a grant of land from the bishop for their basin for water. Ibid. 239.

business touching the community in the King's parliament and elsewhere.[1] But the real struggle seems to have begun about 1327 when much money was spent on lawyers, negotiations with the bishop, and a new charter, and the business was still going on in 1330 with more counsels' fees and messengers to London. Finally in 1335 the town bought a new charter from the king at a cost of £55 and a multitude of gifts to king and queen and bishop.[2] In this year or the next it obtained, among other things, the right to have all wills that affected property in the town proved in the Guild Hall before the mayor and burgesses.[3] The bishop seems to have found means of defeating the burghers' intention in this particular claim; but there still remained the one important question which lay behind all minor struggles—that of the administration of justice in the town—the question whether it was the mayor or an ecclesiastical officer who should preside in the courts, and whether

[1] Hist. MSS. Com. xi. part 3, 240.   [2] Ibid. 213–215.

[3] A will was proved after a proclamation by the serjeant that on such a day it would be read in the Guild Hall before the mayor, and anyone who wished to contradict it must then appear. (Hist. MSS. Com. xi. part 3, 153, 189.) In the earliest wills no mention is made of probate before the ordinary; in later registrations it is recorded that the will had received episcopal probate before coming before the mayor. (Ibid. 155.) The cost of this was what the people desired to avoid.

> "For who so woll prove a testament,
> That is not all worth tenne pound,
> He shall pay for the parchment
> The third of the money all round;"
>
> —Pol. Poems and Songs, ed. Wright, i. 323.

their profits, fines, and forfeitures should go to enrich the treasury of the bishop or of the municipality. The mayor held a court in the Guild Hall twice a week, and had jurisdiction over all transgressions and debts arising by water between the limits of S. Edmondness and Staple Weyre,[1] and he seems now further to have laid claim to the view of frankpledge and the criminal jurisdiction of the Leet Court. The bishop answered with a vigorous retort. In 1347 he assumed the view of frankpledge of the men of Lynn and tenements formerly held by the corporation, and withdrew or threatened to withdraw from the burghers the right of electing their mayor. On this an appeal was made to the king, who sent a royal commission to enquire into the dispute, and meanwhile seized with his own hand the view of frankpledge and the lands, giving the first over for the time to the sheriff of the county and the second to the king's escheator.[2] Possibly there was some attempt at a compromise, but the new charter of 1343 in which the bishop confirmed the liberties granted by his predecessors,[3] even if it may have allowed the mayor's election, left the great question of the courts unsolved. The burghers still debated whether the town officers were not entitled to hold the view of frankpledge, and the husting court, and to have cognizance of pleas—in fact to exercise all the more important rights now monopolized by the bishop; and insisted on the election of their own

---

[1] Hist. MSS. Com. xi. part 3, 207.
[2] Ibid. 205.   [3] Ibid. 189.

mayor. It was in vain that Edward the Third ordered the mayor and community under pain of forfeiture of their liberties to alter their demeanour and not cause prejudice and damage to the bishop;[1] and the whole matter was at last brought before the King's Court in 1352, when the judges decided against the town in every question raised. In spite of the verdict, however, there was one point on which the people refused to submit; and the bishop was compelled to confirm their right to elect yearly one of themselves as mayor, though he enforced a significant confession of subjection by requiring that the mayor should immediately after the election appear before himself or his steward, and swear to maintain the rights of the church of Norwich.[2]

But the burghers never yielded their consent to the decision of the King's justices, and at every provocation loudly renewed their protest. When the bishop visited Lynn in 1377, he demanded that in recognition of his supremacy the town serjeant should carry before him the wand tipped at both ends with black horn, which was usually borne before the mayor himself. For their part they were heartily willing, answered the courteous mayor and aldermen, but they feared that at such a flagrant breach of their ancient customs and liberties, the commons, "always inclinable to evil," would certainly fall on the bishop's party with stones and drive them out

---

[1] Hist. MSS. Com. xi. part 3, 188.
[2] Blomefield, iii. 513. Hist. MSS. Com. xi. part 3, 189, 205.

of the town. But the bishop roughly rebuked the mayor and his brethren for "mecokes and dastards," thus fearing the vulgar sort of people, as if it mattered to him what the common folk should say; and set out on his ride with the rod borne before him. He rode alone with his followers, however, for no burghers would accompany him; and as he went the whole people rose, and with their bows and clubs and staves and stones broke up the brave procession, and put the bishop and his men to flight, carrying off many hurt and wounded.[1] It seems possible that the fray was really excited by the astute mayor and council as a means of making a final breach between the bishop and the common people. But their opponent was too strong for them. The bishop carried his complaint to the King's Council, and "for the transgression done to him in the town" the burgesses barely escaped punishment by spending a sum equal perhaps to two years of the town revenues in fines and gifts to the king, his mother, and others who had "laboured for the community"; besides paying £116 10s. 0d. for the expenses of the mayor, aldermen, and burgesses, in going to London on the business.[2] Seventy years later, after a series of constitutional troubles, the old quarrel as to rights of jurisdiction and the use of the symbols of supreme authority broke out anew. The mayor in 1447 got a grant from the King

---

[1] Blomefield, iii. 516-17.

[2] Hist. MSS. Com. xi. part 3, 222. It would seem that in 1377 the mayor and burgesses were made responsible for the custody of the town, and were ultimately given power of distress for subsidies for its defence. (Ibid. 190, 205.)

allowing a sword to be carried before him [1] with the point erect, the last and highest emblem of absolute jurisdiction. At this outrage to his dignity the bishop interfered promptly and resolutely, and the next year the King had to write that in spite of his good inclinations he must remember his coronation oath to observe the rights of the Church, and that the mayor must henceforth cease from having any sword or mace borne before him. In 1461, however, whether the town had got a new grant from Edward, or was taking advantage of troubled times to re-assert its claim, the common accounts register a payment of 4*d.* for the "cleaning of the mayor's sword," and 6*s.* 8*d.* for "crimson velvet for the sword and for making it up."[2] And when in 1462 the bishop came to the town with a following of sixty armed men, and ordered the gates to be shut after him, the attitude of the people was not to be mistaken, "the mayor and all the commonalty of Lynn keeping their silence" when the bishop was openly defied in the streets by the lord of Oxenford with his fellowship, even though "the bishop and his squires rebuked the mayor of Lynn, and said he had shamed both him and his town for ever, with much other language." So clear was the state of things to the bishop's sixty men-at-arms that "when we met there bode not with him over twelve persons at the most with his serjeant-at-arms, *which serjeant was fain to lay down his mace;* and so at the same

---

[1] Hist. MSS. Com. xi. part 3, 165.
[2] Ibid. 225.

gates we came in we went out, and no blood drawn, God be thanked."[1]

The incident was not one to soften passions or conciliate rivals; but the issue of the strife as compared with the hostilities in the last century shows how the balance of power was shifting. The bishop's resources were being exhausted faster than his pretensions; every trader in Lynn was perpetually reminded that in Norwich, only fifty miles or so distant, the citizens had held their own borough court since 1194, and the higher court with view of frankpledge since 1223. For these privileges they themselves had waited now for three hundred years, and only one settlement was possible. In 1473 the quarrel as to the view of frankpledge was still going on,[2] but the bishop was driven at last to a compromise which preserved his historic claims untouched in theory, while it handed over the real power to the municipality. For the sake of peace he consented in 1528 to lease to the mayor and burgesses the yearly Leet, the Steward's Hall Port, and the Tolbooth Port;[3] besides various dues from fairs and markets, with waifs and strays, and some other rights. A ruder and more effective close was before long put to the quarrel by the sharp methods of the Reformation, when Bishop's Lynn became finally the King's Lynn.

II. If boroughs attached to a bishopric were in a difficult position, the difficulty was vastly increased

---

[1] Paston Letters, ii. 86-7.
[2] Hist. MSS. Com. xi. part 3, 205.   [3] Ibid. 246.

in the case of those subject to the lordship and rule of a monastery. Towns owned by abbot or prior were like all the rest stirred by the general zeal for emancipation, but they were practically cut off from any hope of true liberty. The power with which they had to fight was invincible. Against the little lay corporation was set a great ecclesiastical corporation, wealthy, influential, united, persistent, immortal. All the elements which went to make up the strength of the town were raised in the convent to a yet higher degree of perfection, and the struggle was prolonged, intense, and at the best remained a drawn battle, setting nothing beyond dispute save the animosity of the combatants. Sometimes the defeat of the borough in the fifteenth century was as complete as it had been two hundred years before. Cirencester which had won extended privileges from Henry the Fourth in return for political services in his time of difficulty, was utterly beaten at last,[1] and fell back under the control of the Abbey as completely as St. Alban's had done in earlier times.[2] In other cases the resistance

[1] Proc. Privy Council, i. 127. Beecham's Hist. Cirencester, 154-8.
[2] In 1333 St. Alban's brought its charter to the King's Chancery and renounced there all the liberties contained in the said charter. The keeper of the rolls at their request broke off the seal of wax, and cancelled the enrolment in the Chancery rolls. The townsmen also brought their common seal of silver, which at their request was destroyed and the silver given to the shrine of St. Alban. (Madox, 140.) Common as it was in France for a commune to renounce its freedom, there is scarcely any instance in England save on ecclesiastical property. The case of Dunwich was peculiar and I have met with no other.

was more energetic and sustained, and some slight measure of success was its reward.[1]

As in the case of towns on feudal estates, any borough that possessed traditions of freedom handed down from a state of larger liberties might have some hope of ultimate success, but otherwise rebellion could only issue in defeat so final and decisive as to leave no further room for argument. Under the impulse of the popular movement which seems to have agitated many towns after the rising that took place in the days of Simon de Montfort, the men of S. Edmundsbury kept up for about seventy years a desperate struggle with the abbot who ruled them. For in 1264 it happened that "the younger and less discreet" of the town organized a conspiracy under colour of a Guild called "the Guild of Young Men," and despising altogether the ancient horn of the community set up a new common horn of their own. Three hundred and more of these hopeful conspirators, known by the name of "bachelors," having bound themselves to obey no bailiff save the aldermen and bailiffs of their own Guild, to answer to the sound of their new common horn instead of the old moot horn, and to count all who did not join them as public

---

[1] Occasionally a convent drove a hard bargain. In 1440 an agreement was made between the convent of Plimpton and the commonalty of Plymouth, by which the commonalty was to pay £41 yearly, and if this rent was unpaid fifteen days after quarter day, the officers of the convent might seize all the goods and chattels of the mayor and commonalty and of any burgesses and of any others residing and abiding there which could be found within the borough and the precinct thereof. Madox, 222-3.

enemies,[1] soon found themselves engaged in riotings and in violently resisting the abbot from behind closed gates. On the abbot's appeal to the Crown, however, the town grew frightened; the Guild was annihilated by the help of the more prudent sort, and the insurrection suppressed.

In less than thirty years, however, the burghers were renewing the memory of their old offences— forcing townsmen against their will to go to the hall of the Guild, and take an oath of allegiance to it; levying tolls and taxes, distraining on merchants who sold in the abbot's market to extort money from them; hindering the execution of justice on merchants suspected of selling goods outside that market; and refusing to allow any member of the guild to bring a plea in the abbot's court against any other brother of the guild: while the abbot on his side asserted his right to choose the alderman of the town and to appoint the keepers of the gates. In spite of a compromise made before the king's judges sent the next year to enquire into the case, the same charges were again brought against the men of Bury before a royal commission of judges in 1304. The accused confessed that the abbot was lord of the whole town and its courts, but they still urged a claim to be free burgesses and to have an alderman, and a Merchant

---

[1] The organization of the guild does not seem to have been at all of a democratic or "advanced" kind, but after the pattern of the oligarchic societies of the time. Four men owning goods to the value of 10 marks were elected yearly, by a committee of twelve burgesses, to hold the guild, and summoned to do their duty by two officers of the guild called "les Dyes."

Guild with certain rights of justice belonging to it and with an elaborate code of procedure, and asserted their right to hold meetings for the common profit of the burgesses, and to levy taxes from men trading in the town. All this the abbot denied, whether the right to a Merchant Guild, or pleas belonging to it, or a community, or a common seal, or a mayor; according to him the townsfolk only had a right to a drinking feast, which they maliciously turned into an illegal convention, and if they took any fines it was against the merchant law and the King's peace. The case was given for the abbot. The leaders were fined and put in jail, some of them escaping by payments while others through poverty lay in prison a month.

Once more, however, the burghers took heart, and in 1327 broke into the abbey and forced the abbot to concede to them a community, a common seal, a Guild merchant, and custody of their gates, with other liberties. But their triumph was short; utterly defeated by the forces of abbot and king, they were forced in the concord of 1332 to renounce for ever the claim to a community;[1] and when after the Peasant Revolt there was much general begging for pardon, the men of S. Edmundsbury, who were ordered to sue for their pardons specially, had to find surety not only to the King but to their lord the abbot.[2]

If S. Edmundsbury was one of the most unfortunate ecclesiastical towns Reading was perhaps the most

---

[1] Gross, ii. 29-36. Yates' Bury S. Edmunds, 123-135.
[2] Statutes, 6 Richard II., 2, cap. 3.

fortunate. For Reading was originally a borough on royal demesne, which was granted by Henry the First to the new monastery founded by him.[1] From this time the town lay absolutely in the control of the abbot. He owned all its streams, from which the inhabitants had "chiefly their water to brew, bake, and dress their meat."[2] The mills were in his hands; he did as he chose with the market, controlled the trade, and had the entire supervision of the cloth manufacture. He appointed the Warden of the Guild or mayor, and the various town officers; and claimed a decisive voice in the admitting of new burgesses or members of the Guild, while from every burgher's son who entered the Guild he claimed a tax of 4s., and from every stranger one-half of the fine paid as entrance fee—the sum of the fine being fixed in presence of a monk who might raise objections so long as he was not overborne by the joint voices of six legal men of the Guild. Every burgher in the Guild had further to pay to him a yearly tax of *chepin gavell* for the right of buying or selling in the town.[3] For any breach of the law fines were gathered in to increase his hoard, since all the administration of justice lay in his hands. Before the abbot alone the emblems of supreme authority might be borne, and the mayor when he went in state was only allowed to have two tipped staves carried before him by the abbot's bailiffs.

From the time of Henry the Third there was

[1] Coates's Reading, 49.
[2] Hist. MSS. Com. xi. part 7, 224.   [3] Gross, ii. 208.

unceasing war between the townsmen and their lord. Violent dissensions broke out in 1243, when the burghers "lay in wait day and night for the abbot's bailiffs," and "hindered them from performing their duties," till order was restored by a precept from the King.[1] The townsfolk were appeased by the grant of certain trading privileges; but ten years later the quarrel broke out again. The abbot, as they maintained before the King's Court at Westminster, had taken away their Guild, summoned them to another place than their own Guild Hall to answer pleas, changed the site of their market, and forced them to render unwonted services. An agreement was drawn up before the judges, by which the burghers won the right to hold their corn market in its accustomed place, to own their common Guild Hall, with a few tenements that belonged to it, and a field called Portmanbrok (the rent of which was set apart for the salary of the mayor), and to maintain their Guild merchant as of old. On the other hand the townspeople conceded that it was the abbot's right to select the Warden of the Guild from among the guildsmen, and require him to take oath of fidelity to himself as well as to the burgesses. The abbot might tallage the town at certain times, and his bailiffs were still to administer justice, and might at any time claim the keys of the Guild Hall, sit there to hold pleas, carry off all profits to the abbot's treasury, and fine the burgesses any sum which it was in their power to pay. Finally

[1] Coates's Reading, 49-50.

it was admitted that the meadow beyond the Portmanbrok belonged to the lord.[1]

After an arrangement which left to the abbot all the weighty matters of government, the control of the burghers' trade and a charge on their profits,[2] it was no wonder that before a hundred years were over the inhabitants of Reading, restless and discontented, were again battling for larger privileges. In 1351 the mayor and commonalty refused obedience to a constable appointed by the abbot's steward, claiming for themselves the right to choose the constables, and present them to take their oaths before the king's justices and the justices of the peace instead of before the abbot. At the same time they raised various fundamental questions as to their rights, just as Lynn was doing almost in the very same year. They asked whether the town was not a royal borough and therefore in no way dependent on the abbey; whether the townsmen had not therefore a right to elect their own mayor; and whether that mayor ought not to exercise jurisdiction over the burgesses and commonalty " according to the custom of the borough and Guild "—questions which one and all afforded fair subjects of dispute for the next hundred and fifty years.

[1] Gross, ii. 202-4.
[2] Some of the fines levied were doubtless used for the townsmen's benefit. For example, there were nineteen bridges within the limits of the borough, which after the dissolution of the monastery fell into decay and were repaired in the time of Elizabeth with the stones from the abbey walls. (Coates's Reading, 64.) But material advantages did not take the place of political freedom.

The burghers henceforth gave the abbot no rest. In the long quarrel the Merchant Guild became the real centre of the common activity, just as it did wherever a town subject to a lord temporal or spiritual failed to win independent jurisdiction of its own.[1] For if there were free boroughs where the mayor, with his council and the common assembly of the burghers in which the whole conduct of government was centred, were in name and fact the accepted constitutional authorities; on the other hand in dependent towns where political freedom was still incomplete the Merchant Guild appears as ostensibly the only means by which the will of the community could find expression; as men recognized in it the one society in whose disciplined ranks they might be enrolled to fight for the liberties they claimed, its organization was held to be the most important of their privileges and the truest symbol of their common life; and it necessarily became the bond of fellowship, the pledge of future freedom the school of political energies.[2] In such towns

---

[1] Gross, i., 90–1. The number of burghers in the Guild seems to have been very small. In 1486, 28 burghers paid *chepin gavell;* in 1487, 22 burgesses; and in 1490–93, 31 burgesses. In 1510 there were 45 burgesses. (Coates's Reading, 58.) There were many who paid fines and dues to the abbot who were of the town and not of the Guild, and this class was doubtless encouraged by the convent, following the same policy as the bishop in Lynn. (Hist. MSS. Com. xi. part 7, 172, 175–6.)

[2] The Guilds were naturally looked on with very little favour by the ecclesiastical lords in such cases. There was a conflict between abbot and town at Malmesbury in the time of Edward the First. The burghers claimed to have a Guild of their own

therefore the Merchant Guild had a vitality and a persistent continuity of life which was unknown elsewhere, and was often preserved in full vigour two or three centuries after it had perhaps suffered decay or transformation elsewhere.

This was the case in Reading. The burghers fell back on the Guild as the one authorized mode of association for public purposes, and in its "morghespeche," or "morning talks," the leading townsfolk discussed how the independence of the borough might be advanced. Successive mayors of the Guild, though still to all appearance appointed as officers of the abbot, became really the representatives of the town, identified themselves absolutely with its interests, and readily led their fellow citizens in revolt against the convent. In 1378 the burghers paid about £5 for a new charter; and twice sent the mayor to London to assert their privileges, and to insist that the convent should be forced to bear a just share of the burden of taxation, and pay a part of the tenth demanded by the King. The messengers were lavish with their gifts to judges and officers and lawyers who might befriend them, eels and pike, perches and salmon and capons; and succeeded so well that the town charters were confirmed in 1400, in 1418, and in 1427.[1]

---

people, who alone had a right to trade in the town, and to take certain taxes for the support of the Guild from all traders who were not of it. The abbot refused to allow them to use their rights. The town fell back on its liberties *when it had been a royal borough*, and appealed to the King. (Gross, ii. 173.) See also the precautions taken by the Bishop about the Guild at Salisbury. (Ibid. 209–10.)   [1] Coates's Reading, 53.

In 1391 the burghers carried the dispute about the appointment of constables to the king's judges at Westminster; and seem to have succeeded in this matter too, for in 1417 the mayor elected the constables in the Guild Hall, and the justices of the peace admitted them to office. About 1420 a Guild Hall was built close to the Hallowed Brook, though the burghers complained of being "so disturbed with beating of battle-dores" by the women washing in the brook that they could scarcely hold their courts or do any public business.[1] They made payments for the clock house, and set up a bell for the community,[2] and appointed a permanent salary for the mayor of five marks, to be paid from the Common Chest instead of the uncertain rent of the Portmanbrok. But when they went on to build a new "Out-butchery," and buy "smiting stocks" for butchers not living in the town, the abbot at once saw an attempt to limit his own market profits which he immediately resented, denying the burghers' right to hold their new out-butchery or receive rents from it. They on their side protested that their Guild was a body corporate, having a Common Hall, a seal, and the right of possessing common property; that they held also a wharf, a common beam or weighing-machine, and the stocks and shambles; that they had been granted freedom from toll throughout the kingdom; that they returned two burgesses to Parliament; and were freed from shire and hundred

[1] They got afterwards from Henry the Eighth the church of the Grey Friars for their Guild Hall.
[2] Hist. MSS. Com. xi. part 7, 172-3.

courts; and finally they asserted, to sum up all the rest, that they had held of the King long before the monastery was founded.[1] In 1431 lawyers were appointed to search the evidences in the Common Chest as to agreements between the town and the abbot. At the same time a Register of the Acts of the mayor and burgesses was begun, and continued year after year without break. In 1436 and 1439 payments were made for the writing out of certain articles as to the privileges of the town; and counsel were again employed to look over the evidences in 1441.[2]

Throughout these years the mayor and officers were constantly at Maidenhead, London, or Canterbury, holding consultations about legal business with Lyttleton and the most famous lawyers. They succeeded in buying a charter for their Guild Hall with sums contributed by rich citizens; and gratefully adorned the building with a picture of the King. The mayor of the guild became more and more the representative of the burghers' hopes, and his greatness the symbol of their triumph. They had not only raised his salary in 1459 to ten nobles,[3] but like their

[1] Coates's Reading, 53, 54. All this time matters were made easier for the townspeople by constant talk of loans to the King. In 1420 the town officers went to Wallingford to discuss the matter with the King. There was a loan made in 1430, and another in 1445. Hist. MSS. Com. xi. part 7, 173, 174.

[2] Hist. MSS. Com. xi. part 7, 174.

[3] Under Henry the Eighth, he received £10. (Coates's Reading, 55, 56.) A woman of the town left three silver cups and one gilt cup for the mayoralty in 1479. Public dinners at each election began in 1492, and feasts for the burgesses

brethren at Lynn they got permission from Henry the Sixth to have a mace carried before him; and in 1459 the mace was actually bought.[1] At this extravagance, however, the abbot made a firm stand, and Henry had to send a letter to the Mayor of Reading, just as he had done eleven years before to the mayor of Lynn, ordering that this privilege should remain with the abbot alone as the token of his supremacy. But the mayor possibly gained his point a little later, for in 1487 he was allowed two Mace-serjeants, so it would seem that at least his tipped staves were now borne by his own servants.[2] He secured too for himself and for the burgesses exemption from serving on juries; and in the same year assumed supervision of the cloth trade. In 1480 the burgesses had done away with individual payments of the "chepin gavell" tax to the abbot, by ordering that it should be given from the Town Chest; and in 1486 a citizen bequeathed property for its payment, so that the townsmen were henceforth freed from all personal difficulties in this matter.[3]

Either the question of the cloth-market or that of the mace-serjeants brought the battle to a climax. The abbot absolutely refused to appoint any "master of the guild, otherwise called mayor," and took upon himself to admit such people as he chose to the office of constable.[4] The guild retorted by choosing a mayor for themselves, who nominated his own officers to keep order, while all alike in this emergency gave

at Christmas and Shrovetide. (Hist. MSS. Com. xi. part 7, 180–1, 176.)   [1] Ibid. 180.   [2] Eng. Guilds, 298.
[3] Hist. MSS. Com. xi. part 7, 175, 180.   [4] Ibid. 212.

their services freely, for in 1493 "nothing was paid to the mayor, because neither he nor any one else charged anything on the office."[1] In the case of the lesser offices the burghers held their own, and when in 1499 the abbot appointed two constables, the mayor thrust them out of their places.[2]

But the triumph of the people was short-lived, for in the long run they proved powerless against the great spiritual corporation which ruled over them. In the very next year, 1500, the inhabitants were utterly defeated as to the election of the mayor himself; and as they still protested, there was once more an appeal eight years later to the judgment of the King's Court. The verdict of the judges threw back the whole question almost to the very point where it had stood centuries before at the time of the earlier appeal in 1254, and the brethren of the Guild were declared of ancient time to have had no other right than the power to present from among themselves three persons, of whom the abbot should choose one as mayor. The two constables, and the ten wardmen of the five wards, might be elected by the mayor and commonalty, but they must be sworn in before the abbot. According to ancient custom the name of any proposed burgess must be given to the abbot fourteen days before his election, and a monk must be present for the assessing of his fine of forty shillings, half of which went to the abbot; an alien's fine might be determined by six burgesses, and if they

[1] Hist. MSS. Com. xi. part 7, 176.
[2] Coates's Reading, 52, 53.

affirmed on oath that the fine was reasonable the abbot was bound to accept it. The question of the out-butchery still remained undecided; but the dispute as to the cloth-trade was settled by a compromise. As in the case of the mayor, the town was to choose three men and present them to the abbot, who should then appoint one of the three to be the keeper of the seal for sealing the cloth.[1]

So closed for the moment the long struggle of two hundred and fifty years—a struggle whose gain was small in comparison with all the cost and labour, the civic enthusiasm, the learning and ability which had been lavished on it. The easy passage to freedom by which the royal towns had travelled, the large and regular expansion of their liberties, the liberal admission of their right to supremacy over their own trade and over the higher matters of law and justice, might well kindle in the subjects of abbey and priory a perpetual unrest, and anger deepened against their masters as they saw themselves, in an age of universal movement, bound to the unchanging order of the past, and condemned to perpetual dependence under a galling system of administration which the secular government had abandoned three hundred years before.

[1] Coates's Reading, 54-5. Hist. MSS. Com. xi. 7, 168-9.

CHAPTER X

BATTLE FOR SUPREMACY

WHEN a borough had won from its lord full rights of self-government, its battles were not yet over. The next effort of the town authorities was to secure complete power over all the inhabitants within their walls, so that they might compel all alike to submit to the town courts, and to bear their share of burdensome duties, such as the payment of taxes, the keeping watch and ward, the defence of the town, the maintenance of its trade, or the enlargement of its liberties—in fact to take their part as good citizens in all that concerned the common weal.

For all towns alike, whatever were their chartered rights, had to reckon not only with their own lord of the manor, but with the great people, whether king or noble or bishop or abbot, or perhaps all of them together, who might own a part of the land within their walls, and might all assert their various and conflicting rights, and multiply officials of every kind with courts and prisons and gallows, to vindicate the lord's authority. Thus in Warwick in the eleventh century, when the population was scarcely over a thousand, the King held a hundred and thirteen houses, and various lords and prelates owned a hundred and twelve, while there were nineteen independent burgesses who had the right of sac and soc. So also in the time of Edward the First there were five gallows in Worcester and the district immediately round the city. One belonged to the town, another to the bishop, and a third to the Earl of Gloucester, while two more were set up by the abbots of Pershore and Westminster who held property in the borough; all of which lords and prelates had the right of hanging thieves and rioters in this little community of about two thousand inhabitants.[1]

A new municipality, face to face with these traditional claims, and powerless before the customary rights of property, could only fall back on friendly treaties by which both sides might win advantage from peaceable compromise. As soon as the burghers had won chartered privileges of trade and freedom from toll throughout the kingdom, they had something to offer to their neighbours, and the bargaining began. They could propose to grant protection and a share in their privileges, and would demand in return that the tenants of alien lords should

---

[1] Miller's Parishes of Worcester, vol. I. Rot. Hun., p. 282, 3 Edward I. In Canterbury there were still in 1835 not less than fifteen precincts within the limits of the corporate authority but exempt from its jurisdiction (Rep. on Mun. Corpor., 31). For crown property in York not under municipal law, see Davies' Walks through York, 27–28.

contribute to their taxes and take part in public duties, and perhaps acknowledge, in some respects at all events, the authority of their courts. But the progress of the negociations and their final result underwent considerable modifications, according as the townspeople had to deal with the constable of the King's castle; with some lord who held property in the borough; or with an ecclesiastical settlement, whether cathedral or monastery, planted within the liberties.

I. The Castle Fee was a bit of the royal territory altogether independent of the municipality. In Bristol, for example, the castle had its own market at its gate; and its inhabitants were exempt from the town justice, so that if one of the tenants of the fee committed a crime he was sent to Gloucester thirty miles distant instead of being tried in Bristol itself. Since the castle fee lay outside the jurisdiction of the town, its ditches became the refuge of felons and malefactors flying from the bailiffs, and as late as 1627 it was stated that two hundred poor persons were dwelling within the precincts who mostly lived by begging, besides a number of outlaws, excommunicated people, and offenders who found them a hiding place, and when soldiers and sailors were impressed great multitudes of able men "fled thither as to a place of freedom, where malefactors live in a lawless manner."[1] From his position as the king's lieutenant the governor or Constable of the Castle in important frontier or seaport towns was a very great official, with an authority as military commander

[1] Ricart's Kalendar, 117.

which gave him the right of interference in local affairs, and whose power might easily prove a real danger to municipal institutions.[1] In Bristol, where the mayors after their election "did fetch and take their oath and charge at the castle gate" from the constable as the representative of the King, he was practically the official arbiter in any crisis of town politics, and when a revolt of the commons broke out in 1312 against a handful of merchants who controlled the municipal government, the party in power at once claimed the constable's help against their fellow-townsmen. Thereupon the commons assaulted the castle and built forts against it, so that the forces of three counties which were marched to the rescue by their sheriffs could not quell the riot; but the castle party finally triumphed, the insurrection was violently put down, twelve burgesses banished, the rule of those who had usurped privileges claimed by the whole commonalty confirmed, and the enemy of the Bristol burghers, Lord Maurice of Berkeley, appointed by the King "custos of the castle and town."[2]

It was only however in a few boroughs that exceptional military difficulties made the post of governor one of great or permanent authority, as for instance in Bristol or Southampton. And even in these towns a good understanding was before long established between king and burghers, and powers exercised by

[1] In 1285 the Bristol charter was forfeited because of encroachments on the rights of the constable of the castle. Seyer's Bristol, ii. 74.
[2] Seyer's Bristol, ii. 88–109.

royal officers which impeded the free developement of municipal life were withdrawn without jealous alarms on the sovereign's side, or prolonged agitation on the part of the town. The Bristol mayors were freed by royal charter from the necessity of taking their oath from the constable in 1345. And in towns such as Norwich, where military considerations early became of comparatively little importance, the castle tenants were made to contribute to the city taxes in the thirteenth century, and in the course of the next hundred years, were put unreservedly under the control of the city authorities.[1]

II. There were not very many cases where a lay lord became a formidable enemy to municipal freedom, either from the extent of his property in a town, or from his power of enforcing his claims. Such disputes as did arise were settled in various ways by purchase or friendly compact, or by gaining from the Crown a charter which conferred such rights of control as were necessary for discipline and order. Boroughs on the royal demesne naturally found themselves supported by the King in urging these demands, but the appeal to force always lay behind the legal settlement, and there was occasionally a serious battle before the question of supremacy was finally decided. A bitter fight was waged between Bristol[2] and the

[1] Norwich Doc., Stanley v. Mayor, &c., 25. Here the fee was given to the citizens as early as 1346.

[2] There were also occasional difficulties as to the jurisdiction of Bristol over the Temple fee, which first belonged to the Templars, then to the Knights of St. John of Jerusalem, and was not finally incorporated with the city till 1543. (Seyer's Bristol, i. 134-6.)

lords of Berkeley, who owned Redcliffe, and claimed the river where they had built a quay as part of their lordship; who had their own courts and their own prison; who held their own markets and fair; and who broke the Bristol weights and measures, and refused to take the measures of assize from the mayor even though in such matters he acted as the King's marshal. They fought long and fiercely for their power, even after a royal charter in 1240 had given the jurisdiction over Redcliffe to the mayor.[1] In 1305 an energetic young lord Maurice of Berkeley to whom his father had given Redcliffe Street tried to assert his rights, but at the ringing of the common bell the Bristol men assembled, broke into Maurice's house, took away a prisoner from him, and refused to allow him to hold any court, or to buy and sell any wares in Redcliffe Street. Upon this the young lord, appearing with "great multitudes of horse and foot," forced the burgesses to do suit to him, and cast those who refused into a pit, while the women who came to help their husbands in the fray were trodden under foot. He set free prisoners from the Bristol gaol, assaulted Bristol burgesses at Tetbury fair, claimed dominion over the Severn, and seized the Bristol ships. All this did Maurice, "than whom a more martial knight, and of a more daring spirit, of the age of twenty-four years, the kingdom nor

[1] In 1240 the inhabitants of Redcliffe were combined and incorporated with the town of Bristol; and the ground of S. Austin's by the river was granted to the commonalty by the abbot for certain money paid by the said commonalty. Ricart, 28.

scarce the Christian world then had;" and the
mayor and burgesses left King and Parliament no
rest with their petitions, telling of outrage after
outrage committed by him, till commissioners were
appointed to examine their complaints, and to Lord
Maurice the sequel of this angry business was a
fine of 1,000 marks, afterwards commuted to service
with the King's army with ten horsemen. A few
years later moreover the Bristol men found opportunity to avenge their bitter grudge, for when he
was taken in rebellion the mayor and the commonalty,
" out of an inveterate hatred and remembrance of
former passages," threw into the common gaol every
man who was even suspected of having adhered to
the faction of Maurice.[1] Troubles again broke out
in 1331, and the mayor and burgesses gathered at
the ringing of the common bell for an assault on a
Lord Thomas of Berkeley, destroyed his tumbrill
and pillory, carried his bailiff to the Guild Hall,
and forced him to swear that he would never again
execute any judgements in the courts. The next
year however the town, " taking the advantage of
the time while the said lord was in trouble about
the murder of King Edward the Second in his castle
of Berkeley," settled the matter for ever by an opportune payment to the King of £40, for which the
mayor and burgesses obtained a confirmation of all
their charters, and especially that which granted
that Redcliffe Street should be within their jurisdiction.

No sooner was the dispute finally decided than

[1] Lives of the Berkeleys, i. 177, 196–201.

rancour quickly died away, and the burgesses of Bristol settled down into the most friendly relations with Berkeley castle. The lords of Berkeley took to trading in wool and corn and wine, and went partners with Bristol men in robbing carracks of Genoa as well as in lawful traffic.[1] So far had the wheel of fortune turned that one of the lords who made a treaty of peace with the Earl and Countess of Shrewsbury meekly appeared before the mayor and council of Bristol to give surety;[2] and when he went out to fight at Nibley the Bristol merchants sent men to his help.[3] The alliance was cemented by marriage when a Berkeley in 1475 took to wife a daughter of the mayor of Bristol;[4] and when she died in 1517 the mayor, the master of the Guild, the aldermen, sheriffs, chamberlains, and wardens of Bristol, and thirty-three crafts, followed the coffin with two hundred torches—altogether a multitude of five or six thousand people. A "drinking" was made by the family for the mayor and his brethren in St. Mary's Hall, at which they were entertained with a first course of cakes, comfits,

---

[1] They took to trading about 1367. Berkeleys, i. 365-6. Ibid. i. 23. Thomas Berkeley got leave from Henry the Sixth "for three of his factors to go with the ship called the *Cristopher* with any lawful merchandise, and to sell the same and return and go again. And the year before, this Thomas and two of his partners had the like licence to go with their ship called the *Trinity of Berkeley*, to Bordeaux, and there to unload and load again, and bring any merchandise into England." Ibid. ii. 83, 136.

[2] Ibid. ii. 68. [3] Ibid. ii. 113-4.

[4] The new marquis was very angry at the unworthiness of such a match with so mean blood, and made it an excuse for disinheriting him. Ibid. ii. 172, 173.

and ale, followed by another of marmalade, snoket, red wine, and claret, and a third of wafers and blanch powder, with romney and muscatel; "and I thank God," wrote the steward, "no plate nor spoons was lost, yet there was twenty dozen spoons."[1]

III. Ecclesiastical corporations also nominally held their property in the various towns by the usual feudal tenure, just like the lay lords; and when a borough formally stated its theoretic relations with them both lay and spiritual lords were put on exactly the same level. The "Customs" of Hereford show us the ideal view of these relations as the burghers liked to picture them. "Fees" within the walls[2] were held by both ecclesiastical and lay lords, whose tenants desired a share in the city privileges, and the Hereford men classed them all together under a common description. "There are some lords and their tenants who are dwellers and holders of lands and tenements within the said bounds, which they hold by a certain service which is called 'liberum feodum'; because long ago they besought us that they might be of us, and they would be rated and taxed with us, and they are free among us concerning toll and all other customs and services by us made, but concerning their foreign services which they do, or ought to do, and of old have done, their lords are not excluded by us nor by our liberties; for we never use to intermix ourselves with them in any things touching those tenures, but only with those which concern us, or their tenures which for a time hath been of

[1] Berkeleys, ii. 175, 176.
[2] Journ. Arch. Ass. xxvii. 461.

our condition."[1] Tenants still bound to render feudal services to their lords were not reckoned among the true aristocracy of the freemen, who in admitting them to a limited fellowship marked their sense of the difference of status between the free burgher and the man who was but half emancipated; "and such men ought not to be called citizens or our fellow citizens .... because they are 'natives,' or born in the behalf of their lords, and do hold their tenements by foreign services and are not burgesses." It was only when a tenant bought a house in the city and was in scot and lot with the citizens, that they allowed that he "is free and of our condition; but let him take heed to himself that he depart not from the city to any place into the power of his lord."[2]

But the municipality was perfectly firm in the assertion of the authority which it had a right to exercise over all those who were admitted to the privileges of the common trade, and took a very decided tone with the spiritual as well as with the lay lords. To the Hereford burghers it was obvious that the ecclesiastical tenants only enjoyed a share in the town liberties by the grace of the citizens, and in virtue of "a composition betwixt us and them, which we for reverence to God and to the Church our mother had granted the same unto them; and also for divers alms to be given to our citizens and other poor and impotent of our city in an almshouse by the keeper of the same for ever. And it was not our intentions that these men, the

[1] Journ. Arch. Ass. xxvii. 480.   [2] Ibid. 481.

tenants of the bishop, dean, and chapter should have nor enjoy our laws and customs, unless after the same manner as we enjoy them "—that is, as they went on carefully to explain, every one must acknowledge law as well as privilege, and be subject like the citizens to authority. They were all to be obedient to the Bailiff for the execution of the King's writs; nor could they claim any immunities or independent jurisdiction in the King's highway, seeing that all offenders taken there were to be judged by the city Bailiff. If the peace or the tranquillity of Hereford was disturbed by the tenants of any fee, the city Bailiff, " taking with him the bailiff of that fee and twelve of the most discreetest and stoutest men of the whole city," might " by all way of rigour " compel the offenders to come before them, and force them to end their discords and make amends; if they refused, the whole community " shall account and hold them as rebels; and that they come not among them in their congregations."[1] All bailiffs, whether of Church estates or others, were bound to help the chief Bailiff of the city in apprehending thieves and malefactors and keeping order. A vagabond, even if he were an ecclesiastical tenant, who made a noise at night " to the terror of his fellow-citizens," might be taken up by any inhabitant and brought to the city jail till one o'clock the next day; when, in polite recognition of the lower jurisdictions, he was solemnly handed over in a public place to the bailiff of his own fee, by him to be kept in prison for a day and a night, and then returned to the city

[1] Journ. Arch. Ass. xxvii. 467.

prison, "there to stay until he hath made amends as the Bailiff and commonalty shall think fit." The tenants of the various fees were allowed to plead in the town courts at their pleasure, a privilege not granted to aliens; and in matters touching frank-pledge, or anything "which could not be amended in the courts of those lords," the city claimed rights of arbitration, and power to determine such cases "according to the laws of the city and not according to the customs, unless it be by special favour of the commonalty."[1] All questions concerning lands and tenements in the city were to be decided by the free citizens only; and if ecclesiastical tenants refused to submit to the jurisdiction of the city magistrates and absented themselves from the court, "then our chief Bailiff, calling unto him six or more witnesses of his citizens, shall go to the cathedral church, and there before the chapter shall notify or declare the disobedience of their bailiffs and of their tenants." If the canons would not assist or agree, the Bailiff should announce that he must then proceed himself to administer full justice, though "by his will or knowledge he would not hurt the liberties of their mother the Church." This concession to ecclesiastical sensibilities was apparently looked on by the men of Hereford as a proof of fine magnanimity. "And it was not wont so to be done, but that there was a composition had between us, which we for the reverence of God and the tranquillity of their tenants and our citizens, had granted unto them."

All this story, however, comes to us from the side

[1] Journ. Arch. Ass. xxvii. 480.

of the town, and has something of the ring of a lordly municipal pride; it almost sounds like an ideal view of the compromise between the contracting powers as conceived by the burghers, and one to which the Church party must have demurred. At any rate by whatever means the municipality of Hereford had won a jurisdiction of this sort over the bishop's tenants, it was singular in the possession of such authority, which has no parallel in towns like Canterbury, York, Lincoln, Norwich, Exeter, and many more. But the situation, even as the citizens put it, is so complicated in its arrangements that we could scarcely wonder if a state of truce depending on provisions so elaborate should under provocation be transformed into a state of open war; nor can we question the wisdom of townspeople everywhere in making it their fixed purpose to establish one undivided and supreme law for the government of each community. How important the question at issue really was to the town's life we may see from the story of Winchester.

The mayor of Winchester was at the head of what seems, on paper at least, a powerful and elaborate corporation, worthy of a great city which held itself to have been built "in the age of the world 2995, ninety-nine years before the building of Rome," and "environed with stone walls" exactly 533 years later.[1] A common assembly met twice a year. There were two coroners and two constables, six aldermen of the wards with their six beadles, a town clerk and four serjeants, a council of twenty-four elected every year, and

[1] Gross, ii. 265.

four auditors of this council, besides a body of twelve jurors chosen whenever there was necessity, who sat at "the Pavilion," and with whom the mayor perambulated the liberties to view the rivulets and rivers.[1] The boundaries of the city were apparently marked out by a rough square formed by the walls and ditch; but to the mayor and aldermen of the fifteenth century, the idea that their authority should reach as far as the limits allowed by the girth of the walls would have seemed a far-off counsel of perfection.

For right across the city from the east to the west gates stretched the High Street, cutting the town into two equal halves; and to the south of the High Street one may say roughly that the mayor had no authority at all. Near the west gate stood the King's castle, where municipal law of course did not run. Beside the castle lay the great convent of S. Swithun, and next to it the cathedral, both fenced round by a wall which shut out all lay jurisdiction or intrusion of any kind. Nearer to the east gate lay the palace of the bishop, who was also of course exempt from secular interference, and who ruled with supreme authority over the bishop's Soke that stretched away beyond the gate, and took tolls of all merchandise that passed along the river.[2] His tenants while remaining outside municipal control had still the right to buy and sell all kinds of merchandize in the city which according to the burghers' complaint was to their hurt and loss; and the exceeding difficulty of any regula-

[1] Hist. MSS. Com. vi. 601. Gross, ii. 254.
[2] The bailiff of the Soke was sometimes called the Mayor of the Soke to emphasize his independence.

tion of trade in the midst of this competition of privileged workers, with the ruin of the city treasury which it threatened, are shown by a quarrel between the bishop and the burghers as to a street which the bishop had claimed as his property in 1275; for when people discovered that in that liberty so appropriated they paid nothing, since the city bailiff could not enter it to make distraint, nearly all the clothworkers forthwith withdrew themselves from the other streets and went to live there to the manifest loss of the community, and the great profit of the bishop.[1]

The northern part of the town was more than half given up to fields and gardens, the shops and houses of traders and artizans forming but a narrow settlement that gathered closely along the central street and the lanes that opened from it. And even of this district a part was wholly withdrawn from the city jurisdiction. The Queens, whose "morning gift" Winchester was, lived "tax free" in the Queen's House opposite the King's palace near the west gate, and took rent and tolls from the row of Queen's stalls on the High Street. At the east gate was another belt of ecclesiastical property—the settlements of the Franciscans and Dominicans,—and next to them a group of poor houses depending on S. Swithun's.[2]

[1] Gross, ii. 254. For the way in which a bit of the town under ecclesiastical and not under municipal control might serve as a sort of sanctuary against the tax gatherers, see the complaint of the Bristol commonalty about Temple Street. (Rot. Parl. i. 484.)

[2] They had once been occupied by "good citizens," but all through the Middle Ages were filled by a very poor population. (Kitchin's Winchester, 75.)

Right in the middle of the town, opposite the Guild Hall in the High Street, was the liberty of " Godbeate" belonging to S. Swithun's, where the writ of the King or the authority of the city had no power; and whose church formed a sanctuary always open for ill-doers flying from municipal justice. The very curfew-bell which hung in its tower rang out from land that defied the mayor's authority.[1]

Winchester had not even control of its own gates. The bishop had charge of one; and two were in the hands of the convent, which in times of civil war could freely admit within the city walls the armies of the side opposed to the townsfolk.[2] Even the commerce of the place was taken out of the burghers hands. Not only did the bishop take tolls of the river traffic, but once a year when the great fair of S. Giles' took place he assumed supreme command in Winchester; for the time all civic government was altogether suspended; the bishop closed all shops in and round the town; traders coming with their cloth and woollen goods, their wines, their pottery, their brass-work, or their eastern spices, were subject to his jurisdiction, and handed over to him the biggest share of the profits, which he divided with the various religious establishments in the city.[3] At other times

---

[1] Kitchin's Winchester, 46-7, 75-7.

[2] In 1264 there was a violent fray near the King's Gate, the citizens fighting to keep the monks from admitting the followers of De Montfort. (Ibid. 130.) The convent kept control of the King's Gate till 1520. (Ibid. 132.)

[3] For the bishop's rights during the fair such as tronage, authority to take all weights and measures and bear them to the Pavilion and there make assay, to demand that the people of

the King's chamberlains and the King's clerk of the market regulated business in their master's interest, and collected the dues of the market and tolls on every load carried by man or horse into the town.[1]

Winchester suffered also from the memory of its ancient state as the capital and residence of the West Saxon Kings; and its mayor almost alone among the mayors of English towns in the fifteenth century had to go to London to take his oath of office from the King's judges,[2] just as the mayor of London does to this day. He could win neither freedom nor independence. At home he was beset with dangers; he might be imprisoned by the King for one offence, and punished by the bishop for another.[3]

the city should come to the Pavilion to present cry raised and bloodshed, and other things touching the peace of our Lord the King, see Hist. MSS. Com. vi. 595-605. Compare his powers in Southampton during the same fair. There he might send his bailiff to see that only food was weighed or sold in the town, that no merchant whether resident or not ventured to sell anything except food, that there was no weighing or measuring, that merchants who came with their goods swore they did not bring them to sell at this time. (Hist. MSS. Com. xi. part 3, pp. 67, 68.) The convent also had its own home and foreign trade on a very large scale. (Kitchin's Winchester, 161.)

[1] English Guilds, 353, &c. 358. (Hist. MSS. Com. vi. 495-605.)

[2] This custom, once common (Madox, 152-3), was abandoned in Ipswich as early as 1317, and seems to have generally died out in the fourteenth century, though Gloucester sent its bailiffs to Westminster till 1483.

[3] In 1244 a mayor who had obeyed the King's orders to shut the city gates against a bishop whose election the King opposed, was severely punished by the bishop when he gained possession of his see and palace. (Kitchin's Winchester, 121.) The mayor was thrown into a London prison because a state prisoner had escaped from Winchester. (Ibid. 139.)

Against such odds as the burghers had to face it was almost hopeless for any corporation to contend; and the helpless townsfolk could but show their impatience and discontent in petty quarrels with the convent as to the site of a market, or blindly do battle for worthless Kings such as Henry the Third or Edward the Second if the monks took up the opposite party.[1] The struggle for independence has no fine record of stirring incidents; but that there should have been any conflict at all before the settling down of quiescence and final apathy is a striking instance of the vitality and persistence of municipal institutions.

It is impossible not to attribute to the hopeless situation of the municipality before the rival authorities in the city, and especially the powerful lords of convent and cathedral, much of the calamity of its history. For at a time when prosperity was generally increasing, its fortunes steadily sank. In 1450 the citizens drew a terrible picture of the local distress, not in the vague phrases which we meet with elsewhere when for some special purpose happier boroughs put on a temporary show of distress, but with a minute exactness which betrays the truth and the whole measure of their suffering. Winchester, they declared, "is become right desolate." Nine hundred and ninety-seven houses stood empty, and in seventeen parish churches there was no longer any

---

[1] Compare the action of Norwich. In the Wars of the Roses the Winchester people were, like their bishop Wayneflete, Lancastrian, but they had neither energy nor power to play any important part. (Hist. MSS. Com. vi. 147.)

service. A list is given of eleven streets "that be
fallen down in the city of Winchester within eighty
years last passed"; and in each case an account is
added of the number of householders that had
formerly lived in the street, a hundred, a hundred
and forty, or two hundred, as the case might be, where
there were now but two or three left. Since the last
Parliament held there eighty-one households had
fallen. "The desolation of the said poor city is so
great, and yearly falling, for there is such a decay
and unwin, that without gracious comfort of the King
our sovereign lord, the mayor and the bailiffs must
of necessity cease, and deliver up the city and the
keys into the King's hands."[1] To produce a distress
such as this no doubt industrial causes were at work,
and Winchester probably suffered as Canterbury did
from changes in the woollen manufacture and in
trade routes. But nowhere in any considerable city
do we find a parallel to the utter ruin of this unfortunate community. Nowhere, on the other hand,
were the conditions of municipal life so fatal, if once
prosperity began to dwindle or the pressure of outward circumstances became such as to call on the
resources of the people. Through the breaking up
of the city into separate and independent fragments
the whole burden of any difficulty had to be borne
by the little company of inhabitants governed by the
mayor; and so heavily did the common municipal
charges and expenses fall on the scanty population of
burghers shut into the narrow area which was under
municipal government, and from which alone the

[1] Archæologia, i. 91, 93–4.

authorities could gather the fee-farm and the royal taxes, maintain the bridge and walls, provide householders for the nightly watch, and furnish men and arms for the defence of the city; and we do not wonder that the inhabitants at last began to renounce, or refuse to accept, a franchise which brought such formidable responsibilities, or that they sought to escape from a city doomed to ruin. An attempt was made in 1430 to revive manufacture and commerce by an invitation to all kinds of traders and artificers to come and do business in Winchester free of toll.[1] But the experiment in free trade was quickly abandoned, probably because the corporation could not meet the heavy yearly expenses without the customary taxes levied on trade;[2] and in 1450 the citizens laid a petition before Henry the Sixth, praying him to consider the extent of their distress. They were bound, they said, to pay yearly a rent of 112 marks to the King, "for the which said fee-farm so to be paid your bailiffs have little or naught of certainty to raise it of, but only of casualties and yearly leases £40 or more." There was further a sum of £50 10s. 4d. for the tax of the fifteenth, "the which when it is levyable, some one man in the said city is set unto four marks and some five marks, because your said city is desolate of people." Then came a sum of 60s. to be paid yearly to the Magdalen

---

[1] Gross, ii. 260-1.
[2] Payments for stalls went to the King's ferm. (Ibid. 262.) The question was therefore one of revenue and not one of protection.

Hospital;[1] and besides that there were the expenses of two burgesses to Parliament who cost 4s. a day; " and also the great charges and daily costs the which your said poor city beareth about the enclosing and murage of your said city."[2] To add to all their trouble a grant which the king had made to the municipality in 1439 of forty marks from the ulnage and subsidies of woollen cloths had been withdrawn again; and the commonalty sadly entreat that it may be restored.

The King allowed the payment of the forty marks during the next fifty years, and Winchester made one or two further attempts at mending its fortunes. The people of Southampton had as long ago as 1406 succeeded in obtaining a license from the bishop of Winchester, to buy and sell within their town during the fair of St. Giles;[3] and the mayor and community of Winchester perhaps hoped to follow this example. In 1451 they raised a debate as to the franchises and customs of the fair, and interfered with the bishop's privileges; but their usual ill luck pursued them and they were obliged to submit and give a promise that he should never again be disturbed from having the keeping of the city and the customs aforesaid.[4] A few years later a transient gleam of hope was cast across the unhappy town when the Italian merchants were driven out of

[1] Archæologia, i. 102.
[2] The fraternity of St. John allowed nearly £35 a year towards the maintenance of the bridge and walls.
[3] Hist. MSS. Com. xi. part 3, 77.
[4] Ibid. vi. 595-605.

London in 1456, and in this sudden emergency hired the "great old mansions"[1] which the Winchester traders had allowed to fall into decay, putting the owners to heavy expenses for repairs. But they seem never to have occupied the mansions after all. Perhaps they were disheartened by the sense of failing trade and oppressive taxes; or they possibly feared the dangers that might come to them in a town that had never been allowed powers to govern and defend and deal fairly by its own townsfolk. In any case they left the big empty houses to go to Southampton, and Winchester was none the better.[2]

Winchester was an extreme instance of difficulties which were felt in every other town in a greater or less degree. For scarcely any important borough was without some ecclesiastical settlement within its walls, and everywhere the dispute took the gravest form. With the King or with a neighbouring lord the boroughs might make terms of peace, or impose conditions as conquerors, but their most imposing demonstrations were inevitably routed before the power of the Church. Outbreaks of popular fury in which from time to time the irritation of the burghers found expression have often been represented as symptoms of a spirit of malice and misrule by which an ignorant mob was instigated to attack the most

---

[1] Gregory's Chronicle of London, ed. Gairdner, Early English Text Soc. 199.

[2] A charter of Edward the Fourth still speaks of Winchester as now being "quite unable to pay the fee-farm rent of 100 marks." (Kitchin's Winchester, 174.)

beneficent institution known to their society and with no justification save from their lawless temper seek to appropriate to themselves its privileges and possessions. But the causes of the conflict were more valid and serious. As the instances given in the next chapter prove, the burghers learned by a genuine experience to gauge the beneficence of the Church's claims to temporal authority. There does not seem to have been in England, as there often was abroad, the additional stimulus of religious revolt, for the practical townspeople apparently did not find the slightest difficulty in distinguishing between spiritual influence and secular jurisdiction, mainly perhaps because the power of the ecclesiastical potentates in England was of so limited a kind as to awaken but a moderate fear and equally moderate excitement. But in face of the secular problem created by the presence of a rival authority ruling over half the space enclosed in the town walls—an authority with which no permanent agreement could ever be concluded and which was manifestly fatal to the dignity or the success of municipal government—the boroughs were forced, as a mere matter of self-preservation, into insistent and reiterated demands that this double rule should be abolished, and that there should be but one undivided and supreme control in each community for civil affairs. When the pole-axes and daggers with which they at first sought to enforce their convictions were laid aside, they turned to the law-courts and the paper wars of Westminster to seek a remedy for their grievances; and it is in the records of trials from the middle of the fifteenth century to the Reformation in which the pleadings of both sides may be heard that we find the real justification of the burghers' claim to civic supremacy, and of their determined assaults on the political independence of ecclesiastical communities.

CHAPTER XI

THE TOWNS AND THE CHURCH

In the history of Winchester we may perhaps find a clue to the explanation of that great controversy which for centuries divided the mediæval municipalities and the religious corporations into two hostile armies, —armies that chafed under the restraints of an enforced and angry truce, and from time to time broke into the brief exhilaration of a free fight. There were certain towns, such as Exeter or Canterbury or Norwich, where the municipality was as free as royal charters could make it and acknowledged no dependence on Cathedral or Priory, and where notwithstanding Town and Church were always in arms against one another, and the task of adjusting their mutual relations presented such insoluble difficulties that every other question seemed of easy settlement in comparison with a problem so insistent, so manifold in its forms, so tremendous in its proportions in the eyes of burgher and of ecclesiastic. The convent or chapter, entrenched behind its circuit of walls and towers, with its own system of laws, its own executive, its independent trade and revenues, had practically no interest either in the prosperity or the security of the town, while its keenest activities, whether from the point of view of business or religion, were enlisted in uncompromising defence of ecclesiastical privilege. On the other hand the body of burghers, conscious of the difficulties of government, with a mass of complicated business thrown on their hands and a heavy financial responsibility, nervously keeping guard over their franchises, inspired by a commanding sense of the importance of strict organization, and an ambition stimulated by tradition, success, and capacity, found in common experience reasons for judging that a double system of law and a double authority was the negation of order, peace, or material prosperity in their little republic. Their avowed object was to put an end to this division of the borough into two camps, and to secure for the community the ultimate control of administration within the city boundaries. Hence the issues raised between the townspeople and the clerical order were direct and clear. Questions of temporal and spiritual power, of ecclesiastical jurisdiction, of the immunities claimed by the "clergy," of the gulf that separated the servant of the Church from the citizen of the State—all these things were forced home to the people with the sharpness, variety, and force of practical illustration. The war which in the twelfth century had been waged on behalf of the State and the Church by their great representatives, Henry the Second and Archbishop Thomas, was during the next three centuries brought down into every borough and fought out there in more humble fashion by provincial mayors and ecclesiastics of a circumscribed and stinted fame.

And as the quarrel was long so it was practically universal. It was this that made the struggle so momentous. Few boroughs after all were subject to the absolute rule of ecclesiastical lords; and their attempts to win freedom were local, isolated, without national significance. But all the great towns had one or more ecclesiastical bodies established within their boundaries, and all were able to appreciate the character of the conflict entailed on them. Nor were the consequences of the dispute exaggerated by the combatants on either side. During centuries of strife they had abundant opportunity of gauging its importance—from the time of Edward the First, when, by the enclosing of churchyards and ecclesiastical precincts with walls, the attempt was made to shut in religious authorities within their own limits, and give the town undivided responsibility outside these boundaries—till the time when triumphant burghers saw walls and towers levelled to the ground under Henry the Eighth.

For in the war waged by burghers against clerics who used spiritual authority to create temporal sovereignty, and in this temporal power then found means to enforce spiritual claims,—though the combatants were people of no account, fighting their quarrel out in remote and isolated boroughs, and though the noise of the battle no longer resounded as it had once done throughout Europe,—the conflict was still the same, the questions were as vital for the just ordering of human society, and the tenacity of the opponents was as great as ever. The disputes covered the whole field of practical life. In matters of trade there was not only the rivalry of two trading companies under different conditions of wealth, influence, and protection;[1] but even in the case of individuals there was unfair competition, as when a citizen gave up his dwelling in the town, obtained a corrody in some ecclesiastical house, and claimed the benefits of citizenship without bearing its obligations.[2] Sometimes the burghers found themselves called to defend against the ecclesiastical lawyers a right which had been proved essential to their freedom—the right of being tried only in their own courts—and the commonalty would make ordinances that no process-server should carry or cite elsewhere men or women living in the borough, and the jury of the Leet Court kept watch and made their presentment of summoners, commissary, and clerks, who had dealt lightly with the liberties or goods of the citizens, or called them to distant courts.[3] Or again, the invaluable privilege of having all matters that concerned the commons of the borough tried by a jury of inhabitants and not of aliens, might be put in jeopardy. In Lincoln the dean and chapter had a special grudge against trials "by

[1] See the case of Lincoln, Rot. Parl. i. 156-7.
[2] Hudson's Leet Jurisdiction of Norwich (Selden Soc.).
[3] Cutts' Colchester, 149. Hudson's Norwich Leet-Jurisdiction (Selden Soc.), 17. See pp. xxxvii., xli. The constables of Nottingham at the court leet present the "Master Official (of the archdeacon) for excessive and extorcious taking of fees" for probate of testaments, and for over assessing poor folks and men's servants at Easter for their tythes. (Records, iii. 364.)

people of the same city, which be so favourable one to another that they doubt not to make false oaths, and that because they be encouraged, forasmuch as they have not been before this time convict by foreigners by colour of their franchise." On their complaint "our lord the King, willing, for the cause aforesaid, *to provide for the quietness of the said church*, and full right to be done as well to the said bishop, dean, and chapter and their successors," ordered that henceforth "if any of the parties feel himself grieved of a false oath made by such assize, jury, or inquest, the attaint shall be granted to him, and the record sent by writ into the King's Bench or into the Common Pleas; and that the sheriff impanel the jury of such attaint of foreigners of the county, without sending to the franchise of the said city, and that the justices shall take the same jury of the same foreigners, notwithstanding any franchise granted to the same city, or other usage to the contrary."[1] The question of sanctuary, too, remained a standing trouble, and the bailiffs of the borough who sent town clerks and town serjeants to make proclamation for weeks together at the abbey gate calling upon a debtor who had fled from his creditors to appear for judgement, had small sympathy with the abbot's privileges.[2] Whenever burghers had liberty and opportunity to act on their own judgement they found no difficulty in coming to a decision as to the sanctity imposed by religion on territories

[1] 13 Richard the Second, 1, c. 18. Statute 4 Henry the Fifth, c. 5, repeats with some alterations that of Richard.
[2] 1454, Cutts' Colchester, 150-1.

consecrated to sacred uses. From old premises they drew new conclusions. "As holiness becomes the Lord's House," declared the mayor, jurats, and whole community of Rye in 1483, "in future, to the honour of God and of the glorious Virgin Mary, the parish church of the said town, with the churchyard and the manse of the vicarage thereof, shall be of the same freedom, and with as much liberty as the other houses of the freemen, especially as to arrests and other matters."[1]

There is perhaps no better illustration of the character and conditions of the controversy between town and church than the story of the quarrel between Exeter city and the Cathedral, which has been preserved for us in the letters of an able mayor, who at a very important crisis conducted the case of his fellow-citizens against the chapter, and whose phrases, written in the heat of battle, carry us back into the very midst of a long-forgotten strife. Descended from an old county family which had thrown in its lot with the burghers of Exeter and become traders in the city and leaders in its counsels, John Shillingford was born into a tradition of civic patriotism. His father served as mayor from 1428 to 1430 and was noted for being learned in the law; and John Shillingford himself was mayor three times, and the distinguished leader from 1445 to 1448 of a struggle for independence which was already a hundred and fifty years old.

From 1206 or earlier Exeter had been governed by its own mayor and bailiffs, and the citizens held their town at a fee-farm rent from the King.

[1] Hist. MSS. Com. v. 496.

But a century later the mayor was a mere dependent of the Earl of Devonshire, wearing his "livery" as one of his retainers and acknowledging his protection. However it happened on a certain day in 1309 that the earl and bishop made an attempt to buy all the fish in the Exeter market, leaving none for the townsfolk. Then the mayor, "minding the welfare of the commons of the said city, and that they also might have the benefit of the said market," ruled that one-third of the fish must be given to the citizens. The earl with loud threatenings angrily ordered his rebellious dependent to appear before him. Followed by a tumultuous procession of " his brethren and honest commons of the said city," the mayor went from the Guild Hall to the earl's house, entered his lord's "lodging chamber," and there took off his "livery" coat and gave it back to the earl once for all, the commons meanwhile beating at the door and loudly demanding their mayor, till the terrified earl entreated him to quiet their clamour. The town forthwith passed a law that no citizen should ever again wear "foreigner's livery," and so began the long fight for municipal independence.[1]

For the same two great powers ever kept watch on the Exeter citizens and their market, if by chance there was any profit which could be turned their way. At the town gates the Earls of Devonshire held Exe Island and the adjoining suburb, commanded the navigation of the Exe, forced the mayor to lay aside his mace as he approached the suburb, and sought to recall the days when he had worn their

[1] Freeman's Exeter, 165.

livery. A more dangerous enemy was encamped within the walls. Just opposite the little town-hall rose the great wall with its towers which guarded the bishop's palace, the cathedral, and the ecclesiastical precincts; and within this fortified enclosure ruled an august power that defied the petty upstart forces of the mayor and his group of shopkeepers outside. The conflict of the town with the Earls,[1] if it lasted for something like three hundred years, was still of minor significance. The conflict with the Church was far more dangerous in form and serious in its issues.

The town and the close, as we are told by the mayor in 1448, had "been in debate by divers times almost by time of eightscore years, and that I could never know, find nor read that we ever took a suit against them, but ever stand in defence as a buckler player, and smiter never."[2] Now at last, however, the citizens were resolved "once to smite, taking a suit,"[3] as became the temper and traditions of the fifteenth century when such quarrels were fought out, not with clubs and daggers, but in the "paper wars of Westminster." As the crisis approached the townsfolk made ready for the fray. Determined that their battle should be conducted by the most capable man among them, at Michaelmas, 1444, they elected as their mayor John Shil-

[1] Freeman's Exeter, 84–5, 165–6.

[2] Shillingford's Letters (Camden Society), p. 68. An order of the town had been issued in 1339 that no clerk of the consistory court was to be chosen mayor or bailiff or allowed to meddle with the elections. Freeman's Exeter, 147.

[3] The bishop had taken an action years before in 1432–3. Shillingford's Letters, xiv.

lingford. He refused to accept office, upon which they sent to Westminster and procured a writ under the Privy Seal ordering him either to submit or pay a fine of £1,000, a sum which probably no single individual in Exeter at that time possessed. In February 1445 therefore, he "came to the Guild Hall and there was sworn; and though at the first with an evil will, yet in the end did perform it very well,"[1]—so well indeed that the bishop even saw in "the wilful labour of John Shillingford" the main cause of all "the great hurt and loss of the said church and city."[2]

Once Mayor Shillingford quickly threw down his challenge to the chapter. On Ascension Day, 1445, the city serjeant followed a servant of the chancellor into the precincts, and there arrested him when he was actually taking part in a procession, holding up from the ground his master's golden cope;[3] and two more arrests of clerks followed in a little over a year. A new mayor took his place at Michaelmas 1445, but when in April 1446 the chapter prepared to bring a suit against the town, laying the damages at £1,000, the city again fell back on Shillingford and for the two critical years of the strife he remained supreme magistrate and led the fight as it broadened so as to cover the whole range of the civic life. Party strife ran high, and the inhabitants were soon on terms of open war. On one occasion in the midst of the quarrel, a great stack of wood which lay between the cathedral and the town was set on fire at nine o'clock in the shortest time of

[1] Shillingford's Letters, xxii.-iv.   [2] Ibid. 98.   [3] Ibid. xiv.

the year. This, the burgesses cried out, was done by the ministers of the cathedral to burn down the town. The charge was thrown back in their teeth by the canons, who protested it was set afire by men of the same city deliberately by consent of the commonalty with intent to burn the church.[1] The tossing to and fro of such an accusation gives us a glimpse of the state of feeling that existed. The cathedral party hated the townspeople as a usurping and rebellious mob; while to the townsfolk when their passion was aroused the cathedral within its walls wore the aspect of a fortress in their midst, held by the power of an ancient enemy.

Which was the "smiter" in the quarrel it would be indeed hard to say. The claims raised on either side were absolutely irreconcilable, and each denied with great frankness and conviction every assertion put forward by the other. For convincing proof of its own dignity the corporation boldly carried back its inquiries to some unknown period before the Christian era, when Exeter "was a city walled, and suburb to the same of most reputation;" and recounted how "soon upon the passion of Christ it was besieged by Vespasian by time of eight days; the which obtained not the effect of his siege, and so wended forth to Bordeaux, and from Bordeaux to Rome, and from Rome to Jerusalem, and then he with Titus besieged Jerusalem and obtained and sold thirty Jews' heads for a penny, as it appeareth by Chronicles." They then passed on to its position under the Saxon Kings; and thence came directly to

[1] Shillingford's Letters, 86-7.

the privileges of the mayor, derived from the good old time when bailiffs and citizens held the town in fee-farm from the King, before any monastery or cathedral church was built.[1] All the historical research on this side in fact plainly proved the ecclesiastical authority to be a mere modern usurpation, of no credit or value.

The bishop and chapter for their part ignored the times before Vespasian, and bluntly " say that they doubt of Vespasian's being at Exeter, and so at Bordeaux and Jerusalem, to sell thirty Jews' heads for a penny ; " so coming at once to their main contention, they declared that St. Stephen's Fee was no parcel of the city, as the Book of Domesday would show, and was indeed "of elder time than is the city," for Exeter was nothing more than a borough till the first bishop had been installed there by the Confessor. Indeed they observed that the mayor himself was well known to be an officer of yesterday, since till the time of Henry the Third there " was no mayor nor fee-farm," but the town was governed by the sheriff of the county, and the bishops in their sphere had absolute jurisdiction, " without that time out of mind there were any such mayor, bailiffs, and commonalty known in the city.[2]

But all the arguments of the bishop, " that blessed good man in himself if he must be Edmund, Bishop of Exeter,"[3] as the mayor politely remarked, were thrown away on Shillingford. " I said nay, and proved it by Domesday,"[4] he writes, fully satisfied that my

[1] Shillingford's Letters, 75-6.   [2] Ibid. p. 95-6.
[3] Ibid. p. 1, 43.   [4] Ibid. 10.

lord "had no more knowledge of the ground of this matter than the image in the cloth of arras there"[1]—a melancholy ignorance, "considering his blessedness, holy living, and good conscience." The prelate's history, indeed, like that of his antagonist, was not without reproach. Domesday makes no mention of any separate lands of the Church in Exeter; but copies of Domesday were scarce, and it was tolerably safe to refer to its authority. In any case, however, the daily pressure of circumstance was so strong that it mattered very little to the opposing forces whether ancient history justified their position or no. To the burghers the difficulties of a divided administration, and the humiliation of submission, were made more galling every day by the growing prosperity of the town and the independent temper of the time; while the chapter, confident in the legal strength of their position, had not the least hesitation in forcing on the conflict.

The suit which opened in London in 1447 was complicated and costly,[2] and mayor and law officers and town councillors in Exeter had to put forth all their resources. Perpetual consultations were carried on in the Town Hall with the help of much malmsey; once two plovers and a partridge helped the feast. As time went on the expenses in meat and drink were heavy; judges had to be feasted, and the municipal officers encouraged, and presents were needed for the great folk in London, besides the serious cost of sending messengers continually to London, Tiver-

[1] Shillingford's Letters, p. 43, 44.
[2] Ibid. xiv.–xvi.; Freeman's Exeter, 158-60.

ton, and Crediton. Even after the matter was finally decided the city had to make up in the next year rewards of money, and gifts of fish and wine, for which it was still in debt.[1]

The most arduous and costly part of the work, however, lay in the vast amount of historical and legal research which the case demanded. "It asketh many great ensearches," said Shillingford, "first in our treasury at home among full many great and old records; afterward at Westminster, first in the Chancery, in the Exchequer, in the Receipt, and in the Tower; and all these ensearches asketh great labour long time as after this, to make our articles we have many true against one of theirs."[2] Evidences and documents were read and re-read, and arguments brought from the Black Roll of the city, from Domesday Book, from Magna Charta, from statutes, charters, and letters patent, from the eyres holden at Exeter by the judges of Edward the First, from records of the "customs" under Henry the Third or Edward the Third. The Recorder of Exeter worked hard, and the mayor turned confidently to him when legal questions became peculiarly obscure. It "is dark to my conceit as yet," he writes from London; "but I trust to God it shall be right well with your good information and help thereto; to which intent I send you a roll in the which is contained copies of Domesday, copy of eyres, of charters, and other things that is necessary to be seen in making of these replications. I can no more at this time, but I pray you be not weary to over-read

[1] Shillingford's Letters, p. 143, *et seq*. [2] Ibid. p. 58.

hear and see all the writing that I have sent home to you at this time; and if you be, no marvel though I be weary, and God be with you."¹

Shillingford himself was constantly in London; where the record of one day's work may serve as an instance of his activity. He left Exeter at 6 o'clock on Wednesday morning, and reached London on Saturday at 7 A.M. "That day I had right great business," he says. First he went to the Exchequer to see about Exmouth Port; then to Westminster Hall to speak with various lawyers; after that he visited the chief justice, Sir John Fortescue, and rode with him homeward; then he called on another justice, Sir Richard Newton; from thence he went to commune "with our counsel of our matters;" and in the afternoon proposed to visit the archbishop at Lambeth.² Meanwhile he kept a certain watch over affairs at home, and sent an occasional order as to the conduct of local business in Exeter. "Also I charge Germin (the treasurer) under rule and commandent of J. Coteler, my lieutenant, that he do that he can do, brawl, brag and brace, lie and swear well to, and in special that the streets be right clean and specially the little lane in the back-side beneath the flesh-fold gate, for there lieth many oxen heads and bones, that they be removed away for the nonce against my coming, as soon as I may by cokky's bones."³

From London long letters to the "Fellowship" at home rehearsed every step of the negociations, from the moment when the mayor first "came to Westminster

¹ Shillingford's Letters, 17.   ² Ibid. pp. 67, 68.   ³ Ibid. 23.

soon upon nine of the bell, and there met with my lord chancellor at the broad door a little from the stair-foot coming from the Star Chamber, I in the court, and by the door kneeling and saluting him in the most goodly wise that I could, and recommended unto his good and gracious lordship my fellowship and all the commonalty, his own people and bedesmen of the city of Exeter. He said to the mayor two times 'Welcome' and the third time 'Right welcome, mayor,' and held the mayor a great while fast by the hand, and so went forth to his barge and with him great press, lords and other."[1] In the same way Shillingford notes carefully every detail of the grave ceremonial observed before the arbiters of the city's destiny, when "my lord took his chair and the justices sat with him, and both parties with their counsel kneeled before."[2] Then followed a long argument in which the mayor held his own against the lawyers, and "so we departed, standing afar from my lord, and he asked wine and sent me his own cup, and to no more;"[3] also "my lord in this time did me much worship and openly .... commended me for my good rule at home." When a letter from the mayor was addressed to the lord chancellor, we hear how the recorder "kissed the letter and put it into my lord's blessed hand, and my lord with a glad countenance received the letter, and said that the mayor and all the commons should have Christ's blessing and his, and bade my master Radford[4] to stand up, and so

[1] Shillingford's Letters, p. 6. [2] Ibid. p. 12.
[3] Ibid. p. 12-15, 63. [4] The Recorder of Exeter.

did, and anon my lord brake the letter even while grace was saying, and there right read it every deal or he went to his dinner."

Business in London was best furthered by judicious gifts, and Exeter was constantly called on to send fish to the chancellor—conger eel, 400 of buckhorn or dried whiting, or a "fish called crabs."[1] Or again when the prudent mayor heard the lord chancellor bid the justice to dinner for a Friday, "I did as methought ought to be done. . . and sent thither that day two stately pickerellis and two stately tenches."[2] This proved a very successful venture, as "it came in good season" for the great lords and bishops who dined with the chancellor that day. At one stage of the business indeed the mayor thought it unwise to proceed with his argument until a certain present of fish should arrive. "I tarried and yet tarried because of the buckhorn, the which came not yet, me to right great anger and discomfort by my troth. . . for it had been a good mean and order, after speaking and communication above-said, the buckhorn to have been presented, and I to have come thereafter, and so to have sped much the better; but now it is like to fail to hindering."[3] Whether it was the fault of the treasurer of the town, or of the carrier, he did not know; he was sure each would accuse the other. "Christ's curse have they both," he breaks out, "and say ye amen, *non sine merito*, and but ye dare say so, think so, think so!" At last the buckhorn arrived on Candlemas even—"better late than never," said the

[1] Shillingford's Letters, 146.   [2] Ibid. 9.   [3] Ibid. 23, 150.

irritated mayor. "That day was I at Lambeth with my lord at mass, and offered my candle to my lord's blessed hand, I kneeling adown offering my candle. My lord with laughing cheer upon me said heartily 'Graunt mercy, mayor;' and that same day I abode there to meat by my said lord's commandment; I met with my lord at high table end coming to meatward, and as soon as ever he saw me he took me fast by the hand and thanks enough to; I said to my said lord it was too simple a thing considering his estate to say on his 'graunt mercy,' but if I had been at home at this fair he should have had better stuff and other things. I went forth with him to the midst of the hall, he standing in his estate against the fire a great while, and two bishops, the two chief justices, and other lords, knights and squires, and other common people great multitude, the hall full, all standing afar apart from him, I kneeling by him, and after recommendation I moved him of our matter shortly as time asked." He closed this argument against the prelate's malpractices in his most graceful manner—"I in my leave-taking saying these words, 'My lord have pity and mercy upon that poor city, *Jesus vidit civitatem et flevit super eam.*"[1]

But amid all the fashions of the chancellor's court the mayor never for a moment lost the sense of his own dignity as the representative of a free city. Deferential and scrupulous in paying the grave courtesies of an exact formality, Shillingford was inflexible in all that lay beyond mere ceremonial;

[1] Shillingford's Letters, 37, 38.

for, as he said, "the matter toucheth the great commonalty of the city of Exeter as well as him."[1] "The said mayor," he writes on one occasion, "conceived and knew right well that his said lord bishop took unworthy, as he might right well, for simpleness and poverty to speak or entreat with him. Nevertheless he said, such simple as he was, he was Mayor of Exeter."[2] In every dilemma he fell back haughtily on his own "simpleness," and on his subjection to the town council at home, "having no power, nor nought may do, say, agree, nor assent, without a communication had with my fellowship —a commonalty which is hard to deal with,"[3] added the artful mayor, with a humour which his submissive subjects at Exeter doubtless fully appreciated.[4]

We may safely assume that great labour and cost were not expended without some serious reason by the Exeter citizens—a community of hard-working

---

[1] Shillingford's Letters, 11, 47. [2] Ibid. 43, 45.
[3] Ibid. 32, see 11, 14, 20.
[4] His temper towards ecclesiastical interference and his urbanity in argument are admirably shown in a letter to the bishop's counsel. The rough draft of the letter ends with a fine outburst of anger. "We would fain have an end," he writes, and goes on to ask how it was possible for any one ever to conceive that "John Shillyng, for no dread of great words of malice, disclaunders, language, writings, nor setting up of bulls to that intent to rebuke me and to make me dull to labour for the right that I am sworn to, for truly I will not be so rebuked nor dulled, but the more boldlier." But he struck out this vigorous passage in the second draft in favour of a less belligerent sentence —"for ye may fully conceive that my fellows and I would fain have a good end and peace, praying you to apply your good will and favour to the same." Shillingford's Letters, 25.

practical traders, who knew the value both of their time and their money. And in the mayor's accounts of the proceedings in London we can gather up the long list of grievances which had gone on accumulating within the walls of this little city between Church and State, till the inhabitants found themselves ranged in two hostile armies, to either of which surrender meant ruin and enslavement.

(1) The most burning question at issue was the right of arrest of the bishop's tenants, or within the ecclesiastical precincts. Among many other cases[1] the mayor alleged that of one "Hugh Lucays, tenant of the said bishop, the most, or one of the most, misgoverned men of all the city of Exeter, or of all the shire afterward," who made a fray upon a townsman at the very door of the Guild Hall, and when the sergeant seized him "brake the arrest and went his way" into the church, pursued by the two serjeants. The stewards of the city who followed with the king's mace to keep the king's peace found the church doors shut upon them, and the prisoner "violently with strong hand taken away from them"; and various clerks and ministers of the church, by order of the dean and chapter, fell on them with door-bars, swords, daggers, long-knives, and "Irish skenes," so that "both stewards and serjeants stood in despair of their lives, and scarce escaped out of the church with their lives."[2] This was the mayor's story. The bishop on his part said that Hugh Lucas was an innocent man, who was driven into the cathedral during

[1] Shillingford's Letters, 52-3. [2] Ibid. 78.

divine service by the turbulent mob of burghers brandishing "swords, daggers, and other invasive weapons," and intent only on wickedness and misrule.[1] Then again one of the bishop's servants who had struck a townsman in the eye with a dagger almost unto death, could not be punished because he had been standing within the Close gate, between the cemetery and the city. "Also ofttimes the mayor hath not dared do the law and execution thereof... for now almost every man taketh colour by my lord" the bishop. If any riotous person made a fray, he would run off and "take the church late;" if a man was arrested on Saturday, "he must be delivered to make my lord's work" on Sunday,[2] and by such devices both men and women "by whom the mayor is rebuked" got off scot free. A compromise had been made that the city officers should make no arrests in church or cemetery from the ceasing of Our Lady bell to the end of Compline, but the chapter later laid this against them in evidence that they had no right ever to make any arrest there, "which is to the said mayor and commonalty great vexation, hurt, and hindering; and to misgoverned men, rioters, and breakers of the peace great boldness."[3] The mayor alleged that it was impossible to keep order in face of privileges which rendered the clergy and their tenants practically independent of the law. "Night walking, evil language, visaging, shouldering, and all riotous rule" went on unchecked, seeing that the mayor "could no longer rule the King's people after his laws, nor do right as he is sworn to, for

[1] Shillingford's Letters, 97.   [2] Ibid. 53.   [3] Ibid. 66, 10, 94.

dread of my lord."[1] Just outside St. Peter's Close stood a well-known tavern, and the canons who owned the Broad Gate kept its wicket open almost all the night, " out of which wicket into which tavern cometh the great part of all the rioters into the Close, priests and others," said the townspeople, and there made sleep impossible the whole night long to the neighbours. The canons however held that the " mayor and such dreadful people of his commonalty be the misgoverned people and incomers that they spoke of." According to the clerical party indeed the whole municipal body was altogether sunk in sin; the very town serjeants were " wild and unreasonable fellows," who had even been heard to threaten " that there should many a priest of the Close of Exeter lose his head once of midsummer even;"[2] and as for the tavern, it was wholly the mayor's business to keep order there, unless indeed, as they suggested, it was he himself " that is cause and giver of example to all such misgovernance."[3] This charge, however, which the chancellor had struck out with his own hands, was one about which the mayor did not greatly trouble himself. " As touching the great venom that they meaneth of my living," he wrote to the Fellowship, " I take right nought by and say sadly '*si recte vivas*,' etc, and am right merry and fare right well, ever thanking God and my own purse. And I lying on my bed at the writing of this right early, merrily singing a merry song, and that is this 'Come no more at our house, come, come, come !' I will not die nor for sorrow nor for anger,

[1] Shillingford's Letters, 53. [2] Ibid. 64. [3] Ibid. 93, 104.

but be merry and fare right well, while I have money; but that is and like to be scarce with me, considering the business and cost that I have had and like to have; and yet I had with me £20 and more by my troth, whereof of troth not right much I spend yet, but like, &c. Construe ye what ye will."[1]

(2) It was a further grievance to the townspeople that the bishop claimed the right to hold both a court baron and leet and view of frankpledge, and on this pretence called before himself various pleas and matters that should have been tried before the mayor and bailiffs, thus covetously gathering into his coffers fines on which they themselves had set longing eyes; and moreover that he took to himself any goods seized from felons.[2] There had been angry feeling over the case of one John Barton, whom the town officers pursued for robbing. But as it was a church that he had robbed, and as he had hidden the stolen goods in a tenement of the bishop's, the ecclesiastics, rather than see justice done by the secular power, had shut the door in the face of the municipal officers, and had hurried off the sacrilegious thief into the cathedral, then smuggled him out into a bakehouse, and so conveyed him out of the city; while the stolen goods were kept with a strong hand to the use of the bishop, "to great hurt and hindering of our sovereign lord the King and the said mayor and commonalty."[3]

(3) In all towns where the question of jurisdiction was raised between the townsfolk and the Church

[1] Shillingford's Letters, 16. [2] Ibid. pp. 10, 14, 91, 99, 104.
[3] Ibid. 83–4.

party the quarrel about coroner's inquests ran high. Churchmen and laymen alike had to submit to the coroner's inquest. But chapters of cathedrals and monasteries found it less humiliating to admit within their precincts an officer of the shire than the town officer sent in by a mayor who was for ever keeping his jealous watch at their gates. On the other hand, after their long and determined struggle to be freed from foreign interference, the towns looked with suspicion on the appearance within their walls on any pretext whatever of any official of the shire. In Exeter as elsewhere the city coroner claimed " to corowne prisoners dead in the bishop's prison," but the bishop flatly refused to admit into the precincts any officer save the coroner of Devonshire, and if the municipal coroners on hearing of a prisoner's death appeared at the gates of the Close, they were turned back by "servants of the said bishop, and by his commandment they were let to do their office there; and the said prisoners so dead buried uncoroned."[1]

(4) There was also as might be expected a burning controversy as to the city taxes.[2] The mayor alleged

---

[1] Shillingford's Letters, 83, 84, 99. Compare Norwich, Blomefield, iii. 62. In Canterbury the murder of a citizen by a waggoner of the priory in 1313 gave rise to a hot dispute as to the jurisdiction of the city coroner. The Convent refused him admittance within the priory gates, smuggled in an alien coroner to view the body, and then had it buried by the prior's grooms. The story is given in an Inspeximus of Richard the Second; Muniments of Canterbury.

[2] The distribution of taxes was a matter of special arrangement in the different towns. By the request of the canons the ecclesiastical tenants at Grimsby were not tallaged with the

that he and his deputies had been accustomed to collect in the cathedral precincts a certain proportion of the King's taxes, the ferm, and the sums needed for general town expenses; and Shillingford supported this claim before the lord chancellor by "a long rehearsal thereof from King Edward's time unto this day, how and under what form it was done of old time."[1] Of late however the bishop's tenants had refused to come to the Guild Hall and have their share assessed, "by the commandment of the said bishop menacing the said tenants . . . . to put them out of their tenures. And so they durst not come, set, nor pay as they have been wont to do."[2] The bishop justified his action by a variety of arguments. The King's taxes he probably could not dispute

burgesses (Madox, 270). In Leicester the tenants of the Bishop's Fee just without the walls did suit and service to the Bishop of Lincoln; a compromise had been made in 1281 by which it was decided that the Bishop's tenants should share in certain common expenses, and should in return enjoy the franchises and free customs which had been won by the Merchant Guild of Leicester; but while the burgesses had to bear the charges both of "the community of the town," and "the community of the guild," the bishop's tenants only paid for such matters as touched "the community of the guild," and were not liable for the general town taxes. (Gross, ii. 140–1.) As early as 1189 the Guild of Nottingham obtained the right to raise contributions to the ferm rent from tenants of all fees whatsoever. In Norwich this was given in 1229 (Norwich Doc., Stanley v. Mayor, etc., 5, 6). But the question of collection still remained a burning one, and the itinerant justices having failed in 1239 to settle matters between the convent and the city, the King himself went to Norwich to insist on an agreement in 1241. (Blomefield, iii. 46.) See p. 357, note 4.

[1] Shillingford's Letters, p. 13.   [2] Ibid. 79.

with any show of reason. But with regard to the ferm he employed a comprehensive mode of reasoning which struck at the very foundation of all authority of mayor or commonalty; for that, he said, the town had no power whatever to collect, since Exeter had neither mayor nor bailiffs nor any fee-ferm at all till the time of Henry the Third, and even then the grant was illegally made by Richard of Almayne, who really possessed no rights in the borough.[1] For the taxes connected with municipal expenses, or as the mayor called them, the "citizens' spending," he asserted that his tenants were not legally responsible. In any case he differed altogether from the citizens in his definition of the "ancient custom" by which the payment of the taxes should be regulated,[2] and complained that his tenants had not been duly summoned to take part in the assessment, and "of malice" had been charged in their absence "an importable sum. .... so that there would have remained in the mayor's hands a great sum thereof above the said dime," like as there had remained in other mayors' hands as much as £7 or £5, sometimes more or less.[3]

(5) In one of the most burdensome duties of town life, the keeping of watch and ward, the dependents of St. Peter's fee had sought to throw the whole labour on the citizens.[4] The bishop's tenants

[1] Shillingford's Letters, 96.   [2] Ibid. pp. 98, 108.
[3] For the mayor's defence, see p. x. 107-9.
[4] The tenants of the hospital of S. John in Worcester refused to aid in tallages, to submit to the assize of bread and beer, under the town's officers, and to keep watch and ward. In 1221 they

when they were summoned "to come and keep the watch and the peace came not... but they were forbode upon a great pain, and charged if any of the mayor's officers entered into any tenement of the bishop for to warn any man to come to the watch, that they should break his head."[1] The bishop in fact had ordered that a fine of 40s.—a fine quite beyond the power of an ordinary tradesman to pay—should be levied from any one who dared to serve on the watch. "Whereupon the mayor made right great wayward language to them. The mayor said waywardly he would do more, he would make levy both of the citizens' spending and the fee-farm, and that he would well avow, and bade them of all to inform the Justice thereof, and that he would do the same; and so the mayor did."[2]

(6) "The most disclaunderous article" of all, according to the bishop, was the question of the assize of wine, ale, and bread. While the mayor claimed the assize over the bishop's demesne, the bishop asserted that such assize "of time that no mind is" belonged wholly to the bishop himself, and in no wise

were ordered to do all these things. (Select Pleas of the Crown, Selden Soc. p. 97.) In 1331 Norwich resisted the handing over of three houses to the prior and convent "for that a very great part of the same city which is inhabited, is in the hands of the prior and convent and of other religious persons, whereby the inhabitants are at their distress, and cannot be tallaged to the tallages and aids of the lord the King and of the city aforesaid as tenants should be, nor can they be in assizes, juries, and recognizances, whereby others dwelling in the same city are burdened and grieved more than usual by such gifts and assignments." (Norwich Documents, Stanley v. Mayor, pr. 1884, 24, 25).

[1] Shillingford's Letters, 44-45.   [2] Ibid. 52.

to the mayor.¹ This matter was partly a question of finance, and partly a question of order. So long as wine was first smuggled in by the bishop's tenants, and then sold in the houses of the canons and in the precincts, against " the ordinances and cry " made by the mayor, the town lost the customs which ought to be paid at the port of Exmouth on every pipe of wine ; and as the ferm was paid out of these customs, the bishop's tenants escaped their share of the rent,² and left the whole burden to be borne by the citizens. The corporation further lost the " wine gavell " paid on all wine sold by retail in the town. Moreover fraudulent sellers went unpunished; for instead of allowing the town officers to cast into the canal wine which was condemned by the municipality as " corrupt and not whole for man's body, damnable and which should be damned," the bishop's tenants actually found means to gather from it profits of iniquity; " the which corrupt wine hath been carried to Topsham and there shipped, and so led to Bordeaux, there to be put and melled among new wine, as it shall be well proved if need be." In the same way the weighing of bread was resisted, and the due testing of beer, and the authority of the city set at nought.

(7) There was also a quarrel about who was to get the profits from increased rents of stalls and shops and houses which opened on the market-place,³ and whose value altogether depended on the growth of the market and the town trade. Both the municipality and the church would willingly have seized

[1] Shillingford's Letters, 91-2, 104-5.
[2] Ibid. 92.　　　　　　　　　[3] Ibid. 100, 109.

the " unearned increment." The convent had set up stalls and booths " on the ground of the said mayor and citizens without licence of them asked "—great stalls sixty feet long and over three feet broad, where of old time there had only been shop windows, " the leaves thereof going inward, and none other ne never were." The bishop answered that any one in the town might put stalls outside his own house if he chose ; and in any case, he added, with consistent denial of the authority of the corporation, it was a matter to be punished by the King, if at all, and not by the commonalty. When the townsmen further urged that they had always " of time that no mind is " held their fish-market in Fish Street, a sort of debateable land, which lay outside the cemetery but within the precincts of the close, but that now the dean and chapter had refused to let the market be held there, and had themselves made stairs and gardens encroaching on the street, which moreover cut off the mayor's way to the town walls and towers, the bishop answered in quibbling wise that as there never was such a street as Fish Street, no market could well be held in it, nor could it be encroached upon : what the town chose to call Fish Street, the prelate explained, was in his nomenclature S. Martin's or the Canon's Street.[1]

(8) As in other fortified towns, where the wall of the ecclesiastical precincts ran side by side with the city wall,[2] endless questions were raised as to the

[1] Shillingford's Letters, 84-5, 99.
[2] In Canterbury also the Convent was bent on getting possession of that part of the covered way which lay along its territory.

management and repair of walls and towers, and the control of the city gates, and the use of the narrow way that ran inside the wall for the movement of troops, the carriage of ammunition, and the approach of the city authorities, or of workmen—questions which in time of war or of civil revolt were of vital consequence, and which even in quiet days brought frequent trouble. Each side claimed the lane, and the mayor and corporation objected to the canons who, having back doors opening from the gardens into it, had made it into a mere rubbish heap, so "that no man therein may well ride nor go nor lead carriage to the walls, to the great hurt and hindering of the mayor and commonalty;" and who had further broken up the great drain which had been made to draw off rain water from the town and had carried away the stones. Moreover the commonalty had spent £20 on building a great tower " and right a strong door with lock and key made thereto and fast shut, to this intent there to bring in stuff for the war and defence of the city and other thing more of the said city there to be kept strong, safe, and sure; but whenever this lock, and those of

and the city wall itself so far as it touched the Cathedral precincts. Their first step was taken in 1160, and their final success was not assured till 1492, when the city resigned to the Convent the wall and covered way between Burgate and Northgate with the waste land adjoining, and the chapter was allowed to make a postern and to build a bridge across the foss. Such an arrangement was of course only possible at a time when peace with France, and the close of civil wars and riots at home had freed the town from danger of siege or revolution. (Lit. Cant., i. 60-2, iii. 318-20.) See also Davies' Walks through York, 11, 12.

various postern doors, were repaired · "they have been right spitefully broke up by the bishop, and dean and chapter," and the door of the tower left at all times open so that the canons could throw their rubbish into it. And finally, the canons having fitted one of the town gates with a new lock and key of their own, by night and day "full ungodly carriage have been led in and out." "At which gate also ofttime have been great affrays and debate, and like to have been manslaughter, and divers night-walkers and rioters coming out at that gate into the city, and there have made many affrays, assaults, and other riotous misgovernance against the peace, and broken out over the town walls, and much more mischief like to fall by that gate without better remedy had." To all these charges the canons answered that the lane was their own property, nor had they ever broken any gutter there nor thrown rubbish out; and as to the wall it was the commonalty which "by their frowardness to evil intent," had let it fall down and had not repaired it "in any time this hundred year;" while the towers stood on ecclesiastical ground, "and the bishop sometime had his prison in that tower."[1]

(9) The common use of the cathedral became a further subject of wrangling, as the corporation pressed for sole authority within the tower inclosure and the ecclesiastical party retorted by stricter protection of its own peculiar property. It had been the custom at fair-time to set up booths in the cemetery and even within the church; but the dean and chapter now

[1] Shillingford's Letters, 88, 89, 16.

began to demand tolls, especially from the jewellers' stalls. This the town angrily resented, and the matter was referred to arbitrators, who decided that the chapter had no right to any such tolls within church or cemetery, "for anger and evil will whereof the said dean and chapter by their ministers and servants, ever since have put out all such merchants and merchandize contrary and against the old rule and use, and to the destruction of the fairs and markets."[1] Moreover the canons proceeded to lock the doors of a cloister adjoining the church which was according to the citizens "a common way for the mayor and commonalty" into the cathedral, and "a place of prayer and devotion to pray for all souls whose bones lay buried there." It was in no sense, said the ecclesiastics, a "common way" of the townspeople; it was walled and glazed and had a chapter house and library, and the canons were much offended that "ungodly ruled people, most custumably young people of the said commonalty within the said cloister have exercised unlawful games as the top, 'queke,' 'penny prykke,' and most at tennis, by the which the walls of the said cloister have been defouled and the glass windows all to brost, as it openly sheweth, contrary to all good and ghostly goodness, and directly against all good policy, and against all good rule within the said cloister to suffer any such misruled people to have common entry." The mayor still asserted however that "within time out of mind there was no such cloister there but all open church here, and a common way into the said church." As to the

[1] Shillingford's Letters, 93, 94.

games, "the mayor, bailiffs, and commonalty say that they by the law be not bound thereto to answer."[1]

Amid the endless and vulgar details of all this intricate quarrel, Shillingford held fast to the principles which he saw plainly were of the very essence of any true municipal life. Charters of freedom were of no use if in every question of trade, of police, of finance, of public order, ecclesiastical privilege stepped in and brought all government save its own to an end. All discussions from first to last invariably came back to the one central problem—the right of arrest—and here the mayor was determined that no persuasion should induce him to abate one jot of the city claims. He would give no assent to the bishop's arguments drawn from an alleged friendly agreement which laid down that the town officers should make arrests in the cemetery only, and that they might not arrest there the canons or men wearing the religious habit or their ministers and servants, and steadfastly denied that any such writing had ever been known or proved. Henceforth he would not hear of concession or compromise; "it would seem if I so did that I had doubt of our right where I have right none,"[2] as he said to the lord chief justice. When "my lord himself spake darkly of right old charters," and conjured him to make an end of the matter, "and if I so did I should be chronicled;" the mayor still remained firm.[3] "I held my own, I had matter enough." He was especially pressed in sundry points by the lord

[1] Shillingford's Letters, pp. 85, 86, 101, 110.
[2] Ibid. 9.   [3] Ibid. 20.

chancellor, who as a learned man made merry over the tale of Vespasian's connexion with the city, a piece of history upon which the mayor did not greatly care to dwell;[1] and as former canon of Exeter cathedral he was ready at times to laugh over the stories of his Exeter days, and of the exciting arrests and lively disputes which he so well remembered; "all it was to tempt me with laughing cheer," said the watchful mayor.[2] "At the last fell to matter of sadness, and they spake of God's house, St. Peter's Church of Exeter, and my lord spake of his house, his hall, and the justice the same, how loath they would be to make arrests therein, and said that St. Peter's Church was God's house and His hall, &c., and made many reasons to bring in absence of arrests.[3] They were answered as God would give us grace." The chancellor, as was natural from his old association with the chapter, was especially anxious to bring about a compromise favourable to the church. He proposed that the city should have the view of frankpledge over the whole city and precincts, and should only make arrests ordered by that court; and on the other hand the bishop "to have his courts of his own tenants and to hold pleas of greater sum than the court baron, forty shillings, and spake of forty marks. Upon this mean he sticked fast and thought it was reasonable, and

[1] Shillingford's Letters, 12.　　　[2] Ibid. 10, 19.

[3] The Commons had perhaps some reason to ask in 1371 that none but a layman should have charge of the seal. (Campbell's Lives of the Lord Chancellors, i. 262.) This system, however only lasted till 1378, and in the next hundred years, out of 35 chancellors only eight were laymen.

ever asked of me divers times what I would say thereto, all as I conceived to tempt me, and to consent to a mean; and then I said, my lord, if it please you, ye shall have me excused to answer, for though methought that it were a mean reasonable I dare not say yea, though I have power, for the matter toucheth a great commonalty as well as me, and so that I dare not say unto time that I have spoke with my fellowship at home."[1]

For two years the discussions dragged on at one place or another, till in 1448 an agreement was made between Town and Church "by mean and mediation of Thomas Courtney, Earl of Devonshire, and of Sir William Bonville, knight," and was four days later (Dec. 16th, 1448) confirmed by the Chief Justice of Common Pleas and another Judge. Exeter was forgiven the enormous damages demanded by the convent for the illegal arrests made by the town officers within the precincts two years before—damages amounting to £1,000, or a sum which must have been equal to many years' revenue of the borough. For the rest the arbitration reasserted in definite terms the division of authority against which the city had so vigorously protested. The bishop was left absolute lord of his fee. All he desired—court baron, leet, view of frankpledge, a rule without any disturbance of the mayor, bailiffs, or coroners of the city, and with absolute freedom from distress or arrest, was secured to him for ever. He was only bound not to arrest any of the mayor's subjects in his precincts. As for the mayor

[1] Shillingford's Letters, 11.

and commonalty they retained their ancient powers in the city, but might make no arrests on church lands. They might summon the bishop's tenants to keep the watch in their turn, and might fine them if they refused, making a levy on their goods found *without the Fee*. In the king's taxes and the city murage the church tenants were to take their share, but it was to be raised by their own officers. Lastly the mayor and bailiffs might have their maces carried before them in the cathedral precincts without disturbance.[1] It was decreed that no new charters were to disturb this arrangement;[2] and henceforward the chapter guarded its privileges with accurate solicitude.[3]

This "final" settlement gave to the city all that any lawyer could have given it in the fifteenth century, for lawyers after all could only declare the legal principles that had been laid down in times when the power in the State had been very differently balanced, and the fashioning of the law in these matters had lain in the hands of ecclesiastics. Statesmen like the chancellor moreover could discuss the question with philosophic calm; in the greater concerns of national administration the problem between

[1] Shillingford, 136–140.

[2] In 1463 when Edward granted the city fresh franchises and powers he exempted the close from civic jurisdiction. Freeman's Exeter, 91.

[3] In 1452 the judges held their assize in the hall of the bishop's palace; the King being in the town it was proved to him that holding of assize in the bishop's hall was a breach of the privileges of the church; two traitors who had been condemned were therefore pardoned by the King. Ibid. 89.

Church and State had been decided for them in the days of Henry the Second, by methods as rough and ready as any which burghers of later times had attempted; and they therefore now looked at the townspeople's troubles from afar off. The pressure of difficulty had changed, and whereas it was the people who had once gained profit from ecclesiastical immunities, while kings and statesmen had to bear the violence of the battle for order and the authority of government, now the brunt of the fight fell on the common folk, while rulers at Westminster sat at ease and calmly recounted the old arguments which their greater predecessors had found it necessary to repudiate utterly three hundred years before.

For the experience of Exeter was by no means exceptional or rare, and if we turn to the history of Canterbury or Norwich we find the same record of centuries of passionate strife, with fire and pillage and murder and costly processes of law ending in yet fiercer antagonism. To multiply instances would prove wearisome repetition, but considering the great importance which these questions had for the mediæval burgher, and the gravity of their results in later history, it may be well to note in the history of another town how, with a few superficial differences, the fundamental difficulty was always the same.

In Canterbury, as we might expect, things were yet more complicated than in Exeter, and the situation of the citizens was one of considerable perplexity. From almost every considerable holding in the town some religious corporation claimed a rent charge which had to be deducted in the city accounts. The Convent of S. Gregory declared itself to be in the shire of Kent and outside the city bounds, and as late as 1515 asserted its freedom by refusing to take its share in the payment of a subsidy; when the mayor levied a distress the convent sued him for trespass, and a long and costly lawsuit followed.[1] The hospitals of S. Nicholas at Harbledown and of S. John Northgate were exempted by royal charter from all tallages, aids, and contributions; and their lands and woods in the hundred of Westgate were made free from contribution for the defence of the coast.[2] But these trifling grievances scarcely came into notice beside the troubles caused by greater ecclesiastical powers—the Priory of Christ Church, the Convent of S. Augustine's, and the Archbishop. The old dissensions that had once disturbed their common harmony had all been appeased by means of a complete separation between the property and jurisdiction of the Archbishop and the Convent of Christ Church, which had been finally arranged somewhere about 1260; and by an agreement which was concluded about the end of the fourteenth century, between S. Augustine's and Christ Church, as to their special disputes about ecclesiastical prerogatives, or about the rights of the convents on the high sea, on the quay at Fordwich, in the common meadows at Sturry, and in the neighbouring harbours of Sandwich which belonged to Christ Church, and Stonor which belonged to S. Augustine's.[3] But in the general

[1] Hist. MSS. Com. ix. 150.   [2] Ibid. 169.
[3] Lit. Cant. i., lxi. Sandwich and Stonor were the two ports

peacemaking the city was left out, and the city had its own separate grievances against archbishop, abbot, and prior.

I. For the archbishop possessed certain rights which were exceedingly inconvenient to the borough. In case of a quarrel, he could refuse to ordain Canterbury men, to confirm Canterbury children, or to allow the offices of the Church to sick people, unless the townsfolk swore to obey him in all things. He could forbid his tenants to join in the great city festival of the Translation of S. Thomas. He was known to have cited 140 of the chief citizens to appear before him at Charing, twelve leagues away from Canterbury and without proper victuals, whereas by custom they should be summoned to appear in their own cathedral. Such were the complaints which the struggling town had to make in 1290.[1] His borough of Staplegate, just opposite the palace and within the city boundaries, was surrounded by a wall and exempt from the jurisdiction of both the city and the county;[2] even the royal writ did not run in it. Since his tenants in Westgate and Wingham were free from the town authorities, when Westgate men took to building their houses so near the river that the stream was driven against the city walls with such force as to make them fall, the town was helpless to check the evil, and complained as loudly of the wrong in 1467[3] as it had done in 1290. Or when Wingham men intercepted

of London and therefore of considerable consequence. For the history of Stonor see Boys' Sandwich, 552-5, 658-62.

[1] Hist. MSS. Com. ix. 172-3.
[2] Ibid. 150.　　　　　　　　　　[3] Ibid. 172-3, 141.

for their market the provisions which were on the road to Canterbury, and thus both diminished the tolls of provisions taken at the Canterbury gates and increased the price of food, the corporation had no remedy, for the archbishop's right to hold a market at Wingham could not be denied.[1] Moreover the Whitstaple fishermen, also tenants of the archbishop, were supported by him in 1431 in their claim of a right to sell fish in the city free from any toll save a farthing for each person; and in 1481 when the fishwives refused to pay toll or to sell in a new market built by the citizens, the townsfolk had no resource save to make up out of their own pockets the losses of the tax collector during these troubles.[2] We have the record of yet another quarrel in 1480, when the archbishop seized the tithe of the aftermath in the King's Mead, upon which the mayor immediately collected his posse, marched to the meadow about a mile distant, and there ordered sixteen pennyworth of wine to be served out all round for the refreshment of his troop.[3]

II. With the Abbot of S. Augustine's the city had disputes concerning mill and market. For the "Abbot's Mill" was supposed to injure the City Mill, which lay a little higher up the stream, and the grievance was so serious that in 1415 iron-topped stakes were driven into the river bed by a board of inspectors to mark the highest level for the

---

[1] Hist. MSS. Com. ix. 139, 145.
[2] Ibid. 173.
[3] The cost was entered on the chamberlain's accounts, but there is nothing more to tell how the matter ended. Ibid. 144.

water at the Abbot's Mill, so that the fall might be deep enough for water coming from the wheel of the City Mill.[1] As late as 1522 there was a consultation between the town body and "Milord of S. Austin's" about the fish-market, which ended in a friendly manner with the present of a conger-eel and a bottle of Malmsey to the abbot.

The chief quarrel however was as to the exact limits of the abbot's authority as defined by an agreement drawn up in the thirteenth century, and carefully copied out anew by the city clerk in the fifteenth century; and the nice point under discussion during many generations was whether the abbots, under pretext of infang-theoff, should persist in arresting evildoers in Longport, which was the King's highway and under the jurisdiction of his assignees, the corporation of Canterbury, but which ran for its whole length through the abbey lands.[2] It was only after 1475 that the dispute seems to have come to an end, when the abbot's gallows at Chaldensham were, by the consent of the community and of the convent, broken to pieces. A Baron of the Exchequer and the Recorder of London chosen to arbitrate between the burghers and the monks, were welcomed at Canterbury with a fee for their pains, lodged at the Austin Friars, entertained sumptuously at the town's expense with lavish supplies of choice food and drink,[3] and

---

[1] Hist. MSS. Com. ix. 169–70.   [2] Ibid. 170.

[3] The details as to the costs of many of these feasts are preserved—the claret and wines white and red, and the beer and ale, which recommended a dinner made up for example of a swan, five capons, two geese, a side of brawn, two lambs, four rabbits,

served with three meals a day, "fractio jejunii, jantaculum, et cœna," till finally on a certain afternoon the monks and the corporation met to drink together in honour of the final peace, and the ambassadors set out on their journey homewards, treated to refreshments at every stage from the parting cup at Canterbury to the farewell drink at Newgate. In 1478 they delivered their arbitration at Westminster, and there was a fresh series of "potationes" to celebrate the settlement.[1]

III. The Abbot of S. Augustine's was indeed a far less formidable neighbour than the Prior of Christ Church, between whom and the city there lay centuries of angry controversy. With him also there was of course the usual quarrel about the administration of justice. The Prior had his own gallows, where men were hung for sheep-stealing as well as for murder, and when the see of Canterbury was vacant convicted prisoners who "pleaded their clergy" were handed over to him as their ordinary—an arrangement which evidently must have been a source of much bitter feeling on the part of the townspeople; in 1313, for example, out of nine men who were convicted by a jury in the Assize court of stealing and murder and who all pleaded their clergy, seven purged themselves before the ecclesi-

---

beef, marrow bones, a jowl of salmon, gurnards, roach, bread, spices, salt, vinegar, butter, milk, eggs, lard, and suet. Sacks of coal were always bought for the cooking of these great dinners, either charcoal sold in sacks, or "sea-cole" sold by the tub. Hist. MSS. Com. ix. 146, 163.

[1] Ibid. 143-4.

astical judge and were set free.¹ Moreover the cathedral was turned into a sanctuary, where criminals fled from the just judgment of their fellow citizens. In 1425 Bernard the goldsmith, a stranger from over sea, escaped from the city prison and fled to the cathedral church, followed by the bailiffs and a wild mob of townsmen. As he crouched within the rails of the new monument put up to Archbishop Chicheley, the mob thrust their arms between the bars, seized him and beat him with sticks hidden in their sleeves, and at last tore him out of the enclosure, carried him into the nave, and would have dragged him back to gaol, save for the sudden interference of the commissary, who with his followers drove them back and rescued the prisoner from their hands.²

So also the question of taxes caused much wrangling. Christ Church, which owned within the franchise £200 of rent and five acres of land,³ claimed to be free from any contribution for maintaining the walls of the city⁴ after their circuit had been completed by Archbishop Sudbury and left to the people's care; and this dispute was not settled till 1492, when the convent, having got possession of a part of the wall, undertook to keep that section of it in repair.⁵ With regard to the costs of levying soldiers for the royal service⁶ the citizens decided in 1327

[1] Hist. MSS. Com. ix. 77.　　[2] Ibid. 112.
[3] Lit. Cant. i. 216.　　[4] Ibid. iii. 379, 380.
[5] Ibid. 318–320; Hist. MSS. Com. v. 433–4.
[6] These charges were heavy in the southern towns. For example, Canterbury and Sandwich had to provide Warwick and

to charge a part of this tax on lands held by the convent. The tax seems to have been required only from property in the city, and the archbishop was inclined to give way after discussion with his counsel, "however much those of our Church may wish to do otherwise," but the prior resolutely held out and got a letter of special protection from the King for Church property.[1] At this the city was stirred to the utmost fury. The people held a meeting in Blackfriars' churchyard, and passed a resolution that if the convent still refused they would break their windows in Burgate, disable their mills, drive their tenants out of their houses; that they would allow no one to give, sell, or lend meat or drink to monks, and would seize carts and horses carrying food from their manors and sell them in the market; that they would arrest any monk coming out of the monastery into the city and take his clothes and property; that the monastery should be cut off from the world by a deep trench dug in front of its gate, and that no pilgrim should be allowed to enter the cathedral until he had taken an oath not to make the smallest offering. Finally every man at the meeting swore that he would have from S. Thomas's shrine a gold ring for a finger of each hand.[2] The threat of interference with their pilgrims was a serious matter to the convent, since the whole charge

his garrison with victuals in Calais in 1457. Oman's Warwick, 64.

[1] Lit. Cant. i. 213-222. This quarrel was 100 years old at this time. Hist. MSS. Com. v. 433.

[2] Hist. MSS. Com. ix. 98.

of providing for the comfort and safety of the pilgrims lay with the mayor. Not only was it his office to see that sufficient food was laid up in the city for the pilgrims and to have all the special directions which he judged necessary for their victuals and lodgings set forth on a post which stood before the court hall, but he was further responsible for keeping order among them, and there were occasions when travellers would set out on their journey with just apprehension unless, as happened at Lydd, official messengers from the town were sent before to Canterbury to arrange that its pilgrims might come and go in safety without danger of arrest, and won favour of the mayor's wife by the gift of a quart of malmsey.[1] The corporation had in fact power to make a visit to the shrine so difficult and unpleasant as seriously to affect the flow of offering to the treasury of the saint, and this at a time when the anxiety of the convent about profits was heightened by the pressing demands of the Papal Court for a share in the spoils of its great Jubilee festivals.[2] Money quarrels in fact never failed on either side, and at the very end of the fifteenth century it would seem that Cardinal Morton saw in the old feuds a chance for making Canterbury pay its full tribute to the royal treasury; when in 1494 he issued demands for aid in money or in men for the Scotch war he seems to have

[1] Hist. MSS. Com. v. 521.

[2] The last Jubilee, when the oblations amounted to £600, was celebrated in 1470. In 1520 the Pope demanded a half of the gross receipts, but the archbishop and chapter not being disposed to grant this no Jubilee was held. Literæ Cantuar. iii. xxxv., xxxvi.

sent several blank copies of the summons to his friend Prior Selling to be filled up by him and issued to corporations and citizens whom he thought rich enough to pay. Probably in his directions to the tax-gatherer Prior Selling did not forget old enemies of the convent.[1]

The quarrel as to the town market also lasted on throughout the fifteenth century. There the city magistrates had indeed undisputed control, but it was not always easy to enforce their control on the clever people of the convent. Sometimes the monks attempted to escape from the regulations and tolls of the burgesses by sending to buy their fish at the seaside; and the townsmen protected themselves by seizing any fish so bought on its way to the priory.[2] Other questions arose as to houses belonging to Christ Church which opened inwards on the precincts but had windows looking outwards on the market-place in Burgate just outside the priory gate, from which houses shutters and windows could be let down for the inhabitants to display their wares on market-day, whereat the town was doubly aggrieved both by losing the rent of stalls and by seeing the increasing rent of the houses pass away into the convent treasury. At last in 1493 convent and city sought to make a final settlement of the question. The boundaries of the monastery were defined, including many houses of laymen, and within these limits the town renounced all jurisdiction except over houses and shops which had doors or windows

[1] Hist. MSS. Com. ix. 145-146.
[2] Ibid. v. 433.

opening on the street; while the convent was allowed to distrain on any houses that belonged to it in the city. But in 1500 the quarrel broke out with intenser bitterness, and the mayor violently shifted the market from the prior's gate to the open space near the city church, so that no house held by the convent should have the advantage of opening out upon it. Then ecclesiastical tenants refused to sell in the new market, and city stall-holders treated the convent servants with little courtesy. The citizens fell on the caterer of Christ Church as he was carrying a halibut he had bought from the market to the priory gate, and took it from him, "contrary to all right and good conscience;" and when the prior sent to the seaside for fish, it was seized at the entrance of the town by the citizens, "disappointing in the same the brethren of the place of their dinners."[1] The prior brought his grievances before the London courts, upon which the whole town took up the question with ardour, and the burgesses collected a voluntary subscription to defend their cause. The mayor was charged with the conduct of the suit in London. Ten or twelve citizens were perpetually riding backwards and forwards and hanging about the courts, and the usual expenses entered in the town records for drink, supper, horse-meat, hire of horses to Rochester and hire of barges and cloaks for the travellers from thence to London, down to "threepence paid at Sittingbourne in washing of my shirts."[2] Master Poynings, being at

[1] Hist. MSS. Com. v. 433-4.
[2] Ibid. ix. 146-7. The chamberlain's accounts give the costs of one visit to London of mayor and aldermen

last commissioned by the King to take evidence on the spot, was entertained at a splendid banquet, and finally an exemplification of the market was sent up to the King's Council in London. In 1501 a new messenger from the King "came to the city and on business of the town. Three counsel were paid 10s.; one of them "in the cloister at Paul's when he corrected the copy," got 3s. 4d. and his clerk 12d. The mayor gathered together all the witnesses in a house beside Paul's to rehearse their evidence "against they came into the Star Chamber," and paid for bread and drink and house room for them 16d. At Westminster Hall the three counsel got 3s. 4d. each, and for the three days following the same fees were daily paid. In the Star Chamber Master Roydon paid for examination of sixteen persons at 2s. 4d. a man, 37s. 4d.; two days after fees were again paid to two counsel, and a breakfast given to Sir Matthew Browne. Master Fisher was paid for the fees of the Hilary term 19s. Warrants of attorney cost 4s., and copies of the panels 2s. The counsel had to be looked up in their country houses, and messengers were always crossing Tilbury Ferry to look for "Master Raimond," and give him a retaining fee "to be our counsel," or going to Finchley to seek "Master Frowick," perhaps to find that "he was then ridden to Walsingham, so the said Thomas came to London homeward again." The Master Recorder of London was met coming to the Temple and besought "to be good master to the city," and retained at a cost of 6s. 8d. with a breakfast to his servants in Fleet Street. Then a messenger waited at the Guild Hall for the recorder, and again watched for him "the same day at afternoon at Milord Dawbeny's place, there waiting till the said Master Recorder had supped, and when he came out we besought him to speed us, for the time of the forfeit passed not three days; which answered that he was sore occupied and might not entende it so shortly, where we took him 6s. 8d., and then he bade us wait on him on the morrow in the Temple. The next day when Mr. Recorder had contrived the bill and corrected it, for his reward 6s. 8d. Paid for a pike given to Master Mordaunt 3s. 4d." The mayor then sent to Canterbury to direct that some gift should be sent up which

tarried not because of death,[1] but spake with Mr. Mayor at S. Andrew's Church, the which showed him the market and so he departed to Dover," followed by a messenger of the mayor hurrying after him with presents of fish, game, poultry, and wine. Then new ambassadors were sent from the city to the King at Richmond, and the paying of fees, and costs for eating and drinking went on merrily. But the citizens won the day in the end, for the Canterbury market is still held by S. Andrew's Church and was never brought back to the priory gate.

Even the control of the river brought its troubles, for whenever a question arose as to embanking and straightening the bed of the stream, the prior and the mayor met in the meadows about Chatham with their followers and carried on consultations refreshed by the usual supply of meat and drink. Business however was done at these parties, and the river turned from its meandering course from one side of the valley to the other into the straight channel in which it now flows.[2] The question of the mills was less easy to

might be used in "making friends"; and several members of the Common Council travelled up with two trouts (one trout cost about 10s.) and ten capons. The witnesses examined in the Star Chamber each got 6s. 8d. and their travelling expenses; after their examination they adjourned to the buttery for an entertainment, and paid "in reward to the officers of the King's buttery for their good cheer 12d. and to the cook of the King's kitchen 8d." Besides all this there was a great deal of feasting and drinking in eight of the London inns, in Southwark, Cheap, Fleet Street, Paul's Chain, and Holborn. Hist. MSS. Com. ix. 147.

[1] The Plague. Hist. MSS. Com. ix. 147.
[2] Ibid. 150.

settle, with the dependent problems as to damming the water and dredging the shallows. A settlement made in 1431 to prevent the injury of the city mill failed to end disputes, and in 1499 the prior dug a trench which drew away the water from it, upon which the citizens destroyed the trench and proceeded to make a dam for the conservation of the water running to their mill. The prior in his turn cut the dam; whereupon the mayor called out his posse to fight the matter out in the meadows by the river, apparently routed the enemy's forces, seizing their arms, and the next day in his wrath removed the market to its new place, as we have seen.[1]

So ended the fifteenth century in Canterbury amid a storm of invective and free fighting. The mayor protested that the prior, in addition to all his other crimes, had taken away the mace from the city serjeant, and had allowed the city ditch to be befouled. The prior retorted by accusing the mayor of riotous conduct, and breaking of boundaries and building of bridges and diverting of water-courses to his damage, and not only this, but of having for malice and grudge to the prior and convent broken the old custom of the citizens' gathering at Christmas at the tomb of Sudbury to pray for his soul for the great acts he had done for the city, so that they now withdrew their prayers from thence to hold their service under the prison house called Westgate. Indeed they even refused to join the noblemen who brought the King's offering to S. Thomas at the Christmastide feast.

[1] Hist. MSS. Com. v. 433-4.

As usual, however, all this mighty turmoil ended in nothing. The mayor was indicted by the convent for riot, and the verdict of the jury went against him, but no particular result seems to have followed; and though the persevering prior then had the case brought before the Star Chamber in 1501, it was passed over for want of leisure.[1]

Practically the same story was repeated at Canterbury as at Exeter and in every other city where there was a similar conflict.[2] Money and skill and labour and passion were expended without measure, and finally the courts adjudged that all must remain as it had been when the municipality scarcely existed three hundred years before, an order which statesmen possibly thought the safest course in the presence of opposing forces, neither of whom was strong enough to win, and neither of whom could dare to lose. But this was not the end of the matter. Through these three hundred years the towns had gathered strength, perfected their machinery of government, and realized their own might. Wealthy, highly organized, very centres of rationalism in politics and common sense in business, their controversy with the Church, singularly free as it was from theological pre-occupation, was inevitably in all questions of temporal government more keen and resolute in the fifteenth century than ever before. It was vain to renew attempts in one town after another to appease irreconcilable quarrels by arbitra-

[1] Hist. MSS. Com. v. 434.
[2] The dispute in Norwich was brought before the king's court in 1512. Documents, Stanley *v.* Mayor, &c., pr. 1884, 50–64.

tions and compromises which left the real problem untouched, and the century before the Reformation was everywhere a time of restless dissatisfaction, and of spasmodic revolts against the alien ecclesiastical settlements which throve on the town's wealth, and could never be absorbed into the town's life. For a little space matters hung in the balance, and then came the crash of the Reformation. In the bitterness of feeling that grew out of the long struggle of the burghers, we have a measure of that temper of virile independence which created the boroughs of the Middle Ages; and as we stand now under the walls of Canterbury Cathedral and see its glory shattered and its carved work broken in pieces, we may well wonder whether in that great ruin there was no other motive at work than the fanaticism of a religious awakening.

CHAPTER XII

CONFEDERATION

THE fact that the English burghers took so impatiently the one hindrance that lay in their path to independence and supremacy is itself a proof of the habit of prosperity and success which they were accustomed to accept as part of their natural heritage in the pleasant place where their lot had fallen. How little they had at any time to reckon with opposition is obvious from the striking fact that they never found themselves compelled to form any kind of union or alliance for common purposes. Here the story of English boroughs is in vivid contrast to that of the continental towns. The powerful confederations formed in European countries by towns battling against tremendous odds to protect their commerce, liberty, and law, had no parallel among the comparatively peaceful and regular conditions of English life, where self-government was so easily attained, and where trade was so generally secure, that the necessity never arose for the creation of any such associations.

Towns on the royal demesne stood in no need of any combined effort to defend their freedom; and the towns on ecclesiastical lands or feudal estates that had grievances to complain of were few, scattered, and subject to so many different lords that combination among them would have been wholly impossible. Organized common action was therefore practically unknown among the English boroughs; for the loose tie of affiliation which bound together communities of which one had adopted the charter and copied the customs of another was a bond so slight as to be scarcely recognized,[1] and implied no mutual obligations whatever. In moments of excited strife or rapid constitutional growth a borough might undoubtedly become fired by the example of a near neighbour, or catch the contagion which spread from some community more advanced in its experiments and daring in its pretensions; but these movements of sympathy, of voluntary affiliation, of emulation, never resulted in any kind of federation or alliance. For the developement of its liberties each borough was ultimately left to depend only on its own resources; while such societies as were constituted in later days in England for trading purposes took the form of federations of men not of towns.[2]

There was but one exception to this general rule,

[1] Gross, i. 241–281.
[2] See the saying of Bacon quoted by Anderson in his Origin of Commerce, ii. 232. "I confess I did ever think that trading in companies is most agreeable to the English nature, which wanteth that same general vein of a republic which runneth in the Dutch and serves them instead of a company; and therefore I dare not advise to adventure this great trade of the kingdom,

and in the Confederation of the Cinque Ports we have the single illustration in England of an association of towns created and maintained for common interests. From Seaford in Sussex to Brightlingsea in Essex ports and villages were bound together into one society. To the original group of the Five Ports— Hastings, Sandwich, Dover, Romney, and Hythe, whose alliance probably reaches back to the time when the English learned war and commerce from Danish masters—the two Ancient Towns, Winchelsea and Rye, had been added immediately after the Norman Conquest; and what with the desire of these seven to divide their burdens of taxation and war charges with the neighbouring villages, and the readiness of the villages on their side to seek admission to the Port privileges,[1] an association had in course of time been evolved consisting of seven head Ports with eight corporate and twenty-four non-corporate members,[2] all gathered under the rule of the Lord Warden. To the last they bore traces of foreign influences in the name of Jurats by which they called their "portmen," and of Barons which they gave to their "freemen." But amid the curious vicissitudes of

which hath been so long under government, in a free or loose trade."

[1] Boys' Sandwich, 770. The Custumals of Dover, Sandwich, Romney, Rye, and Winchelsea, are given in Lyon's Dover, ii. 267–387.

[2] The Ports with corporate members were:—Hastings: (Seaford, Pevensey). Sandwich: (Fordwich, Deal). Dover: (Folkestone, Faversham). Romney: (Lydd). Rye: (Tenterden). Hastings had six non-corporate members; Sandwich six; Dover seven; Romney four; and Hythe one; each of which was governed by a Deputy sent by the head Port.

their history, and the odd incidents of their ownership in times when it seemed natural and simple to grant away the very frontier defences of England to Norman counts and Breton dukes and abbots of Fécamp and monks of Canterbury,[1] and in later days after English kings had realised the advantages of themselves owning the main gates by which their country opened on the European world,[2] these communities remained firmly united under their federal government.[3] The King's writ did not run in the Ports unless it bore the seal of the Lord Warden. Exempt by charter from serving on juries, assizes, or recognizances outside their own

[1] Dover had always remained in the King's hands, but Hythe and Romney belonged to the Archbishop, while Sandwich had been given to Christ Church, Canterbury, and Hastings, Winchelsea, and Rye had been handed over to the Abbey of Fécamp. A few details about the relations of Fécamp to its possessions at Hastings, Winchelsea, and Rye, may be found in Leroux de Lincy's Abbaye de Fécamp, pp. 289, 294, 300, 327, 331; and a notice of the tax called *aletot* which was paid by the inhabitants of Rye to Fécamp, p. 299. The two parish churches of Hastings, being part of the alien priory of Fécamp, were never appropriate or belonging either to the College of S. Mary or to the Priory. They were afterwards granted away by Henry the Eighth (Horsfield's Hastings, i. 448). The Counts of Eu held the Castle with the whole of the rape of Hastings and the manor till their estates were forfeited by rebellion about 1245 and given by Henry the Third to his son Edward. Moss' Hastings, 3–4, 63.

[2] There was a considerable change in the century that followed the complete political separation of England from the Continent. Henry the Third got back Rye and Winchelsea, and at least the Castle of Hastings if not more; and Edward the First Sandwich; while Hythe and Romney remained with the Archbishop.

[3] For rights possessed in the time of Henry the Second see Hist. MSS. Com. v. 454.

territory,[1] the freemen could be impleaded only in their own courts.[2] No prisoner from the Ports could be summoned by the Judges to Westminster, and in the case of an express order from the King " some demur should be made to the first mandate till it be known with certainty it is his pleasure,"[3] while on the other hand any stranger who committed a crime within their liberties might be claimed by the mayor and jurats from any lordship in the realm, even from the King himself.[4] They had even, after a fight which lasted for generations, successfully resisted all attempts to bring their local jurisdiction within the general judicial system of the kingdom, and the Justices Itinerant were shut out from crossing their boundaries or sitting at their Court of Shepway.[5] Ancient privileges were jealously guarded. "New Acts of Parliament," they said, "ought not to alter the free customs."[6] No deodand was given to the Crown

[1] Confirmed by Edward the First, 1293. Rot. Parl, i. 101. There were no coroners in the Cinque Ports except the mayors of the various towns. Lyon's Dover, ii. 269, 347, 371, 303.

[2] A writ of error lay to the Shepway Court only from any of the Ports; but from the Shepway finally there might be an appeal to the King's Bench. (Boys' Sandwich, 697, 771.) A mayor of Sandwich accused of assaulting the sheriff's bailiff refused to answer except at the Court of Shepway. (Ibid. 661.)

[3] Lyon's Dover, ii. 304. See Rot. Parl. i. 332. For the charter of Edward the Third see Boys' Sandwich, 568-9.

[4] Boys, 470-1.

[5] Montagu Burrows' Cinque Ports, 73-4. The Cinque Ports joined Simon de Montfort against the King. Possibly this revolt was due to the limits fixed to their territory by Henry in 1259-60, for a little later the Barons' party extended those limits. (Ibid. 107.) It was in this war too that they finally secured freedom from summons before the King's Justices.

[6] Boys' Sandwich, 445. "Within the Cinque Ports there

"because it never was the custom here."[1] If an ecclesiastical officer came from Canterbury to make an inventory of the goods of a Sandwich man who had died without a will, he was not allowed to act because it was contrary to the ancient customs and liberties of the town.[2] Their corporate dignity was officially recognized on great occasions of State, such as the coronation of a King or the consecration of an Archbishop, when the envoys of the Cinque Ports were treated with special honour and sat at the right hand table in the hall; and each of the Ports in turn sent representatives to carry the canopy over the newly-crowned King, and after the ceremony to bear it back with its silk hangings, its spears, and its silver bells, as the town's spoils.[3]

As to the idea or principle which held this society of towns together and the purpose which it was meant to serve, the definition given by a minister of the Crown would probably have been very different from that given by a baron of the Ports. To a statesman the confederation of the Cinque Ports was organized in the interests of the whole country, and maintained as the bulwark of national safety; and the policy of West Saxon rulers, of Danish conquerors, of Norman kings, of Angevin statesmen, had all alike aimed at the increasing of its public utility. Holding their posts in the first line of defence against invasion, the Cinque Port towns were bound to keep a sufficient number

is no trial by jury as in other places." Ibid. 452. For the system of compurgation see p. 465.
[1] Ibid. 468.   [2] Boys, 681.
[3] Hist. MSS. Com. iv. 1, 425; v. 496; ix. 151.

of men within their walls for defence against the enemy, and watch that inhabitants were not driven away by the imposition of undue local taxes; they had to bear heavy costs for ordnance, ammunition, fortifications; to set a nightly watch in every borough and at every dangerous creek or harbour; to have armed forces ready to meet the first brunt of attack, while their citizens might expect in time of war to see their houses sacked and burned again and again. They had to provide every year fifty-seven ships and 1,197 men with provisions for the defence of the kingdom,[1] and if these were not enough in number or in size greater ones and more were required of them. If they hesitated to comply with such demands, or if they were shown not to have held firm against the invader, they were roughly reminded of the bargain on the terms of which alone all their privileges were held, and saw their charters and franchises seized into the King's hand.[2]

This view of the organization of the Cinque Ports for the public service was visibly represented in the rule of the King's officer, the Lord Warden of the Ports and Constable of Dover Castle. His authority the men of the Cinque Ports were never for a moment

---

[1] Boys' Sandwich, 682.

[2] In 1395 Romney contributed nearly £10 to the maintenance of the liberties of the Cinque Ports, and in 1407, 1408, and 1409, it had to spend over £5 each year in payment for such purposes. The renewal of these charters on one occasion cost Hythe £17 as its share. (Hist. MSS. Com. v. 535, 537.) These payments were over and above the sums which had to be given for the charters of each separate Port, and which were also a heavy cost.

allowed to forget; and the Lieutenant of Dover or his messengers, continually riding round the Ports with message or proclamation or to "make inquisition,"[1] were everywhere helped on their way by dinners, breakfasts, pipes of wine, or a play at the public expense. From Dover came proclamations " warning us of the Danes"; ordering "that no man should quarrel with other for none old sores"; commanding " to arrest the men who came from beyond sea without leave and without billets"; or to seize ships for crossing over to Flanders; calling out vessels " to watch the sea"; or to serve the King in siege or battle during the French war; summoning men "to keep the Castle of Dover"; or decreeing the amount of benevolences to be paid to the King.[2] The subjection of the whole confederation to his rule was publicly recognized every year in the Court of Shepway, when at his summons there came from every port the mayor and a little group of jurats carrying with them the required gifts and dues, wine and swans and fish and spices to furnish breakfast for officials and suitors at the court; or costly offerings to soften the hearts of wardens and judges, and induce them on their first entering into office to look favourably on their subjects. Before them as they sat on either side of the Warden on the open plain near Lympne [3] proclamation was made as to the taxes to be raised by the confederation, the special military

[1] Hist. MSS. Com. v. 545.
[2] Ibid. 525, 494, 517-18, 520.
[3] The usual number was four or five. Lyon's Dover, i. 251. Romney sent six. Ibid. ii. 342. For the capons, geese, etc., with which they came laden see Hist. MSS. Com. v. 534.

services required of the freemen, or the new decrees issued by the Government; and special offences against the Crown were judged. A whole community might be charged with a breach of the King's peace,[1] or an aggrieved corporation made application that officers of the Ports should be sent to help in the arrest and punishment of some stranger who had committed a crime in their town; and prisoners from the various towns accused of coining false money, treason, or counterfeiting the King's seal,[2] were tried, and if found guilty were forthwith tied on a sledge, drawn round the circuit of Shepway, and hanged on the spot.[3]

Nor did the authority of the Warden end at Shepway. As Constable of the Castle he had his court-martial in Dover.[4] As Admiral he could order a "quest of the Admiralty" to be held on the sea-shore, or perhaps at some one of the Ports which had offended against the laws of the confederation —a calamity which the town at once sought to avert by negociations and bribes " that he should not hold the court." As Chancellor he issued precepts and summonses as to the services to be performed by the Ports in return for their privileges, and exercised in his court of chancery the complicated jurisdiction that gradually arose out of these records. There were moments when the King was stirred to a recollection of his sovereignty—moments when the towns had pushed independence too far, or when the treasure in the royal coffers had fallen low; then

---

[1] In 1281 the mayor and townsmen of Sandwich were accused of assaulting the sheriff's bailiffs. Boys' Sandwich, 661.
[2] Ibid. 462.   [3] Lyon's Dover, i. 254.   [4] Ibid. 1., 260-1.

from Westminster a writ of enquiry would come as to the privileges of the Ports, delegates were summoned from the various towns to appear before the Warden, and might find themselves kept many days and nights at Dover [1] while "inquisition was made for the King." Sometimes they were ordered to assemble on the sea-shore. Sometimes the Warden came down the steep path of the castle hill to the tiny church of S. James, set in the first little reach of level ground below the walls of the fortification, and there the jurats came up to meet him from their lodgings in the town below, and after days of discussion probably returned home with heavy news of fines to be levied for buying a new charter, or for getting the confirmation of some doubtful privilege.

In the authority of the Warden we see the view held at Westminster about the uses of the Cinque Ports and the main object of their existence. To the people on the other hand the association had another and wholly different character. So completely was all the business of the Warden's court at Shepway looked on by the portsmen as the King's affair, and so slight was their sense of participation in it, that they presently gave up attending it altogether, leaving the Warden at last to preside in solitary state. In course of time even the ancient site was abandoned, and instead of the annual assembly at Shepway the president only summoned an occasional court of appeal to be held at Dover, [2] and there, surrounded

---

[1] In 1410 jurats from Romney spent three days and three nights at Dover at such an inquisition. Hist. MSS. Com. v. 538.

[2] From about 1471 the court only met at Shepway for the in-

by a group of lawyers to advise him, sat on the chalk cliff fronting the castle to hear certain cases immediately touching the King's interest.[1] Meanwhile the barons of the Ports had their own tradition of independence and self-government; and the popular belief as to the object and meaning of the confederation was embodied in another court which sat on the Broad Hill, near Romney—a court where the Lord Warden had no seat.[2] It was there that the whole interest of the people centred, as turning their backs on the King's courts and leaving him to conduct through the Lord Warden the matters which were his peculiar business, they occupied themselves with the management of their own special affairs. For to the fisherman of the coast the confederation of the villages was in its origin and working simply a great trading company of the Ports for the protection of their staple business, the herring fishery, and for the preservation of their ancient customs of harbourage and sale on the strand at the mouth of the Yare—a matter which became of absorbing importance when their monopoly was threatened by the fishermen of Yarmouth, so that from the time of John onwards they could only preserve their interests by ceaseless vigilance and by costly appeals to King and Parliament, and Council.[3]

stallation of the Lord Warden and the presentation of the courtesy of £100 offered him on the occasion by his subjects. Montagu Burrows' Cinque Ports, 186. Hist. MSS. Com. v. 539.

[1] It only took cognizance of five points, high treason, falsifying money, failure of ship service, false judgment, and treasure box.

[2] Montagu Burrows' Cinque Ports, 66-7, 73-5. See the agreement of the Ports drawn up in 1358. Boys' Sandwich, 560-3. [3] See Rot. Parl. i. 32, 332

In the eyes of the barons therefore the great assembly of the confederation was that which yearly met to discuss the business of the Yarmouth fair. And this was in the strictest sense a court of the people themselves, summoned only by common consent,[1] presided over by the chief magistrate of each Port in turn, and in which every town was represented by its mayor or bailiff, three elected jurats, and three commons. The sheltered harbour of Romney formed a sort of natural centre of the Ports, and the delegates met for business on the Broad Hill or Bromhille of Dymchurch close by, whence they possibly took the name of Brodhull, a name which in later days when the first site was forsaken and forgotten and the delegates met in Romney itself, became changed into "Brothyrhill" or Brotherhood.[2]

On the first day of meeting the business, as befitted an association for trading purposes which dated back to the time when the herring fishery was the staple trade of the Ports, was invariably the Yarmouth fair, and the court heard the report of the bailiffs of the last fair who stood bare-headed before them, and elected their successors who were to govern the coming fair.[3] But other interests had grown up

[1] Every year a letter was sent to each Port asking "whether a Brotherhood or Guestling is necessary to be arreared this year," and when the common consent was given the summonses were issued. Burrows' Cinque Ports, 177.

[2] Hist. MSS. Com. iv. i. 427.

[3] These four bailiffs aided by a provost chosen by the Yarmouth commonalty, took over the keys of the prison, issued all ordinances and held pleas. This went on till 1663. (See Hist. MSS. Com. v. 553, 533, 535, 539-43.) Boys' Sandwich, 576-7. But the question of the Yarmouth fair gradually declined

round the assembly hill. The seafaring population, masters and mariners of trading barges, saw in the union of Ports the power which regulated the relations of seamen on either side of the Channel. To the taxpayers it was a voluntary association for the equitable adjustment of their burdens. And all the inhabitants alike recognized its importance for maintaining against lords of other franchises the privileges which had been granted them in return for their services.[1]

On the great day when the Yarmouth fair was under discussion the Court of Brotherhood sat alone; but on the following days when other work was to be done—the distribution between the various towns of the taxation[2] ordered at Shepway, the discussion of commercial relations,[3] the care of the common cor-

---

in importance, and in the fifteenth century became relatively of so little consequence that the Brodhull decreed in 1515 that the yearly report of their bailiffs sent to Yarmouth might be dispensed with. (Lyon's Dover i. xii.)

[1] Lyon's Dover i. iv. v.

[2] It was already well established in the fourteenth century, and possibly much earlier, that orders of the Court of Shepway as to the taxes required for the King or for the general purposes of the Ports became the basis of agreements made between the Ports at the Brodhull concerning the share of taxes to be paid by each Port. See Burrows' Cinque Ports, 180-1.

[3] In 1412 a curious agreement between the mariners of France and England was signed by Romney and Lydd, and probably by all the ports from Southampton to Thanet. It provided that if any master or mariner were captured the only ransom to be asked on either side should be six nobles for the master and three for the mariner with 20 pence a week board for each; a fishing boat with nets and tackles was to be set free for 40 pence; any man taken on either coast should be charged no ransom, but a gentleman or merchant who was taken might be charged any

porate privileges of the confederation [1]—the Court of Brotherhood was joined by the Court of Guestling, probably a descendant of the ancient Hundred Court once held in the old town of Gestlinges near the border-line of Kent and Sussex.[2] To this court each town might send the mayor, two jurats, and two commoners; so that if all the delegates came the number of the united assemblies would be seventy-seven; as a matter of fact however in the time of Henry the Sixth the business was done by about thirty members.[3] All the important affairs of the

ransom that his captor chose. In case of any dispute, arbitrators were appointed; if these were disobeyed 100s. was to be paid on one side to S. Nicholas at Romney, on the other side to the Church of Hope All Saints. (Hist. MSS. Com. v. 537-538.) The arrangement as to the place of payment of the fine was doubtless different in each town of the league. The common serjeant of Hythe in the same year rode to Dover to get a copy of the composition for his own town. In a disputed case when the plaintiff and defendant seem to have been of Romney, questions touching the "Law of Oleron," i.e., the Law Maritime, were decided "by the judgment of the masters of ships and boats of the vills of Hastings, Winchelsea, Sandwich, and Dover," that is, a majority of the seven towns. (Hist. MSS. Com. vi. 543.)

[1] At any time the court might be summoned to redress a wrong, and not only the jurats and commonalty of a town but any aggrieved person whatever in the whole confederation might claim that a Brodhull should be summoned if he was wronged on any point touching the charters, usages, or franchises of the Ports. Burrows' Cinque Ports, 181.

[2] Ibid. 177-8. The Guestling sometimes sat separately for special business, generally perhaps at Winchelsea, for the affairs of the three Sussex Ports. For an instance in 1477 see Hist. MSS. Com. v. 489.

[3] Moss's Hastings, 21. The importance of the Guestling Court gradually declined and in 1601 the Brotherhood Court

Cinque Ports practically lay in their hands, and their decisions, registered as Acts of the Brodhull by the Common Clerk of the Cinque Ports,[1] became the law of the whole confederation.

Constantly reminded of their ancient covenant and confederation by imminent perils, arduous exertions and recurring taxes, trained to habits of vigilance and mutual support, the Cinque Ports kept a jealous watch against the slightest infraction of the privileges of their united body. But there was one matter with which the confederation had nothing whatever to do. Subject to a variety of jurisdictions, some of them depending on the King, some on the Archbishop, some on a bigger neighbouring town, the special liberties of each borough had been developed under very different conditions; and the whole association took no heed of the defence of the liberties of any single Port against its lord, or the enlargement of the privileges of any one member of their society as apart from the whole.[2] The corporate existence of the united Cinque Ports was a thing altogether apart from the corporate existence of each town within it; and indeed combination for any purpose of securing local liberties would have been out of the question in a confederacy where a

(then near its own extinction) passed a decree that the yearly Guestling might be abolished. Lyon's Dover i. xii.

[1] Hist. MSS. Com. v. 539.

[2] Burrows (Cinque Ports, 238) suggests that Lydd, like the supposed case of Faversham, might have owed its incorporation under a mayor and jurats to the Court of Shepway. He does not give any reasons for this supposition. Lydd was under the Archbishop; Faversham under the abbot until the suppression of the abbey. Ibid. 234.

certain outward uniformity was but the screen of endless diversity, and towns bound together by special duties and privileges were widely separated from one another in all the conditions of government.[1] This is very evident if we compare the situation of Sandwich and Romney—much more so if we consider the position of any of the subordinate members of the Ports.

I. For many centuries Sandwich belonged to the monks of Christ Church, Canterbury, and so long as it was a humble little port powerful kings like Eadgar, Cnut, Henry the First, and Henry the Second had been content to have it so, and with indifferent acquiescence confirmed the monastic rights over the town. But when in the course of time Sandwich became the port through which almost the whole of the continental trade with England passed, when its commerce and revenue increased till it stood far before Dover in importance,[2] when it was the chief harbour from which monarchs or their ambassadors set sail for France, or from which armies were sent forth in time of war, the King

---

[1] Dover and Sandwich were the first of the Ports to have a mayor, the mayors of Sandwich being continuous from 1226. Then came Rye and Winchelsea about 1297. The other three, Hastings, Hythe, and Romney, were ruled by bailiffs till the time of Elizabeth.

[2] For goods imported into Sandwich see Boys, 435-9, 658-9. Iron was brought from Spain and Cologne and wine from Genoa; all kinds of skins, and furs, with silk, spices, and frankincense from the Levant. For the taxes on merchandise, cellars, and warehouses see Hist. MSS. Com. v. 458. Under Edward the Third it fitted out for the King's service 22 ships with 504 mariners. Boys, 783-4.

began to look more seriously on the powers exercised over it by the convent. An inquest ordered by the Crown in 1227 reported in favour of the rights of Christ Church over Sandwich, but by judicious bargaining matters were finally arranged to the royal satisfaction. At the price of a grant of lands in Kent Edward the First bought the town, and though the monks were still allowed certain lands and houses free from municipal charges, and continued to receive large sums from the wharf which was known as Monkenkey with its crane for loading and unloading ships,[1] and from the warehouses enclosing it, they had to abandon their powers of taxing at discretion all passengers and goods which crossed the bounds of their territory.[2]

The Sandwich people had elected their own mayor since the beginning of the thirteenth century; while the royal interests were now looked after by a bailiff appointed by the King.[3] The townsmen however kept a jealous watch over their own prerogatives. When in 1321 Christ Church obtained a royal writ to protect their property from the town taxes the mayor and community refused to accept it because it had been issued to the King's bailiff, and the

---

[1] Literæ Cant. i. lxix.—lxxii. Hist. MSS. Com. ix. 74. Boys' Sandwich, 663. Edward the Third completed the process in 1364. Ibid. 669.

[2] In 1422 an agreement was made that the corporation should go in and out on the quay freely, and use the monks' gate, "to provide for the guard and the defence of the town." The ground along the quay was to be deemed a highway. Ibid. 671.

[3] Under a patent of white wax because Sandwich would not obey an Exchequer patent under green wax. Boys, 441, 404, 435–457.

convent had to get a new writ.¹ The bailiff's powers were carefully defined and kept in strict subordination to those of the mayor. He collected the King's dues on goods brought into the town;² and it was he who summoned the Hundred Court every three weeks to meet in S. Clement's church for view of frankpledge, for pleas of land, questions of trespass, covenant, debt, battery, bloodshed, and so on;³ but he could not hold the court without the mayor's leave, nor issue the summonses without the mayor's orders.⁴ The mayor for his part, if he was elected in S. Clement's, the church where the courts of the King were held, had his seat of government in S. Peter's, a church that stood in the very centre of the town near the Market-place and Common Hall, and in whose tower the "Brande goose bell" hung which summoned jurats and council men to the Common Assembly, and rang out the hours for the market. He gathered the Town Council for business to S. Peter's, and in S. Peter's he sat every Thursday, and if business required it on other days, to judge the people.⁵ Though the bailiff sat by his side and took part in the business of the court, yet for offences against

¹ Literæ Cant., i. 46–48. In 1324 the convent however repeated the offence. Ibid. 118–120. ² Boys' Sandwich, 435.
³ Pleas of the Crown were held at Sandown in a place called the Mastez either on the Monday of the Hundred Court or any other Monday. Ibid. 443. ⁴ Ibid. 457.
⁵ Ibid. 311, 501. The mayor is the judge and gives such judgment as he thinks proper, whereas the bailiff has nothing further to do with the business than to receive the amercements. Ibid. 459.

the corporation the mayor and jurats might punish the freemen "without consulting the bailiff or any one else."[1] To them belonged the entire regulation of trade and the management of weights and measures, for "the bailiff has nothing to do with this business." In no case was he allowed to interfere with the town market; "that business belongs wholly to the mayor and jurats," the town customs declared.[2]

II. Sandwich in fact after it had passed to the Crown enjoyed the full freedom common to the royal boroughs. Bound only by allegiance to the general law of the Cinque Ports it long maintained, as we shall see later, a real independence of local life and a vigorous democratic temper. But in Romney, in the very port where the general assembly of the Cinque Ports held its deliberations, the conditions were wholly different. For a moment Romney like other towns enjoyed its share of profits in the growing trade of the country.[3] The vintners engaged in the wine trade rose from ten in 1340 to forty-eight who headed the list of taxpayers in 1394; a new ward was called

[1] Boys' Sandwich, 527. See also 450.
[2] Ibid. 510, 536-7.
[3] Hist. MSS. Com. v. 533-4, 535, 537, 539, 541-2. In 1340 Romney was divided into thirteen wards, and 941 persons above fifteen were assessed to the subsidy granted to the King that year. The whole sum assessed was £48 9s. 6d. Forty-five persons were assessed in Old Romney at 43s. 6d. The receipts from taxes, rents, etc., in 1381 seem to have been nearly £180. (Boys, 799-801.) Romney seems to have come to the height of its prosperity about 1386. One barge was built 1386; one in 1396; one in 1400; one hired in 1420. (Ibid. 535-40.)

after its cloth-dealer Hollyngbroke;[1] and merchants from Prussia, Holland, Spain, and Flanders, citizens of Bristol and of London, men from York and from Dorset gathered within its walls. But a doom was already on the town. As early as 1381 it had begun its vain struggle against winds and tides which silted up its port, destroyed its river channel, and forced the Rother into a new bed. Dutch and Flemish engineers had been called over to make scientific sluices and barriers, and the whole population had been summoned out to dig a water-course, but in spite of incessant efforts the men of Romney saw their trade driven into other ports.[2] The forty-eight vintners of 1394 had sunk to forty-four in 1415, to five in 1431, and to one in 1449.[3] The burghers were being steadily ruined, and the story of their decay remains registered in the long lists of citizens who pledged their goods for debt, giving in promise of payment saddles, cups, table-cloths, helmets, cloths, which were delivered by the creditor into the hands of the bailiff for keeping in the Common Hall "according to custom," and when the day of payment had passed were appraised by bailiff and jurats, often at half or a quarter of the value at which they had been first declared, and handed over to the creditor.[4]

Through good and evil fortune moreover Romney

[1] This was an old family in the town, for in 1314–15 complaint was made that Hugh Holyligebrok and the community were sheltering and defending robbers and felons so that the country could not get justice on them. Rot. Parl. i. 324.
[2] Hist. MSS. Com. v. 535–42.
[3] Ibid. 535–42.   [4] Ibid. vi. 543–4.

had to maintain a constant struggle for freedom. The Archbishop of Canterbury was lord of the manor, and appointed, subject to the ratification of the Lord Warden, the bailiff of the town,[1] choosing if it seemed good to him one of his own servants or squires, and by a curious exception from the general law having liberty to select a publican.[2] The bailiff fixed the days for holding the market. He gathered in the Archbishop's dues, made sure that his share of any wax, or wine, or goods cast on the shore from wrecks was handed over, and that the jurats collected in proper time the capons and swans and cygnets which had to be sent to him, or that a porpoise taken by the fishermen should be duly despatched to the lord. The common horn sounded twice at the market-place and at the cross to summon the people to his court.

The question of government and of the bailiff's position was however always in debate. The "best men of the town" rode to Archbishop Courtenay "to know his will and what he proposed to do against their liberties"; and for the following century the Romney men were always on the watch, and heavily taxed in gifts and bribes "to protect the liberty of the town that the said lord might not usurp it."[3] The bailiff's power indeed was strictly limited. So far as the administration of justice went he was

[1] Hist. MSS. Com. iv. 1, 425, 429; Ibid. vi. 541.

[2] Bailiff and jurats were allowed to hold taverns of wine and ale "notwithstanding their office, so that they do not sell more dear on account of their office." Lyon's Dover, ii. 337.

[3] Hist. MSS. Com. v. 534, 535, 539, 543, 544.

absolutely controlled by the twelve jurats who were
yearly elected "for to keep and govern the port and
town;"[1] and "in case the bailiff do other execution
than the sworn men have judged against the usage
of the town" they might fine him £10 to the commons.[2]
But this was not enough. In 1395 the
jurats made suit to the Lord Archbishop to "put
his bailiwick into the hands of the community of
Romney at ferm,"[3] and for the century which followed
they were always seeking for some means of gaining
complete control of the government. For lack of
better security a simple expedient was discovered.
The townspeople allowed a custom to grow up that
the Archbishop should not be expected to appoint
a new officer every year, but that whoever was sent
to the town should be understood to hold his post
permanently. When in 1521 the prelate complained
that the jurats would not let his bailiff enter
Romney[4] they answered that when there was no
bailiff in the town the Archbishop might send a new
one, but that the accustomed bailiff who had been
admitted seven or eight years ago was still living

---

[1] The twelve jurats were summoned by the common horn to
assemble for business in the parish church until they hired a room
in 1410 to hold their meetings and to store the goods of the community;
in 1421 they built or repaired a common house with
thatched roof and glass windows, an exchequer table covered
with green cloth, and a bell to ring for the election of jurats. A
book of customs was probably drawn up under Richard the
Second, a small seal made in 1389, and a bell in 1424. Hist.
MSS. Com. v. 534, 537, 540, 541, 546.

[2] Lyon's Dover, ii. 313-14.

[3] Hist. MSS. Com. v. 535. [4] Boys' Sandwich, 806-8.

and was "of good name and fame," and so the place was not void; moreover, they said, a bailiff must make his appearance with certain formalities and "be of good opinion," but this new man had not been sent with the proper forms. The fixity of tenure[1] which the townsfolk thus raised to the dignity of a "customary" right was a real guarantee that the bailiff should no longer be a mere dependent holding his post at the pleasure of a distant master, trembling under the apprehension of hazarding his employment by preferring the interests of the commonalty to those of his lord, and only intent on heaping up treasure against the day when his credit and employment should come to an end. He became more and more identified with the townsfolk among whom he lived, and on whose approval he was made dependent by their contention that he should hold office so long as he was, in their opinion, "of good name and fame."

But the burghers were still dissatisfied with so precarious a tenure of independence. There was a proposal which came to nothing to unite the bailiff and jurats of the town with the bailiff and jurats of the marsh; but in 1484 the people profited by the troubles of Richard's reign to plan a thoroughgoing revolution.[2] They set up a mayor for themselves, and sent to have a silver mace made at Canterbury under the very walls of the Cathedral precincts. The Archbishop

---

[1] One bailiff appointed in 1415 was only ratified in 1421. (Hist. MSS. Com. iv. i. 429.) The contrast with the habit in other boroughs is very striking. [2] Hist. MSS. Com. v. 547.

called in the help of the Crown and the great people of the London law courts, and after much battling and negotiation the matter was ended before the year was out by a Privy Seal being sent down to Romney to depose the mayor. Before a generation had passed away however the struggle broke out again with new vigour, and in 1521 town and prelate were again quarrelling over all the old grievances.[1]

The main point of the burghers' argument was to deny the Archbishop's assertion that "the town is all bishopric." The jurats contended that "from all time" they had had the privileges of one of the capital Five Ports, that their grant of "streme and strond" of the sea and all other rights came to them from the King and not the Archbishop; and that they held the greater part of their town directly from the Crown,[2] on which land the Archbishop had no right to enter, and the commonalty had rights of justice. So also the Archbishop had no right to the marsh and pasturage of four hundred acres which had once been creek and haven, but had been left dry land since about 1380 by the withdrawal of the sea a good half-mile from the town, for this "void place" left by the main course of the stream through the town belonged to the King. Arguing therefore from this fiction of being on royal soil the jurats went on to claim the popular control of justice which was used in royal boroughs, and frowardly kept the courts without the bailiff,

[1] Boys' Sandwich, 806-8.
[2] For notices in Domesday on this point see Burrows' Cinque Ports, 48.

boldly asserting in their own defence that he was at the best but a minister of the King's courts in Romney and not a judge; for if the town courts were in fact courts of the King, they were under the royal grants and charters which ordained that mayor and jurats, or bailiff and jurats, *elected by the people*, were to hold courts, hear pleas, and have fines and amercements and other profits of leets and law-days; and therefore since the bailiff of Romney was not elected by the commons he was clearly excluded and had nothing to do in the said courts save as minister and executioner, and any record of pleas before him was void. In times past, they declared, he had merely been allowed to sit among them by favour, and not of duty. The fines raised at leets and law-days they claimed for the town's use, saying that these had only been given to the most Reverend Father by the favour of the jurats to obtain his good lordship; but that he had never any right whatever to leet or law-day, fine or amercement. So persistent were their protestations of independence that it seems as though ultimately the Archbishop's heavy wrath settled down to rest on the town. When Cranmer leased out the bailiwick of Hythe to the townspeople,[1] he refused to give to

---

[1] In 1412 Hythe sent two of its citizens to London to see the Archbishop and the Lord Chancellor and succeeded in winning some relief from the ancient customary services to the King. In the fifteenth century the Archbishop sometimes appointed the bailiff of Hythe, and sometimes leased out the appointment to the town for a term of years. Cranmer leased it out for ninety-nine years. It only got a mayor under Elizabeth. (Burrows'

Romney a similar lease—a gift which it had begged of Courtenay a hundred and fifty years before. Cranmer's lordship indeed came to an end at the Reformation, but even then Romney was for a time governed by its senior jurat, and it was not until 1563 that it seemed to have sufficiently purged its iniquity, and that Elizabeth finally allowed its people to elect a mayor.

III. From the instances of Sandwich and Romney it is evident that the bond which existed between the chief Ports only served certain definite ends, and had no influence whatever on the developement of local liberties or the intimate relations of a borough to its lord. And if this was the case with the leading Ports, still less was it possible for the subordinate members of the confederation to look for aid in their private controversies. Romney itself for example in the midst of its struggle with the Archbishop was engaged in a resolute effort to retain its own hold over its dependent town of Lydd. There also the Archbishop of Canterbury was lord of the manor, both of the town and of a great part of the grazing land round it known as Dengemarsh, in which lay the fishing-station of Lydd, Denge Ness; while the rest of Dengemarsh was divided between the Abbot of Battle, the Castle of Rochester, and Christ Church, Canterbury, all alike ready to raise at any time questions of disputed rights. As far as the Archbishop was concerned the townsmen had commuted

Cinque Ports, 215, 217-218; Hist. MSS. Com. iv. i. 434, 429. Boys' Sandwich, 811.) One man was bailiff for six years from 1389; and a wealthy publican for two years from 1421.

their services at his court of Aldington for a yearly payment, and became "lords in mean" of their own borough—possibly in the time of Henry the Sixth when they first began formally to use the style of Bailiffs, Jurats, and Commonalty of Lydd; but the Archbishop's seal with the mitre was still used in deeds for selling or letting land.[1]

But Lydd was further subject to Romney as "member of the Town and Port," and in token of this submission their custumal was kept at Romney. If they wanted to ascertain their rights they had to send a messenger to the superior town; and an entry in the accounts of Lydd tells how the corporation paid eightpence to "the servant of Romney bringing authority of having again our franchise." Romney claimed to make awards on disputed questions, interfered about the Lydd markets, and ordered inquisitions as to whether they had been wrongfully held.[2] Moreover as the inhabitants of Lydd "were contributors to Romney before all memory," their officers had year after year to present themselves before the jurats of Romney in the Church of S. Nicholas carrying their accounts and such payments as were demanded by their rulers.[3] Even after the men of Lydd had been given by Edward the First the same liberties and free customs as the other barons of the Cinque Ports, the sum of their taxes was fixed by Romney.

[1] Hist. MSS. Com. v. 531-2. [2] Ibid. 525-6, 532, 536.
[3] In 1403 "Jurats of Lydd and Dengemarsh made account in the church of S. Nicholas at Romney before the Jurats there of all their outlays and expenses." Ibid. 536.

Among many masters the corporation was kept in a perpetual ferment. The boundaries of its territory were not finally decided till 1462, and the quarrel with Battle on this point kept lawyers and town clerks busy hurrying backwards and forwards between London and Lydd, or riding to Canterbury to get the Abbot's charter, or to Winchelsea to meet the Abbot's counsel.[1] For a hundred years moreover the town kept up the long struggle to free itself from the supremacy of Romney. Already in 1384 deputations from both the towns met in Dover to discuss the terms of agreement between them with the Warden, and from that time lawyers were kept constantly at work, and a counsel seems to have been permanently employed in London, besides the deputations of bailiff, common clerk, and jurats sent there as well as to Dover, Sandwich, or Canterbury, and the messengers despatched with "courtesies" for the Lieutenant, the Seneschal, or the Clerk of Dover Castle, the Mayor and Clerk of Dover town, the Archbishop of Canterbury and his steward, the Common Clerk of Winchelsea and so on; while the salary of the Town Clerk, Thomas Caxton, probably a brother of the great printer, was raised again and again, so as to secure the services of the most skilful lawyer and able administrator in all the country round.[2] Even in a trifling matter of taxation it was not till 1490 that the town was able to make a composition for a fixed yearly payment.[3]

IV. In the same way Sandwich had the mastery of

[1] Hist. MSS. Com. v. 524-5. [2] Ibid. 522, 524, 526, 528.
[3] Ibid. 516, 532.

the little town of Fordwich,[1] which lay fifteen miles higher up the river and claimed dominion over a tiny territory reaching back from the water's edge on either side as far as a man in a boat on the river could throw an axe of seven pounds called "Taper-axe." The inhabitants elected every year a mayor, treasurer, and jurats to govern them and preserve the liberties of the town. The mayor with a black knotted stick as badge of his office, held his court of justice. He appointed every year four freemen to act as arbitrators in case of trespass, and if any townsman refused to accept their decision or tried to carry the cause to another court, he was fined the enormous sum of a hundred shillings, or thrown for a year into the town prison, a filthy hole of nine feet square which still exists. In capital cases the mayor could give sentence of death, and order the prosecutor if he won his suit to carry the condemned criminal to the "Thefeswell" and himself throw him into it with hands and feet tied, "knebent" as it was called.[2]

Fordwich however had been granted by the Confessor to S. Augustine's, Canterbury.[3] The Abbot owned the soil of the town; his bailiff lived within its walls and presided over the Hundred Court which he summoned by his officer "Cachepol"; he had his own prison; he was entitled to fines and forfeitures

[1] Hist. MSS. Com. v. 606–7.
[2] It was a common custom in the Cinque Ports for the accuser to be executioner. Burrows' Cinque Ports, 76.
[3] The customs levied by S. Augustine's on the imports at Fordwich quay were to be the same as those collected by Christ Church at Sandwich. Hist. MSS. Com. v. 443.

from felons and fugitives; and he claimed certain customs on all imports, and asserted a right to control the fisheries of the river so as to supply his monks at the fasting seasons.

The convent of Christ Church, Canterbury, owned on the other hand a quay at the highest point to which ships could pass up the river; to this quay wine, alum, Caen stone, etc., were brought for the use of the monastery, and endless quarrels were developed out of its trading monopolies.[1]

As a member of the Port of Sandwich the town was subject to certain regulations and taxations which Sandwich had a right to impose. When the chief Ports met to assess and distribute taxation among themselves, the voice of the lesser members of the confederation was never heard, and the dependent towns had simply to pay such proportions of the sum due as their masters ordered, and there were naturally frequent signs of grumbling and dissatisfaction.[2] The severe protectionist laws which the Fordwich people passed against Sandwich as to the use of the common quay with the crane possibly indicates some attempt at encroachment which it was possible to resist as well as to resent.

Under the rude pressure of rival jurisdictions on every side, and from which there was no escape, the corporation needed constant vigilance in looking after its own interests. Like every other town big and little in the fifteenth century Fordwich made careful research into the true limits of its chartered

---

[1] Literæ Cant. iii. 358. Hist. MSS. Com. viii. 326.
[2] See case of Old Romney. Hist. MSS. Com. v. 544.

rights, and the clerk wrote out new copies of their custumal and of the old record of their boundaries. In the only point where they had a chance of success its burghers fought with steady pugnacity for their privileges. Protesting that they held a monopoly of the quay where the ships were unloaded, they refused the customs demanded by S. Augustine's, claimed the whole control of the river and of the three weirs which were made every year at the beginning of the fishing season, and at last forced a compromise which left the convent only the produce of a single weir.

If the lesser members of the Ports which were themselves corporate bodies, such as Lydd or Fordwich, could expect from their superiors no help in achieving independence, the non-corporate members were yet more completely withdrawn from the chance of assistance; for the seven great towns of the association would have looked with little tolerance on any revolt in their dependent villages.[1] Undoubtedly the inhabitants of the Cinque Ports had their full share of the democratic temper that ruled in the trading towns of the eastern coast from the Wash to the Channel. Rebellion was in the air; and the labourers and miners of Kent and Sussex had an evil reputation in the Middle Ages as being most prone to civil dissensions, "as well for that they can hardly bear injuries as for that they are desirous of novelties."[2] There was never a rising in which they were

---

[1] For the difficulties which attended the government of a group of dependent villages by the head town see Lyon's Dover, i. 26-29. See also the relations of Sandwich and Stonor. Boys' Sandwich, 547-8. [2] Polydore Vergil, 84.

not the most eager partizans of the revolutionary side. The men of Kent crowded after Cade. Hastings sent eleven soldiers to help him; Rye begged for his friendship; and Lydd sent its constable on horseback to meet him, wrote him a letter of excuse for not joining him, and presented him with a porpoise.[1] When Warwick took up the cry of Cade they rallied to his side; and when he brought back Henry the Sixth in 1470 they again gave him support.[2] In the internal politics of the towns we meet the same temper; and however obscure and insignificant were the struggles of the Ports and of the humble villages that gathered around them, they reveal to us the militant spirit of self-assertion which was stirring in

---

[1] Archæologia Cantiana, vii. 234; Hist. MSS. Com. v. 520.

[2] See especially the account of Canterbury in Hist. MSS. Com. IX. 176-7. Lydd incurred heavy expenses in the war of 1460. In Rye there is an entry of 19s. 3d. for the expenses of the mayor, bailiff, common clerk and four jurats at Dover, " going and returning on carrying the men's quarters, when the mayor and bailiff with four jurats were sent under the heaviest penalty, and on pain of contempt of our lord the King." Another two pence was spent in giving them a drink of malmsey before dinner (Hist. MSS Com. v. 492, 493); and the same year " the men of the Lord Warwick entered the town with a strong band and took down the quarter of the man and buried it in the churchyard." In 1470 Romney and the other Cinque Ports supported Warwick against Edward, 1469-70. (Hist. MSS. Com. v. 545.) For Lydd, p. 525; and Sandwich, Boys' Sandwich, 676. At the return of Henry the Sixth from October 1470 to April 1471, an entry in Lydd records " on the second Sunday after the feast of St. Michael the Archangel in the year of King Henry the Sixth." (Hist. MSS. Com. v. 525.) The clerk did not know what year to call it. For the sufferings of Kent in the war see Warkworth's Chronicle, 21-22.

every hamlet in England. But with this sturdy spirit of municipal freedom the question of federal organization had nothing whatever to do. We have seen that the trading privileges won in early days by the joint action of the towns were confined to the supervision of the herring fair at Yarmouth, and that the association never developed into a great commercial league after the imposing pattern of the towns of Picardy or of the Rhine. Still less did the union resemble any of the federative republics formed across the water in Ponthieu or the Laonnais for mutual aid against the enemies of their peace or liberties.[1] There is no evidence that the confederation of the Cinque Ports afforded to its members any security of municipal freedom, or any extension of the rights to be won from their several lords; and as a matter of fact this group of favoured towns does not seem to have made the slightest advance on other English boroughs, either in winning an earlier freedom, or in raising a higher standard of liberty. In fact the history of the sixteenth century was to prove that there was no more formidable opposition to the growing democracies in the Kent and Sussex towns than the respectable official company that gathered at Romney and ate together the annual feast of the Court of Brotherhood.

[1] Luchaire, Communes Françaises, 77, etc.

INDEX

A

Abbotsbury, convent at, 203
Adamson, William, lease of Liverpool ferm to, 271, *note* 2
Admiral, appointment of mayor as, 234; his jurisdiction, *ib.*, *note* 2; of Norwich, 245; of the Cinque Ports, his jurisdiction, 392
Adventurers, Merchant, 90; their rivalry with Staple and Hanse, 94, 95; organized by charter, 95, 96; by Henry VII., 96; growth of their privileges, *ib.*; settlement at Antwerp, 97, 98; struggle for free trade in cloth in the Netherlands, 99-101; struggle with the staplers, 101-103; with Hanseatic League, 103-111; organization in Norway, Sweden, and Denmark, 106; supported by Henry VII., 111, 112; their triumph in the north, 114; progress from Edward III. to Henry VII., 122
"Advocantes," 190
Alderman of the staple, 46, 48
Aldington, archbishop's court of, 409
Aletot, tax paid by Rye to Fécamp, 387, *note* 1
Alexandria, centre of Mediterranean traffic, 77
Alien, judicial combat in Fordwich with, 221, *note* 2

Almshouses, 41, *note* 2
Amusements in towns, 145-153
Andover, punishment for breach of public duty in, 181, *note* 2
Antwerp, trade of English Adventurers at, 94; capital of the Merchant Adventurers, 97, 98; succeeds Bruges as a centre of commerce, 100; conference at, 113
Apprentices, kept only by burghers, 182
Apprenticeship, in towns, sought by country labourers, 194
Archers of Reading in 1371, 16, *note*
Arms, view of, at Bridport, 15, 16; at Reading, 16, *note*
Arrest, disputes about rights of, 351-352, 364-367, 372
Assemblies in the towns, 223
Assize of wine, bread, and ale, controversy as to, in Exeter, 358-9
Attorneys, their numbers in Norfolk and Norwich limited, 58
Augustine's, S., convent of, Canterbury, its agreement with Christchurch, 369; disputes with the town, 371-3; owner of Fordwich, 412; compromise with Fordwich, 414
Aylesbury, evasions of watch and ward in, 133
Aynesargh, Richard de, lease of Liverpool to, 271, *note* 2

B

Bailiff, commander of the town in war, 128; his appointment as king's steward and marshal, 236; capital, of Hereford, 229, 319-320; election of, in Liverpool, 270; of wards in Norwich, 240, 243, 245, 246; of Romney, 404-406; of the king, in Sandwich, 400-402

Bailiff-errant, his duties, 205

Baltic, English Merchant Adventurers in, 95

Barge, the admiral's, 245; common, of towns, 87, 140; of Ipswich, 85, *note* 2; of London, 87, *note* 3; of Romney, 87, 88

Barnstaple, granted to Sir John Cornwall and the Countess of Huntingdon, 253; its ferm, &c., in 1273, *ib.*, *note* 3; its traditions as borough in ancient demesne, 253-255; byelaws of, 254; "Burgesses of the Wynde" in, *ib.*; complaints of lords of, about authority claimed by burghers, *ib.*; inquisition as to franchises of, 255; charters, *ib.*; market, 253, *note* 3; Long Bridge, *ib.*; its wealth in thirteenth and fourteenth centuries, *ib.*; seal, 225, *note*

Barons of the Cinque Ports, 386

Barton, John, thief in Exeter, 354

Battle, services due from its burgesses, 171, *note* 2; its quarrel with Lydd about boundaries, 411; abbot of, owner of land in Lydd, 409

Beaufort, Cardinal, 214

Bedford, opposition to commission of enquiry in, 268, *note* 1

Beer, its introduction, 57; English, exported to Flanders, *ib.*

Bell, the common, 161, 180; of Bristol, 314, 315; of Hereford, 127; Reading, 304; Romney, 405, *note* 1; Brandegoose, at Sandwich, 401; of church, 153; the curfew, 324

Bell-foundries, 55

Benecke, captain of Danzig privateers, 109, *note* 2

Bergen, staple set up by English adventurers at, 95; English expelled from, 107

Berkeley, owned by lay noble, 227; privileges leased to the burghers of, 263; relations with its lords, 264, 267; lords of, their fight with Bristol, 313-315; their trading, 316

Berkeley, Lord James, 266

Berkeley, Lord Maurice, 265, 266 312, 314-315

Berkeley, Lord Thomas, 315

Berkeley, Lady, daughter of Mayor of Bristol, 316; her funeral, *ib.*

Bernard, the goldsmith, his escape from prison, 374

Berwick, government of, given to one of the Berkeleys, 264

Bier, the parish, 202

Billeting, forbidden in Bristol, 210, *note* 3

Birmingham, 200, *note* 2; its bridges, 20; its guild, *ib.*

Bishops as lords of towns, 281

Blackwall, entrepôt of Dinant copperworkers at, 56

Bondmen, not to be admitted to franchise in York and Bridgenorth, 196

Bonvil, Sir William, 41, *note* 2, 267, 268, 366

"Booners," 141

Bordeaux, its trade, 87, 118, 119, 316, *note* 1; taken by the French, 119

Boroughs, English, their importance in fifteenth century, 1; created by Edward I., 11, *note* 3; representation in Parliament, 24, 25; conditions of claiming the property of, 218; importance of corporate succession of, 219; classification of, 227; sympathy of king with, in questions of rival jurisdiction, 232-3; local self-government in, 233-237; extortion in, 235, *note* 1; advantages gained by, in times of state troubles, 237; anxiety of king about democratic movement in, 247,

note 3; granted to nobles, 253, note 2; in "ancient demesne," 227, 246, see Towns
Borough Court, or Portmote, attendance of burghers required at, 180; wills enrolled in, 200, note 1; at Norwich, 239
Borough English, 222
Boston, house of the Hanseatic League at, 110
Boulogne, soldiers from Reading at, 16, note
Boundaries, preservation and perambulation of, 134
Boy Bishop, 148
Brass, guns made of, 55, note 4
Bribes, system of, in the towns, 211-217
Brickmaking, its beginnings in England, 56
Bridges, repair of, 144; the Long, at Barnstaple, 253, note 3; at Birmingham, 20; Canterbury, 19; Exeter, 144; London, ib., Nottingham, ib.; Reading, 301, note 2
Bridgenorth, payment to players forbidden in, 152; franchise of, 196; complaint of the jurors against the sheriff's bailiffs, 207, note 1
Bridgewater, burgages held by clergy at, 175, note
Bridport in the thirteenth century, 202-203; in fourteenth century, 15; in fifteenth century, 15-16; views of arms at, ib.; fraternities in, ib.; Toll Hall and Guildhall at, ib.; bell foundries at, 55-56; collection for improving its harbour, 143, 144; rector and parishioners, 157; bequests for the church, 159, note; manufactures at, 202; payments in kind for ferm, 204-5; advantages of its obscurity and distance from court, 210
Brinklow, his political ideas, 60, note 4
Bristol made a shire, 12; gives a benevolence to the king, 27, note 2; disputes with Genoese merchants, 91, note 2; its contribution for protection of traders, ib., note 3; new channel dug for the Frome at, 142; billeting forbidden in, 210, note 3; revolt of the Commons, 312; charter forfeited, ib., note 1; mayor of, freed from oath to constable, 313; obtains jurisdiction over Redcliffe, 314; fight with lords of Berkeley, 313-315; difficulties as to jurisdiction of Temple fee, 313, note 2; incorporation of Redcliffe with, ib., note; burgesses' petitions to King and Parliament, 315; assault on Lord Thomas of Berkeley, ib.; payment for confirmation of charters, ib.; sends men to Lord Berkeley's help at Nibley, 316; the castle fee in; 311; constable of castle, 312; grant of ferm, 238, note 3; dispute about ferm, 253, note 2; S. Mary's Hall at, 316; Fellowship of Merchants, 89; paving, 18, note; common bell, 314, 315; gaol, 315; watch on S. John's Eve, 149; compass first used in England by its men, 107; trade with Gascony, 119; traders from, settle in Bridport, 15; sail to Iceland, 107; Flemish weavers in, 193.
Britanny, commercial treaty with, 112
Broad-cloth first mentioned, 52
Broad Hill, court held on, 394, 395
Brodhull, register of its acts, 398; see Brotherhood
Brotherhood, court of, 395-398; see Brodhull, Guestling
Bruges, the staple at, 45; made staple for English cloth in Flanders, 113, note 3; decline of its weaving trade, 65
Building in towns in fifteenth century, 18, 19
Burgage rents, 13, note 2
Burgage tenure, 170-173, 200, note 2
Burgesses, in the empire, first mention of, 11, note 1; decayed, in Preston, 190, note 3; of the Wynde in Barnstaple, 254; their qualifications, 170, 171; crafts-

E E 2

men and foreigners admitted as, 173 ; *see* Burghers, Citizens
Burghers, mode of admission of, 178-9 ; duties, 180-181 ; privileges, 181-185 ; responsibilities and services, 185-188 ; punishment of, for refusing [to serve in municipal offices, 187, 188 ; their duties confined to town, 188 ; the exclusive character of the poorer, 195 ; claim to have their own courts, 220 ; growing importance in the country, 257 ; their seals, 175 ; *see* Burgesses, Citizens
Burgundy, Henry VII.'s alliance with, 4 ; charter to Merchant Adventurers in, 96
Burgundy, Duke of, grants charter to English Merchant Adventurers, 96

C.

"Cachepol" of abbot of S. Augustine's, 412
Cade, Jack, his supporters in Cinque Ports, 415
Calais, the staple at, 46 ; captain of, 49 ; mint at, *ib.* ; Likedelers of, 90 ; election of governors of Merchant Adventurers held at, 96, *note* 6
Cambridge, first notice of bricks at, 56, *note* 3
Canal-makers, Dutch, 193
Cannyges, of Bristol, 84, *note* 1, 89, 107
Canopy, at coronation of King, carried by representatives of Cinque Ports, 389
Canterbury, royal borough, 227 ; extent of its jurisdiction, 3, *note* ; Henry VII. received at, 37, *note* ; quarrels with Sandwich, 163, *note*; Henry VII.'s breve to enable inhabitants to resist demands of King's purveyors, 210, *note* 1 ; payment to be excused from sending ships to the war, 213, *note* 3 ; relations with York and Lancaster, 215, 216 ; refusal of citizens to appear at the King's Court at Westminster, 230, *note* 2 ; property exempt from corporate authority 310, *note* ; dispute as to jurisdiction of city coroner, 355, *note* 1 ; dispute with S. Augustine's, 371-2 ; with Christ Church, 135-6, 373-382 ; with convent of S. Gregory, 369 ; bridge, 19 ; charters, expenses connected with, 211, *note* ; cathedral, its jubilee festivals, 376 ; church of S. Andrew, 380 ; Blackfriar's churchyard, 375 ; first main drain, 20 ; expenses of feasts, 372, *note* 3 ; town festival, 149 ; price of admission to freedom, 178, *note* 5 ; municipal debts, 140, *note* 1 ; gifts, 214-216 ; hospitals, 369 ; Swan inn, 216 ; loans to King, 27, *note* 2 ; market, 371-2, 377-80 ; mayor, probate claimed by, 200, *note* 1 ; mace, 381 ; king's mead, 371 ; mill, *ib.*, 372, 381 ; minstrels, 145, *note*; paving, 18, *note* ; plays, 146 ; protection of burghers, 185 ; provision for pilgrims, 375-6 ; punishment for drawing knife, 132, *note* 2 ; extortions of sheriff, 207 ; Staplegate, 370; trade with Bordeaux, 118 ; walls and gates, 129, *note* 1 ; Westgate, 370, 381 ; *see* Augustine's (S.), Christ Church
Canterbury, Archbishops of, 177, *note* 2, 369-371, 409
Cardiff requests copy of Hereford customs, 228
Carlisle, its "frelidge," 180 ; help granted towards payment of ferm in, 231, *note* 2 ; liberties forfeited, 247, *note* 4
Carpets, manufactory of, at Ramsey, 57
Castile, commercial treaty with, 120
Castle Coombe, cloth sold at, 54, *note* 1
Castle, constable of, his authority, 311-12
Castle Fee, its independence of the municipality, 311
Catalonia, commercial treaty with, 120
Caxton, Thomas, town clerk of Lydd, 411

INDEX

Cemetery, booths set up in, at fair-time, 362
Chaldensham, the breaking to pieces of the abbot's gallows at, 372
Charters, power of the King to withdraw, 211-12; payments for the confirmation of, 211; of incorporation, 219, note 1; see Barnstaple, Bristol, Canterbury, Ipswich, Leicester, Lincoln, Liverpool, Lynn, Northampton, Norwich, Nottingham, Plimpton, Reading, Winchester
Chepin gavell in Reading, 299, 306
Chepstowe, its trade with Iceland and Finmark, 107, note 1
Chest, the parish, 202; the common, of Reading, 305, 306
Chester, raid of Baldwin of Radington on, 130; affray at, ib., note 1; town festival, 149; liberties forfeited, 247, note 4; silting up of harbour, 270
Chester, Earl of, Liverpool granted to, 270
Children of citizens, age of taking up duties of citizenship, 194; of non-burgesses, age of beginning work, 194-5
Chimneys of tiles or brick, houses to be provided with, 194
Christ Church, Canterbury, its agreement with S. Augustine's, 369; ownership of Sandwich, 399-400; owner of land in Lydd, 409; quarrels with Fordwich about the quay, 413; see Canterbury
Christopher, the (ship), 316, note 1
Church, hostile to the formation of communes, 279, note 2
Church-ales at Plymouth, 160, 161; at Yaxley, 161, note
Churches, parish, their various uses, 153-156; apportionment of seats, 154; townspeople lay rectors of, 157; various expenses, 158-161; bequests for, 159; rebuilding of, in 15th century, 18
Churchyards and ecclesiastical precincts enclosed by walls, 335
Cinque Ports, their treaties with "French Shipmen," 4, note 1; house of elected mayor or jurat who declined to serve, pulled down, 187; jurats and barons of the, 386; confederation of, 386-399; privileges, 387-389; ownership of, 387, notes 1 and 2; justices itinerant shut out from, 388; writ of error in, 388, note 2; no trial by jury in, 388, note 6; support Simon de Montfort, 388, note 5; heavy charges for defence borne by, 389-390; payments for maintenance of liberties of, 390, note 2; monopoly threatened by Yarmouth, 394; jealous watch against infractions of privileges, 398; accuser often executioner in, 412, note 2; confederation affords no security to members against their lords, 414; various jurisdictions, 398; admiral of, 392; no coroner in, 388, note 1; trading privileges, 414-415; confederation, unlike confederations abroad, 415; supports Cade, ib.; supports Warwick, ib.; courts of, see Brotherhood, Guestling, Shepway
Cirencester, 295
Citizens, their busy life, 161; independence, 177; laws passed in Norwich and Worcester to compel men to become, 190; age for taking up duties, 194; outnumbered by the unenfranchised classes in the towns, 196; distinguished from "natives" in Hereford, 318; see Burgesses, Burghers
Clarence, Duke of, present from Canterbury to, 215
Clergy as citizens, 175, note
Clisbeath, fight on, 267
Clock, the town, 182
Clock-house, payments for, in Reading, 304
Cloth, altered conditions of production, 54; sold in London, ib. note 1; taxes on, 81, note 1; struggle for its free importation into Netherlands, 99, 100; undressed, its export forbidden, 110; terms of sale and finishing, granted to Henry VII. by Flanders, 113, note 3; woollen,

its export allowed to Portuguese, 121, *note* 2; manufacture protected by government, 66, 67; attempt to confine its export to London, 69; dressing of, disputes about, 70; seal for sealing it, in Reading, 308; broad, 52; *see* Trade

Cloth-workers, rivalry with wool-growers, 68

Clothiers distinguished from drapers, 67

"Clothing, Great," of Worcester, 138, *note*

Coal, its early use in London, 55, *note* 1

Cœur, Jacques, 114

Colchester, its condition, c. 1300, 14; progress in the 14th cent., *ib.*, 15; burghers not to be appointed in any quest or assize outside the borough, 188, *note* 2; Norwich system of government imitated by, 238, *note* 2; gallows, 2, *note*; moot hall, 14; wool hall, *ib.*

Cologne, Hanse of, 75, 76, *note* 1

Commerce, treaties of, 66; government protection of, 66, 67; by sea, its early routes, 75-77; between England and the Baltic, 83; its two great routes, 83; in hands of foreign carriers, 83, 84; growth of private enterprise, 88, 89; transferred from foreign carrying vessels to those of English adventurers, 94; *see* Trade, Treaties

Common, rights of, 136, 137, 181

Commons, House of, relation of boroughs to, 24; control over taxation, 25, *note* 3; height of power in early 15th century, 26; petition for working of mines, 55, *note* 1; *see* Parliament

Communes, the Church hostile to the formation of, 279, *note* 2; of France, contrast between their history and that of the English towns, 29-32

Communitas, its meaning, 167-168; early government, 169-171

Compass, its first recorded use in England, 107

Compurgation, 221, *note* 2

Conesford Ward, Norwich, 239-40

Confederation, contrast between English boroughs and Continental towns as to, 384-385; of Cinque Ports, 386-99, 414-416

Constable, dispute about election of, in Reading, 304, 306; of the castle, his authority, 311-312

Convents, towns subject to, 227, 295

Copes, regulations about use of, at Plymouth, 158

Copper works at Dinant, 56; in England, *ib.*

Cornwall, Sir John, Lord of Barnstaple, 253

Cornwall, its silver mines, 55, *note* 1; tin works, 83

Coroner, business of, 203; dispute in Exeter about the jurisdiction of, 355; of Devonshire, 355; in Cinque Ports, 388, *note* 1

Corpus Christi, guild of, 150, 151

Coteler, J., lieutenant of mayor of Exeter, 346

Court, the papal, its demands from Canterbury cathedral, 376; *see* Admiralty, Borough, Brotherhood, Curia Comitatus, Guestling, Hundred, King's, Leet, Orphans, Portmote, Sheriff's, Shepway, Steward's Hall Port, Tolbooth

Craft guilds, 150

Crafts, their formation into close companies, 195

Craftsmen, their political importance, 60; admitted as burgesses, 173

Cranmer, his refusal to lease out bailiwick of Romney to townspeople, 408-9; his lease of the bailiwick of Hythe to townspeople, 408,

Cranbrooke, cloth sold at, 54, *note* 1

Crete, English merchants buy wine in, 116

Criers in the towns, 161-162, 180

Cunningham, Sir Thomas, 98, *note* 5

Curfew bell in Winchester, 324

Curia Comitatus at Norwich, 239

Customs, Hereford, 317; copy of, asked for by Cardiff, 228

INDEX

D

Danzig, English cloth-dealers at, 95; English colony at, 104, note 6
Dartmouth, its parish church, 157, note 2
Davison, Sir W., 98, note 5
Dean, Forest of, its forges, 54
Demesne, ancient, boroughs in, 227-229
Dengemarsh, 409
Denge Ness, 409
Denmark, English traders expelled from, 66; Henry VII.'s treaty with, 113
Derby, franchises of, forfeited, 247, note 4
Derby, Earl of, Liverpool granted to, 270
Devon, its silver mines, 55, note 1
Devon, Earl of, his fight with Lord William Bonvil, 267-8
Devonshire, the coroner of, 355
Devonshire, Earls of, 266, 366; conflict of Exeter with, 339, 340
Dinant, its relation to the Hanseatic League, 82, note 3; copper-workers of, their trade with England, 56
Disfranchised table, 181
Domesday, 343, 344, 345; of Ipswich, 225
Dominicans, their settlement in Winchester, 323
Doncaster, 269, note
Dorchester, extent of its jurisdiction, 3, note; sheriff's court at, 203, 204
Dorset, its silver mines, 55, note 1
Dover, member of Cinque Ports, 386; ownership of, 387, note 1; church of S. James, 393; the Lord Warden's court of appeal held at, 393-394; meeting of deputations from Lydd and Romney at, 411; punishment of thief, 221, note 2; lieutenant of, 213, note 1, 391; castle, constable of, 390, 392
Drain, at Canterbury, 20; at Exeter, 361
Drapers distinguished from clothiers, 67; of London, their first charter, 52, note 3
Duel in Leicester, 221, note 2; freedom from, in Lincoln, ib.
Dunwich, 238, note 3

E

Ecclesiastical estates, towns on, 227, 277-281; tenants of, their attitude in the towns, 191, 192
Edmund Crouchback, 269, note; 270, 271
Edmund, Bishop of Exeter, 343
Edward I., boroughs created by, 11, note 3; charter to Norwich, 242; grant to Lydd, 410
Edward II., advantages to towns of disorders under, 237
Edward III., his dealings with the staple, 45, 46; relations with Florentine merchants, 78, 79; borrows money of Lübeck merchants, 83; advantages to towns of his commercial policy, 237
Edward IV., his relations with the Hanse, 109-110; grants fresh franchises to Exeter, 367, note 2
Egypt, Venetians driven out of, 114
Elbing, market at, 104
Election of town officers, 224, 235
Empire, first mention of burgesses in, 11, note 1
Enclosure of churchyards and ecclesiastical precincts within walls, 335
Engineers, Dutch and Flemish, employed in England, 142, 143, note, 403
England, its comparative unimportance in Europe in thirteenth century, 32, 33; character of its history in fifteenth century, 35-44; classes of its population c. 1453, 60
English language, prayers in, used by a Norfolk guild, 42, note
Escheator, the King's, 208; appointment of mayor as, ib., note 1; term of office, 234, note 3
Essex, Dom Robert, manufactures silk at Westminster, 57, note 2
Exe Island, 339

Exeter, its early government, 338 ; jurisdiction of Earls of Devonshire in, 339 ; disputes with them, 266, 339; with the cathedral, 340-368 ; discussion between bishop and mayor, 155 ; election of Shillingford as mayor, 340, 341; grant of Richard of Almayne to, 357 ; grants of Edward IV. to, 367, *note* 2 ; almshouses at, 41, *note* 2 ; right of arrest in, 364-366 ; assize of wine, bread, &c., 358-9 ; bridge at, 144 ; Broad Gate, 353 ; great drain, 361 ; Canon's-street, 360 ; controversy as to common use of cathedral, 362-364 ; as to jurisdiction of coroner, 355 ; cathedral close, 352, 353, 355 ; provision for ferm in, 359 ; Fish-street, 360 ; price of admission to freedom, 178, *note* 5 ; gates, dispute for control of, 361, 362 ; Guildhall, 341, 351, 356 ; hospitals, 41, *note* 2 ; law against livery, 339; market, *ib.* 359, 360 ; St. Martin's-street, 360 ; paving of, 18, *note* ; bishop's prison, 362 ; St. Peter's fee, 357 ; Recorder, 345, 347 ; maces, 339, 367 ; Black Roll, 345 ; S. Stephen's fee, 343 ; town-hall, 344 ; great tower, 361-2 ; warden of the poor, 41, *note* 2 ; controversy as to watch and ward, 357, 358 ; wine gavell, 359

Exeter, Edmund, bishop of, 343

Exmouth, port, 346, 359

Export trade, revenue from, under Henry VII. and VIII., 58 ; industrial changes occasioned by, 67 ; disputes caused by, between merchants and artizans, 70 ; *see* Trade

Extortion in the boroughs, 235, *note* 1

F

Fairs and markets forbidden to be held in sanctuaries, 156 ; forbidden on Sundays and feast days, 156, *note* ; of Ripon, 130 ; of Tetbury, 314 ; St. Giles's, at Winchester, 324, 329 ; at Yarmouth, 395, 396, 415

Fastolf, Sir John, 259, *note* 2 ; 267, *note* 1

Faversham, its incorporation under mayor and jurats, 398, *note* 2

Fécamp, abbey of, its relations to Hastings, Winchelsea, and Rye, 387, *note* 1

Fees on admission to freedom of town, 178 ; in kind at Wells, *ib.*

Fellowship, Merchants', in Bristol, 89 ; in London, attempt to monopolize the export of cloth, 69 ; of the mayor of Exeter, 346, 353, 366

Felon, dispute about the seizure of the goods of, in Exeter, 354

Ferm of towns, collection of, 205 ; settlement of, connected with election of mayor, 218, *note* ; provision for payment of, 231, *note* 1, 244, 359 ; leasing out of, 238, *note* 3, 247, *note* 4

Festivals, local, 149 ; complaints of their decay, 151 ; jubilee, at Canterbury cathedral, 376

Feudal estates, condition of towns on, 250, 251 ; lords, struggle of the boroughs with, 198-200, 255-257

Finance of towns, 138-141

Fines paid to be free of holding municipal offices, 187, *note* 1 ; of borough or manor courts, granted to citizens, 231

Fineux, Master John, justiciar, 214

Florence adopts free trade, 117 ; Henry VII.'s commercial treaty with, *ib.* ; its trading importance, 78 ; loans of its merchants to Edward III., *ib.*, 79 ; commercial revival after acquisition of Leghorn, 79

Folkestone, punishment of thief at, 221, *note* 2

Fordwich, 227, 369 ; under mastership of Sandwich, 411, 412 ; extent of its territory, 412 ; jurisdiction of Abbot of S. Augustine's, *ib.*, 413 ; quarrels with Christ Church about quay, *ib.* ; regulations and taxations imposed by Sandwich on, *ib.* ; compromise with S. Augustine's

INDEX

as to control of river and weirs, 414 ; capital punishment in, 412 ; judicial combat with alien in, 221, *note* 2 ; Hundred court, 412 ; jurisdiction of mayor, *ib.* ; its officers, *ib.* ; prisons, *ib.* ; Thefeswell, *ib.*
Foreigners, admitted as burgesses, 173, 178, *note* 5 ; limitation of their rights, 184
Forfeiture of town privileges, 247, *note* 4 ; of citizenship, 179, 180
Fortescue, Sir John, chief justice, 59, 346
France, condition of people in, as described by Fortescue, 59
Franchise forfeited by forsaking town for a year and a day, 179 ; refusal to take up, 186, 328 ; to be confined to members of craft guild, 195, 196 ; bondmen born not to be admitted to, in York and Bridgenorth, 196 ; of Lynn, controlled by the Bishop of Norwich, 286 ; *see* Freedom
Franciscans in Winchester, 323
Frankpledge, view of, dispute in Lynn about, 290, 294
Fraternities at Bridport, 16
Freedom, municipal, ways of winning, 177, *note* 1 ; mode and terms of admission to, 178, 179 ; lost by breach of public duty, 180 ; mode of recovery in Hereford, 180, *note* 3 ; classes shut out from, 189, 190
Freemen, their decrease in Romney and Winchester, 190
Freeman's prison, 185
Free-traders, their settlement outside the towns, 192, 193
"Frelidge" at Carlisle, 180

G

Gallows and pit, right of, 2, *note*
Gallows of prior of Christ Church, Canterbury, 373 ; the abbot's, at Chaldensham, 372 ; of Colchester, 2, *note* ; Southampton, *ib.* ; Worcester, 310
Gaol, the common, of Bristol, 315
Gascony, its trade with England, 119

Gates, dispute about control of, in Exeter, 362 ; in Winchester, 324
Gate, the Broad, of Exeter, 353
Gaunt, John of, 253, *note* 2, 260, *note* 2, 270
Gavell, the wine, in Exeter, 359, *see* Chepin
Genoa, its trade, 79, 80 ; bank of S. George, 80 ; relations of its traders with England, 114, *note*, 115 ; proposal to forbid trade with, 116 ; disputes of its merchants with those of Bristol, 91, *note* 2
Germin, treasurer of Exeter, 346
Gestling, drowning of felons in the, 221, *note* 2
Glass, English, forbidden in Beauchamp Chapel at Warwick, 56, *note* 4
Glass-painting, early English, 56
Gloucester made a shire, 12 ; owned by King, 227 ; custody of, given to one of the Berkeleys, 264 ; bell foundries at, 55, 56 ; paving of, 18, *note*
Gloucester, Duke of, at York,216,217
Gloucester, Earl of, his gallows at Worcester, 310
Godbeate, liberty of, in Winchester, 324
Goldsmiths of London, their wealth, 58
Grendon, Simon, Mayor of Exeter, 41, *note* 2
Griffith, David ap, grant of ferm of Liverpool to, 275
Grimsby, regulation as to taxes in, 355, *note* 2
Guestling, courts of, 397 ; *see* Brotherhood
Guild at Birmingham, 20 ; of Corpus Christi, 150, 151 ; of Young Men at S. Edmundsbury, 296, 297 ; shipmen's, at Hull, 89, *note* 2 ; of merchants at Lynn, 89 ; at Malmesbury, dispute about, 302, *note* 2 ; of Nottingham, rights of taxation given to, 355, *note* 2 ; of Totnes, 251, 252 ; of Our Lady and S. George at Plymouth, 158 ; at York, 42, *note*, 89, *note* 2
Guilds, festivals of, 150
Guild Hall, *see* Hall

INDEX

Guild Merchant, its importance in dependent towns, 302, 303; of Ipswich, 224, 225; Leicester, 355, note 2; Liverpool, 270; Lynn, 286, 288; Reading, 300, 303, 304; Totnes, 175, note; claimed by S. Edmundsbury, 297, 298
Guns, English-made, their superiority, 55

H

Hadley, cloth sold at, 54, note 1
Hall, the common, of Romney, 129, note 2, 403, 405, note 1; of Sandwich, 401; the guild, of Bridport, 16; Exeter, 341, 351, 356; London, 378, note 2; Lynn, 283; Reading, 300, 304, 305; Winchester, 324
Hanse of Cologne, 75, 76, note 1; Flemish, in London, 76
Hanseatic League, 81, 82; its carrying trade, 83; disputes with Lynn merchants, 91, note 2; struggle with English Merchant Adventurers, 103-111; gathers fleet against England, 109; supports Edward IV., ib.; Edward IV.'s treaty with, 110; its guildhall in London, ib.; house at Boston and Lynn, ib.; its decline, ib., 111; negotiations with Henry VII. at Antwerp, 113; expels English traders from Denmark, 66; succeeds Hanse of Cologne in the carrying trade, 77
Harbledown, hospital of S. Nicholas at, 369
Harbours, making and improving, 142-144
"Harry Grâce à Dieu," the, 84, note 1
Hastings, 386; castle, 387, note 1
Haute, William, lord of the manor of Bishopsbourne, 216, note 2
Hemp, grown at Bridport, 202
Henry III., advantages to towns of his reign, 237; charter to Liverpool, 270; to Norwich, 242
Henry IV. supports the Merchant Adventurers, 95, 96, 105, 106; advantages to towns of his political insecurity, 237; charter to Norwich, 245-6
Henry V. forbids English trade with Iceland, 106; plans a royal navy, 86; advantages to towns of his financial needs, 237
Henry VI., Canterbury associated with the party of, 215; advantages to towns of tumults of his reign, 237; charter to Barnstaple, 255
Henry VII., his position among English sovereigns, 73, 74; received at Canterbury, 37, note; enforces Navigation Act, 94; patron of the Merchant Adventurers, 96, 111, 112; international treaties of commerce, 66; renews treaty with Brittany, 112; treaties with Burgundy, 4; commercial treaty with Florence, 117; with Riga, 113; with Scandinavia, ib.; with Venice, 118; confirms treaty of Utrecht, 112; negotiations with Hanseatic League at Antwerp, 113; treatment of Lombards, 116; secures protection for English merchants in Bordeaux, 119; stipulations for free trade with Spain, 120
Herbert, bishop of Norwich, 282
Hereford, municipal almshouse at, 41, note 2; duties of its citizens to their chief magistrate, 126; town bell, 127; mode of recovery of freedom, 180, note 3; the burghers' account of their freedom, 199, 200; law against maintainers or protectors, 220, 221; trial by combat abolished, ib.; customs, 317; relations with lay and ecclesiastical lords and their tenants within its liberties, 317-320; distinction drawn between "citizens" and "natives," 318; authority over those privileged to trade in town, 318, 319; capital bailiff, 229, 319, 320; punishment of a vagabond, 319, 320; tenants of various fees allowed to plead in the courts of, 320; refusal to give Cardiff copy of customs, 228, 229
Highway, the king's, sale of merchandise in, 156
Holcraft, Thomas, ferm of Liverpool let to, 275
Holland, engineers from, employed

INDEX

at Hythe, 142, 143, *note* ; at Sandwich, 142
"Holland" linen made in England, 57
Hollingbroke, ward in Romney named after, 402, 403
Horn, the common, 161 ; at Dover, 178, *note* 5 ; of S. Edmundsbury, 296 ; of Romney, 404, 405, *note* 1
Hospital at Exeter, 41, *note* 2 ; at Sandwich, *ib.*; the Magdalen, Winchester, 328, 329 ; of S. Nicholas, Harbledown, 369
Hospital of S. John, Worcester, refusal of its tenants to aid in taxes, &c., 357, *note* 4
House built by burgher as security on admission to freedom, 179 ; of burgher must be kept in proper repair, *ib.*, 180 ; of stone, 193 ; the Queen's, at Winchester, 323
Hull, shipbuilding at, 89 ; shipmen's guild at, 89, *note* 2
Hundred, freedom from officers of, 232, 233
Hundred court in Fordwich, 412 ; Sandwich, 401
Huntingdon, perambulation of its boundaries, 134, *note*
Huntingdon, Countess of, owner of Barnstaple, 253
Huy, burgesses at, 11, *note* 1
Hythe, ownership of, 227, 387, *note* 1 ; member of Cinque Ports, 386 ; payment towards renewal of Cinque Ports charters, 390, *note* 2; Cranmer's lease of bailiwick to townspeople, 408 ; appointment of bailiff, *ib.*, *note* ; grant of mayor to, *ib.* ; new harbour made at (1412), 142, 143; subscriptions for new steeple, 160, *note*

I

Iceland, English Adventurers in, 106, 107
Income-tax in towns, 139
Incorporation, charters of, 219, *note* 1
Industry, revolution in, during 14th and 15th centuries, 39, 40, 44, 45 ; changes in, 67, 70, 71 ; relations of government to, 67, 70-72; state protection of, 72, 73
Inferiores, in Lynn, 193, *note*
Inns of London, 378, *note* 2; bailiffs and jurats allowed to hold, in Romney, 404, *note* 2; the "Swan" at Canterbury, 216
Intercursus Magnus, 112
Ipswich, archbishop of Canterbury given right to trade in, 177, *note* 2; general assembly, 224 ; barge, 85, *note* 2 ; charter from John, 223, 224 ; charter withdrawn, 247, *note* 4 ; Domesday Roll, 225 ; election of officers, 224 ; Guild Merchant, *ib.*, 224, 225 ; ordinances, 224 ; arrest of Scotch priests, 230, *note* 3 ; common seal, 225 ; guardianship of sea, 234, *note* 2
Ireland, its trade with Liverpool, 270
Irishmen, feeling against, in the towns, 173, 174, *note* 1
Iron, trade in England, 54; increase in price, 55 ; imported from Sweden and Spain, 55
Italy, merchants of, their privileges in England, 78 ; expulsion from London, 329, 330 ; hire houses in Winchester, 330 ; settle in Southampton, *ib.*

J

Jewry of Bishop's Lynn, 283
John, advantages to towns of his money difficulties, 237 ; charter to Ipswich, 223 ; to Liverpool, 270 ; to Lynn, 283
Jurats of the Cinque Ports, 386
Jury, citizens from twelve years old might serve on, 184 ; exemption from serving on, granted to burghers of Reading, 306 ; payments to "friendly," 212 ; no trial by, in Cinque Ports, 388, *note* 6
Justices, itinerant, shut out from Cinque Ports, 388 ; of the Peace, 247

K

Kent, men of, their evil reputation in Middle Ages, 415

428 INDEX

Kiln of feudal lord, 199
King, the, and Commons, 25, *note* 3, 26; his sovereign rights, 207-209; various officers of, who visited the towns, 208-210; power of, to withdraw or question the value of charters and ancient customs, 211, 212; as lord of manor, 229-232; his sympathy with borough in questions as to rival jurisdictions, 232, 233; his difficulty in finding sufficient officers, 234; power of granting privileges beyond that of other lords, 263, *note* 2; loans to, 27, *note* 2, 305, *note* 1
King's court, 208

L

Labour, division of, 67; forced, in towns, 141, 142
Landowners, unfavourable conditions of life of, 258-268
Language, English, prayers in, used by a Norfolk guild, 42, *note*
Laonnais, federative republic of, 415
Law, king's, and town law, 236, *note*
Law day, business done at, 203
Law Merchant, 48
Lawsuits, increase caused by growth of trade, 58; of nobles, 266
Leet in Norwich, 240, 242, 243
Leet court, 336; in Lynn, 288, 294; in Norwich, 230, *note* 3; in Nottingham, 336, *note* 3
Leghorn won by Florence, 79
Leicester, owned by lay noble, 227; dispute about election of mayor, 235, *note* 2; town property, 269, *note*; charter from Edmund Crouchback, *ib.*; regulations as to taxes, 355, *note* 2; Guild Merchant, *ib.*; duel in, 221, *note* 2; petition for abolition of "borough English" in, 222
"Libel of English Policy," 61, 62; the second, 62-64
Likedelers of Calais, 90
Lincoln, charter of, 238, *note* 2; complaint about trials in, 336, 337; freedom from duel, 221, *note* 2
Linen manufacture, its beginnings in England, 57

Lisbon, commercial treaty with, 121
Lisle, Lord, his death at Nibley Green, 267
Liverpool, burgages in, 172; takes place of Chester as landing place, 270; trade with Ireland, *ib.*; common seal, *ib.*; election of bailiffs, *ib.*; charter from John, *ib.*; from Henry III., *ib.*; granted to constable of Lancaster Castle, *ib.*; resumed by John, *ib.*; to Earl of Chester, *ib.*; to Earl of Derby, *ib.*; to Edmund Crouchback, *ib.*; passed by marriage to John of Gaunt, *ib.*; Quo Warranto in, *ib.*, 271; first mayor, 218, *note*, 271; leases of fee form, 218, *note*, 270, 271; liberties usurped by Edmund Crouchback, 271; dependence on lord, 272; reverts to crown, *ib.*; petition of burgesses, *ib.*, *note* 3; relations with Molyneux and Stanley, 273-276; grant of ferm to David ap Griffith, 275; ferm let to Thomas Holcraft, *ib.*; granted to corporation, *ib.*; revenue, 273, *note* 1
Livery, 339; town laws against, 257, 268; supplied from lord's estate, 260
Loans, voluntary, from towns to the king, 27, *note* 2
Lombards settled in London, 81; their relations with Edward IV., Richard III., and Henry VII., 116; persecution of, in London, *ib.*
London hires out its common barge, 87, *note* 3; bell foundries in, 55, 56; first notice of bricks in, 56, *note* 3; bridge of, 144; drapers of, 52, *note* 3; cloth sold in, 54, *note* 1; use of coal in, 55, *note* 1; wealth of its goldsmiths, 58; guildhall, 378, *note* 2; Flemish Hanse of, 76; guildhall of Hanseatic League, 110; inns, 378, *note* 2; Italian merchants expelled from, 329, 330; Lombards in, 81, 116; house of Cologne merchants in, 76, *note* 1; Merchants' Fellowship of, its attempt to monopolize export of cloth, 69;

annexes Middlesex, 219, *note* 3 ; Recorder of, 372, 378, *note* 2 ; silk manufacture in, 57, *note* 2; settlers from, at Rye, 17 ; effort to concentrate foreign trade in, 69 ; paviour from, employed at Southampton, 18, *note* ; great play acted in, 145

Longport, Canterbury, disputes about rights of arrest in, 372

Lübeck, head of the Hanseatic League, 81, 82 ; succeeds to financial importance of Florence, 79 ; its merchants farm the English wool tax, 83 ; lend money to Edward III., *ib.* ; rent English mines, *ib.*

Lucas, Hugh, arrest of, in Exeter, 351

Lydd, expenses incurred in war, 415, *note* 4 ; fine for refusing to take journey on town business in, 187 ; incorporation under mayor and jurats, 398, *note* 2 ; assessment of income tax, 139, *note* 2 ; imitates Romney jetty, 143, *note* ; liberties given by Edward I. to, 410 ; quarrel with Battle about boundaries, 411 ; loan to Thomas Dygon, 139 ; minstrels at, 147 ; plays, &c., at, 148 ; provision for poor in, 41, *note* 2 ; Portuguese in, 122, *note*; use of archbishop's seal in, 410 ; its services at archbishop's court commuted for yearly payment, 409, 410 ; its hired ships, 87 ; style under Henry VI., 410 ; subjection to Romney, 410, 411 ; town clerk, 411 ; watch on S. John's Eve, 148

Lynn under Bishop of Norwich, 227, 282 ; granted by Bishop Herbert to monks of Norwich, 282 ; repurchased, 283-4 ; charters from John, 283 ; of 1335, 289 ; from bishop, 290 ; struggle between bishop and town, 287-294 ; petition for relief from demands of king's bailiffs, 285, *note* 1 ; expenses of bribes, 214, *note* 3 ; Church of St. Margaret, 283 ; disputes with the lords of Castle Rising, 284-5 ; various courts held by the Bishop of Norwich, 285-6 ; courts leased by bishop to burghers, 294 ; municipal debt, 140, *note* 1 ; franchise controlled by the Bishop of Norwich, 286 ; dispute about the view of frankpledge, 290, 294 ; guildhall, 283 ; guild of merchants, 89 ; Guild Merchant, 286, 288 ; house of the Hanseatic League, 110 ; cross set up by hermit at, 175, *note*; "Inferiores," 193, *note* ; Jewry, 283 ; Leet court, 288, 294 ; Tolbooth court, 286, 288 ; the authority of the mayor limited by the Bishop of Norwich, 286 ; disputes of merchants with the Hanse, 91, *note* 2 ; lends money to the king, 27, *note* 2 ; payment of players, 145, *note* ; growth of shipping, 87 ; taxation for Church expenses, 158, *note* 3 ; trade with Iceland forbidden, 107, *note* 1 ; wealth in the thirteenth century, 286 ; proving of wills at, 289

"Lyvelode," 139

M

Maces, at Canterbury, 381 ; Exeter, 339, 367 ; Norwich, 246 ; Reading, 306 ; Romney, 406

Maintenance, statute of, 221, *note* 1 ; town laws against, 257

Malmesbury, dispute about guild at, 302, *note* 2

"Maltodes," 139

Malvern, fifteenth century glass at, 56, *note* 4

Manchester, qualifications of burghers in, 170, *note* 2 ; charter, 181, *note* 3

Mancroft, ward in Norwich, 240

Manufactures, growth of, in England in fourteenth and fifteenth centuries, 44, 45, 67 ; of cloth, 52-54 ; of wool, in Normandy, 119

Manufacturers, rivalry with merchants, 68

Marienburg, treaty of commerce made at, 104, *note* 6

Mariners of England and France, agreement between, 396, *note* 3
Market, the king's clerk of, 208; payments for freedom of, 192; market at Barnstaple, 253, *note* 3; Canterbury, 371-2, 377-380; Exeter, 359, 360
Marshal of king's house, extent of his jurisdiction, 209
Mastez in Sandwich, 184, *note* 5
Matthyessone, Gerard, Dutch engineer employed at Romney, 143, *note*
Mayor, election of, 12; its connexion with settlement of fee-farm rent, 218, *note* 1; various offices given to, 231, 233, 234, 236; position between the king and townspeople, 236-7; of Bristol, charter to the, 313; his daughter's marriage with Lord Berkeley, 316; of Canterbury, his office respecting pilgrims, 376; of Exeter, his dependence on the Earl of Devonshire, 339; of Fordwich, his jurisdiction, 412; of Hythe, 408, *note*; of Leicester, dispute about election of, 235, *note* 2; of Liverpool, first election of, 218, *note*, 271; of Lydd, 398, *note* 2; of Lynn, his authority limited by Bishop of Norwich, 286; dispute with the Bishop about jurisdiction, 289-94; his sword, 293; of Norwich, rights of jurisdiction given to, in 1403, 245-6; made mayor of Staple, 245; his salary, *ib.*; his sword and maces, 246; appointed King's Escheator in Norwich, *ib.*; of Reading, provision for his salary, 300, 304, 305; his mace, 306; disputes about election, *ib.*, 307; of Romney, 409; deposed by Privy Seal, 407; of Sandwich, 400; his power to arrest on suspicion, 184, *note* 5; of Winchester, 325; of the Staple, 46, 48
Mediterranean, its trade, 77, 78
Melton, action against townsmen for not baking bread at lord's oven in, 199, *note* 1

Memling's Last Judgement, its adventures, 109, *note* 2
Mendip, mines in, 55
Mercers of York, 89, *note* 2
Merchant Guild, *see* Guild Merchant
Merchants, their aversion from foreign war, 64; rivalry with manufacturers, 68; associations of, 88; increase in their number, 89; Fellowship of, at Bristol, *ib.*; guild of, at Lynn, *ib.*; Italian, their privileges in England, 78; of London, seek to monopolize foreign trade, 69; Statute of, 156
Middlesex annexed to London, 219, *note* 3
Mill of feudal lord, 199; at Canterbury, 371-2, 380-1
Mines, English, 55; rented by Lübeck merchants, 83
Miners of Mendip, riot of, 55; of Sussex, 415
Minstrels, 147; of Canterbury, 145
Mint at Calais, 49
Moleyns, Bishop of Chichester, his Libel of English Policy, 61, 62
Molyneux, Sir Richard, his relations with Liverpool, 273-276
Monkenkey, Sandwich, owned by Christ Church, Canterbury, 400
Montault, Robert of, his struggle with Lynn, 284-5
Montfort, Simon de, Norwich and Winchester against, 242; supported by Cinque Ports, 388, *note* 5
Moot Hall at Colchester, 14
Morgespeche of Guild of Reading, 303
Morpeth, 227
Mortmain, Statute of, 219, 246-7; extended to cities and boroughs, 219, *note* 2
Morton, Cardinal, 211, *note*, 376-7
Music, its developement in England in fifteenth century, 44

N

"Natives," their distinction from citizens in Hereford, 318
Navigation Act, the first, 84; put in force by Henry VII., 94; of 1489, 112, 119

INDEX

Navy, mediæval idea of its origin and use, 75; planned by Henry V., 86; merchant, its character, 92; its inefficiency as a royal navy, 93

Netherlands, rivalry with England in the cloth trade, 65, 66; English traders in, 98-101

Newgate, leet of, in Norwich, 242, 243

Nicholas of the Tower (ship), 89

Nibley Green, battle of, 267, 316

Nobles, their patronage sought by towns, 216; honours paid to, 256; dress and state, *ib.*, 257; decay and poverty, 257; stores of treasure, 259; money difficulties, *ib.*; dependents, 260; borrowing and debts, 261-2; leasing out privileges to townspeople, 263; frequent absences from home, 264, 265; heavy consequences of rebellions and civil wars to, 265-266; feuds and lawsuits, 266-268

Non-burgesses, 193-196

Norfolk, cloth-making in, 52, *note* 1; worsted manufacture, 54; increase of lawsuits, 58; traders robbed by Danes, 91

Normandy, beginning of its woollen manufactures, 119; Henry I.'s charters to towns in, 172, *note* 1

Northampton, charter of, 238, *note* 2; collection of arrears of ferm, 205-6

Norton Mandeville, cloth sold at, 54, *note* 1

Norwich, its condition before Henry II.'s time, 238; charter of Richard I., *ib.*; of Henry III., 242; of Edward I., *ib.*; of Henry IV., 245-6; sided with king against De Montfort, 242; authority exercised by Parliament over, 235, *note* 2; liberties forfeited, 243, 247, *note* 4; petition in 1307, 243-4; made county, 245; made staple town, 245; sues for repayment of a loan to the king, 27, *note* 2; twelve of its citizens distrained for the city's debt to the king, 140; action in Wars of the Roses, 37, *note*; under the protection of Suffolk, 216; rivalry with Yarmouth, 163, *note*; admiral appointed in, 245; its burghers freed from arrest for debt, 242; four bailiffs, 240, 245, 246; bell foundries, 55, 56; Borough Court, 239; castle fee and its tenants, 240, 241, 244, 245, 313; law passed to compel men to become citizens, 190; church of S. George, 243; exemption from clerk of the market, 208, *note* 2, 245; ditch, 242; exports in 1374, 88, *note* 2; ferm, 238; provision for, 244; guild of S. George, 150; system of government imitated by Yarmouth and Colchester, 238, *note* 2; inhabitants in thirteenth century, 171, *note* 3; increase of lawsuits in, 58; four leets, 240; leet of Newgate, 242, 243; amercements ordered by Leet Court, 230, *note* 3; mayor of, his salary, 208, *note* 1; his rights of jurisdiction, 245-6; his sword and maces, 246; made mayor of Staple, *ib.*; made King's Escheator, *ib.*; payment for charter, 238; petition against players, 152; Provost, 238, 239; seal, 246; sheriffs, *ib.*; municipal taxation, royal interference with, 219, *note* 4, 241, 355, *note* 2; adventures of a thief, 243; tolbooth, 239; four wards, 239, 240; towers and walls, provision for repairing, 245, *note* 4

Norwich, Bishops of, *see* Herbert, Lynn

Nottingham, borough in ancient demesne, 227; charter, 238, *note* 2; franchise forfeited, 247, *note* 4; foreigners to pay £10 for admission to freedom, 178, *note* 5; payment for liberties, 232, *note* 1; rights of taxation given to the guild, 355, *note* 2; "booners" in, 141; "borough English," 222, *note* 1; bridge, 144; burgages, 172; court leet, 336, *note* 3; pledges, 178, *note* 4; pleas concerning trade, 58

Novgorod, 77, 111

O

Official, the Master, of the archdeacon at Nottingham, 336, *note* 3
Onterdel, Dutch engineer employed at Romney, 143, *note*
Oporto, commercial treaty with, 121
Orphans, Court of, 41, *note* 2
Outbutchery built in Reading, 304
Oven of feudal lord, 199 ; of householders at Preston, *ib.*
Oxford, first notice of bricks in, 56, *note* 3

P

Palmer, John, of Exeter, 41, *note* 2
Parliament, representation of towns in, 4, 7, 24, 25 ; Brinklow's criticism on, 60, *note* 4 ; authority exercised by, in Norwich, 235, *note* 2 ; expenses of members of, in Winchester, 329; *see* Commons
Paston family, stores in their house, 259, *note* 2
Paston, Sir John, 260, 265
Paston, Judge, 265
Pavilion, the, in Winchester, 322
Paving of towns, 18, *note*
Payments from towns for the confirmation of charters, 211, 303 ; for liberties, 232, 238 ; for deliverance from feudal obligations, 198 ; in kind at Bridport, 204-5
Peasant Revolt, 196, 237
"Penny prykke," game of, 363
Pershore, Abbot of, his gallows in Worcester, 310
Philip, Archduke, makes Bruges the staple for English cloth in Flanders, 113, *note* 3
Picardy, commercial league of, 415
"Piers Ploughman," picture of English life in, 21 ; dealings with the social problems of the day, 22 ; his theory of King and Commons, 25, *note* 3, 26
Pilgrims to Canterbury, provision for the safety and comfort of, 375, 376
Pillory, 252, 315

Pit and gallows, right of, 2, *note*
Pirates attack English Adventurers 90, 91
Pisa, English wool merchants at, 117
Plays, 145-148
Players, petition against, in Norwich, 152
Pledges required of candidates for citizenship, 178
Plumpton family, their money difficulties, 261
Plumpton, Sir John, 130
Plumpton, Sir William, 265, 266, *note* 1
Plimpton, charter of Baldwin of Redvers to, 263, *note* 2 ; agreement of the convent of, with Plymouth, 296, *note* ; rope yarn made at, 202
Plymouth, its agreement with the convent of Plimpton, 296, *note* ; money collected for S. Andrew's by church ales, 160, 161; regulations about the use of copes, 158 ; the guild of our Lady and S. George, *ib.*; of Corpus Christi, 151 ; incorporation of tailors, *ib.*
Ponthieu, federative republic of, 415
Portmanbrok in Reading, 300, 304
Portmen in Ipswich, 224
Portmote, *see* Borough Court
Portugal succeeds Venice in the Eastern trade, 121 ; commercial treaty with, *ib.*
Pratt, William, builds the first main drain at Canterbury, 19, 20
Preston, its various lords, 253, *note* 2 ; qualifications of burghers, 170, *note* 2 ; their privileges, 190, *note* 3, 198, 199 ; punishment for breach of public duty, 181
Prison of the bishop, in Exeter, 362 ; freeman's, 185 ; the abbot's, at Fordwich, 412
Privy Seal, *see* Seal
Probate, claimed by the Mayor of Canterbury, 200, *note* 1 ; at Lynn, 289
Provost of Norwich, his election, 238; his duties, 239; replaced by four bailiffs, 240

INDEX

Prussia, English traders banished from, 66
Purveyors, the king's, 210

Q

Quay at Fordwich, quarrels about the, 413; of Sandwich, agreement between Christ Church and Sandwich about, 400, *note* 2
"Queke," game of, 363
Quo Warranto in Liverpool, 270

R

Radford, Recorder of Exeter, 345, 347
Radington, Baldwin of, 130
Ramsey, carpet and tapestry manufactories at, 57; tenants of King's Ripton transferred to the Abbey of, 228, *note*
Reading, originally on royal demesne, 299; its subjection to the Abbot, *ib.*, 227; struggle with him, 300, 301, 303-308; confirmation of charters, 303; archers, 16, *note*; view of arms, *ib.*; bell, 304; nineteen bridges, 301, *note* 2; the Hallowed Brook, 304; chepin gavell in, 299, 306; common chest, 305, 306; constable, 304, 306; guild merchant, 300, 303, 304; guildhall, 303, 304, 305; exemption from serving on juries granted to burghers, 306; loans to the king, 305, *note* 1; the mayor, his salary, 304, 305; his mace, 306; disputes about his election, 306, 307; register of his acts, 305; Morgespeche, 303; Outbutchery, 304; Portmanbrok, 300, 304; seal for cloth, 308; contribution of soldiers under Edward VI., 16, *note*
Reap-silver, 171, *note* 2
Recorder of Exeter, 345, 347; of London, 372, 378, *note* 2
Redcliffe, dispute about ownership of, 314, 315; incorporated with Bristol, 314, *note*
Redvers, Baldwin of, his charter to Plimpton, 263, *note* 2
Religion among English townsfolk in 15th century, 42
Rhine, commercial league of the, 415
Ricart of Bristol, his notices of political events, 37, *note*
Richard I., advantages to towns of his money difficulties, 237; his charters to towns, 238
Richard III.'s dealings with York, 27, *note* 2
Richard of Almayne, his grant to Exeter, 357
Riga, Henry VII.'s commercial treaty with, 113
Ripon, its fair, 130; fight at, in 1441, *ib.*
Ripton, King's, tenants of, transferred to the abbey of Ramsey, 228, *note*
Rising, Castle, disputes between the lords of, and the bishop of Norwich, 284; its rights in Lynn pass to Edward III., 285
Roan, John, Flemish engineer employed at Romney, 143, *note*
Rochelle, its wine trade with Romney, 88
Rochester, the King's hackney-men in, 209, *note* 3; castle of, owner of land in Lydd, 409
Roll, the Black, of Exeter, 345
Romney under Archbishop of Canterbury, 227; member of Cinque Ports, 386; ownership of, 387, *note* 1; struggle for freedom, 404-409; claim to be a royal borough, 407-408; struggle with Lydd, 409, 411; auditing of town accounts, 139, *note* 2; bailiff, 404-406; bell, 405, *note* 1; Cranmer's refusal to lease out bailiwick to townspeople, 408-409; common barges, 87, 88; decay of burghers, 403; book of customs, 405, *note* 1; commerce, 87, 88; common hall, 129, *note* 2; 403, 405, *note* 1; common horn, 404, 405, *note* 1; care of common lands,

VOL. I   F F

136, 137; decrease of freemen, 190; bailiffs and jurats allowed to hold inns, 404, *note* 2; government by senior jurat, 409; places of assembly of jurats, 405, *note* 1; grant of mayor, 409; mayor deposed by Privy Seal, 407; silver mace, 406; payment for maintenance of liberties of Cinque Ports, 390, *note* 2; plays at, 148; silting up of its port, 403; punishment of elected mayor or jurat who refused to serve, 188; seal, 405, *note* 1; sluices, 143, *note*; assessment of taxes, 402, *note* 4; trade, 402-403, 88; wards, 402, *note* 4

Roofs of tiles or brick, houses to be provided with, 194

Ropes, made at Bridport, 202

Rosiers. at Canterbury, dispute for jurisdiction over, 135, 136

Rother, river, 403

Rotherham college, its red brick, 56, *note* 3

Rowley, William, 120, *note*

Russia, Henry VII.'s attempt to secure trade with, 113

Rye, ownership of, 387, *note* 1; member of Cinque Ports, 386; growth, 17; auditing of its accounts, 139, *note* 2; expenses for war, 415, *note* 4; tax for its fortification, 129, *note* 1; London merchants in, 17; building of its quay, 142, *note* 2; rights of sanctuary forbidden in, 338; its "schipwrite," 88, *note* 2; trade, 88; gifts to poor, 41, *note* 2; wards, 17

S

Sailors, in seaports, 194

St. Albans, ownership of, 227; renounces its liberties, 295, *note* 2; its seal, *ib.*

St. Edmundsbury, its agricultural services, 171, *note* 2; dispute with abbot, 296-298; Guild of Young Men, 296, 297; claims a merchant guild, 297, 298; common horn, 296; seal, 298

Salford, qualification for citizenship in, 170, *note* 2

Salisbury, bell foundries at, 55, 56; cloth sold at, 54, *note* 1; relations between citizens and bishop, 281, *note*

Sanctuary, question of, 337-8; in Canterbury Cathedral, 374; rights of, forbidden in Rye, 338

Sandwich, member of Cinque Ports, 386; port of London, 369, *note* 3; ownership, 387, *note* 1, 399, 400; freedom as royal borough, 402; refuses loan to the king, 27, *note* 2; quarrels with Canterbury, 163, *note*; mastery of Fordwich, 411-413; common assembly, 401; Hundred court, *ib.*; powers of King's bailiff in, 400-402; church of S. Clements, 401; of S. Peter, *ib.*; engages a Dutchman to make a new dyke, 142; harbour, 369; privilege of burghers, 185; market-place and common hall, 401; the Mastez in, 184, *note* 5; its mayor manager of the hospitals, 41, *note* 2; his power to arrest on suspicion, 184, *note* 5; mayor and jurats, 400-402; Monkenkey, 400; punishment of men charged with homicide or theft, 221, *note* 2; of elected treasurer who refused to serve, 188; penalty for wounding in, 132, *note* 2

Scarborough, its complaint about ferm, 247, *note* 4

"Scavadge," 142, *note* 1

Scot-ales, 206, 207

Scotland, war with, Morton's demands for, 376, 377

Scots traders at Veere, 98, *note* 5

Schonen, English cloth dealers at, 95

Seaford, 386, *note* 2

Seaports, their duties, 128, 129

Seals, 175-6; English, their fine workmanship, 225, *note*; of Archbishop of Canterbury used in Lydd, 410; of Barnstaple, 225, *note*; of Doncaster, 269, *note*; Ipswich, 225; Liverpool, 270; Norwich, 246; for sealing the cloth in Reading, 308 ; of Romney, 405, *note* 1 ; St. Albans, 295, *note* 2 ; of S. Edmundsbury, 298 ; of Lord Warden of Cinque Ports, necessary to make King's writ valid, 387 ; the Great, request that only laymen should have charge of, 365, *note* 3 ; the Privy, writ of, 341 ; mayor of Romney deposed by, 407

Security required by town on admission of man to freedom, 179

Self-government in the towns, 1-3, 218

Selling, Prior, of Christ Church, Canterbury, 377

Serfs, conditions of their emancipation in towns, 174, *note* 3

Shepway, court of, 388, 391-394, 396, *note* 2

Sheriff, jurisdiction of the, 203-4 ; appointment of deputy by, 204 ; assessor and collector of royal taxes and rents, *ib.* ; duties as head of shire forces, *ib.*; tyranny and extortion of, 206 ; hatred of, expressed in popular ballads and books, 207 ; term of office, 234, *note* 3 ; business at Bridport, 204 ; modes of extortion in Canterbury and Bridgenorth, 207 ; court at Dorchester, 203, 204 ; of Norfolk, his Curia Comitatus at Norwich, 239 ; jurisdiction there, 246 ; of Norwich, 246

"Shewage," 142, *note* 1

Shillingford, John, 338, 340-341, 346-348, 350

Shipbuilding for aliens, 86 ; at Hull, 89 ; at Woolwich, 84, *note* 1 ; its costliness, 87

Shipmen's guild at Hull, 89, *note* 2

Shipping, native and foreign, regulation of, 84 ; its conditions in England, 85, 86 ; growth in seaport towns, 87 ; trade taken under State protection (1489), 112

Ships, English and foreign, sizes of, 84, *note* 1 ; English, dispute with Flemish, 92, *note* 2 ; *see* Christopher, Grâce, Harry, Nicholas, Trinity

Shire officers, 203-207 ; freedom from them, 232-3

Shrewsbury, wearing of liveries forbidden in, 268, *note* 2.

Shrewsbury, Countess of, her agreement with James, Lord of Berkeley, 266

Silk, its importation forbidden, 110 ; manufacture, its beginning in England, 57 ; carried on by women in London, *ib.*, *note* 2

Silver mines in England, 55, *note* 1

Skenes, Irish, 351

Soke, the bishop's at Winchester, 322

Soldiers, charges of levying for royal service, 374

Somerset, its silver mines, 55, *note* 1

Southampton, owned by King, 227 ; burgess imprisoned for its rent, 140, 141 ; liberties forfeited, 247, *note* 4 ; its aqueduct and water supply, 19, *note* ; constable of castle, 312 ; gallows, 2, *note* ; licence to buy and sell during S. Giles' Fair, 329 ; Italian merchants at, 78, 81, 330 ; paving, 18, *note* ; provision for poor, 41, *note* 2 ; ship, 85, *note* 2 ; rights of Bishop of Winchester in, during fair of S. Giles, 324, *note* 3

Spain, English trade with, 120, 121

Stalls, in Exeter market place, 360 ; the Queen's, in Winchester, 323

Stanley, John of, 130

Stanley, Sir John, his relations with Liverpool, 273-276

Staple, the, 45 ; its wanderings under Edward III., *ib*, 46 ; fixed at Calais, *ib.* ; mayors and aldermen of, *ib*, 48 ; English towns of, 46 ; rules, 46-48 ; authority, 48 ; merchants of, monopolize export of wool, 49 ; of Calais, its money transactions with the captain and the Government, *ib*, 50 ; decline, 51 ; struggle against Merchant Adventurers, 101-103 ; Mediterranean merchants freed from its control, 78 ; appointment of mayor as mayor of, 234 ; set up by English adventurers at Bergen, 95 ; for English cloth in

Flanders, placed at Bruges by Archduke Philip, 113, *note* 3
Staplegate at Canterbury, 370
Statute of Maintenance, 221, *note* 1; of Merchants, 156; of Mortmain, 219, 246-7
Steel-yard, the, 83, 109, 110
Steward of King's house, his jurisdiction, 209
Steward's Hall Port of Lynn, 294
Stonor, harbour of, 369
Sturgeon, Nicholas, 44, *note* 1
Sturmys of Bristol, sends a ship to the East, 115
Sturry, 369
Sudbury, Archbishop, 374
Suffolk, Duke of, 216
Sussex, miners of, their evil reputation in Middle Ages, 415
Swithun, S., the convent of, at Winchester, 322, 323, *see* Winchester
Sword, of mayor of Norwich, 246; of mayor of Lynn, 293

T

Tailors at Plymouth incorporated, 151
Taperaxe, 412
Tapestry factory at Ramsey, 57
Taverner, John, builds a "carrack" at Hull, 89
Tax on wool farmed by Lübeck merchants, 83
Taxation, changes in, 27 *note* 1; of cloth, 81, *note* 1; illegal, controlled by Commons, 25, *note* 3; internal, of towns, 139, 355-357; interference with, in Norwich, 219, *note* 4
Temple Fee, Bristol, 313, *note* 2
Tennis, game of, 363
Tetbury fair, 314
Teutonic Order banishes English traders from Prussia, 66
"Thefeswell" in Fordwich, 412
Thiefdown, 221, *note* 2
Thomas, S., feast of translation of, 370
Tin-works, Cornish, rented by Lübeck merchants, 83

Tolbooth at Norwich, 239; Court at Lynn, 286, 288; Port, at Lynn, 294
Toll hall at Bridport, 16
Tolls of cloth-exporters and staplers compared, 52; on export, 90, *note* 2; for Merchant Adventurers, fixed by charter in Burgundy, 96; freedom from, granted to burghers, 183
Topsham, 359
Totnes, jurisdiction of the lord's bailiff in, 252-3; disputes between lord and tenants, 252; poverty in 1449, 159; wooden belfry replaced by stone tower, 160; Guild under Henry II. and John, 251; rights claimed by, 251-2; Merchant Guild, 175, *note*; waterbearers, 157, *note*
Towns, English, their importance in fifteenth century, 1; significance of their history, 8-10; beginning of municipal history, 11; contrast of their history with that of French communes, 29-32; their lowly beginnings, 33; relation to the Government, 27; importance of their internal administration, 20; their contribution to the reorganization of society, 23, 24; progress up to fourteenth century, 10-12; in fourteenth century, 13; place in history of fifteenth century, 40-44; fallen condition in 1835, 5, 6; attitude in Wars of Roses, 164; ratify Henry VII.'s treaties with Burgundy, 4; their self-contained and self-dependent life, 125; changes in their condition through increase of industry and commerce, 171; amusements in, 145-153; assemblies, 223; "common barges," 140; preservation of boundaries and "liberties," 134; common lands, 136, 137; common revenue, 139; competition and commercial jealousy in, 163; corporate property, 138; criers, 161, 162, 180; duties, 4; duty of citizens to chief magistrate and community, 126; military duties, 129-131; military discipline,

127, 128 ; freedom of election, 5 ; its decay, 6, 7 ; festivals, 149, 152, 153 ; financial responsibility, 140, 165-167 ; refusal to take up the franchise, 186 ; forced labour in, 141, 142 ; extent of their jurisdiction, 3, 190-193, 333-8 ; right of criminal jurisdiction in, 2 ; election of mayor, 12 ; officers' duties and responsibilities, 186 ; representation in Parliament, 4, 7, 24, 25 ; patronage of nobles sought by, 216 ; paving of, 18, *note* ; political feeling in, 60, 61 ; privileges forfeited, 247, *note* 3 ; their protection extended to men who were not free citizens, 189; provisions for relief of the poor, 41, *note* 2 ; ranks and classes of men in, 189-196; conflicting rights in, 309-311 ; their self-government, 1-3 ; self-taxation, 2 ; distribution of taxes in, 355, *note* 2 ; regulation of trade, 2, 3 ; watch and ward, 132, 133 ; water-supply in, 19 ; condition of the working classes in, 195 ; public works, 141 ; on ancient demesne, 227-229 ; dependent on other boroughs, 227, *note*; on ecclesiastical estates, 227, 277-281 ; on feudal estates, 250-1 ; subject to monastic rule, 295 ; sea-port, their duties during Hundred Years' War, 128, 129 ; of the Staple, 46 ; *see* Boroughs

Townspeople lay rectors of parish church, 157 ; their temper in the fifteenth century, 165,

Tracy, Henry de, holder of Barnstaple, 253 *note* 3

Trade, its regulation in towns, 2, 3 ; early associations for protection of, 32 ; increase of lawsuits concerning, 58 ; revolution in fifteenth century, 51 ; endeavour to exclude foreigners from, 73 ; attempts to protect it from piracy, 91 ; right of, given to burghers, 182 ; payment for rights of, 189 ; with the East, monopolized by Italians, 114 ; diverted from Venice to Portugal, 121 ; English, with Bordeaux, 118, 119, 316, *note* 1; with Genoa, proposal to forbid, 116 ; with the North, 106, 107, 114 ; of Florence, 78, 79; foreign, Bishop Moleyns's views of, 61,62 ; an anonymous "Libeller" on, 62-64 ; London attempts to monopolize, 69 ; injured by war with France, 64, *note*; of Romney, 403 ; free, adopted by Florence, 117; of the country, formidable rival to protected trade of towns, 193 ; between Liverpool and Ireland, 270 ; of the Mediterranean, 77, 78 ; State protection of, 72, 73 ; its results at Venice, 80 ; by sea, its early routes, 75, 77 ; Venetian, bill against, proposed in Parliament, 115 ; of Winchester, 324, 328; in beer, with Flanders, 57 ; in cloth, its rise, 51-54, 94, 95 ; rivalry in, between England and Flanders, 65-66 ; in iron, 54 ; in wool, 45, 49, 51; in wine, between Aquitaine and England, 118-120; from Rochelle to Romney, 88 ; struggle between England and Venice for, 116-118 ; licenses for trade given to lords of Berkeley, 316, *note* 1

Traders in the towns, 189-192 ; privileged, living outside towns, 192-3

Treaties of commerce, Henry VII.'s, 66 ; with Brittany, 112 ; with Castile and Catalonia, 120; Henry VII.'s, with Florence, 117 ; with Portugal, 121; with Riga and Scandinavia, 113; of Marienburg, 104, *note* 6; of Utrecht, 110 ; of 1475, 1486, 1495, 119, *note* 2 ; of 1496 (*Intercursus Magnus*), 112

Trials, complaint about, in Lincoln, 336-7

Trinity of Berkeley (ship), 316 *note* 1

Tumbril, 252, 315

U

Under-sheriff, appointed by sheriff, 204

Unenfranchised class, increase of, in towns, 196
Utrecht, treaty with the Hanse made at (1474), 110; confirmed by Henry VII., 112

V

Veere, depôt of Scottish traders at, 98, *note* 5
Venice, its state-protected trade, 80; its trade with Southampton, 81; diverted to Portugal, 121; bill to forbid its carrying trade proposed in Parliament, 115; driven out of Egypt, 114; struggle of English merchants with, 116; Henry VII.'s agreement with, 118
Vitalien Brüder, 90

W

Waits, 145
Walls, provision for repairing in Norwich, 245, *note* 4
Wards in Norwich, 239, 240; in Romney, 402, *note* 4; in Rye, 17
Warden, the Lord, of the Cinque Ports, towns under the rule of, 386; his authority, 390-394; powers as Constable of Dover Castle, as Admiral, as Chancellor, 392; his seal, necessary to make King's writs valid, 387
Warden of the Poor at Exeter, 41, *note* 2
Warwick, its various lords, 309 310
Warwick, Earl of, the Kingmaker 257-8, 415
Watch and ward, 132, 133; controversy about in Exeter, 357-8
Water supply in towns, 19, *note*
Wayneflete, Bishop of Winchester, 326, *note*
Weald, iron trade in, 54
Weavers of Chester, their riot in 1399, 130, *note* 1; English and foreign, their rivalry, 65; Flemish, their struggle against importation of English cloth, 99-101; in Bristol, 193

Weights and Measures, Act of 1429, 3, *note*
Wells, under Bishop of Wells, 227; fees in kind at, 178
Westgate, Canterbury, 381; Archbishop's tenants of, 370
Westminster, silk manufactory at, 57, *note* 2; Abbot of, his gallows in Worcester, 310
Westwick, ward in Norwich, 240
Weymouth, ownership of, 227
Whitstable, rights claimed by Archbishop of Canterbury's tenants, of, 371
Wikham, John, "schipwrite" of Rye, 88, *note* 2
Wills, enrolled in borough courts, 200, *note* 1; probate of, at Lynn, 289; claimed by Mayor of Canterbury, 200, *note* 1
Winchelsea, ownership of, 387 *note* 1; member of Cinque Ports, 386; punishment of thief at, 221, *note* 2
Winchester, owned by King, 227; charter, 238, *note* 2; sided with King against De Montfort, 242; its reputed antiquity, 321; poverty, 190; decrease of freemen, *ib.*; dispute between bishops and burghers, 323; fight between citizens and monks, 324, *note* 2; distress and poverty in fifteenth century, 326-330; Lancastrian sympathies, 326, *note*; heavy burdens, 327-9; petition of burghers to Henry VI., 328, 329; ferm, fines, and expenses in 1450, *ib.*; grant of forty marks to, from ulnage and subsidies of cloths, 329; various alien bodies within its liberties, 322-324; common assembly, 321; boundaries, 322; castle, *ib.*; corporation, 321; curfew bell, 324; S. Giles' fair, 324, 329; fraternity of S. John, its payment towards maintenance of walls and bridges, 329, *note* 2; provision for ferm, 328, *note* 2; franchise refused, 328; experiment in free-trade, *ib.*; friars, 323; Magdalen hospital, 328, 329; mayor, 325; control of gates, 324; liberty of Godbeate,

ib.; Guildhall, 324; High Street, 322, 323; Italian merchants in, 330; King's officers in, 325; town officers, 321, 322; expenses of burgesses to Parliament, 329; Pavilion, 322; perambulation of liberties, *ib.*; the Queen's House, 323; Queen's stalls, *ib.*; convent of S. Swithun, 322; Bishop of, bribes to, 214; his authority over trade, 324; palace, 322; rights of his tenants, 322-3; Soke, 322
Windsor, Dean of, gift from Canterbury to, 214
Wines, variety of, 215; Rhine, ordered to be carried only in English ships, 110; *see* Trade
"Wine gavell" in Exeter, 359
Wingham, Archbishop of Canterbury's tenants of, 370-1
Women carry on silk manufacture in London, 57, *note* 2; their management of great estates, 265
Wool, beginning of its manufacture in Normandy, 119; export of, 45, 49; under Edward III., 50; decrease in fifteenth century, 51; tax on, 49; farmed by Lübeck merchants, 83
Wool Hall at Colchester, 14
Wool-growers, rivalry with cloth-manufacturers, 68
Woolwich, ship built at, 84, *note* 1
Worcester, protection of burghers, 184; law passed to compel men to become citizens, 190; common coffer, 138, *note*; "Great Clothing," *ib.*; gallows, 310; hospital of S. John, 357 *note* 4

Working-classes in towns, condition of the, 195
Worsted manufacture in Norfolk, 54
Wynde, burgesses of the, in Barnstaple, 254

Y

Yarmouth, owned by King, 227; rivalry with Norwich, 163, *note*; made staple town, *ib.*; imitates Norwich system of government, 238, *note* 2; riotous population of sailors, 194; threatens monopoly of Cinque Ports, 394; its fair, 395, 396, 415
Yaxley, church-ales at, 161, *note*
Year gift, 206
York, owned by King, 227; its corporation made justiciars for preserving rivers, 234, *note* 2; dealings with Richard III., 27, *note* 2; reception of Duke of Gloucester, 216, 217; guilds at, 42, *note*; 89, *note* 2; mercers at, 89, *note* 2; territory, 3, *note*; its franchise, 196; dispute about payment of troops, 131, *note* 3; riot about common lands, 137, *note* 2
York, Archbishop of, his attack on Ripon in 1441, 130
York, Duchess of, gifts from Canterbury to, 215
Yorkshire, early brick buildings in, 56, *note* 3
Ypres, decline of its weaving trade, 65

END OF VOL. I.

www.ingramcontent.com/pod-product-compliance
Lightning Source LLC
Chambersburg PA
CBHW032010300426
44117CB00008B/965

978-3-33709-457-7

Town Life in the Fifteenth Century - Volume 1 is an unchanged, high-quality reprint of the original edition of 1894.
Hansebooks is editor of the literature on different topic areas such as research and science, travel and expeditions, cooking and nutrition, medicine, and other genres. As a publisher we focus on the preservation of historical literature. Many works of historical writers and scientists are available today as antiques only. Hansebooks newly publishes these books and contributes to the preservation of literature which has become rare and historical knowledge for the future.

ISBN/EAN: 978-3-33709-457-7
www.hansebooks.com

hanse